advisory editor in american history

arthur mann

the winning of the midwest

social and political conflict, 1888-1896

richard jensen

The University of Chicago Press

Chicago and London

International Standard Book Number: 0–226–39825–0
Library of Congress Catalog Card Number: 71–149802

The University of Chicago Press, Chicago 60637
The University of Chicago Press, Ltd., London

contents

Contents

Democracy as a way of government presupposes that politicians depend closely upon the opinions of the entire people and, therefore, that political changes follow social developments. The Midwest in the 1890s provides an arena for the observation of democracy at work in America. More specifically, this study tries to discover the basic political beliefs, values, and wants of Americans by examining the voting patterns of the electorate, the activities of various religious, ethnic, and economic interests, and the efforts exerted by politicians and party organizations to ride the tides of public opinion to political power.

Election campaigns illuminate the nature of democracy and the political system directly. Oddly, historians have seldom studied the ways candidates appealed for votes and the reasons men voted as they did. Most historical studies focus upon the nominating process, explaining how it happened that Bryan or Eisenhower or Taylor or Harding defeated his rivals at the convention. Such research is valuable, but it concentrates so heavily upon the maneuvering of a few leaders that the voters, upon whom victory depended, are lost sight of. Voting analysis involves very difficult techniques, and most historians have avoided the masses of statistics that must be digested before clear patterns emerge.[1] Quantitative methods, however, are now rapidly being taken up by historians, and voting studies are becoming fashionable.[2] While this study is not exclusively, or even primarily, quantitative, it would have been impossible to arrive at or verify its results without using statistics.

Election campaigns provide exciting material for research because the people considered them important. Midwesterners have never treated the act of voting lightly; their sense of civic duty and their belief in democratic participation in the affairs of government prevent that. It will appear that nineteenth-century voters

1. Frederick Jackson Turner and several of his students did attempt quantitative election analysis early in the twentieth century; their approach collapsed because their methodology was inadequate. Richard Jensen, "American Election Analysis: A Case History of Methodological Innovation and Diffusion," in Seymour M. Lipset, ed., *Politics and the Social Sciences* (New York, 1969), pp. 226–43.
2. See Robert Swierenga, ed., *Quantification in American History* (New York, 1970).

were, if anything, far more involved in politics than their descendants are today. The 1890s witnessed unusually hard-fought contests in which the voters were forced back upon their deepest beliefs, their strongest loyalties, and their most urgent needs. These elections illuminate the nature of American society and politics at the grass roots as well as, or better than, any events since the Civil War.

The dominant forces that animated the electorate were party loyalty and, more fundamentally, religion. Economic or class antagonisms (which some historians have insisted upon as the "real" issues) existed too, but seem to have been of lesser importance. (The Appendix assesses in elaborate detail the relative importance of religion and occupation for parts of the Midwest in the 1870s.) Religion, in conjunction with racial and ethnic loyalties, was a central fact of life to most Americans, and could hardly have failed to affect their political behavior. Indeed, in England, Ireland, France, Germany, Spain, Italy, Canada, and various smaller states, politics at the time included heated disputes between various clerical and anticlerical forces. The roles of the church, the state, and language in elementary education were everywhere salient—and nowhere more so than in the Midwest in 1890.

The polarization of religious value systems manifested itself in the United States chiefly through the moralistic crusade for prohibition. It is possible to argue that from the 1830s to the 1930s no debate at the local level agitated this country more, year in and year out, than the question of controlling alcohol, unless it was the contests between Democrats and Republicans or Whigs. Chapter 3 explains the religious polarization of the Midwest; chapter 4 provides a case study of prohibition in Iowa in the 1880s; and chapter 7 contrasts the crusading moralists with the professional politicians. Chapters 5 and 10 discuss other facets of religious, cultural, and moral values in the elections of 1890 and 1896. Economic matters are not ignored—how could one overlook the worst depression of the era? Chapters 8 and 9 gauge the impact of the depression, while the tariff and monetary issues raised by the major candidates are discussed throughout the book.

Before the importance of social conflict can be appreciated, the operations of parties and election campaigns must be understood. The opening chapter sketches the nature of campaigning in the 1880s, while chapter 6 investigates the changes in party operations that occurred during the 1890s. The descriptions of party operations are not meant to be comprehensive. Much research needs to be done on the life cycle of the politician; for example, who sought public office, why, at what age, and how did they advance their careers? Nor is this a political history of the region; there is little discussion of the ordinary affairs of legislative, administrative, or judicial government. As for voters, the evidence that most men voted as their fathers or grandfathers did means that attention should turn to the origins of party affiliation and to the mechanisms that maintained, or weakened, those loyalties over long stretches of time. A full history of party affiliation would focus on the 1830s and the 1850s, and cannot be attempted here. The evidence at hand does, however, strongly indicate that religion was the basis of partisanship for most families.

The religious hostilities and economic hardships of the era produced a dizzy series of electoral turnabouts. In 1888 the Midwest seemed safely Republican; within two years the Democrats achieved a decisive advantage. Yet in 1894, in the midst of depression, the Republicans scored the most massive landslide in modern American history. In 1896, despite William Jennings Bryan's brilliant efforts, William McKinley solidified the GOP's newly built coalition into a standing majority that lasted until the New Deal.

The most striking contrast between the politics of the 1890s and the 1970s comes from the much higher levels of party loyalty and popular participation in the earlier period. The people, furthermore, demonstrated a significantly higher level of information about public affairs in the 1890s. Loyalty to one's religious or ethnic heritage was also much stronger then.

Only in two grave circumstances did numbers of voters fail to support their traditional party. They did this, first, if the old party grossly disappointed them, usually in an economic crisis. During the depression of 1893–96 everyone considered it the duty of President Grover Cleveland to return the country to prosperity.

When he failed, every identifiable group of voters slashed its support of his party.

The second circumstance, far more fascinating, came when outside loyalties—religious, ethnic, or ideological—conflicted with party loyalty. Some men resolved the tension by denying its existence; others stayed home and refused to vote; some switched parties or cast a protest ballot for a minor party. When ethnic or religious issues spilled over into the political arena, polarizing the parties, the results were unpredictable. Hostility between religious groups and between metropolitan and rural areas thus deserve special attention. When cultural conflict interacted with economic distress, the result was violence, as demonstrated by the case of the coal miners (chap. 9).

The politicians were the men immediately affected by unrest at the grass roots. If out of power, they tried to fan discontent; if in power, to quench it or channel it against the opposition. Power went to the politicians who won the support of the people, and they showed remarkable flexibility and imagination in adjusting the tenor of their appeals and the image of their parties. Unfortunately, some politicians sought to win power through fraud, bribery, or coercion. They seldom were successful, as chapter 2 makes clear. The legitimate reactions of the politicians, and their initiatives in creating a political system into which ethnic and religious issues would not intrude, are as central to this study as the voting patterns of the citizenry. The politicians responded to unrest by liquidating the traditional style of campaigning and ushering in the modern era of American politics.[3] Cynics mesmerized by the supposed corruption of the politicians, or the "failure" of the system to grapple with the "true" issues (invariably involving radical economic changes) have misunderstood American democracy and have failed to appreciate the genuine accomplishments of the decade.

Few historians—certainly not this one—are unmoved by the

3. For a generalized interpretation, see Richard Jensen, "Armies, Admen and Crusaders: Types of Presidential Election Campaigns," *History Teacher* (January 1969) 2:33–50. Walter Dean Burnham, *Critical Elections and the Mainsprings of American Politics* (New York, 1970), examines some of the effects of this transformation on voting and turnout patterns.

crises of their own time. This study was written while Barry Goldwater and George Wallace, Eugene McCarthy and Martin Luther King, Jr., were conducting their moralistic crusades against the corruption and injustice they perceived in American government and society. Their work, and the behavior of their followers, made it possible to understand forgotten crusaders like William Hoard, Frances Willard, and Bryan himself. Television was almost as valuable in writing this book as microfilm readers. The book was finished in the midst of campus turmoil that taught the author more than any book could about emotionalism and irrationality in times of crisis. Sometimes it seemed like the turmoil of 1894 all over again! The events of the 1960s helped underscore the two basic modes of political expression of the 1890s, crusading moralism on the one hand and countercrusading pluralism on the other. Did the political system of the 1890s work? The answer depends upon one's view of current events. My answer is yes, if one is asking whether a satisfactory state of stability was reached that won the active support of the majority of the people. I have too deep a commitment to pluralistic democracy and to full political participation to approve of any alternative to them.

The "Midwest" of this study comprises the six states of Illinois, Indiana, Iowa, Michigan, Ohio, and Wisconsin. Fully a quarter of the national electorate lived there, so this is more than a small-scale case study. Both parties recognized the region was decisive in the electoral college. From 1860 through 1912, the GOP only twice failed to select its presidential candidate from Ohio, Illinois, or Indiana, while in nine of these fourteen elections the Democratic nominee for vice-president came from one of the same three states. Economically and culturally, the six states were fairly similar. Furthermore, they all had been free-labor states which were settled, gained statehood, and reached political maturity between the Revolution and the Civil War. They thus escaped the angry memories of both the Federalist era and Reconstruction.

No effort has been made to cover all the elections of the period in each state, although all the major ones are mentioned. Certain campaigns receive special attention if they set the model for the entire region, as they did in Indiana in 1888 and Ohio in 1891.

Sometimes a campaign marked a major upheaval, as in Iowa in 1889 or Wisconsin in 1890, and could not be ignored. Otherwise, the choice typified significant regional patterns—as in Michigan in 1894, for example, or Illinois in 1892. By comparing the different states, the common elements stand out more sharply, while personalities or other factors peculiar to a single state can be downplayed. Occasionally municipal elections revealed the trend of affairs between general elections. The youngest states, Iowa and Wisconsin, claim disproportionate attention since their political systems had not quite reached the stability of older areas, and thus their political battles were more intense and their voting shifts more dramatic.

Laymen seem to believe the Midwest was a hotbed of agrarian Populism in the 1890s, and that most farmers spontaneously abandoned Tweedledum or Tweedledee to support the radical reformers who voiced the people's innermost convictions and needs while exposing the sham and hypocrisy of the old order. Populists may have had some success in the racially torn South, and in the thinly settled states further west, but they were hardly a serious factor in the Midwest. They carried one obscure farm county in western Iowa in 1894, their best year, together with a small industrialized county in northern Michigan in 1892 where the lumberjacks had been unionized. They never attained 10 percent of the vote in any state, and usually had to settle for much less. Probably most of the midwesterners who voted Populist were not farmers at all, but coal miners, railroad workers, lumberjacks, doctrinaire socialists, and middle-class utopians. More details are in chapter 9. The silverites, led by Bryan, were a different group all together, and deserve full treatment (chapter 10). To the extent that minor parties highlight the strengths and the weaknesses of the major parties rather than the minor parties' own pretensions, they are worth investigating. The Prohibition party meets the criteria far better than the Populists for the Midwest.

Years of statistical investigation went into this book, and rather little shows. Elaborate correlational and multivariate analyses proved valuable in spotting patterns of stability and change, and in indicating fruitless lines of research. The interesting patterns, however, have all been expressed in terms of aggregate trends and poll results.[4] Many of the tables are based on samples of counties, wards, or townships which had relatively homogeneous populations. Chapter 5, for example, has tables showing the trend over time of the vote in twenty-one rural German Catholic townships in Wisconsin that had been settled for a long time.[5] Whether all Wisconsin's rural German Catholics followed exactly the same pattern cannot be known, since many voted in more heterogeneous townships. The trends in sample areas, however, probably reflected the true trend without gross distortion. Well before Gallup the politicians were using interviews to predict the election results, and whenever possible the poll results have been indicated, together with the estimates made by shrewd political observers who probably had access to secret polls.

The debts I have incurred greatly outnumber the footnotes. I shall long be grateful to the American Studies Department at Yale, and the History Department at Washington University, where I was nurtured, prodded, corrected, and encouraged for eight busy years. Special thanks are due to friends who willingly criticized various drafts, particularly W. Dean Burnham, Samuel P. Hays, Paul Kleppner, Rosalind Mael, Arthur Mann, C. Vann Woodward, and Robert Zemsky.

4. On the methods, see Charles Dollar and Richard Jensen, *Historian's Guide to Statistics* (New York, 1971). For examples of the statistics, see Paul Kleppner, *The Cross of Culture* (New York, 1970), or Roger Wyman, "Wisconsin Ethnic Groups and the Election of 1890," in Swierenga, *Quantification,* pp. 239–73.

5. The Midwest in the late nineteenth century was just entering the melting pot stage. Voters whose fathers were born abroad will be described as immigrants, or as "German," "Irish," "Norwegian," and so on, without hyphenation. As the grandson of Danish and Italian immigrants to the Midwest, I am aware of their sensitivity to ethnic slurs. I have tried to avoid stereotypes, and yet tell the story as I saw it, without whitewashing the unpleasantries.

The Battle of 1888: General Harrison in Indiana

> The whole state is a blazing
> torchlight procession from one
> end to the other.
>
> Senator Daniel Voorhees[1]

One hot afternoon late in July, 1888, a large delegation of enthusiastic Republicans journeyed the hundred miles from Urbana to Indianapolis to meet their candidate for president, to pledge their support, to wish him well, and to listen to his wisdom. They brought a band, and some men wore gaudy five-dollar uniforms and carried replicas of log-cabins, cider-barrels, coons, and eagles. The campaign emblems recalled the "Log Cabin and Hard Cider" campaign of 1840, which carried William Henry Harrison to the White House and opened an era of mass participation in democratic politics that was strangely and wonderfully new to the world. Three of the visitors had voted for the old Harrison, and now were striving to elect his grandson. Little did they realize that this would be the last old-fashioned election campaign in the nation's history.

"Tippecanoe's" grandson, Benjamin Harrison, welcomed the group and spoke to them of the sublime importance of the electoral process in American democracy:

> It is fortunate that you are allowed, not only to express your interest by such popular gatherings as these, but that you will be called upon individually, after the debate is over, to settle this contention by your ballots. . . . We ought to elevate in thought and practice the free suffrage that we enjoy. As long as it shall be held by our people to be the jewel above price, as long as each for himself shall claim its free exercise and shall generously and manfully insist upon an equally free exercise of it by every other man, our Government will be preserved and our development will not find its climax until the purpose of God in establishing this Government shall have spread throughout the world—governments "of the people, by the people, and for the people." (Cheers.)[2]

1. *New York Herald*, September 28, 1888.
2. Speech of July 24, 1888, in Charles Hedges, ed., *Speeches of Benjamin Harrison* (New York, 1892), p. 56.

Harrison's words were not merely idle platitudes. Already in the Southern states many thousands of Negroes were restrained from voting; later disenfranchisement devices would keep nearly all the rest from the ballot box. In an effort to win Southern electoral votes (and thus lessen dependence on New York) the Republicans were soft-pedaling the powerful issue of fraud, intimidation, and violence in Southern politics, which was rapidly losing its democratic veneer. In the Midwest, however, every adult male citizen could vote, along with women, in school elections, and, in several states, immigrants who had not completed the process of becoming citizens. The ideal of full participation in politics on the part of all the voters was strong in the Midwest. The Iowa GOP had long before stated the norm:

> It is not only the right but the duty of every good citizen, at the party caucuses, in the party conventions, and at the polls, to use his best efforts to secure the nomination and election of good men to places of official trust.[3]

Participation was more than an ideal, it was a reality. The national elections of the 1880s brought more than 80 percent of the northern electorate to the polls. In 1896 turnout soared above 95 percent of those eligible in Illinois, Indiana, Iowa, Michigan, and Ohio. (In Wisconsin that year the turnout was "only" 85 percent—still higher than that in any state of the Union in any election after 1908.) In state and local races the turnout was lower, usually 60 to 80 percent, but still higher than twentieth-century rates.[4]

The simple act of voting, itself difficult enough in an era of poor roads and slow transportation, was only one manifestation of popular participation in politics. Midwesterners turned out by the tens of thousands to march in parades, shout themselves hoarse

3. State platform of 1878, in *Appleton's Annual Cyclopedia and Register of Important Events of the Year 1878* (New York, 1879), p. 453; this important yearbook will be cited hereafter as *Ann. Cycl.*
4. Turnout data is based on unpublished estimates by W. Dean Burnham, and was computed by dividing the number of males over twenty-one (estimated by linear interpolation of census returns, after deducting the estimated number of ineligible recent immigrants) into the total vote cast for president. See also Burnham, "The Changing Shape of the American Political Universe," *American Political Science Review* (1965), 59: 7–28.

at rallies, picnic at barbecues, and listen to long-winded speeches on hot summer afternoons. Exactly how many joined in the fun, and in the more prosaic work of attending conventions, distributing literature, contributing money, and talking up the candidates cannot be exactly estimated, but all indications point to a much higher rate of participation than the 10 or 15 percent typical of the 1950s and 1960s.[5] Perhaps people who lacked electronic amusement and commercialized sports sought entertainment from the political arena. Certainly they found enough spellbinders, oddballs, cranks, and demagogues to fill a three-ring circus in every county. "What the theatre is to the French, or the bull-fight or fandango to the Spanish, the hustings and the ballot-box are to *our* people," noted one shrewd observer. "We are all politicians, men, women, and children."[6] Yet the evidence points to a much deeper involvement than the analogy with television or baseball might suggest. Men spoke of political attachments in the same breath as loyalty to religion; for as one Presbyterian historian explained, "Every man . . . is expected to stand up for the creed of his church as he does for the platform of his party."[7]

The electorate followed political developments, recognized politicians, and understood the issues. They sat through hours of speeches without a break, not only to display their support of favorite candidates but also to soak up the details and the minute points of the tariff, the money question, educational policies, prohibition laws, and the myriad of minor issues that erupted from time to time. Financial questions, despite their inherent technicality, proved to be the most popular topics for occasions when an orator really wanted to stir up his audience. Routinely the newspapers published lengthy texts of major speeches, and there is no evidence that the subscribers hurried by them to the sports page (there

5. See William H. Flanigan, *Political Behavior of the American Electorate* (Boston, 1968), pp. 12–25, 95–98; and John H. Kessel, *The Goldwater Coalition* (Indianapolis, 1968), pp. 329–34, for summaries of modern participation levels.

6. Joseph Baldwin, *Party Leaders* (New York, 1855), p. 278.

7. Robert Ellis Thompson, *A History of the Presbyterian Churches in the United States* (New York, 1895), p. 252. In 1885 Senator Henry Blair of New Hampshire would wax lyrically, "We love our parties as we love our churches and our families. We are part of them." *One Hundred Years of Temperance* (New York, 1886), p. 85.

were no comics). James Bryce understood the situation in the 1880s:

> It is not that [nineteen of twenty voters] are incapable of appreciating good arguments, or are unwilling to receive them. On the contrary, and this is especially true of the working classes, an audience is pleased when solid arguments are addressed to it, and men read with most relish the articles or leaflets, supposing them to be smartly written, which contain the most carefully sifted facts and the most exact thought.[8]

In 1888 the tariff was the focus of elaborate argumentation from both sides. President Cleveland devoted his entire annual message for 1887 to the problem of tariff reform, developing his argument down to the point where he was analyzing the costs and profits in growing wools of different quality. The spectacle of the chief executive lecturing the nation on the minutiae of wool prices, and expecting to win reelection thereby, can be understood only when it is realized that millions of men (few of whom had ever shorn a sheep) considered the tariff to be the paramount matter of national concern and the tax on wool a significant battleground for American elections. The Wisconsin Democrats were so pleased with Cleveland's address that they made elaborate plans to distribute 85,000 copies of it in English, German, Polish, Czech, Norwegian, and Swedish across the state in 1888, along with a million other documents. However, the "stiff Republican" postmaster at Lavalle, Wisconsin, reportedly distributed most of the presidential documents "in his outhouse, and to parties that he knew would do the same with them."[9]

Although midwesterners read a good many pamphlets, and often had a chance to shake a politician's hand, they relied primarily on newspapers for political information. Circulation far exceeded the number of voters in most counties, suggesting that the great

8. James Bryce, *The American Commonwealth* (New York, 1894), 2:250; see also William D. Foulke, "Campaigning in the West," *North American Review* (1893) 156: 126–28.

9. B. S. Barney (sic) to Ellis B. Usher, February 29, 1888, for quote; W. J. Mize to Usher, March 28, 1888; "Memorandum on 1888 Campaign," all in Ellis B. Usher MSS, Wisconsin State Historical Society. Albert T. Volwiler, "Tariff Strategy and Propaganda in the United States, 1887–1888," *American Historical Review* (1930) 36: 76–96; and Dorothy Fowler, *John Coit Spooner* (New York, 1961), p. 115.

majority of men subscribed to at least one paper—a daily for city-dwellers, a weekly for rural folk—and perhaps a religious paper too. In 1886 the Midwest published 340 dailies and 2900 weeklies, totals that were almost exactly the same as the numbers of television and radio stations, respectively, for the entire nation in the mid-1950s. Except for a few metropolitan papers with statewide circulations, the sheets were tailored for local distribution. Practically every hamlet of any importance had at least one weekly, although small budgets demanded the heavy use of patent insides and stereotype plates sent out from Chicago with an ample quota of political news (Republican or Democratic according to order, though occasionally a hilarious mixup occurred and a staunch Republican weekly published an issue that delighted the Democrats). Small cities, of, say, 10,000 population usually supported two or three dailies and four or five weeklies for the rural hinterland. Cities of 20,000 to 40,000 population in the late 1880s, like Aurora, Canton, Council Bluffs, Fort Wayne, Oshkosh, and Sioux City boasted from three to five dailies, while Des Moines (50,000) had five, Detroit and Cleveland (200,000 and 260,000) eight each, Cincinnati (300,000), fourteen, and Chicago (1,100,-000) eighteen daily newspapers in several languages.[10]

The papers were short, usually only four to eight pages an issue, yet the editors crammed immense amounts of political news into their small-type columns. Measurement of space allocated to election news shows that thin metropolitan dailies provided twice as much information as their bulky successors did half a century later.[11] As the first Tuesday in November drew near, the

10. *Ann Cycl. 1886:* 633–35; S.N.D. North, *History and Present Condition of the Newspaper and Periodical Press of the United States* (10th Census Report) (Washington, 1884); Frank C. Mott, *American Journalism* (New York, 1962), pp. 478–80, 590; and for all the details, N.W. Ayer & Sons, *American Newspaper Annual* (Philadelphia, 1880–1900).

11. This section is based primarily on a reading of thousands of issues of dozens of newspapers across the Midwest. See also Robert Batlin, "San Francisco Newspapers' Campaign Coverage: 1896, 1952," *Journalism Quarterly* (1954) 31:297–303, and Irene B. Taeuber, "Changes in Content and Presentation of Reading Material in Minnesota Weekly Newspapers 1860–1929," *ibid.* (1932) 9:281–89, for statistics. Two pioneer efforts at content analysis of the distribution of newspaper space that remain particularly valuable are in the *New York Voice,* March 29, 1888, and Delos F. Wilcox, "The American Newspaper: A Study in Social Psychology," *Annals of the American Academy* (1900) 16:56–92.

pages spilled over with reports of yesterday's rallies and announcements of tomorrow's schedules. Three or four columns of editorials examined the day's developments thoroughly, for most of the editors were prominent party leaders.

The midwestern papers flourished because they were semiofficial party organs and furnished the main channel of routine communication between party workers and the rank and file. Reports and interpretations of significant developments locally, in the various state capitals, and in Washington provided the cues to appropriate attitudes and opinions. Nowhere else could a loyal partisan, whether county chairman, precinct captain, or average voter, find the arguments, the slogans and clichés, the boasts and excuses, the facts of national, state, and local political doings that fed his curiosity, whetted his enthusiasm, and satisfied his need to understand the course of events. Recognizing the critical importance of the press, the parties subsidized struggling foreign-language papers, linked subscription drives to political canvasses, and rewarded editors with printing contracts and posts of profit, honor, and power.

The news was almost as biased as the editorials. The weaknesses of the opposition grew into fatal flaws, their blunders magnified into heinous crimes against American liberties, and their policies metamorphosed into evil designs of conspiratorial juntas. The editor's own party rarely stumbled, its principles remained ever pure and self-evident, its rallies were uniformly crowded to the rafters (while the opposition inevitably suffered poor attendance), and the party was always marching to victory. When victory did come it was due to sound principles, superior organization, invincible leadership, and the basic good sense of the people. If perchance an election brought defeat, the causes were unnatural: heavy rains downstate, overconfidence or treachery in the ranks, vile frauds at the polling places, or wicked deception by the enemy.

The only explanation for the high participation in politics on the part of the common man was intense partisanship and loyalty to party. In both urban and rural areas the vast majority of midwesterners, at least 90 percent, were firmly committed to either the Republican or Democratic standard. Third parties rarely held more than 5 percent of the vote, and then only when strong loyalties to labor unions came into play. Comprehensive door-to-door party canvasses, a typical feature of the period, revealed that less than 5 percent of the adults failed to acknowledge a party preference. A sample of thousands of interviews conducted by nonpartisan directory makers in Illinois and Indiana in the mid-1870s disclosed that only 2 percent of the men were without a party. By contrast, a third of the Northerners in the 1950s and 1960s claimed to be "independent" of party, or never voted, while only a third acknowledged they were "strong" Republicans or Democrats.[12]

Partisanship ran deep in the Midwest. The Civil War was a living memory; more than anything else it fused the loyalty of Republicans to the "grand old party" that had saved the Union and abolished slavery—just as it fused the loyalty of Democrats to the poor man's party which had defended constitutional liberties in an era of despotism and corruption, and fought bitterly to prevent "miscegenation" and the "flooding" of the region with Negroes. From father to son the loyalty passed. The hundreds of thousands of new immigrants who had come to the Midwest since the war usually adopted without question the loyalties of their kinsmen who had participated in the critical events of the 1850s and 1860s.

The politicians did not leave all to tradition, for the median voter was only thirty-seven years old in the 1880s, and thus had been eligible to vote only after the end of war and Reconstruction. Instead, the Republican leaders refreshed memories by recalling

12. Flanigan, *Political Behavior,* p. 39; *The People's Guide: A Business, Political and Religious Directory of Hendricks Co., Indiana. . . .* (Indianapolis, 1874). The publishers, Cline and McHaffie, lived in the county and had little difficulty obtaining detailed information from their neighbors. In Washington Township, a typical rural area, they recorded 162 Republicans, 78 Democrats, a "neutral" shoemaker, a "neutral" wagonmaker, a nontalkative sawmiller, and an "Old Whig" farmer. The vote in 1872 was 207 Republican and 104 Democratic, so a fourth of the voters were overlooked. They seemed to have voted the same as the canvassed men did, so there is little reason to suppose they were any more independent. It is significant, however, that three of the four nonparty men were nonfarmers. The Democratic poll of Trempeleau County, Wisconsin, in September, 1888, tabulated 1,592 Democrats (43.9%), 1,635 Republicans (45.1%), 178 Prohibitionists (4.9%), 153 "dissatisfied republicans" (4.2%) and only 61 "independents" (1.7%); the poll is in the Usher MSS.

the glorious and the treasonable episodes of the 1860s, and by frequently nominating war heroes like General Harrison. The Democrats reinforced party loyalty by warning that monopolistic Eastern wealth and extremism had corrupted and controlled the GOP, so only the Democrats could be trusted to preserve American liberties. Furthermore, every midwestern state in the 1870s and 1880s experienced a revival of those issues, especially prohibition, that reinforced the underlying determinants of party loyalty.

The prevalance of party loyalty was evident in the focus on national issues in races where national problems had no bearing. Candidates for state and local office were more likely to take stands on the tariff than on local taxation. In the larger cities, however, a movement can be discerned in the 1880s (and especially after 1893) to elect aldermen and mayors without regard to national issues or even party labels. The *Wisconsin State Journal,* a banner Republican paper, in endorsing the incumbent Democratic mayor of Madison for reelection in 1892, explained that "true reform in municipal government is to be sought through the divorcing of its politics from state or national politics." It went on:

> A body of men in a municipality may be interested in . . . street improvements, better water supplies, cheaper gas, better educational facilities, etc., and oppose the ideas of [others who agree with them] entirely upon the ways of raising national revenues, the kind and quality of money to have in circulation, and having free trade between nations rather than restrictions by tariff duties.[13]

On the whole, however, municipal contests followed national themes except when prohibition or law-and-order was central, while local races in rural areas revolved around personalities.[14]

13. *Wisconsin State Journal* (Madison), March 16, 1892 (editorial).

14. "Unless some special reason intervenes, [local rural] contests are always of a most neighborly and friendly kind. Sound, safe, practical and honest business men are what all seek. Villages and cities usually recognize party lines, but are not tied down to them. . . . [Big city municipal] contests do not afford good partisan battleground, though the form of party division is gone through with." *Milwaukee Journal,* March 22, 1890 (editorial). See also Bryce, *American Commonwealth,* 1:619–20; Merle Curti, *The Making of an American Community* (Stanford, 1959), chaps. 12, 13; and on the movement for nonpartisanship, *Proceedings of the Second National Conference for Good City Government . . . The First Annual Meeting of*

The strength of partisanship was also manifest in the relative absence of ticket splitting. In legislative, state, and presidential contests rarely did more than 5 percent of the voters split their tickets. The result was a striking uniformity in the total vote for all members of a ticket. In Iowa in 1890, for example, the low man out of eight on the Republican state ticket received 190,007 votes, while the high man polled 191,774, a variation of less than 1 percent. In the 1880s each state used private ballots, that is, each voter brought to the polls a ballot provided by party workers and already marked. This system was prone to abuse, especially bribery and multiple voting. Between the elections of 1888 and 1892 all the midwestern states introduced the Australian secret ballot, which made fraud more difficult and ticket splitting easier. The mechanical change in ballot form could not upset party loyalty, however, and in the early 1890s ticket splitting remained uncommon. In Iowa in 1894 the leader of the GOP state ticket polled 229,480 votes, while the low man received 228,565, a variation of less than one half of 1 percent. In minor local contests, however, ticket splitting was already common in the 1870s.[15]

The prevalence of intense partisanship produced a remarkable familiarity with the issues. Not that most of the voters were trained experts (less than half had schooling beyond the eighth grade). Rather, adherence to the standard of a great party gave a man a share of the prestige of the party and its leaders; it was, said James G. Blaine, "the patriotic pride of every man in its ranks that he has been a member of it and has shared its responsibilities, its triumphs, its honors." Belief in the party's precepts and confidence in its policies gave the citizen an understanding of public affairs. The symbols, speeches, and slogans provided an easy guide to respectable, comprehensive, and satisfying judgements and opinions on the questions of the day. To forfeit the self-confidence

---

the National Municipal League and of the Third National Conference for Good City Government (Philadelphia, 1895, printed together), especially p. 22 ("We are all slaves, or nearly all of us, to parties"), pp. 42–44 (on Sioux City), pp. 55–57 (Cleveland), p. 88 (Minneapolis), pp. 242–43 (upstate New York), pp. 374–71 (Indianapolis), and pp. 467–68.
15. Jerrold G. Rusk, "The Effect of the Australian Ballot Reform on Split Ticket Voting: 1876–1908," American Political Science Review (1970) 65: 1220–38, finds very little effect before 1904.

and esteem associated with what Blaine referred to as "party fealty, political principle, personal pledges, ancient prejudices, hoary tradition, boasted record," was to cast one's self adrift in confusions and bewilderment.[16] Not many men could analyze issues clearly without a party to guide them, to tell them what was true or false, relevant or misleading, good or evil.

A man who was uncomfortable with his party's position did not split his ticket, and almost never switched parties save in grave crises. Instead, if his displeasure was great enough, he simply stayed away from the polls on election day. Since off year contests were not as important or exciting as presidential elections, the turnout usually dropped 10 or 15 percent. If one party was on the defensive—its leadership divided or disgraced, its treasury depleted, its workers apathetic, its rank and file disgruntled, and its opposition united and thirsty for the kill—the turnout of its supporters dropped precipitously while that of the opposition held up. Since the basic distribution of partisanship in the electorate was normally very stable, most of the fluctuation in relative party strength from year to year was due to variation in turnout rates.

Turnout was doubly important since the two parties were very evenly matched in the 1880s, both in the Midwest and in the nation at large. Nationally, less than two percentage points separated the total Democratic and Republican vote for congressmen in the elections of 1878, 1880, 1884, 1886, and 1888. In 1880 Garfield edged Hancock by only 7,000 votes, and Cleveland's edge in 1884 over Blaine was 70,000 out of 10 million votes cast. The Midwest was almost as close; Blaine ran only 90,000 ahead of Cleveland out of 3 million votes cast regionally. In half the Midwestern counties (157 out of 312) casting more than 4,000 ballots in 1884, the winner's plurality was less than 10 percent. Clearly a small shift of votes, a sharp drop in turnout, or a little fraudulent manipulation of returns could decide the winners in

---

16. James G. Blaine, *Political Discussions: 1856–1886* (Norwich, 1887), p. 447, from a campaign speech in South Bend, Indiana, October 18, 1884; ibid., p. 110, referring to the effects of Horace Greeley's independent candidacy, July 27, 1872. On the relation between loyalty, dissent, and party strength, see Albert O. Hirschman, *Exit, Voice, and Loyalty: Responses to Declines in Firms, Organizations, and States* (Cambridge, 1970).

races for the legislature, Congress, the statehouse, and even the White House.

The major parties adjusted their basic strategies to the two main facts of political life, intense partisanship and very close contests. Elections were treated like battles in which the two main armies (parties) concentrated on fielding the maximum number of troops (voters) on the battlefield (the polls) on election day. Party organization resembled that of an army (many leaders had been officers in the war), with the head of the ticket as commanding general, the lesser candidates as officers of the line, and party officials as staff officers. Even the language of politics was cast in military terms. From the *opening gun* of the *campaign* the *standard bearer,* along with other *war-horses fielded* by the party, *rallied* the *rank and file* around the party *standard,* the *bloody shirt,* and other *slogans.* Precinct *captains aligned* their *phalanxes shoulder-to-shoulder* to mobilize votes for the *Old Guard.* Meanwhile the *Mugwumps* warned that the *palace troops* sought to *plunder* the treasury; their *strategy* was to *crusade* against the *myrmidons* of corruption. Even a *man on horseback* could not have saved the *lost cause* with his *jingoism.* But party *headquarters* changed *tactics* and emptied its *war chest* to buy *mercenaries* and *Hessians.* Finally the *well-drilled fugelmen* in the *last ditch* closed *ranks,* overwhelmed the enemy *camp,* and divided the *spoils* of victory.[17]

Discipline and enthusiasm were the watchwords for campaign managers. Bolters or sulkers incurred the public wrath of stinging editorials, while faithful officers could reasonably expect nomination to a suitable office. (The policy of rotation in office meant that very few men served more than one or two terms in the state legislatures.) Power in the parties rested with the county committees, whose main task was to guarantee a high turnout, and with the state committees which supervised the distribution of scarce resources, especially money, literature and orators, and decided on the optimum mix of issues to use.[18]

17. William Safire, *The New Language of Politics* (New York, 1968), p. 262; Hans Sperber and Travis Trittschuh, *Dictionary of American Political Terms* (New York, 1964).
18. Jesse Macy, *Party Organization and Machinery* (New York, 1904), chaps. 8, 13; Albert V. House, "The Democratic State Central Committee of Indiana in 1880," *Indiana Magazine of History* (1962) 58: 179–210.

In 1888 the critical states were New York and Indiana; the strategists realized that a minute shift of votes (actually less than 1 percent) would swing those states and decide the outcome in the electoral college. The winner would become president, determine national policy, and have control of the distribution of some 100,000 patronage places (one per hundred voters) to reward his army. Republican prospects were bright. In New York the GOP was united after years of dissension, while the Democrats, as usual, were feuding bitterly. For victory General Harrison relied on the skills of the local party chieftans. "I have acted upon the theory that I was too far from the seat of war in the East to direct the movement of our forces," he explained.[19] Indiana was Harrison's home, and it had not seen a Hoosier in the White House since Benjamin's grandfather, another famous general, had led the Whigs to a smashing victory in 1840. The Republicans proposed to carry Indiana and the Democrats had to stop them.

By the end of September the Indiana battle reached a peak of intensity, thrilling even the most hardened Hoosiers. Harrison had promised at the national convention to carry the state without outside help, but a Republican poll of voters' intentions early in September showed Cleveland in the lead. To lose Indiana was unthinkable; to win at the price of becoming subservient to victorious powers in the Eastern GOP was intolerable. The candidate therefore assumed personal control of the campaign and overruled the national committee's strategy of concentrating its resources on the doubtful states in the East. He requisitioned the outstanding orators and spokesmen of the party to come and stump Indiana for him, diverted national campaign funds to Indianapolis, and stepped up his own unprecedented "front porch" campaign.

More than 10,000 political speeches, delivered by 2,500 orators and spellbinders, filled the crisp October air in Indiana. Battalions

19. Benjamin Harrison to James Clarkson, October 27, 1888, quoted in Harry J. Sievers, *Benjamin Harrison* (New York, 1959), 2:417. Sievers has the fullest account of Harrison's campaign in 1888; see also Allan Nevins, *Grover Cleveland* (New York, 1932) pp. 383–442; R.C. Buley, "The Campaign of 1888 in Indiana," *Indiana Magazine of History* (1914) 10: 162–85; Clarence J. Bernardo, "The Presidential Election of 1888" (Ph.D. diss., Georgetown University, 1949); and for overall strategy, Robert Marcus, *Grand Old Party: Political Structure in the Gilded Age, 1880–1896* (New York, 1971), pp. 101–50.

of 5,000, even 10,000, enthusiastic citizens assembled at little crossroad villages on two or three days' notice to watch the floats and parades and listen to the bands and speakers and to picnic and politick. A man could scarcely escape the tumult. The GOP distributed scores of thousands of leaflets, speeches, posters and pamphlets among the half million Hoosier voters. Some 300,000 explanations of Harrison's sterling record on the liquor question assuaged the qualms of the moralists (the pious General was a temperate Presbyterian) and the drinkers too (he did not favor prohibition). Another 300,000 fliers refuted the persistent lie that Harrison considered a dollar a day to be a fair wage. Special editions of German newspapers flooded the immigrant settlements, and the general press worked overtime to meet the demands of the voters. For men who cared to weigh the arguments, various high tariff groups broadcast 60,000 copies of Congressman McKinley's eloquent defense of protectionism, as well as 30,000 each of Congressman Reed's and Senator Frye's slightly more prolix utterances. And for those who could merely display their colors, some 300,000 lithographed portraits of the general were available, and uncounted bushels of tin buttons. The quarter million Hoosier Republicans were armored for battle.[20]

Their intrepid general fought in the front ranks, and hardest of all. From mid-July to the eve of the election, Harrison on the front porch of his Indianapolis home welcomed 110 delegations of well-wishers, totaling nearly 200,000 persons. He shook hands with perhaps 100,000 of the Hoosiers among them, and had a few words for each of the 20,000 visitors from Illinois, the 14,000 from Ohio, and the thousands more from about the country. The highlight of the Indiana campaign came on October 11, when James G. Blaine, the magnetic hero of the rank and file, came to Indianapolis. For an hour and a half 25,000 marchers stepped smartly before the reviewing stand. With forty bands, scores of flag-decked floats, the gaudiest uniforms and the shrillest music and the loudest cheers, they came. A thousand blue-garbed veterans, another thousand mounted cavalry, two dozen Negro clubs with 2,500 marchers, Irish contingents, and "Carrie Harrison"

20. *Indianapolis Journal,* November 4, 1888; *Chicago Tribune,* October 3, 7, 1888; Claude Bowers, *My Life* (New York, 1962), pp. 7–10.

girls' groups—all came to honor Blaine and whoop it up for Harrison and for the applause of the 100,000 onlookers. Some spectators claimed it was the biggest parade ever held outside of New York, while everyone agreed it was the greatest in Indiana history.[21]

Harrison's addresses to the regiments of visitors were his pride and his achievement. Without notes, although not without careful preparation, he delivered seventy-nine major speeches, short, pithy, warm and gracious, and well suited to the needs of the daily press. Harrison escaped the repetition, monotony, and hyperbole that typified the stump speeches of the day, and won the admiration of many hostile observers. Save for one vacation trip to Ohio, Harrison refused to tour the country as Blaine had done in 1884. "I have great risk of meeting a fool at home," he confided, "but the candidate who travels cannot escape him."[22] To forestall the possibility of being greeted by a "Saloons, Sacraments, and Sedition" echo of the "Rum, Romanism, and Rebellion" epithet that soured Blaine's canvass in 1884, Harrison and his staff read and edited advance texts of the visitors' statements. The front-porch campaign worked smoothly, without a serious mishap, much to the delight of the skeptical party professionals. Harrison was "the ablest political strategist I have ever known," wrote his top aide. Strong "in the details of organization and the selection of methods," he continued, the general was "a superb strategist and tactician in political warfare."[23]

In 1888, the purpose of the rallies and speeches was not to create a new coalition of voters, or to convince men of the validity of the party position, but to reactivate the loyalties and enthusiasm of the party faithful. Secondarily, they worked to hold or win over

21. *Indianapolis Journal,* October 12, 1888; *Indianapolis Sentinel,* October 12, 1888; *Chicago Tribune,* October 12, 1888; Sievers, *Harrison,* 2:371–72, 404–5; statistics from Hedges, *Harrison's Speeches,* esp. pp. 170–71.

22. B. Harrison to Whitelaw Reid, October 9, 1888, cited in Sievers, *Harrison,* 2:405–6.

23. Louis T. Michener, memorandum on "The Harrison Campaign for the Nomination in 1888," Michener MSS, Library of Congress. See also Michener's memoranda "Harrison's Speeches in 1888," "Party Organization in Indiana," and "The Battle in the State, 1888"; Sievers, *Harrison,* 2:331, 359, 372; *Chicago Tribune,* October 28, 1888 (editorial); *Saint Louis Globe-Democrat,* October 13, 1888 (editorial).

wavering voters, to capture new voters, and to frustrate or complicate the opposition's parallel efforts. "It is a mistake," cautioned one experienced Wisconsin organizer, "to suppose that political successes are the results of accidents, or are brought about by a sudden change of heart on the part of the people." Not many converts, he went on, "are made during the heat of a campaign by speech-making, however eloquent it may be."[24] The deeper implications of such theorizing were soon to unfold, but in the midst of the battle of 1888 it was the first duty of every party worker to make sure that his men were all in line and touching elbows, as President Cleveland put it.[25]

Harrison, the scion of America's foremost political dynasty, and an accomplished professional politician in his own right, directed the thrust of the campaign toward both the Republican regulars and the potential recruits. Septuagenarian Republicans were canvassed in an effort to locate the surviving supporters of William Henry Harrison in 1836 and 1840, and to organize them into "Tippecanoe" clubs. The Republican campaign emphasized the symbols of continuity with the Whig tradition and with the Lincolnian heritage of the Grand Old Party itself. "There is no older Republican in the United States than I am," Harrison claimed, for "my first presidential vote was given for the first presidential candidate of the Republican party." That party, he boasted to the Indianapolis Tippecanoe club, steadfastly defends the "principles which were dear to you as Whigs. . . . chief among these were a reverent devotion to the Constitution and the flag, and a firm faith in the benefits of a protective tariff."[26]

About half the midwestern voters in 1888 were, in varying degrees, committed to the principles of Republicanism, and a slightly smaller number to those of the Democrats. Symbolically, the GOP claimed to be the party of national legitimacy, the vehicle for the salvation of the Union in its historic days of crisis, and the party of moral achievement, the destroyer of slavery. The Democrats

24. E.C. Wall to W.F. Vilas, November 30, 1892, in Vilas MSS, Wisconsin State Historical Society.
25. Cleveland to Governor Isaac Gray (of Indiana), September 29, 1888, in Nevins, *Cleveland,* p. 435, and in Allan Nevins, ed., *Letters of Grover Cleveland* (Boston, 1933), p. 190.
26. Hedges, *Harrison's Speeches,* pp. 17, 38–39.

claimed to be the party of the common man, the bulwark of the Constitution, defending the little people against the encroachments of paternalistic and corrupt power wielded by greedy monopolists and Eastern moneybags. Jackson and Jefferson were the demigods of the Democratic party, and Lincoln it honored as the hero of a great rival party that had since been captured by the rich and the privileged. The tension between the symbols of the parties underlay the issues and the personalities of the era. Not manufactured "images" or advertising slogans, but meaningful symbols recalled from times of crisis permitted the ordinary citizen to participate wholeheartedly in the political process.

Party affiliation, like church membership, was a deeply rooted commitment. Fathers inculcated in their sons with a loyalty to the family party. Brash young men, of course, sometimes revolted over parental control. In Indiana in 1888, the Democrats admitted that in Republican areas some first voters were breaking with their Democratic family heritage and supporting Harrison. Evidently the enthusiasm of their friends and the encouragement of the young ladies of the Carrie Harrison clubs proved especially convincing. The Democrats claimed that in their bailiwicks (where "Frankie Cleveland" clubs were active) Republican youths were announcing for Cleveland.[27]

So evenly matched were the rival armies that neither dared to rely on traditional loyalties alone. Since every potential vote had to be polled or forfeited, the campaign directors concentrated on publicizing their candidates and platforms, and organized the parades and speechfests to invigorate the laggards and encourage the faithful. Yet there were dangers in overly vigorous campaigns. "Boldness is not always wise," cautioned one Ohio Republican leader. "I never saw it fail," he elaborated," that when you go into the enemy's stronghold you only arouse his soldiers to vigorous action."[28] The politicians usually avoided goading the opposition,

27. *New York Tribune*, October 19, 26, 1888. Young men, one editor noted, "inherit their political sentiments, just as they inherit their religion." *Saint Louis Republic*, October 28, 1896.

28. *Detroit Free Press*, October 9, 1896. The Democratic leader in Madison, Wisconsin, told his state chairman in 1888: "In Democratic strongholds there ought to be marching clubs and torch light processions. It is the only way that you can get into line certain Democrats. It has a tendency

and a few years later revised their campaign tactics radically so as to keep all the benefits of active campaigning for their own party. The participants in rallies and parades were the fully committed foot soldiers of the rival armies, but by instilling a "will win" psychology, the demonstrations spurred the party workers to canvass their precincts more thoroughly and to make sure that no likely voter stayed home or strayed into the enemy's camp. The parallel with the strategy of the ministers and priests suggested itself to the politicians. "Revivals and missions in the church," theorized one, "are the same as speech-making and torchlight processions during the last days of a campaign."[29]

Harrison realized that flaming oratory would excite the delegations in his yard, but would read poorly in the thousands of newspapers that broadcast his words across the land. He therefore blended with his gracious remarks incisive statements on the burning issues of the campaign. The heart of his message was the gospel of the protective tariff. His convictions rested upon the classical American principle of the harmony of all legitimate interests and the reciprocal dependence of all social classes. "It is not possible," he felt, "for one class to be highly prosperous while all other classes are suffering . . . there is an interdependence in all our business and social relations."[30] The progress of the nation demanded the prosperity of all groups. The benefits of the protective tariff, he pointed out, "are felt by all classes of our people—by the farmer as well as by the workmen in our mills; by the man who works on the street as well as the skilled laborer who works in the mill; by the women in the household, and by the children who are now in the schools and might otherwise be in the mills."[31] The crowds cheered, and they were not being bamboozled. Harrison was not the minion of mysterious forces somewhere, he was the spokesman for his party and for the millions of men who cherished their allegiance to it.

---

to solidify a portion of our voters who, unfortunately, have not enough intelligence to be solidified by 'ideas.' Of course in places where Republicans are in the majority I would not advise any torch light processions etc." J.L. O'Conner to E.B. Usher, October 29, 1888, in Usher MSS.

29. Wall to Vilas, November 30, 1892, Vilas MSS.
30. *Ann. Cycl. 1896:* 274–75.
31. Hedges, *Harrison's Speeches,* p. 157.

"The Republican party," Harrison proclaimed, "holds that a protective tariff is constitutional, wholesome, and necessary."[32] The GOP, he said, offered not a fixed schedule of tariffs, but a principle, a commitment to the preservation of the American market for American producers, and the maintenance of a scale of wages for American workingmen. Harrison pitched his appeal to the rapidly growing body of factory and mill workers ripe for enlistment into Republican ranks. To railroad workers the candidate explained that high wages in industry induced high wages for them too, but even if not "your fellowship with your fellow toilers in other industries would lead you to desire" a tariff to protect them.[33]

The future of America, the GOP believed, lay with the city and the factory. A high protective tariff was not a burden but a blessing, for it was the primary governmental instrument available to encourage the rapid development of industry in a predominantly agricultural region. By raising the demand for American-made products, the tariff raised the wages of American workingmen and (sotto voce) stimulated the flow of skilled, industrious Europeans to our shores. Excessive profits, the GOP admitted, were socially undesirable. But, they replied uncertainly, competitive free enterprise would guarantee that profits were, or eventually would become, only equal to a fair return to the invested capital and entrepreneurial talent that had been stimulated to enter industry. Quickly turning from profits to general prosperity, the Republican's vision beheld tradesmen, merchants, miners, and railroad workers sharing in the new prosperity of urban America. And last, the farmer would benefit as a rich, growing, reliable domestic market paid handsome prices for his foodstuffs; no more would the farmer have to depend on an erratic world market that one year might be normal but the next year glutted and ruinous. This argument had little appeal for cotton planters in the South and wheat farmers on the plains, who would continue to sell their products on a world market; but, no matter, the Republican vision was built on success in the Midwest and the East.

32. Ibid., p. 110.
33. Ibid., pp. 48, 75–76.

Where the Republicans found opportunity the Democrats saw only crisis and corruption. The high tariff unnaturally interfered with the course of economic development, was unnecessary, and—what especially frightened Cleveland—had already produced a dangerous surplus in the federal treasury, which thereby became

> a hoarding place for money needlessly withdrawn from trade and the people's use, thus crippling our national energies, suspending our country's development, preventing investment in productive enterprise, threatening financial disturbances, and inviting schemes of public plunder.[34]

For Cleveland and the party he led, the justice and wisdom of the remedy was equalled only by its urgent necessity. The high protective tariff, "the vicious, inequitable, and illogical source of unnecessary taxation," had to undergo radical revision downward. The tariff was a tax on American consumers, and ought to be levied only as a source of needed revenue for essential programs. Cleveland recognized that the nation's two or three million factory workers wanted protection from "what is called the pauper labor of Europe," but he argued that "the standard of our laborer's life should not be measured by that of any other country less favored." Furthermore, every laborer was a consumer too, and therefore paid extra for goods manufactured under a protective umbrella; he ought to welcome a reduction of the cost of living. To this line of argument the Republicans answered that cheap prices meant cheap wages and cheap men, pointing repeatedly to the wretched condition of European and Oriental labor. "Less work and lower wages are the inevitable result of the triumph of the principles advocated by the Democratic party," Harrison warned.[35]

The Democrats' most effective rhetorical thrust, one guaranteed to excite the crowds, linked the protective tariff to the alarming growth of trusts. Men read uneasily of the growth of monopolistic combinations in oil, sugar, milk, binding twine, barbed wire, even whiskey. The 1888 Democratic national platform declared:

> The people are betrayed, when, by unnecessary taxation, trusts

34. "Third Annual Message to Congress," December 6, 1887, in George F. Parker, ed., *The Writings and Speeches of Grover Cleveland* (New York, 1892), p. 73.
35. Ibid. 78, 80–81; Hedges, *Harrison's Speeches,* p. 184.

and combinations are permitted and fostered, which, while unduly enriching the few that combine, rob the body of our citizens by depriving them of the benefits of natural competition.[36]

The Republicans met the issue by promising antitrust legislation in their platform, but Cleveland pressed on, in one letter hurling sharp terms like "perversion," "deception," "extortion," "tribute exacted from the people," and "appeals to selfish interests." The theme endlessly repeated on the stump was that the protective tariff was a species of corruption designed to fatten the rich (from whom the Republicans would "fry the fat" for campaign contributions) and that only Democratic reform could restore American virtue.[37]

Both Cleveland and Harrison wanted to wage the campaign honestly and squarely on the tariff issue. The Democrats' concentration on lower tariffs, the Republican nominee felt, meant "the enemies of the [protective tariff] system have left their ambuscades and taken to the open field, and we are to have a decisive battle over this question."[38] Nevertheless, he did have to fend off snipers. Harrison repeatedly denied Democratic allegations that he opposed trade unions, had insulted the Irish, or sneered at workingmen. Rather, he retorted, the Democratic insinuations, designed "to poison the minds of the workingmen against the candidate of the party that stands in this campaign for the principle of protection to American labor," were "utterly false."[39] Similarly, the widespread rumors that he proposed to open the floodgates of immigrant Chinese coolie labor were malicious and unfounded.[40]

36. Kirk Porter and Donald Johnson, *National Party Platforms, 1840–1964* (Urbana, 1966), p. 78. The "twine trust" particularly outraged wheat and oats growers in 1888, and midwest farm groups sponsored boycotts. Chester Destler, "The People's Party in Illinois, 1888–1896" (Ph.D. diss., University of Chicago, 1932), pp. 36–37.

37. Parker, *Writings of Cleveland*, pp. 88–89; see *Chicago Daily News Almanac for 1891* (Chicago, 1891), pp. 164, 167, 170, 172; Horace Merrill, *William Freeman Vilas* (Madison, 1954), p. 53; Festus P. Summers, *William L. Wilson and Tariff Reform* (New Brunswick, 1953), pp. 68–69. On fear of the trusts, see *Ann. Cycl. 1889*: 793–97, *1896*: 273; Sanford D. Gordon, "Attitudes toward Trusts Prior to the Sherman Act," *Southern Economic Journal* (1963) 30:156–67; and Hans B. Thorelli, *The Federal Antitrust Policy* (Baltimore, 1955).

38. Hedges, *Harrison's Speeches*, p. 180.

39. Ibid., pp. 183–84.

40. Ibid., pp. 88–89; Buley, "1888 Campaign," pp. 35, 38; for Democratic

The Democrats, of course, placed their main emphasis not on slanders but on legitimate campaign tactics. In Indiana they could match neither the galaxy of oratorical stars nor the unprecedented enthusiasm of the Republicans. Harrison lacked Blaine's magnetic personality, but he was a Hoosier, and the GOP workers mingled state pride with the hope of federal patronage in undertaking their thorough campaign. To neutralize that fieldwork, the Democrats brought in their most prestigious leaders. "The key to the situation is Indiana," mused Democratic Senator Daniel Voorhees, so there the Democrats must wage "war against the unjust taxation of American labor for the benefit of the enriched idlers and pampered monopolists."[41]

The most popular and effective spokesman for the national ticket proved to be its junior member, the "Old Roman" Allen G. Thurman of Ohio. Thurman undertook a dignified and extensive eleven-week canvass, in which he traveled five thousand miles and delivered eighty-nine speeches, a remarkable achievement for a man in his mid-seventies, and a model for Bryan's vastly more exhausting tour eight years later. Thurman concentrated his energies on Indiana and Ohio, and reiterated the Democratic principle of "Tariff for Revenue Only" before some 140,000 listeners. "I would like to know," he usually asked them, "how taxing a laboring man on everything from the crown of his head to the sole of his feet is going to enrich him." The tariff, he emphasized, "raises the price and taxes him until the poor man can hardly make enough money, even if he gets a few cents more wages in the day, to support himself and his little family if he has one. And yet they say that this is for the benefit of the laboring man!"[42] Crude and homespun as they were, Thurman's speeches attracted the crowds; but the farmers followed his logic perhaps better than the protected laboring man.

allegations see *The Campaign Text Book of the Democratic Party . . . 1888* (New York, 1888), pp. 375–77, 407–10; for the Republican rebuttal, George Dawson, *Republican Campaign Text Book for 1888* (New York, 1888), pp. 140–55.

41. *Indianapolis Sentinel,* August 5, 1888.

42. Quoted *Detroit News,* August 23, 1888; see *Indianapolis Sentinel,* November 4, 1888; *New York Times,* November 5, 1888; Buley, "1888 Campaign," p. 42.

The top of the ticket, President Cleveland, remained secluded in the White House, attending to affairs of state. The president was not, however, totally detached from the campaign. Besides consulting with his managers and delivering a few speeches, Cleveland busied himself with vetoes to nullify special pension laws Congress was passing to aid veterans and the widows of veterans. Cleveland pointed out that many of the bills were ill-advised, but with unconcealed sarcasm he discovered subtle technicalities, which other men would have overlooked, to justify denying relief and to preserve the pension list as a "Roll of Honor."

Naturally the veterans resented Cleveland's niggardly attitudes, and he had long suffered strained relations with the veterans' organization. The Grand Army of the Republic, President Cleveland once declared, "has been played upon by demagogues for partisan purposes, and has yielded to insidious blandishments."[43] Cleveland's hasty decision to return captured Confederate battle flags to the Southern states, his veto of the Republican-sponsored bill to pension all disabled veterans, and his refusal to attend the GAR convention—all during the year 1887—had compromised his relations with the nation's million and a half Union veterans (the Confederate veterans loved these actions).

The Republicans, with the support of local GAR posts, played up General Harrison's distinguished war record, while ridiculing Cleveland for having paid for a substitute to serve in his place. "Will he send another substitute?" queried GAR men when Cleveland cancelled his visit to their encampment. More specifically, the Republican platform denounced Cleveland's vetoes and promised a more generous pension program. Many Republicans suggested that the nagging surplus which had been building up in the federal treasury be eliminated by giving pensions to all veterans, or at least to all the disabled ones. Harrison encouraged the talk. "My countrymen," he exhorted, "it is no time now to use an apothecary's scale to weigh the rewards of the men who saved the

43. Nevins, *Cleveland,* pp. 328–30, 338; see also *Democratic Campaign Text Book,* pp. 168–94; Donald McMurry, "The Soldier Vote in Iowa in the Election of 1888," *Iowa Journal of History* (1920) 18:335–56; idem, "The Political Significance of the Pension Question, 1885–1895," *Mississippi Valley Historical Review* (1922) 9:19–36; and, for the most comprehensive treatment, Mary Dearing, *Veterans in Politics* (Baton Rouge, 1952).

country."[44] No one was quite sure exactly what the General proposed to do about pensions if elected, and the leadership of the GAR itself did not consider the time ripe to demand across-the-board pensions, or even pensions for men with disabilities acquired after the war. The organized veterans, however, had more confidence in Harrison's sensitivity to their needs, both material and psychological, than in callous Cleveland's. By the tens of thousands they flocked to Harrison's porch, to hear his clever words, to shake his hand, and, while the cheering went on, perhaps to snag a souvenir splinter from his fence.[45]

The Democratic candidate for governor of Indiana, Colonel C.C. Matson, had loudly proclaimed in Congress his support for lavish pensions. His opponent, General A.P. Hovey, however, was the president of the Service Pension Association, and had led the congressional battle for service pensions, land bounties, and assorted other boons for the boys in blue. Corporal Tanner, the legless spellbinder of the GAR, toured Indiana swearing "God help the surplus" if Harrison won, and charging (accurately) that Matson had actually used his power in Congress to block pension legislation. The Indiana GAR, contrary to the wishes of the more cautious national leaders, easily swung into the Republican army. Local posts advised their members to "vote as they shot"—against the Democrats. "Under the pretext of having a soldier candidate," grumbled a prominent Democratic veteran, the Indiana GAR was "prostituted by its designing leaders to political uses," and "became a machine in the hands of republican politicians to awaken enthusiasm among the people on the one hand, and to beat down opposition to their candidates, both personal and political, on the other."[46]

The veterans inevitably played a major role in the 1888 campaign, especially in the Midwest, where four hundred thousand of them (35 percent of the total) lived. Their power and symbolic

44. Hedges, *Harrison's Speeches,* p. 71.
45. Dearing, *Veterans,* pp. 362, 366, 370–74, 377–79.
46. Statement of G.R. Koontz (President of "Democratic Union Soldiers' and Sailors' Veteran Association"), in *Indianapolis Sentinel,* January 7, 1889. See Dearing, *Veterans,* pp. 367, 387, 391; *Chicago Tribune,* September 8, 1888; Buley, "1888 Campaign," 44; McMurray, "Soldier Vote," pp. 175–182, and Wallace Davies, *Patriotism on Parade* (Cambridge, 1955), p. 205.

role far exceeded their proportion of the population. The war had ended only twenty-three years before, and the veterans, who averaged about fifty years of age, occupied the highest rungs of power in politics and business. They still remembered the war, and their sons, now rapidly entering into full citizenship, constituted in some places 60 percent of the new voters. The Sons of Veterans, a fairly recent organization, worked with their elders in the GOP to instill loyalty to the party of the Union. "The history of the war was falsified, democratic ex-soldiers were stigmatized as rebels and every possible influence was brought to bear, from debasing importunity to scandalous vilification, to prejudice the sons of veterans against the democratic party," or so ran the disgusted complaints of Cleveland supporters.[47]

Most of the 80,000 members of the 1,100 Republican clubs organized in Indiana in 1888 were first voters or sons of veterans. Harrison, of course, linked his appeal to them with the need for a protective tariff. He invited "these young men who were too young to share the glory of the struggle for our political unity to a part in this contest for the preservation of our commercial independence."[48]

Despite their prestige gained in the nation's service, the veterans were controversial. The Republican claim that they had "championed the soldiers' cause at all times and in every possible manner," coupled with the indictment that the Democrats were "just as bitter toward the veterans who buried secession in the long and unknown trenches of the South as [they were] in the copperhead days of the draft," was choice bloody-shirt waving.[49] But it rang too shrill. In fact there was a reaction underway against veterans. Many voters, dubious of the need for generous pensions for vigorous men, complained that "the soldiers want everything." The GAR commander reacted to the news of Cleveland's returning the Confederate flags by cursing, "May God palsy the hand that wrote that order! May God palsy the brain that conceived it, and may

47. Koontz in *Indianapolis Sentinel,* January 7, 1889. See *Chicago Tribune,* October 19, 1888; *New York Tribune,* October 19, 26, 1888; and Bureau of the Census, *Report on Population . . . Eleventh Census: 1890* (Washington, 1897), v. 1, pt. 2, p. 803.
48. *Ann. Cycl. 1888:* 780–81; Hedges, *Harrison's Speeches,* p. 174 for quote.
49. *Iowa State Register* (Des Moines), November 2, 1889 (editorial).

God palsy the tongue that dictated it!" By no means did all temperate men applaud this outburst. The GAR had again disgraced itself by vilifying the president of the United States.[50]

The GOP too often and too loudly boasted of the large number of old soldiers it honored with high or lucrative offices. In 1882, nearly half of the men appointed by Republicans in Washington were Union veterans; the patronage plums distributed by the Democrats (who controlled the Senate) more often went to Confederate veterans. In the Iowa legislature elected in 1893, 70 percent of the eligible Republicans, but only 39 percent of the eligible Democrats, claimed war service. In the Wisconsin legislature of 1889, only two of the thirty-six veterans sat on the Democratic side of the aisle.[51]

The great majority of the soldiers who voted in the field in 1864 supported Lincoln, and in the next two decades the Republicans retained the affection of most of these. The sick and disabled veterans at the Ohio Soldiers and Sailors Home, for example, voted three to one for Harrison. The inmates at the Dayton veterans' hospital gave President Cleveland an icy reception when he visited there in 1887, and the next year gave him only 20 percent of their votes.[52]

---

50. Davies, *Patriotism,* pp. 257–60; Nevins, *Cleveland,* pp. 332–38; Dearing, *Veterans,* pp. 352–60.

51. Dawson, *Republican Campaign Text Book,* pp. 190–92; *Iowa Official Register* (Des Moines, 1894), pp. 35–41. Twenty-three of the 38 Iowa Democrats and 66 of the 112 Republicans had been eligible to serve in the war; 46 of the Republicans but only 9 of the Democrats actually had served. The differences in Iowa, and in the Wisconsin legislatures of 1889 and 1891, were statistically highly significant, but probably only reflected the fact that most veterans were Republicans. With a smaller pool of veterans available, the Democrats may actually have exerted more effort in enlisting them for office.

52. Curiously, the trend of voting at the supposedly isolated veterans' hospitals paralleled the statewide patterns, although the hospitals remained the strongest Republican precincts in the Midwest. The precincts were Soldiers' Home precinct in Erie County, Ohio, Jefferson Township in Montgomery County, Ohio, and Ward #3 (Ward #2 after 1889) of Wauwatosa Township, Milwaukee County, Wisconsin. For the wartime soldiers' votes, see *Tribune Almanac* (New York, 1862–1866), or *Ann. Cycl. 1864:* 39, 577, 630, or W. Dean Burnham, *Presidential Ballots: 1836–1892* (Baltimore, 1955), pp. 305, 459, 487, 505, 533, 723, 881. Note that the soldiers had been somewhat more Democratic in 1862, *Ann. Cycl. 1862:535.*

Yet the Republicans realized that they could not automatically count on the veterans' votes; too many straws in the wind warned them. A Republican poll of 26,000 Indiana veterans in 1880 showed that 69 percent were Republicans, 25 percent Democrats, and 6½ percent Greenbackers. Four years later the GOP found that 30 percent voted for Cleveland. In 1888 a prominent Democrat nearly became commander of the GAR.[53] Furthermore, many veterans, especially those outside the GAR and those too healthy to qualify for the promised pensions, seemed to admire Cleveland's pledge to make the pension list a roll of honor, not a dole.

The Republicans could not afford the loss of votes or enthusiasm from any quarter, least of all from the veterans. Yet the issues that influenced the Civil War and Reconstruction were dead or dying, and the new issues were mostly economic. For Benjamin Harrison, however, economics was not the dismal science. Realizing that relatively few veterans were factory workers, but that half were farmers and all were consumers, Harrison linked protection of the nation by the soldiers with protection by the tariff. "The Republican party," he emphasized, "has walked upon high paths. It has set forth before it ever the maintenance of the Union, the honor of its flag, and the prosperity of our people. It has been an American party in that it has set American interests always to the front."[54]

Harrison wooed the Irish vote too, and as always managed to interject the tariff issue. The great majority of the Irish were Democrats, but there was a substantial block of "Blaine Irish" Republicans. They had voted for Blaine in 1884, partly attracted by his strong Catholic connections, but most of them already shared the same cultural outlook as the Republicans. Harrison realized that the "Blaine Irish" tended towards teetotalism and strict codes of sexual morality. Ingeniously he merged the themes of protection of the home and protection of home markets and home rule for Ireland. "Who, if not Irish-Americans," he asked, "should be

53. "The number of Ex-Union soldiers in Indiana and their politics in 1880," manuscript in Benjamin Harrison Papers, Library of Congress, series 14, microfilm reel 143; *Indianapolis Journal,* July 21, 1888; *Chicago Tribune,* April 14, 1890, October 1, 1894.
54. Hedges, *Harrison's Speeches,* p. 59.

able to appreciate the friendly influences of the protective system upon their individual and upon their home life?"[55]

Subtle speeches did not gain Harrison a tenth as many Irish votes as a crude trap sprung by some California Republicans. In August Cleveland had gained the praise of Irishmen, who had long distrusted him, by demanding a retaliatory law against British and Canadian encroachments upon American fishing privileges. The Irish were not fishermen, but they were intensely hostile to England, and applauded every twist of the lion's tail. The GOP saved its trump until October 24, when they broadcast a private letter from the British ambassador, Lord Sackville-West. The duped diplomat suggested to one "Murchison," whom he supposed was a naturalized Englishman honestly seeking advice, that Grover Cleveland was the candidate most amendable to British interests. Cleveland hurriedly handed the meddling ambassador his passport, but the Republicans had something to chant about: "John Bull rides the Democratic party and we ride John Bull."[56]

Hardly had the Republican poster paint dried when the Democrats played their final trump. On October 31 the *Indianapolis Sentinel* published a confidential letter to the Indiana county chairmen from W. W. Dudley, Harrison's friend and the treasurer of the Republican national committee. Dudley had incautiously advised them to "Divide the floaters into blocks of five, and put a trusted man with necessary funds in charge of these five, and make him responsible that none get away and that all vote our ticket." There would, he assured them, "be no doubt of your receiving the necessary assistance through the National, State and County committees,—only see that it is husbanded and made to produce results."[57] The "floaters" were venal men who sold their votes to the

---

55. Ibid. p. 125; See Theodore Roosevelt's letters of July 14 and October 19, 1888, in Henry Cabot Lodge, ed., *Selections From the Correspondence of Theodore Roosevelt and Henry Cabot Lodge* (New York, 1925), 1:69, 73; and the *Nation* (August 7, 1884), 39:101 (editorial); *New York Times,* October 17, 1888.

56. Hedges, *Harrison's Speeches,* p. 177. On the incident generally, see Nevins, *Cleveland,* pp. 412, 428–31; Ellis Oberholzer, *A History of the United States* (New York, 1937), 5:58–64; and Florence Gibson, *The Attitudes of the New York Irish Towards State and National Affairs: 1848–1892* (New York, 1951), pp. 412–21.

57. The *Chicago Herald,* November 4, 1888, and *Indianapolis Sentinel,* cover the story fully.

highest bidder, and the Democrats with astounding speed distributed half a million copies of the letter in Indiana alone.

The Republican leadership stood accused of wholesale bribery of voters in the home of their holier-than-thou candidate himself, and by the hand of his long-time aide. The fiasco was the outcome of Harrison's overemphasis on Indiana and his failure to untangle the lines of authority in the party. The national committee had no business contacting county leaders, let alone dictating strategy, without authorization from the state chairman. Dudley wanted to make sure that the national committee (and he personally) received full credit for the special attention devoted to Indiana. When the story broke the Indiana chairman repudiated the letter and denied vehemently that Dudley had anything to do with the state campaign. The Republican press tried to blunt the Democrats' new issue by crying forgery, but to no avail. Dudley, a former pension commissioner, had long been suspected of dirty politics, and no one trusted him in his hour of disgrace, not even Harrison (who never spoke to him again). The Democrats now had their own snappy slogan, "blocks of five," to rally their ranks in the closing hours of the contest.[58]

Bribery was not wholly foreign to Indiana politics. "This infamous practice," thundered the *Shelbyville Daily Republican* in 1885, "kept up year after year by both parties, has brought about a state of affairs that cannot be contemplated without a shudder." "Good judges," the newspaper confessed, "estimate that fully a third of our voting population can be directly influenced by the use of money on the day of election."[59] In 1886 William Fishback, Harrison's former law partner, had exposed the bribery and corruption that disgraced Indiana elections. The state was so closely balanced between the parties that whoever controlled the 20,000 or so floaters would capture the state. Ever since 1876, Fishback charged, Indiana reeked with corruption.[60]

58. Sievers, *Harrison,* 2:302–03, 418–21; Marcus, *Grand Old Party,* pp. 143–44.

59. Editorial, May 2, 1885, quoted in J. Wetnight, "1882: The Year that Shelby County Went Republican," *Indiana History Bulletin* (September 1963) 40:146.

60. William Fishback, *A Plea for Honest Elections* (Indianapolis, 1886), copy in New York Public Library, and partially quoted in Joseph F. Dunn, *Indiana and Indianans* (Chicago, 1919), 2:730–35. Cf. *Indianapolis Sen-*

The point of Dudley's letter had actually been to warn the local workers that the Democrats had been saving their money for a last-minute vote-buying spree. One Democratic county chairman, for example, had instructed his pollsters to "mark every one who has to have money as a 'float.' Those who have to be bought are not 'doubtful' but are 'floats.' Look closely after every one. Let not one escape."[61]

But the Indiana GOP hardly needed the national committee's advice. The Republicans had their own polls, and ample funds, and were ready to thwart a Democrat steal by preemption. The time-honored procedure, once a float had been purchased for $5 or $10, was to keep him out of the clutches of the other party until voting time. The floater received a premarked party ballot, which he had to drop publicly into the ballot box. Then he would receive a token redeemable by the precinct "boodle" man. Apparently, the floaters were mostly poor Negro townsfolk, although city dwellers and farm hands of both races often doubled their weekly income on election day. Careful polls turned up 18,000 to 20,000 "voters for revenue only" in Indiana in 1888, about double the number estimated in 1876.[62]

On election day, 1888, both parties were ready to play the boodle game, but all the curious reporters alerted by the publicity given to the Dudley letter made the work more dangerous than ever. "Lying, debauchery, bribery and all manner of corruption were employed!" screamed one Democratic newspaper, but it could cite only the generosity of Republican workers in buying drinks for prospective friends of the tariff.[63] No "blocks of five" were discovered, although in Bloomington a few floaters were penned up overnight, and in Terre Haute one man complained that he received counterfeit money for his genuine vote. The election was the cleanest in Indiana in years, but Democratic law of-

tinel, January 2, 1889; Robert LaFollette, "The Adoption of the Australian Ballot in Indiana," *Indiana Magazine of History* (1928) 24:105–14; and Marcus, *Grand Old Party,* p. 58.

61. Exposed by *Chicago Tribune,* October 11, 1888.

62. Dunn, *Indiana,* 2:740; *New York Herald,* October 22, 1888; *New York Times,* November 2, 4, 1888; *Chicago Herald,* November 2, 1888; *Civil Service Chronicle* (March, 1889) 1:78.

63. Editorial in *Columbus City Post* (Indiana) quoted in *Indianapolis Sentinel,* November 12, 1888.

ficers arrested several hundred Republican workers and attempted
to indict Dudley in federal court. No convictions resulted, and
Dudley escaped prosecution, although he did not escape infamy.[64]
After investigating the charges and countercharges of bribery
in Indiana's notorious First Congressional District, the House
Committee on Elections declared it "a matter of congratulations
for the country" that "neither party has been able to support
the charge. The only proper inference is that no such evidence
was available and the charges were unfounded." The committee,
controlled by Republicans, thereupon agreed that the Democratic
candidate had won the district fairly, by twenty votes.[65]

By election day, the sixth of November, Harrison was under-
standably weary from addressing so many delegations, juggling
so many issues, and attending to the many details of campaign
management. His ticket mate, gubernatorial candidate Hovey, must
have been even more exhausted, for he had spoken to a million
Hoosier faces and shaken 200,000 hands, or so he boasted.[66]
After the grueling, frenzied, and occasionally dirty campaign, Harrison and Hovey must have been somewhat frustrated to discover
that they had not managed to increase the GOP's 1886 plurality
in Indiana. The frustration cannot have been too serious, however, for they both carried the state by 2,000 votes out of half a
million—and Benjamin Harrison was the next president. Every
state in the Midwest hoisted the Republican banner. Harrison ran
a full 120,000 ahead of Cleveland in the 3.3 million votes of the
region, although he trailed the president by over 200,000 votes
in the 8 million cast elsewhere in the nation.

Harrison carried 343 of the 533 midwestern counties, a mediocre
performance for a Republican. He became the first GOP candidate since Frémont to lose Marion County (Indianapolis). Cleve-

64. *Nation* (November 22, 1888) 47:406, 412; letter of Mason J. Niblack
in F.J. Stimson, *The Methods of Bribery and its Prevention at our National
Elections* (Cambridge, 1889), pp. 16–18; Martha Gresham, *Life of Walter
Q. Gresham* (Chicago, 1919), 2:603–13; *Indianapolis Sentinel*, November
9, 10, 12, 15, 17, 1888; cf. *Chicago Herald*, November 7–9, 1888, and L.J.
Woolen to G. Cleveland, September 11, 1892, in the Grover Cleveland Papers, Library of Congress, series 2, microfilm reel 71.
65. Charles H. Rowell, *Digest of Contested-Election Cases in the Fifty-
First Congress* (Washington, 1891), p. 189.
66. *Chicago Herald*, October 25, 1888.

land carried Chicago, but Harrison eked out an 800 vote margin in Cook County as a whole, thus narrowly retaining a traditional Republican stronghold. Wayne County (Detroit), normally Democratic, yielded its highest Democratic plurality in history. Cuyhoga County (Cleveland, Ohio) gave Harrison a plurality of only 2,000, the smallest since Frémont. Hamilton County (Cincinnati) and the Western Reserve (in northeast Ohio), however, gave the Republicans enough support to give Ohio to Harrison by 21,000 votes out of 840,000. Milwaukee County, with the largest plurality it had ever given a Republican, kept Wisconsin safely in the GOP column, and showed that the Democrats had not gained in all the industrial centers. Iowa, normally a safe state, again went Republican, but serious trouble already was threatening Republican hegemony there.

In Indiana the aggregrate voting patterns of 1888 were virtually identical to those of 1886. Hoosiers tenaciously clung to their party affiliations. Landslides were rare; congressional districts, counties, townships, even precincts hovered about a delicate equilibrium. Although the Republicans won a majority of the popular vote in 1888, and there was hardly any ticket splitting, the Democrats grabbed ten of the thirteen congressional districts, and gained eight seats in the legislature. "Gerrymandering!" cried the Republicans with righteous anger, but a little luck would have swung the districts the other way.

The voting patterns among Indiana's ninety-two counties revolved around three dimensions; rural versus urban, Yankee versus Southerner, old-stock white versus immigrant and Negro. Table 1 displays the Republican share of the aggregate popular vote in the three main groups of counties from 1880 to 1896.

Among the forty-nine most rural counties, the nineteen Yankee counties usually were about .5 percent more Republican than the thirty non-Yankee counties, an insignificant difference. The four rural Yankee counties with large Negro or immigrant populations in 1880 (Adams, Pulaski, Starke, and Vermillion) were 7 or 8 percent less Republican than the group as a whole, but in no other category did the differential amount to more than 2 percent. In sum, the rural counties displayed a uniform pattern. The forty-three most urban counties, which cast over 60 percent of the total state vote, were slightly more Republican than the rural counties

Table 1

Republican Percentage of Total Popular Vote in Indiana, 1880–1896, by Categories of Counties[67]

Category	1880	1884	1886	1888	1890	1892	1894	1896
49 most rural	48	47	48	48	45	45	49	49
43 most urban	50	49	49	49	45	46	51	53
19 urban & Yankee	54	53	52	53	49	50	55	55
24 urban & non-Yankee	48	46	47	47	42	44	49	51
Statewide	49	48	49	49	45	46	50	51
Winner	GOP	Dem.	GOP	GOP	Dem.	Dem.	GOP	GOP

before 1896, when these urban counties suddenly became Republican strongholds. The non-Yankee urban counties were less Republican than either the Yankee urban counties or the rural counties, but were the scene of the greatest Republican gains in 1896, when they carried the state for McKinley.

A variety of conflicts and rivalries raged fiercely in Indiana: Southerners distrusted Yankees, the southern part of the state resented the northern part, Methodists feared Catholics, hard-money men ridiculed inflationists, natives denounced immigrants. Yet the struggle between Democratic and Republican loyalties was more than a reflection of other struggles; in Indiana it was itself a basic source of political conflict, and gave election campaigns in that state a fervor and intensity normally unknown elsewhere in the Midwest. "Things never died down from one campaign to the next," recalled Will Hays, who went from Indiana to become Republican national chairman. "It was one round of

67. The 49 rural counties had less than 20 percent of their 1900 population in cities of 2,500 or more; in the 67 old-stock counties, 75 percent or more of the voters in 1900 had native-born white parents. The 38 Yankee counties were those in which 48 percent or more of the 1880 population that had been born outside Indiana had been born in New York, Pennsylvania, or Ohio. *Compendium of the Tenth Census* (Washington, 1883), pp. 464–69, 501–3, and Bureau of the Census, *Abstract of the [Thirteenth] Census with Supplement for Indiana* (Washington, 1913), pp. 599–615, supplied the data.

committees, caucuses, conventions, elections, victories, defeats—and then the whole thing over again."[68] The other states approached elections not as ends in themselves but as the vehicle for the resolution of more basic conflicts.

Harrison's victory in 1888 did not result from his intensive campaign, for the voting patterns duplicated those of the 1886 election, which had been fought before Cleveland forcibly introduced the tariff issue. Rather it reflected, for the last time, the stabilizing influence of party loyalty and army-style campaigns. However, the campaign was not without its far-reaching effects. Not only was Harrison in the White House but he had given the nation a criterion by which to judge his administration. Not many Americans understood the tariff in 1888, but Harrison's assurance that high duties would develop American industry, protect the workingman, and provide a home market for agriculture sounded sensible. Cleveland's abstractions about the burden of the tariff did not convince the people. The policy of encouraging the industrialization of America might raise prices, as the Democrats repeatedly charged, but the Republicans promised even higher raises in wages. The GOP would have its opportunity to redeem its pledges, and the people would render their verdict in the midterm elections of 1890.

The embittered Democrats charged that Harrison won not because of the excitement of the people with a thorough dedication to industrialization, but simply because of bribery and corruption. The election of 1888 in the Midwest was less corrupt than formerly, but the purity of the ballot, so loftily praised by Harrison, was in question. Charges of bribery, fraud, and coercion were repeated biennially for the next decade. The next chapter will consider the merit of these charges.

68. *Memoirs of Will Hays* (New York, 1955), p. 64.

2

Fraud, Bribery and Coercion:
The Honesty of Midwestern Elections

> Coercion of voters is not only [an]
> un-American, unpatriotic and
> despotic usurpation of the rights
> of a free citizen, but it is a wrong
> that will inevitably recoil upon its
> perpetrators . . . . [Without free
> majorities] a political victory would
> be barren of results worthy of a
> great party.
>
> Mark Hanna[1]

So close were the elections of the 1880s, especially that of 1888, that the historian must confront the possibility that fraud, bribery, and coercion actually determined their outcomes. If elections really failed to represent the true will of the electorate—if the basic principles of mass participation democracy failed in practice —then elaborate analysis of campaigns and voting patterns is an exercise in cynicism and futility.

It is easy to accept the fulminations of embittered losers at face value, to conclude with the Indiana Democratic platform of 1890 that "the electoral vote of Indiana was obtained for Harrison and Morton by the most flagrant crimes against the ballot-box ever perpetrated in an American commonwealth," to endorse the 1892 Populist platform's charges that "corruption dominates the ballot-box . . . the people are demoralized . . . the newspapers are largely subsidized or muzzled, public opinion is silenced," or to agree that McKinley's victory in 1896 represented "the consummation of a conspiracy to defeat an honest vote of the people by bribery, fraud, and intimidation."[2] But the historian has to be

1. *New York Tribune*, October 22, 1896.
2. *Chicago Daily News Almanac for 1891* (Chicago, 1891), p. 166; Kirk Porter and Donald Johnson, *National Party Platforms; 1840–1964* (Urbana, 1966), p. 89; letter of L.F. Wilson of Shelbyville, Indiana, to William Jennings Bryan, November 6, 1896, in Bryan MSS, Library of Congress. Matthew Josephson developed the conspiracy interpretation to high theory in *The Politicos: 1865–1896* (New York, 1938); see also Richard Hofstadter, *The American Political Tradition* (New York, 1948), chapter 7.

more careful, especially in view of the long history of a "corruption" theme in American politics.

This chapter examines every known major case of significant election fraud, bribery, and coercion in the Midwest for the period together with a few cases that were never publicly known. Successful dirty politics, by definition, is never discovered, yet men who are firmly convinced of the existence of an evil conspiracy to defraud their rights are stimulated by the *absence* of reliable evidence to condemn the enemy all the more for his fiendishly clever techniques. It is vastly easier to make blanket allegations of illicit, secret activities than to disprove them; almost always there is a grain of truth in the charges. The historian confronted with a conspiracy interpretation realizes that men in distress typically turn first to such theories or myths to explain their misfortunes.[3] The myth of massive corruption so cleverly conceived that it cannot be detected is a ghost story. It scares some people, and that is its purpose; as one historian has noted, "much of the talk that circulated at the time was mere rumor, designed to shock respectable voters and encourage local supporters to work harder for their own side."[4]

Party managers, nearing the climax of an extremely close contest, convinced by scraps of intelligence the historian should dismiss as rumor, often decided to act first, thus prompting the opposition to fall back on its emergency plans, and thus confirming the original rumors. Who could be surprised if fraud took place under such circumstances? On the other hand, illegal practices were extremely dangerous. As the Dudley "blocks of five" incident shows, the man who got caught suffered infamy and the opposition was handed a powerful issue in the crucial final hours of the campaign. The American voter is always afraid of dirty work, and if some comes to light he is apt to react very strongly. Both parties, therefore, watched closely for any evidence, no matter how slight, and typically issued wild charges on election eve of dangerous plots afoot. Such charges kept everyone on his toes. After the returns were in, the losers often grumbled about irregularities; the

3. See Richard Hofstadter, *The Paranoid Style in American Politics* (New York, 1964), especially the title essay.
4. John A. Garraty, *The New Commonwealth: 1877–1890* (New York, 1968), p. 303.

winners never did. If solid evidence existed, however, legal remedies were available, especially in national elections. The candidates were not so blind that massive irregularities could have gone undetected, yet the midwestern record in this respect is remarkably clean. By contrast, nearly every closely contested election in the rural South in the late nineteenth century was besmirched by frauds, irregularities, coercion, or even violence, and many winners were unseated after careful congressional investigations. By nineteenth-century standards, American or European, the midwestern elections were quiet, decorous affairs—hard fought, but basically honest.

From the time of James Bryce's *The American Commonwealth* (1888) to Edwin O'Connor's *The Last Hurrah* (1958) the great city machines have engaged the attention, and usually the indignation, of political observers. The natural milieu of fraud and corruption in the Midwest was the great metropolis. There the pecuniary rewards for shady maneuvers were immediate and large, and the consequences less likely to involve disgrace or prison. The reformers of the day focused their ire on New York, Chicago, Philadelphia, Boston and a few of the other cities, convinced that wicked "machines," as they have been termed, bought and sold votes and favors, and manipulated government to sabotage the public interest. Intriguing though the politics of trolley franchises and sewer contracts may be, the strictly local operations of city politics lie beyond the scope of this study, for there is no evidence that these contests for power and money directly affected the social aspects of the normal voting behavior of the masses of honest citizens.

The cities, once they had grown large enough to afford sufficient jobs, contracts, and minor patronage positions, became inwardly directed feudal polities. In the lowest estate were the local precinct or ward bosses, men in direct contact with the people and the primary dispensers of relief, jobs, legal aid, and petty patronage. The realm of the ward healers was the slum, the teeming precincts crammed with unacculturated European immigrants, drifters, criminals, and transients.

In Detroit the precincts fronting the river fell under the political domain of the proprietors of grimy hotels, beanshops and saloons.

John Coughlin and William Conner, who fed more than a thousand men a day at a nickel or a quarter each, controlled the Democratic organization in the notorious First Ward. A lone Republican worker, a saloon-keeper on Cadillac Square, struggled vainly to hold down the opposition strength. Come election day, however, Detroit's Republican leaders knew how to neutralize Coughlin and Conner:

> Sad to say [said a Democratic newspaper], some of these democratic warriors . . . have been known to desert the sacred principles of democracy for a pecuniary consideration and support the republicans with might and main, but such little things are not treasured up for future retaliation by the party at large. In the river precincts of the first everything goes. It is the inalienable right of every free man to work and vote for whom he pleases, and to call them to account for any such political inadvertency would be considered undemocratic.[5]

Nor was it considered fair sport to prosecute any of the ward bosses for their professional work, although their foot-sloggers might occasionally spend a few days in jail to amuse the citizenry and to keep the vote brokers faithful to their agreements.

Every large city gossiped about deals between local bosses and the leaders of the opposition. Undoubtedly more money exchanged hands in the vivid imaginations of the reformers than in the poor slum wards themselves. The corrupt techniques at which the machines were most adept—multiple voting, cemetery registration, ballot-box stuffing, fraudulent naturalization of ineligible immigrants, bribery of poll watchers, and falsification of election returns —were chiefly used to win city elections. In primaries, mayoralty races, aldermanic campaigns, and other local contests (which nearly always were held apart from state and federal elections), the winning of a precinct or a ward carried immediate and tangible returns. The outcomes of state and federal elections, were, by comparison, of trivial importance to the realities of machine politics. The local machine workers were not in line for gubernatorial or presidential patronage; their rewards came from city hall. Consequently, in a

5. *Detroit News,* June 14, August 29, 1891. For systematic descriptions of political conditions in every Detroit precinct, see also the issues of June 21, 28, July 5, 12, 19, 26, August 9, 16, 23, 30, September 6, 13, 20, 27, October 4, 1891.

metropolis like Chicago, with major elections every six months, and intraparty contests even more often, the machines let the state party take care of the "uninteresting" state and federal elections.

Chicago, with a million people in 1890, already was large enough, and growing rapidly enough, to have its own self-contained political system. In Cincinnati (1890 population 300,000), Cleveland (260,000), Detroit (210,000), and Milwaukee (200,-000), the party machines had at least partially weaned themselves from the state organizations. No other midwestern cities had as many as 110,000 people in 1890, or displayed the local independence of these largest five. No big city machine politician in the Midwest achieved national, or even statewide, stature. Mayors Hazen Pingree of Detroit and George Peck of Milwaukee did, indeed, rise from city hall to the governor's mansion, but each was a "blue-ribbon" businessman candidate who achieved power in local politics, not after a rise through the system, but in a time of crisis when the local organization went beyond its ranks to head a ticket with a man of character and prestige.[6]

Bribery for votes for state and federal officials did flourish, however, in several scattered, isolated rural areas. In Indiana, the floaters congregated in the sleepy towns along the Ohio River where poor Southerners had settled. Undoubtedly the worst example of corruption of the ballot ever known in American history came in Adams County, Ohio. Adams was a hilly expanse of scrub land stretched out along the Ohio River a bit to the east and south of Cincinnati. The Revolutionary War veterans, Virginians mostly, who had settled in and near Adams County had produced a galaxy of distinguished progeny: Ulysses S. Grant, Senators Allen Thurman, Joseph Foraker, and Albert J. Beveridge, Ambassador Whitelaw Reid, and eight governors of Ohio.

6. The literature on metropolitan machines is of course, voluminous. On the relationship between machine politics and the patronage system, see James Q. Wilson, "The Economy of Patronage," *Journal of Political Economy* (1961) 69:369–80; see also Eric McKitrick, "The Study of Corruption," *Political Science Quarterly* (1957) 72:502–14, and James A. Bryce, *The American Commonwealth* (New York, 1895), 2:120–30. On Chicago, see especially Claudius Johnson, *Carter Harrison I* (Chicago, 1928). Clifton Yearley, *The Money Machines* (Albany, 1970), links party finances and municipal corruption. The best local study is Zane Miller, *Boss Cox's Cincinnati* (New York, 1968).

America changed after the Civil War, but Adams did not; it lapsed into stagnation. The railroads bypassed the county, and even the single telegraph line to the county seat was torn down. The people had mostly supported the North during the war, and that helped the Republicans pull even with their rivals in county elections, which became fierce annual contests. In 1867, the practice of buying votes began, and by 1871 the backwoods county fully endorsed the practice. At first the vote sellers consisted only of the poorest folk (95 percent of whom were old-stock, white Protestants); soon more and more men accepted the shiny five-dollar gold pieces, or sometimes even the twenty-dollar bills, that five minutes of their time was worth on election day. The vote buyers were the most reputable and trustworthy pillars of the community—schoolteachers, professional men, businessmen, Methodist elders. By the 1890s fully 90 percent of the voters in Adams County, and probably considerable numbers in nearby areas, were voluntarily engaging in the bribery. Although vote *buying* had long been illegal, vote selling only became illegal in 1896. But the sellers would not permit the politicians to end the practice. Finally in 1911 a local judge called a halt, and 1,690 men, more than a fourth of the electorate, pleaded guilty to selling their votes, paid five-dollar fines, and lost their suffrage for five years. The other vote sellers of Adams County escaped the penalty, as did those in neighboring counties, but the elections became pure again.

In 1887 the Democrats spent $25,000 in Adams, and the GOP nearly as much. Nine-tenths of the money came from local contributions, although state leaders as prominent as Mark Hanna occasionally aided with the funding. Curiously, the massive bribery helped neither party. Adams kept a remarkably consistent record of almost exact equality between the parties. Whether a Democratic landslide swept the state or the Republicans were scoring massive gains, troubled the stable voters of Adams hardly at all. Apparently neither party could afford a landslide.[7]

7. *Cincinnati Commercial-Gazette,* September 14, 1889; Albion Z. Blair, "Seventeen Hundred Rural Vote Sellers," *McClure's Magazine,* (November 1911), pp. 28–40, and Genevieve Gist, "Progressive Reform in a Rural Community: The Adams County Vote-Fraud Case," *Mississippi Valley Historical Review* (1961) 48:60–78.

Since most honest men were firmly loyal to their party, the purchase of votes did not greatly affect the outcome of elections in rural areas. Yet the practice, whether systematic or sporadic, greatly disturbed the reform-minded citizens and the economy-minded politicians. "It is a humiliating fact," the governor of Iowa admitted in 1890, "and yet one that is criminal negligence to ignore, that some men are corrupt enough to buy, and others base enough to sell, the noblest birthright of an American citizen."[8]

More relevant to the outcome of elections, and more disturbing, was the falsification of election returns by party or government officials. In the 1880s and 1890s serious cases arose in Ohio, Indiana, and Michigan. In 1885 some Democrats in Cincinnati improved a "208" on a tally sheet to a "508," and a "726" to a "926." Trivial as the alterations may seem, they added 500 votes to the Democratic column, elected fourteen men to the state legislature, and threatened to give the Democrats control of the state senate. After weeks of turmoil, the Republicans gained command of the legislature by ousting the fraudulently elected Cincinnati senators. The GOP remembered the incident for some years at campaign times.[9] In Indianapolis in 1886, the Democratic county chairman, Sim Coy, rearranged sixteen votes on the official tally sheets, just enough to elect a judge of criminal court. The Republicans pounced on Coy, and after three trials he landed in jail for eighteen months. Upon his release, Coy immediately won reelection to the city council, but lost his party chairmanship and soon left the state.[10]

8. Inaugural address of Horace Boies, February 27, 1890, in Benjamin F. Shambaugh, ed., *The Messages and Proclamations of the Governors of Iowa* (Iowa City, 1904), 6:276. On corruption in Connecticut, see J. McCook, "The Alarming Proportion of Venal Voters," and "Venal Voting: Methods and Remedies," in *Forum* (1892) 14:1–13, 159–77. V.O. Key made a bibliographical and theoretical review of *The Techniques of Political Graft in the United States* (Chicago, 1936); cf. M. Ostrogorski, *Democracy and the Organization·of Political Parties* (New York, 1902), 2:343–50.

9. *Cincinnati Commercial-Gazette,* September 1, 1889; Joseph Foraker, *Notes of a Busy Life* (Cincinnati, 1917), 1:218–23; *Ann. Cycl. 1885:* 673; *1886:* 731. For Republican use of fraud as campaign fodder, see Benjamin Harrison's speech of November 26, 1887, in *Independent* (July 26, 1888) 40:944.

10. Joseph Dunn, *Greater Indianapolis* (Chicago, 1910), 1:293–97; Simeon Coy, *The Great Conspiracy* (Indianapolis, 1889).

More heinous than the simple frauds in Indianapolis and Cincinnati were the Michigan referenda cases of 1894. A statewide referendum on a constitutional amendment to raise the salaries of elected state officials passed narrowly in the spring of 1893. The overwhelming margin of support given by the economically prostrate mining counties of the upper peninsula sparked an investigation into the accuracy of all the returns. Not only were the official counts proven fraudulent, but it soon became evident that the votes for the referendum in 1891 raising salaries, as well as those for the prohibition referendum in 1887, had been doctored. The investigators found that in Detroit the simple expedient of adding a "1" before the actual returns in scores of precincts enabled the salary increases to pass and prohibition to fail. Six junior clerks had done the dirty work, but four high elected officials were implicated. Governor John Rich, a Republican, acted with dispatch. He removed his secretary of state, the state treasurer and the commissioner of the land office, all Republicans. The attorney general, a Greenbacker elected with Democratic support, and the secretary of state went on trial, but hung juries saved them from the penitentiary. In the fall elections, Governor Rich led the GOP to its greatest victory in Michigan history.[11] Nowhere else in the Midwest were serious cases of fraud reported in the 1880s and 1890s.

The alleged corruption at the polls and in the tally rooms ignited a nationwide movement for election reform in the late 1880s. Three days after the presidential election of 1888, the *Indianapolis Sentinel,* the voice of Indiana Democrats, declared "The supreme duty of the next legislature is to pass an election law which will forever free Indiana from the scandal and disgrace to which it is now exposed every four years."[12] Lame duck Governor Isaac Gray, a Democrat, instructed the legislature that:

> It is manifest that the public faith in the purity of elections has become shaken, and the feeling is widespread that the decision at the ballot box no longer reflects the honest judgment of a majority of voters.

11. *Ann. Cycl. 1894:* 486–87; *1897:* 528; *Detroit News,* January 22, 23, February 5–9, 12, 16, 24, June 25, 1894.
12. *Indianapolis Sentinel,* November 9, 1888.

> You can render the state no more exalted service than to frame and enact such laws that will go as far as legislation can accomplish to prevent the corrupt use of money, preserve the secrecy of the ballot, secure fair elections, and punish by the severest penalties all who may be guilty of committing fraud upon the ballot box, or bribery or attempting to bribe any elector, or of corrupting in any manner the suffrages of the people.[13]

Incoming Governor Hovey, a Republican, squirmed at the unsubtle allusions to Dudleyism in Gray's address, but admitted "there is reason to believe that the ballot has been polluted."[14] The Democratic legislature was in a reforming mood, and passed a stiff law against vote buying (but not against vote selling) that ended the practice in Indiana, and instituted the Australian system of secret voting that seemed to work so well in England. By guaranteeing a private booth in which the voter could make his decision, the Australian system frustrated attempts to bribe voters, for there would be no way to know if the corrupt bargain had been kept. In place of ballots printed by the various parties, the system further provided for a single uniform ballot, to be handed by the election officials only to qualified voters. The old system had produced too many comic cases of candidates losing offices because of typographical errors in printing their names; occasionally a clever opponent would even circulate ballots with deliberately misspelled names. Referenda on constitutional amendments often failed because the parties refused to include the question on their ballots.[15]

The Australian ballot immediately became a popular reform, especially among Democrats, labor leaders, and political scientists. In Wisconsin, the Republicans enacted the new system in 1889. In Ohio the Democrats passed the reform in 1891. In Michigan

13. Charles Roll, *Indiana* (Chicago, 1931), 2:341–42.
14. Ibid. 2:342. See Robert LaFollette, "The Adoption of the Australian Ballot in Indiana," *Indiana Magazine of History* (1928) 24:114–20.
15. *Ann. Cycl. 1889:* 434: *Chicago Daily News Almanac for 1890* (Chicago, 1890), pp. 159–60. *Literary Digest* (1889) 2:49. After an abortive attempt to introduce the Australian ballot in Michigan in 1885, the first success came in Wisconsin, which in 1888 required secret ballots for all Milwaukee elections. *Nation* (April 12, 1888) 46:290, (November 22, 1888) 47:407.

the Republicans began the reforms in 1889, and the Democrats enacted the full Australian system in 1891. Illinois adopted the reform in 1891 and Iowa, after several years of squabbling, in 1892. By 1889 every midwestern state also provided a system of registering the eligible voters of the larger cities, usually those of 2,500 or more population. Save for isolated pockets of corruption, the elections of the Midwest entered an era of honesty.[16]

The only specific charges of widespread corruption or bribery after the reforms came in a long open letter by John Peter Altgeld several months after the 1896 election. As the Democratic governor of Illinois during the campaign, and a leader in the silver movement, Altgeld had ample opportunity to detect voting irregularities. He found one precinct in Springfield, near his mansion, where 182 unregistered Negroes named Jones had voted—but for whom, he could not say. The thrust of his main argument was that 157,223 votes in Illinois were illicit; they had to be, he maintained, because in 1896 217,223 more voters turned out than in 1892, when every legal vote had been cast—and population growth could account for only 60,000 new voters.[17] Altgeld rejected the perfectly obvious fact that not everyone had voted in 1892, and that the turnout in 1896 soared much higher. The number of males over twenty-one in Illinois in 1890 was 1,083,000. The total vote cast in 1892 was only 874,000, and in 1896, after four more years of population growth, the vote was 1,091,000—a huge turnout, indeed, but well within the bounds of plausibility.[18]

Challenged by the chief election officer of Cook County with the fact that more than a third of the election judges in Chicago were Democrats or Populists, Altgeld responded that many of his own appointees were "working hard for the Republican ticket; some openly and others secretly."[19] Altgeld, who had pardoned Democrats convicted of election fraud, insinuated that the Republi-

16. *Ann. Cycl. 1889:* 450, 559, 727–30, 826–27; *1890:* 448, 694–95; *1891:* 364–65, 527, 691; *1892:* 358.

17. John Peter Altgeld, *Live Questions* (Chicago, 1899), pp. 712–13.

18. The number of males over twenty-one in Illinois in 1900 was 1,401,-000. Of these, 467,000 had been born abroad, but most had immigrated to America before 1891 and thus were eligible to vote in 1896. *Ann. Cycl. 1896:* 771, 793; *Abstract of the [Thirteenth] Census With Supplement for Illinois* (Washington, 1913), pp. 216, 609.

19. Altgeld, *Live Questions,* p. 719.

cans spent $2 million to $5 million to bribe the election judges in Illinois' 2,000 townships, to colonize "thousands of negroes," in Ohio River counties, and illegally to vote the "very ignorant foreign-born people."[20] Altgeld, whose bid for reelection had collapsed along with Bryan's presidential bid, had few kind words for the victors, who "spread a moral leprosy over this country, and who use the government as a convenience to make money for corporations,"[21] but he was unable to uncover any significant cases of bribery or fraud, or find enough evidence to initiate any prosecutions or other legal actions. The midwestern elections of 1896 were honest.

Even in honest elections, however, the returns could be garbled by careless counting and tabulation of the vote. Local panels of election judges from both parties had the responsibility to count the votes and certify their accuracy. In the hectic hour after the polls closed, with the entire state hungry for quick returns, errors inevitably crept into the counts and often were never rectified unless one party demanded an expensive recount. Many ballots rejected because of technical errors should have been counted. The only scholarly study of recounts suggests that perhaps 1 percent, possibly 2 percent, of the ballots are incorrectly tabulated or rejected. Generally the errors favor the party of the majority of the panel of election officials, but statewide or countywide the errors tend to cancel each other. Only in very close elections did error become a crucial factor, and Congress and the state legislatures sat through many weary hours deciding on the relative merits of two claimants to a contested seat. At the conclusion of the deliberations, the seat generally went to the majority party.[22]

20. Ibid., pp. 717–21, 702, 516–21. The Democrats made many wildly exaggerated estimates of the GOP campaign chest—the larger it was supposed to be, the more ominous it became; thus the Democrats elicited almost hysterical fears of the corrupt power of Hanna's money. Their strategy is considered in chapter ten.

21. Ibid., p. 692.

22. See Samuel Eldersveld and A. Applegate, *Michigan Recounts for Governor, 1950 and 1952: A Systematic Analysis of Election Error* (Ann Arbor, 1954), pp. 38, 174–76; Chester A. Rowell, *A Historical and Legal Digest for All the Contested Election Cases in the House . . . 1789–1901* (Washington, 1901).

More abhorrent to the democratic spirit of free, fair elections than the fraud of politicians and bribery of citizens was the coercion of men to vote contrary to their true wishes. Not blithely would a man risk the subtle disapproval of his family and friends by quitting his party and going over to the opposition. Whatever the discomfort endured by the mavericks, the spontaneous coercion of close associates aided the Democrats as much as the Republicans, and probably had no net effect on the outcome of elections. Partisan conflict within families was sometimes a serious matter, but seems to have been infrequent. The sharing of cultural, religious, social, and economic attitudes and conditions, and the family origins of the party identification, minimized the number of family cleavages. In the Midwest of the period, moreover, both major parties, and in certain circles one or another of the minor parties too, were considered acceptable organizations for membership, at least before the bitter 1896 campaign. The Republican father of a Democratic son probably was disappointed, but not shocked or shaken—boys, after all, did have to sow their wild oats. The comfort derived from mingling with men of like viewpoint doubtless tended to homogenize the political opinions of small groups of friends. Most midwesterners knew someone who delighted in fierce argument, but for themselves preferred the quiet of congenial companionship.[23]

23. Contemporary data on family relations, are, of course, hard to find, but see Newell Sims, *A Hoosier Village* (New York, 1912), p. 58. The absence of conspicuous family feuds based on political tensions constitutes perhaps the best evidence. For relevant modern studies see Arthur S. Goldberg, "Social Determination and Rationality as Bases of Party Identity," *American Political Science Review* (1969) 63:5–25; M. Kent Jennings and Richard Niemi, "The Transmission of Political Values from Parent to Child," ibid. (1968) 62:169–84; Gabriel Almond and Sidney Verba, *The Civic Culture* (Boston, 1965), pp. 94–104; Herbert McClosky and Harold Dahlgren, "Primary Group Influences on Party Loyalty," *American Political Science Review* (1959) 53:757–76; for a theoretical orientation, Bernard Berelson and Gary Steiner, *Human Behavior* (New York, 1964), pp. 557–84; Robert Lane, *Political Life* (Glencoe, 1959), pp. 108–11, 197–202; and Robert Dahl and Charles Lindblom, *Politics, Economics, and Welfare* (New York, 1953), pp. 97–106. Republican workers in Minneapolis in 1896 found "a reluctance on the part of [Republican] workingmen to say what they intended to do . . . their reluctance being based on a desire to avoid the pressures likely to be brought upon them by their associates." *Detroit Free Press,* October 7, 1896.

The informal pressures of family and friends could become quite serious in the case of supporting third parties. Ministers and priests constantly flayed the Populists and Socialists as evil gangs of anarchistic fiends. The Prohibitionists fared better at the pulpits of the Protestant ministers, but squirmed under the sting of Republican wrath. "They are in reality," young Theodore Roosevelt thundered, "bitter and unscrupulous partisans and they follow blindly the lead of a host of vindictive and discredited politicians."[24] A Prohibitionist preacher in Iowa complained that whenever a man inclined toward the third party, "he is denounced as a traitor, a turn-coat, a dud, a pharisee, a mugwump, or some other of the pet names or opprobrious titles by which the party slave-drivers seek to terrify the rank and file into submission, and keep the party lines unbroken." It took great courage, the minister continued, to overcome the "power of slang and abuse and vituperation."[25]

One governor of Iowa, who had himself switched parties a few years earlier, conceded that party loyalty itself exerted the greatest coercive force. "In place of the deliberate judgement of the citizen has come the relentless demand of party ties. Men often shrink from the performance of the most sacred duty imposed by citizenship, because of the political ostracism to which they are subjected if they dare assert an opinion in conflict with the creed of their party."[26] While some men "vote in blind obedience to party ties they will not sunder," and for others the "empty name of a political organization is too often the embodiment of their faith," the governor demanded an Australian ballot to prevent even worse abuses:

> Self-constituted overseers pursue those who stop to consult their conscience or exercise their reason. . . . The strong overcome the weak, employers too often control employees, the rich direct the poor, and all of these rob in a degree the nation and the

24. Speech, December 13, 1888, in *The Works of Theodore Roosevelt* (New York, 1925), 16:133.

25. Frank Haddock, *The Life of George C. Haddock* (New York, 1887), pp. 325–26.

26. *Dubuque Herald,* October 8, 1889, campaign speech of Horace Boies.

State of . . . the deliberate judgement of those who exercise the almost sacred privilege of the elective franchise.[27]

Coercion, given the sacredness of the franchise, had to be shrouded in secrecy. But Americans are a brave enough people to yell when their arms get twisted. And the politicians are bold and clever enough to make political capital out of instances, or even suspicions, of coercion. Indiana's Democratic chairman ascribed the Republicans' success in 1888 to their hard work and to "the intimidation and coercion of employees by their employers." The purpose of the pressure, he suggested, was to protect the tariff. "Hundreds of Democrats," in his home of New Albany alone, he charged, "voted against their own convictions under the coercion, actual or constructive, of those who employ them."[28]

The mechanics of "constructive coercion" were illustrated by the patterns of party affiliation of 725 Moline, Illinois, factory workers in 1877. Only 19 percent of the men were Democrats, and nearly all the rest acknowledged a Republican affiliation. At the Deere plant, 26 percent of the employees were Democrats, while at the rival Moline Plow Company only 10 percent were. The city as a whole voted only 30 percent Democratic in 1876. John Deere, an active Republican and former mayor, was noted for his liberal and benevolent attitude toward labor, while the proprietors of the Moline Plow Company, all Republicans, achieved no such distinction. The foremen at the Deere plant were much more likely to hire Democrats. Thus 20 of the 64 German Protestants at Deere were Democrats, compared with only 2 among the 25 at Moline Plow, and 6 among 36 at the city's other factories. The hiring practices at the factory gate apparently favored Republicans, or else the Democratic applicants lost interest in working alongside so many Republicans.[29]

The dark secrets of voter manipulation, if not actual coercion, had developed into a precise art. Preparing for the 1890 campaign, Louis Michener, the Indiana Republican chairman, confidentially

27. Boies' Inaugural Address, February 27, 1890, Shambaugh, *Messages,* 6:275–76.

28. *Indianapolis Sentinel,* November 10, 1888.

29. *The Past and Present of Rock Island County, Illinois* (Chicago, 1877), pp. 245, 318–60.

advised his lieutenants to "see the employers and foremen who are our friends and see that they give employment, as far as possible to the right kind of men, even if they have to send outside of the state for them."[30] These tactics were necessary, Michener explained, because:

> The enemy are now engaged in moving men from one close township, county and legislative district to another. Their farmers and employers are hiring such men only as they can use on election day. Many of their farmers rent their farms to such men only. We must see that our men are provided for.[31]

Michener further warned that the Democrats were trying to control trade unions, Granges, and farmers' alliances. Infiltrate trusted men inside each, he urged, and "please have our folks understand the advantage of dissensions in the ranks of the enemy, and lay their plans accordingly. Much good can be done in this way."[32]

Charges of employee coercion appeared infrequently before 1896. In April, 1892, 150 Polish sawmill laborers near Manistee, Michigan, complained that they had been fired for voting contrary to the wishes of their bosses at the recent local election. The sawmill had been owned by a prominent Republican, but he went bankrupt in 1890 and the mill was run by receivers appointed by a Democratic judge.[33] A few years before, the third-party Prohibitionists, whom Republicans considered responsible for Blaine's defeat in 1884, found themselves harassed from New York to Iowa. In upstate New York their candidate, John St. John, "was burned or hanged in effigy in many towns, preachers who had voted

---

30. "Confidential Memorandum," October 5, 1889, in Benjamin Harrison Papers, Library of Congress, (microfilm reel 23).

31. Ibid.

32. Ibid.

33. *Tenth Annual Report of the [Michigan] Bureau of Labor and Industrial Statistics* (Lansing, 1893), p. 1221. In 1884 Norman Kelly, an Ohio quarry owner, explained to his fifty men that the victory of Democratic free trade would necessitate the reduction of his work force. On election day, Kelly inspected the ballots of his employees to see whose jobs would be safe. Congress thereupon unseated the innocent beneficiary of Kelly's work. William Mobley, *Digest of Contested Election Cases* (Washington, 1889), pp. 439–44.

for him were dismissed from their pulpits, [and] business men were boycotted."[34]

Since Reconstruction, the Republicans had assumed a stance of moral superiority on election methods that embarrassed and angered the Democrats. Charging that Southern Democrats prevented tens and hundreds of thousands of Republican Negroes from voting, the GOP pledged itself to enact a federal election bill to implement the Fifteenth Amendment. The Republican line of attack climaxed in 1890, but a coalition of Democrats and dissident Republicans finally filibustered the Lodge election bill to death in the Senate.[35] To cover their opposition to civil rights legislation, the Democrats charged that factory owners and other large employers were forcing their men into voting Republican. Although duress of voters was a federal crime, no indictments were brought. Trade unions in the 1880s demanded the Australian ballot to forestall intimidation, but raised no explicit charges of illegal activities against any employers in the Midwest.

The cry of coercion waxed loudest during the campaign of 1896. Senator Jones, the Democratic chairman, in the wake of a bitter defeat, charged that the Republicans used "every kind of coercion and intimidation . . . including threats of lock-outs and dismissals, and impending starvation."[36] Beginning about Labor Day, Bryan and the Democrats alleged that corporations, insurance companies, banks, and railroads were forcing their employees and debtors to support McKinley, or at least to renounce free silver. "Not a corporation or trust," claimed the leading Democratic paper in Indiana, "but is using every effort to intimidate its men and compel them by whatever they see fit to endorse McKinley and the corporation platform." Bryan, however, coupled his condemnation of the practice with the advice that the secret ballot insured freedom from reprisals; even if a man had to announce for McKinley to save his job, he could and should safely vote for Bryan.[37]

34. *The Political Prohibitionist for 1887* (New York, 1887), p. 100.

35. Richard E. Welch, "The Federal Elections Bill of 1890: Postscripts and Prelude," *Journal of American History* (1965) 52:511–26; Stanley P. Hirshson, *Farewell to the Bloody Shirt* (Bloomington, 1962).

36. *New York Times,* November 6, 1896.

37. *Indianapolis Sentinel,* September 7, 1896 (editorial) for quote. William J. Bryan, *The First Battle* (Chicago, 1897), pp. 379, 571, cf. pp. 123, 305.

Blatant coercion did exist in scattered places on a small scale. The Democratic national committee had made repeated calls for coerced men to quietly let them know about it, but few responses came back. In St. Louis a prominent merchant fired a dozen of his junior executives and clerks for supporting Bryan on company time; the Democrats immediately held protest rallies and initiated legal action. The merchant hastily retreated, rehired the men, apologized publicly, and closed his store early on election day. The well-publicized affair, unhappy Republicans felt, cost McKinley thousands of votes.[38] A half-dozen sawmill workers in Michigan lost their jobs for arguing free silver too vociferously, as did a Bohemian blacksmith in Nebraska, a station agent in Iowa, and sixteen railroad laborers in Illinois. If more than fifty midwesterners lost their jobs for supporting Bryan, the Democrats certainly did not know of it.[39]

In a few instances the silverites attempted some duress of their own. In Des Moines, Iowa, the "Farmers' and Laborers' Association" ordered a boycott against a score of prominent opposition merchants, but local Democrats, mindful of Bryan's advice against such ventures, squelched the plan.[40] The decrepit Knights of Labor tried to organize "Minute Men of 1896" to "make the punishment for interference with the free ballot adequate to the crime." Trade unions in Milwaukee boycotted merchants who were paying their men double wages in Mexican silver "dollars" worth fifty cents. An attempt to organize a nationwide boycott against the Miles Drug Company, the maker of Alka-Seltzer and a vigorous pro-

---

38. *St. Louis Republic,* October 13, 14, 1896; *Review of Reviews* (1896) 14:525; Robert Durden, *The Climax of Populism* (Lexington, 1965), p. 140.

39. *Indianapolis Sentinel,* September 28, 1896; *Detroit News,* November 6, 1896; *Omaha World-Herald,* September 19, 21, October 8, 1896; Thomas Butler to Bryan, November 7, 1896; Bryan MSS. When the Democratic governor of Missouri charged that the Alton railroad coerced its employees, the line's president denied the charge and offered a $1000 campaign contribution to the Democrats if they could prove it. The governor backed down, but still insisted that propaganda campaigns against free silver amounted to intimidation. *St. Louis Republic,* September 29, 1896.

40. *Omaha World-Herald,* October 15, 1896; Democratic farmers near Springfield, Illinois, threatened to boycott a local plow company that was supposedly trying to coerce its *customers* to vote for McKinley: it is hard to see how a small plow factory could have tried that. *St. Louis Republic,* October 10, 1896.

ponent of the gold standard, apparently fizzled.[41] When the *Milwaukee Journal,* the leading Democratic paper in Wisconsin, bolted Bryan, it lost half its subscribers in three weeks and nearly went bankrupt. The *Indianapolis Sentinel* managed to swallow Bryan, but refused to support free silver. Circulation and advertising plunged and the paper went bankrupt.[42] From Iowa, a coal-mine operator wrote Bryan, "I have in my employ about 600 men. We gave you all but 81 (Swedes mostly) of this vote."[43] The majority of employees in the other coal mines of the Midwest were supporting McKinley.

As part of their assault on the financial community, the Democrats charged that insurance companies were threatening to foreclose overdue mortgages if Bryan lost, or promising better terms if McKinley won. Insinuations spread that silverite farmers were threatened with immediate foreclosure. Bryan repeated the charges, but in evidence cited only an anonymous letter written to an obscure London newspaper and relying on "a relative in Iowa" for its information.[44] Surely a man who had just traveled 18,000 miles and spoken to hundreds of thousands of farmers could have found better evidence of a supposedly widespread phenomenon. None of the hundreds of farmers who wrote to Bryan during and after the campaign claimed to have been coerced or even approached by their creditors. Many did assert that other farmers had been coerced, but their language followed closely the charges and insinuations being printed in the Democratic press.[45] Insurance agents had indeed explained to policy holders and mortgagees that bankruptcy and liquidation would face the companies if the free coinage of silver started, but the agents, not daring to risk the wrath of the farmers or the Democrats, made no threats to Bryan

41. *St. Louis Republic,* October 6, 1896, for K. of L.; *Peck's Sun and Saturday Star* (Milwaukee), August 1, 15, 1896; cf. Joseph Schafer, Jr., "The Presidential Election of 1896" (Ph.D. diss., Univ. of Wisconsin, 1941), pp. 330–36.

42. Will Conrad, et al., *The Milwaukee Journal* (Madison, 1964), pp. 47–49; Joseph Dunn, *Indiana and Indianans* (Chicago, 1919), 2:757–58.

43. Hamilton Browne to Bryan, November 4, 1896, Bryan MSS.

44. Bryan, *First Battle,* pp. 617–618. Bryan also claimed that bankers "tyrannized" and threatened silverite businessmen. Ibid., p. 583.

45. The Populist party leaders in Minnesota also made the charge, omitting names, dates, and places. *Omaha World-Herald,* October 28, 1896.

supporters and promised no bonuses for voting the "right" way. At the height of the campaign the huge Equitable insurance company hedged its betting on the election by purchasing an expensive full-page, nonpolitical advertisement in Bryan's own newspaper, the *Omaha World-Herald*.[46]

The anxiety engendered by Bryan's free silver panacea led many shopkeepers to place orders with their jobbers contingent upon McKinley's election. Apparently a few factories received contingent orders too. The provisions to cancel orders if Bryan won, however, were generally kept secret. The Democrats, not the Republicans, publicized such contracts to support the coercion charges. Canadian firms, presumably without interest in domestic American politics, but likewise threatened by free silver, also placed contingent orders.[47] The president of the Deere plow company explained that his firm, like most other manufacturers, was a heavy borrower from banks. Free silver inflation would thus reduce his debts, except that the resulting crisis of confidence would disrupt and probably destroy the intricate financial infrastructure of the economy—that part of America which Bryan did not understand, but did hate. Worried by Bryan's chances, Deere explained, banks were refusing to grant loans to businesses since they might be repaid in fifty-three-cent silver dollars. The financial stringency in the weeks before the election was not some sort of Republican plot, but the result of retrenchment in the face of possible panic and disaster.[48]

Financial and manufacturing concerns warned their customers of the dangers inherent in a Democratic victory. Bryan, they explained, simply did not understand the economy, and in the name of justice for the "producing classes" would plunge everyone into the depths of another depression. Over 90 percent of the country's

46. Ibid., September 27, 1896; such ads were uncommon. Indiana farmers received postcards from one Chicago mortgage company, asking how they would vote, but advising, "You need not sign your name." *Indianapolis Sentinel*, September 26, 1896.

47. *Chicago Daily News Almanac for 1897* (Chicago, 1897), pp. 436–44 for Chicago jobbers; *Detroit Free Press*, October 15, 1896; Schafer, "Election of 1896," pp. 337–38; James Barnes, "Myths of the Bryan Campaign," *Mississippi Valley Historical Review* (1947) 34:400; Bryan, *First Battle*, p. 617.

48. *Detroit Free Press*, October 18, 1896.

business was transacted not in cash but in checks and negotiable instruments. The Democratic platform called for the abolition of "notes intended to circulate as money," a policy that would have immediately produced total financial chaos.[49] In western Iowa an undertaker received a letter from a supplier predicting that "the coffin business would be greatly depressed in the triumph of free coinage."[50] The day after the election, business picked up.[51] Across the nation gold-hoarding stopped, factories and shops reopened, new construction began, bank loans became easy to get, and the era of McKinley prosperity was foreshadowed.[52]

The Democrats' charges of coercion were not entirely without foundation. Large factories, especially in the East, ordered their men to participate in the massive "sound money" parades. Mark Hanna, the Republican chairman, on the other hand, gave his six-hundred iron-mine employees in northern Michigan three hours off, with pay, to listen to Bryan. More often, factory employees had to listen to Republican speakers, who usually focused their remarks on gold versus silver and avoided candidates and party labels. The railroads were the most active employers in lining up their men. The roads had immense debts of bonds and mortgages outstanding, usually payable in gold. Their rates were fixed by law in dollars, and sudden inflation would bankrupt every railroad in the country, throwing their men out of work, crippling the nation's transportation, and wrecking whatever remained of the financial system. The Rock Island Railroad hired a dozen pro-gold orators; other lines distributed posters, pamphlets, gold badges, and membership blanks for the Railroad Men's Sound Money Clubs ("blankety blank blanks," Bryan called them, seeing only the tools of coercion).[53]

49. Speech of E.H. Pullen, president of American Bankers' Association to annual convention, in *St. Louis Republic*, September 23, 1896. Porter and Johnson, *National Party Platforms*, p. 98.

50. *Omaha World-Herald*, September 13, 1896.

51. "Well, we scared em like the Devil anyhow," one Bryanite consoled his defeated hero; W. Wintersteen to Bryan, November 6, 1896, Bryan MSS.

52. Barnes, "Myths," pp. 387–89; *Literary Digest* (November 21, 1896) 14:89.

53. On Hanna, *Detroit Free Press,* October 15, 1896; for Bryan quote, *Indianapolis Sentinel,* September 4, 1896, and *First Battle,* pp. 362–63; on the railroads, *Review of Reviews* (1896) 14:392–93; on coercion, *Indian-*

Fear troubled the voters of the Midwest in 1896, and with good reason. The hard times that had begun three years before persisted. Too many factories were closed, too many businesses bankrupt, too many men unemployed to allow much confidence. The factory laborers still working did not fear their employers; rather they shared the fears of capital that free silver would bring calamity. Bryan's own words, "burn down *your* cities and leave *our* farms, and your cities will spring up again as if by magic,"[54] hardly warmed the soul or delighted the imagination of the city-dweller. While the commerce of the nation desperately sought confidence, Bryan ridiculed such demands, finding "in the Bible a rebuke of the same kind of confiidence which is being preached today."[55] Many Democrats privately maintained that another panic was inevitable and that free silver would be the ideal cathartic to purge the economy of its rotten structures. And if that ruined the moneyed classes, they deserved no less. Hundreds of silverites writing to one Chicago newspaper cited their belief in the need for panic as their reason for supporting Bryan, and the candidate himself did little to discourage such views.[56] Much as the Democrats exploited fears of the mysterious "money power," the Republicans played upon the anxieties of the workingmen by emphasizing over and over again that no man's job would be secure if Bryan got the opportunity to wreck the economy.

Few observers were surprised, therefore, when secret polls and estimates of the voting intentions of midwestern factory workers showed a heavy preponderance for McKinley. In Moline, the patterns of party loyalty that had existed twenty years before persisted. The Moline Plow employees were still 90 percent Republican, and the Dimock, Gould factory hands increased their Repub-

---

apolis *Sentinel,* September 7, 22, 1896, Schafer, "Election of 1896," pp. 333–36, and Philip Foner, *History of the Labor Movement in the United States* (New York, 1955), 2:339–40.

54. Bryan, *First Battle,* p. 205, from the "Cross of Gold" speech, emphasis added.

55. Ibid., p. 543.

56. *Chicago Record,* October 31, 1896; *Review of Reviews* (1896) 14:393. At Rock Island, Bryan replied, "I was accused of saying that the free coinage of silver would result in a panic. I have not said so. I do not believe it." *Washington Post,* October 25, 1896. Cf. Thomas Beer, *The Mauve Decade* (New York, 1926), pp. 56–57.

lican preference to over 90 percent. The Deere men were still more Democratic, about 27 percent preferring Bryan, and two new factories reported in September that half their men preferred the Nebraskan. In downstate Illinois, secret polls of 3,480 railroad employees and 9,750 factory workers revealed that 86 percent and 82 percent, respectively, supported McKinley. At the Studebaker plant in South Bend, Indiana, 70 percent of the men, by secret ballot, favored gold, and most of the silverites were Democrats, immigrants from Eastern Europe. The polls were not random samples, of course, and generally the Republican owners released only glad tidings. But the uniformity of the results, their correlation with the election returns, and the striking similarity of the Moline samples of 1877 and 1896, suggest that the midwestern factory workers were overwhelmingly Republican by choice.[57]

Late in the campaign McKinley rejected the allegations of massive coercion:

> There are some who seem to think that the best way to get on in this world is to be against one another. They are disturbed whenever they discover that the employer of labor and labor itself are on good terms, and whenever that occurs they commence crying, "Coercion!" It is not "coercion," it is cooperation, the one working with the other for the public good and for their advantages severally.[58]

McKinley's words hardly comforted the Bryan man forced to march under the gold banner. The problem of psychological pressure, especially as exerted by foremen, remained, and was best explained by a silverite railroad man in Indianapolis:

> Of course the companies are not taking clubs and beating men over the head if they refuse to vote for McKinley, but they are going at the work just as effectively. We are compelled to keep quiet and read the literature thrust in our faces and listen to McKinley talk and hear Bryan denounced as an anarchist, but we are not allowed to say a word in reply. The republican employees go around shooting off their mouths about McKinley,

---

57. *Chicago Tribune*, September 21, 29, 1896. The Democrats retorted that Republicans suppressed a poll of eight hundred Armour stockyard workers, 84 percent of whom supposedly endorsed Bryan. *Omaha World-Herald*, September 29, 1896.
58. *New York Herald*, October 27, 1896.

hoping to advance their own interests with the company, while we are compelled in self-defense to pretend to fall in the procession.[59]

The Democratic fright over the losses due to coercion grew to obsession. The independent and fair-minded *Chicago Record* conducted a huge straw poll of midwestern voters in September and October. It mailed out 833,277 postcard ballots, at an expense of nearly $60,000, to all registered voters in Chicago and to 10 percent of the voters in twelve midwestern and adjacent states. The Democrats suspected a trick, and many refused to participate. In Chicago, the Democratic national headquarters intemperately denounced the poll:

> The whole scheme is one of fraud and debauchery, and may be taken as the first step in a conspiracy to do away with popular elections under the law, and place the molding of public opinion in the hands of millionaires and corporations.[60]

The *Record* nevertheless persisted, and called in eminent mathematicians to adjust the data and take account of the refusals. They retabulated the 240,000 cards returned and predicted McKinley would capture 57.95 percent of the Chicago vote (he actually got 57.91 percent), but were unable to make equally accurate predictions for the rest of the region.

Aside from the harassment of some Democrats, the effects of coercion were not significant and did not alter the outcome of the election. Anyone who believed that Bryan represented the best hope for the nation could have voted for him in complete secrecy. Laborers whose Democratic proclivities clashed with the advice or demands of their employers could have most easily responded by not voting at all, or at least not for presidential electors. Very few

---

59. *Indianapolis Sentinel,* September 22, 1896. A Bryanite railroad worker in Clinton, Illinois, explained that not the managers but "a few understrappers" impelled "by Republican enthusiasm," are "encouraging the spirit of intimidation and coercion." *St. Louis Republic,* October 11, 1896. In a large East St. Louis packinghouse "nearly all the foremen . . . are going to vote for Bryan. A foreman usually sees to it that the men under him vote as he does." Ibid. October 6, 1896.

60. *Omaha World-Herald,* October 14, 1896; *Chicago Record,* October 24, 28, 30, 31, 1896, and Charles Dennis, *Victor Lawson* (Chicago, 1935), pp. 169–77.

men took the latter path. Throughout the Midwest the turnout soared to record highs—over 95 percent in many precincts. And the manufacturing centers voted for McKinley. In eighty-five cities where Cleveland's plurality in 1892 had reached 162,000, McKinley led Bryan by 464,000. Bryan carried only one midwestern city of 45,000 or more, the Democratic stronghold of Fort Wayne, Indiana. Except in Wisconsin, McKinley did better in the cities than in rural areas, although in Wisconsin, Michigan, and Illinois, Bryan's strength was concentrated slightly more in the cities than Cleveland's had been in 1892. The farmers, too, were not coerced. "As a rule," explained one keen Bryanite reporter, the farmers were "free from the domination of any clique or combination and do not hesitate to tell where they stand."[61]

Perhaps the best evidence that coercion did not determine the outcome in 1896 comes from the 1900 election. The Democrats uncovered a few instances of employees being forced to march in GOP parades in Chicago, where 2,000 lumberyard workers rioted when forced to listen to a Republican speaker. The Democratic national headquarters concluded, "while direct intimidation methods have been reported in but a few instances as yet, word is being passed around that only the re-election of McKinley will mean jobs." That was indeed the word, for McKinley's promises of continued prosperity (the depression was over) swept him to an even larger landslide over Bryan in 1900.[62]

Coercion did not determine men's votes—rather they weighed the promises and historic performances of the parties against their own values and beliefs. In the process their religious outlook was the most important factor. To understand the basic forces in midwestern politics it is necessary to survey the religious beliefs and divisions of the people.

61. Quote from *Omaha World-Herald*, September 19, 1896; *Ann. Cycl. 1896:* 672.
62. *St. Louis Republic*, September 26, 1900, for quote, September 29, 30, Oct. 9, 16, 22, 27, 1900, for other stories, none of which indicate that coercion played a role in 1900. See also Carl Degler, "American Political Parties and the Rise of the City," *Journal of American History* (1964), 51:47–49.

3

Pietists and Liturgicals:
The Religious Roots of Partisanship

> The preachers of Iowa with the
> exception of those in the ritual
> churches and a few Presbyterians
> . . . have been on the stump
> for legal prohibition, declaring
> that the use of alcoholic drinks
> is the source of all sin.
>
> *Iowa City Press*[1]

Religion was the fundamental source of political conflict in the Midwest. Religion shaped the issues and the rhetoric of politics, and played the critical role in determining the party alignments of the voters. This chapter focuses on the long-run relationship between religion and partisanship; later chapters will explore the linkages between religion and issues in specific elections.

Three dimensions of religion impinged on political behavior. Theologically, a man's view on the deepest questions of salvation was basic to his sense of morality and his judgment on the proper course of action for a Christian citizen. The two polar theological positions, pietistic and liturgical, expressed themselves through the Republican and Democratic parties, respectively. Second, religion organized men into cohesive groups—congregations and denominations—which exerted intense pressure toward uniformity of outlook. The members of a congregation worshipped together, did business with each other, intermarried, and discussed political questions intimately over long periods of time. In the case of inwardly directed immigrant groups, like the German Lutherans or Irish Catholics, the congregation and denomination provided a stable basis of identity in the strange new American society. Religion intensified the separateness of the immigrants and transformed them into distinct subcultures.[2] Religion was politically

1. Quoted in *Iowa State Register* (Des Moines), July 12, 1882. John P. Irish, editor of the *Press,* was a former Democratic state chairman.
2. See especially Frederick Luebke, *Immigrants and Politics* (Lincoln, 1969), pp. 33–52, and his "The Immigrant Condition as a Factor Contributing to the Conservatism of the Lutheran Church—Missouri Synod," *Concordia Historical Institute Quarterly* (1965) 38:19–28.

more important than culture, for partisanship followed religious lines more closely than cultural divisions. A German Catholic was more likely to vote the same as an Irish Catholic than a German Methodist. Yankees and Southerners constituted visible subcultures in the Midwest, yet the political views of a Methodist of Southern extraction resembled those of a Methodist of Yankee extraction more than a neighboring Baptist who also claimed a Southern heritage. Third, the denominations as organized institutions with highly influential leaders took stances on public issues from time to time, and communicated those views to the membership through such well-established channels of communication as Sunday sermons, auxiliary societies, regular conventions, and, especially, widely read periodicals.[3]

Theological orientations can be traced through the sermons, pamphlets, convention records, periodical articles, and books produced by the more articulate clergy and laymen. The role of the congregation as a small group can be examined through reports of newspapers and travellers, autobiographies, and especially through interviews taken in Indiana and Illinois. For the most part, however, the historical sources bear primarily on the organized activities of the denominations, hence most of the analysis must be based on the level of denominations, bearing in mind that the other two levels were always of importance.

A voter's denominational preference, which involved all three levels of religion, was highly correlated with his party preference. (It will be assumed that religious preference was prior to partisanship; the former may have determined the latter, but not vice versa.) Tables 2, 3, and 4 show the party preferences in the mid 1870s of 3,300 midwestern voters living in fifteen townships in four counties stretching from Rock Island, Illinois, to Indianapolis. The patterns revealed in these tables probably held for the entire Midwest, and perhaps for the entire North (they did not hold for the South). The data comes from four county directories that attempted to enumerate the occupation, nationality, religion, and partisanship of every voter and taxpayer. The enumerations were based on interviews in the field, and appear highly reliable,

3. See Donald Mathews, "The Methodist Schism of 1844 and the Polarization of Antislavery Sentiment," *Mid-America* (1968) 51:3–23.

with the caveat that unskilled workers, farm laborers, and transients were more likely to have been overlooked than more established citizens.[4]

The tables demonstrate that certain groups, especially the old-stock Quakers, Congregationalists, Methodists, and Disciples of Christ, and the Swedish Lutherans and Methodists, numbered few, if any, Democrats in their midst, while the various Catholic groups harbored few Republicans. Very few men listed third party preferences (although the Greenbackers and Prohibitionists were recruiting support at the time). Demographic analysis (reported more fully in the appendix) indicates that region of birth and age were

Table 2

Party Preference by Denomination, Hendricks County, Indiana, 1874[a]

Denomination	% GOP	% Dem.	% none/other	N
Friends (Quakers)[b]	96.4	1.2	2.4	83
Christian-Disciples of Christ[b]	73.6	23.7	2.7	291
Methodists[b][c]	72.8	21.9	5.2	232
Presbyterians[d]	64.3	31.4	4.3	70
Universalists[b]	58.3	42.7	0	12
Missionary Baptists[b]	57.4	38.6	4.0	101
Miscellaneous Protestant[e]	50.0	33.3	16.7	12
No Denomination listed	47.0	48.3	4.6	699
Regular Baptists[f]	17.0	78.7	4.3	94
Roman Catholics[f]	4.2	83.3	12.5	24

a: Liberty, Lincoln, Marion, Middle, Union and Washington Twps.
b: Predominantly pietistic
c: Includes African Methodists, who were also pietistic
d: Mostly Cumberland Presbyterians (pietistic)
e: Mixed pietistic and liturgical
f: Predominantly liturgical

SOURCE: *The People's Guide: A Business, Political and Religious Directory of Hendricks Co., Indiana* (Indianapolis, 1874).

4. The men less likely to have been included were also less likely to vote; for example, most farm laborers were under twenty-one.

only weakly correlated with party preference; although the Civil War had ended only a few years before, men of Southern extraction were only slightly more likely to be Democrats than their neighbors. On the other hand, occupation did affect partisanship, as is

Table 3

Party Preference by Ethnicity and Denomination, Geneseo, Illinois, 1877[a]

Ethnic group	Denomination	%GOP (of two-party total) [b]	N
Old Stock	Congregationalists[c]	96.5	74
	Unitarians[d]	96.0	25
	Methodists[c]	91.4	70
	Baptists[c]	90.9	22
	Presbyterians[e]	72.5	29
	Miscellaneous Protestant[e]	80.0	20
	No Denomination listed	69.0	400
Swedish	Methodists[c]	100.0	7
	Lutheran[c]	98.5	65
German	Methodists[c]	85.7	7
	Lutheran[f]	66.7	60
	No Denomination listed	48.4	60
	Roman Catholic[f]	25.0	16
Irish	Roman Catholic[f]	0.0	52
Other	Roman Catholic[f]	7.7	13
Total		70.1	920
Actual vote (Governor, 1876)		68.1	827

a: Includes city and rural township; although Geneseo City had a population of only 3,400 at the time, fewer than a fifth of all midwesterners lived in larger cities.

b: Republican share of the two-party total. Excludes men who gave no party preference, and 29 listed as "independent," of whom 7 were German Lutheran and 11 listed as no denomination.

c: Predominantly pietistic.   d: Religious style uncertain.

e: Mixed pietistic and liturgical.   f: Predominantly liturgical.

SOURCE: *The History of Henry County, Illinois, Its Taxpayers and Voters* (Chicago, 1877).

demonstrated in the Appendix. The chief factor, however, was religion, and the explanation for its importance in determining party preference requires a review of the nature and role of religion in the Midwest in the middle nineteenth century.

The most revolutionary change in nineteenth-century America was the conversion of the nation from a largely dechristianized land in 1789 to a stronghold of Protestantism by midcentury. The revivals did it. From the 1780s to the early twentieth century uncounted thousands of itinerant preachers—Methodists, Baptists, Presbyterians, Congregationalists, Disciples, and others—went to the people, warning of damnation and holding out the promise of salvation. Their success was remarkable everywhere. By 1890 more than 70 percent of the midwestern population was church-

---

Table 4

Party Preference, Old-Stock Voters by Denomination, Eight Illinois Townships, 1877–1878

Denomination	%GOP (of two-party total)[b]	N
Congregationalists[c]	82.0	39
Methodists[c]	75.0	289
Disciples of Christ and Cumberland Presbyterians[c]	71.8	220
Lutherans (General Synod)[c]	60.5	38
Unitarians[d]	60.8	18
Presbyterians[e]	57.7	108
Baptists[e]	55.7	61

a: Lincoln City, Elkhart, Sheridan and Chester Townships, Logan County: Black Hawk, Buffalo Prairie, Port Byron and Rural Townships, Rock Island County.
b: Republican share of two-party total; see Appendix for the patterns for the entire population, and further analysis.
c: Predominantly pietistic.
d: Religious style uncertain.
e: Mixed pietistic and liturgical.

SOURCE: *The Past and Present of Rock Island County, Illinois* (Chicago, 1877); *The History of Logan County, Illinois* (Chicago, 1878).

---

affiliated; of these, five out of nine belonged to the revivalistic camp. (See table 6 for details.)

The revivals induced a theological confrontation that raged throughout the century.[5] Led by Charles Grandison Finney of Oberlin, Nathaniel Taylor of Yale, Edward Park of Andover, and S.S. Schmucker of Gettysburg, the revivalist theologians abandoned the predestination doctrines of orthodox Calvinism and rejected the conservative, established Anglican, Catholic, and Lutheran dogmatism. The opponents of revivalism, led by John Nevin at Mercersberg (Reformed), Charles Hodge at Princeton Seminary (Presbyterian), Carl Walther at Concordia (German Lutheran), Augustus Strong at Rochester (Baptist), Charles Porterfield Krauth at Philadelphia (Lutheran), and John Hobart at General (Episcopalian) recognized the threat posed by the revivalists to the historical and ritualistic foundations of their faith and fought back brilliantly, sparking a theological and liturgical renaissance in their denominations.

Disputes over revivals broke out in every denomination, aligning the faithful into prorevival, or "pietistic," and antirevival, or "liturgical," camps. While this conflict was not the only divisive force in American religion,[6] it was the most intense and long standing until the very end of the century, when the revivals declined sharply in importance and moderates sought to clear the air of the old bitterness. Until the mid-1890s the conflict between pietists and liturgicals was not only the noisiest product of Amer-

5. The best treatments of the religious background are: Robert Baird, *Religion in America* (New York, 1856); Winthrop Hudson, *Religion in America* (New York, 1965); Timothy Smith, *Revivalism and Social Reform* New York, 1957); and H. Shelton Smith, Robert T. Handy, and Lefferts A. Loetscher, eds., *American Christianity* (New York, 1963), esp. vol. 2, chaps. 12, 13, 15, 18. T. Scott Miyakawa, *Protestants and Pioneers* (Chicago, 1964), although imaginative is unreliable. Three good state studies are Willard Allbeck, *A Century of Lutherans in Ohio* (Yellow Springs, 1966); L. C. Rudolph, *Hoosier Zion: The Presbyterians in Early Indiana* (New Haven, 1963); and John F. Cady, *The Origin and Development of the Missionary Baptist Church in Indiana* (Franklin, Indiana, 1942).

6. Anti-Catholicism was widespread, but its political impact in the 1890s was weak, since both Catholics and many anti-Catholic Lutherans, Episcopalians, and Baptists favored the Democratic party. Cf. Clifton J. Phillips, *Indiana in Transition, 1880–1920* (Indianapolis, 1968), p. 463, and Robert Cross, *The Emergence of Liberal Catholicism in America* (Cambridge, 1958), pp. 52–53.

ican religion, it was also the force which channeled religious enthusiasm and religious conflict into the political arena.

The liturgical, or "high church," outlook consisted of much more than simple opposition to revivalism. It stressed the positive values of the institutionalized formalities and historic doctrines of the old orthodoxies, whether Calvinist, Anglican, Lutheran, Catholic, or Jewish. Salvation, the focus of all Christianity, required faithful adherence to the creeds, rituals, sacraments, and hierarchy of the church. The quintessence of the liturgical style appeared in Catholicism's lavish use of ornamentation, vestments, stylized prayers, ritualized sacraments, devotions to relics and saints, all supervised by an authoritarian hierarchy led by the pope, whose infallibility was proclaimed in 1870. Comparable ritualism developed rapidly among Episcopalians in the middle and late nineteenth century, while German Lutherans, orthodox Calvinists ("Old School" Presbyterians and many Baptists) increasingly stressed theological scholasticism and fundamentalism.

One key element in the liturgical outlook was particularism, the belief that the denomination was the one true church of God and that most outsiders were probably damned. The attitude was strong among Catholics, German Lutherans, Landmarkean Baptists (a movement inside the Baptist denomination), high-church Episcopalians, and predestinarian Presbyterians. The church itself would attend to all matters of morality and salvation, the particularists believed, hence the state had no right to assert a role in delineating public morality. Voluntary moralistic social-action groups that were not an integral part of the church structure were illegal, unscriptural, and unnecessary, since they threatened to remove the determination of good and evil from the hands of properly anointed church leaders. Opposition to independent or interdenominational missionary and temperance societies led to a rupture of the Presbyterian denomination in 1837, nearly ruined the long-run growth of the Baptists in the 1830s, led to a great crisis over "Americanism" in the Catholic church in the 1890s, and fueled a controversy over the independence of seminaries in the Presbyterian fold in the 1890s.

Heresy, pride, and insubordination (matters totally outside the concern of the state) were the cardinal sins for the liturgicals. Consequently they devoted their intellectual resources to neoscholastic theology and their financial resources to building seminaries and parochial schools that would insulate their adherents from the follies of the aggressive pietistic denominations. The success of the Catholics and German Luthcrans in building strong networks of parochial schools in the last third of the century seemed to pietists to be a threat to the public school system they controlled, and touched off an unusually bitter political controversy that climaxed in the elections of 1890 in Wisconsin and Illinois. The hostility of the pietists only encouraged the liturgical forces to redouble their efforts. The courageous pursuit of duty was the highest virtue for the liturgicals, and the most outstanding exemplar of this trait was the son of a Calvinistic Presbyterian minister, Grover Cleveland.[7]

The pietistic outlook flatly rejected ritualism. It showed little regard for elaborate ceremonies, vestments, saints, devotions, or even organ music. Theologically the key to pietism was Arminianism, the idea that all men can be saved by a direct confrontation with Christ (*not* with the church) through the conversion experience. The revival was the basis of growth—the preaching of hellfire, damnation, and Christ's love, the "anxious bench" for remorseful sinners, the moment of light wherein a man joyously gained faith and was saved forever.[8] The revivals worked; from 1800 to 1886 the Methodists gained in membership at the compound rate of 4.6 percent per year, while the total population grew at only 2.8 percent per year.[9] The liturgicals grew rapidly too —not because of revivals but by baptizing all their children as infants (not just those who had a conversion experience in adolescence or adulthood) and by working hard to raise the religious aspirations of millions of immigrants who came from liturgical backgrounds in Europe.

7. Robert Kelley, *The Transatlantic Persuasion* (New York, 1969), is especially interesting on the influence of religion on Cleveland.
8. James Findlay, *Dwight L. Moody* (Chicago, 1969), pp. 192–261, and William G. McLoughlin, *Modern Revivalism* (New York, 1959), are good on theology. See also Rudolph, *Hoosier Zion,* pp. 118–50, and Washington Gladden, ed., *Parish Problems* (New York, 1887), pp. 311–16.
9. Bureau of the Census, *Historical Statistics of the United States, Colonial Times to 1957* (Washington, 1960), series A 2, H 541. Adequate statistical studies of denominational growth are badly needed. For a model British study, see Robert Currie, *Methodism Divided* (London, 1968), pp. 85–111.

The pietists not only demanded a conversion experience as a condition of membership (a requirement softened as the century grew old), but also insisted on continuous proof of genuine conversion in the form of pure behavior.[10] The Methodists did not hesitate to expel members whose conduct was unbecoming a true Christian; the liturgical churches only expelled heretics. Creeds and formal theology declined in importance for the pietists; heresy was never a major concern. Denominational boundaries softened, and pietists frequently switched church membership, a process that would have excited great alarm had it become common among liturgicals. The pietists cooperated generously in numerous voluntary societies; they banded together to distribute Bibles, Christianize the world, abolish slavery, and enforce total abstinence.

Pietists struggled with liturgicals in every denomination. In most cases one group or the other secured the upper hand, driving the minority to silence, schism, or transfer to a more congenial denomination. By the 1860s the Methodists, Congregationalists, Disciples, United Brethren, and Quakers in the Midwest were predominately pietistic. The Episcopalians and Catholics were predominately liturgical, although a kind of pietism had important support among Catholic bishops. The Presbyterians were fragmented, with liturgicals in control of the Old School and United bodies, and pietists in control of the New School and Cumberland bodies. (The Old and New Schools, calling a truce to theological disputes, reunited in 1869, and in 1906 Cumberland joined them.) The Baptists were fragmented too. The small Freewill body was intensely pietistic; the even smaller Primitive (or "Anti-Mission") body, fiercely Calvinistic. However the large numbers of "Regular"

10. The very success of the revivals meant that as the century neared an end most of the new members of the pietistic churches would be children of members who had entered by revivals. A sort of "half-way" entrance requirement emerged, as Christian nurture at home, faithful Sunday school attendance, and good character substituted for the conversion experience. Fewer members were expelled for misbehavior, in large part because there was little overt immorality among pietistic church members. See Earl Brewer, "Sect and Church in Methodism," *Social Forces* (1952) 20: 400–408; Robert Ellis Thompson, *A History of the Presbyterian Churches in the United States* (New York, 1895), pp. 239–41; H. Shelton Smith, "Evangelical Christian Nurture," *Religion in Life* (1948) 17: 548–49; Washington Gladden, *The Christian Pastor and the Working Church* (New York, 1898), pp. 381–89.

Baptists had no central authority to provide theological unity; probably most were pietistic, with scattered pockets of Calvinistic and high church Landmarkean believers playing important roles in places like Hendricks County (see table 2). Lutherans, whose numbers grew rapidly with the immigration of hundreds of thousands of Germans and Scandinavians, were divided into three camps with semi-independent synods shifting frequently from one camp to another as the tides of theological disputation rose and fell. The liturgical German Lutherans, gathered into the Synodical Conference under the leadership of the Missouri Synod, were the most militant and disputatious religious group in the nation until the rise of the Jehovah's Witnesses in the twentieth century. The pietists, led by the old-stock (formerly "Pennsylvania Dutch") General Synod and the Swedes in the General Council, were thoroughly revivalistic. The General Council, although it included pietists, also included many articulate liturgical Lutherans and attempted to steer a middle course.

Round after round of withdrawals and schisms, mostly reflecting pietistic-liturgical conflict, produced a remarkable proliferation of smaller denominations in America; by 1890 the Census Bureau counted no fewer than 143 bodies.[11] These smaller groups (like the Holiness and Pentecostal sects) played no great role in midwestern politics, but their continual formation indicated that pietistic-liturgical tensions persisted well into the twentieth century.

The bridge linking theology and politics was the demand by pietists that the government remove the major obstacle to the purification of society through revivalistic Christianity, institutionalized immorality. Specifically, the midwestern pietists demanded Sunday blue laws, the abolition of saloons, and, in the prewar era, a check to the growth of slavery, or even its abolition. Many pietists, identifying the heavy influx of Catholic immigrants (especially the Irish) as the chief source of the corruption of politics and the decay of the cities, and ultimately as a barrier to the success of the revival movement, also supported nativist movements. The liturgicals, as a rule, opposed Sunday laws and prohibition, denounced abolitionists, and avoided nativist movements.

11. Frank Mead, *Handbook of Denominations* (New York, 1965), and, especially for statistics, H. K. Carroll, *The Religious Forces of the United States* (New York, 1912), provide guides to each denomination.

The church, they insisted, should attend to morality, not the government. Although they were no more pleased with the evils of drunkenness and saloons than the pietists, the liturgicals rarely supported total prohibition and never demanded total abstinence as many pietists did. Furthermore they never denounced slaveholders as sinners, though many agreed that slavery was an evil thing. The liturgicals saved their strong condemnations for the pietists—"fanatics" they always called them—and grew fearful that the pietists would capture control of the government to impose different standards of morality.[12]

The liturgicals' fears were well grounded. Beginning in the 1820s and 1830s the pietists established a grass-roots network of reform societies that demanded governmental action against slavery and saloons. In the late 1830s the pietists renounced the concept that moderation in drinking was an acceptable social standard; they demanded total abstinence and total legal prohibition of the manufacture and sale of all alcoholic beverages, including wine and beer. (The condemnation of fermented wines, including communion wines, struck the liturgicals as unscriptural, antisacramental and anti-Christian.) The pietistic congregations fell into line, and in 1851 secured their first great triumph, total prohibition in the state of Maine. Immediately the tempo of reform quickened. Prohibition laws or constitutional amendments were enacted in Illinois and Ohio in 1851, Michigan in 1853, Iowa and Indiana in 1855; steadfast German opposition in Wisconsin in 1853 was all that prevented a complete sweep of the Midwest. In 1853, 1854, and 1855 the primary forces reshuffling party allegiances in the Midwest were the pietistic antiliquor, antislavery and anti-Catholic crusades. The Democratic party everywhere adopted the liturgical position, usually with some success, while a new Republican party emerged as the chief vehicle of pietistic reform. After 1855 the pietists largely abandoned temperance movements to concentrate

12. For a similar view, see Paul Kleppner, *The Cross of Culture* (New York, 1970), pp. 71–91. Kleppner argues that pietists emphasized "right behavior" and liturgicals "right belief." The pietists themselves thought what one believes is more important, since it determines conduct. The vast majority rejected the notion that right conduct is more important than correct beliefs. See the survey of Methodists conducted in 1959, in Herbert Stotts and Paul Deats, *Methodism and Society: Guidelines For Strategy* (New York, 1962), p. 328.

on antislavery, while the Republican party backed away from nativist and dry platforms to permit a broadening of support among voters who were repulsed by pietistic crusaders.[13] It seems reasonable to hypothesize that when party lines reformed in the 1850s, the great majority of midwestern (and eastern) pietists entered the Republican party, while the great majority of liturgicals became Democrats. The data in tables 2-4 suggest that the unchurched voters fell midway between the two camps, probably dividing their votes about equally. It is also reasonable to postulate that the continuity of party loyalty among individuals and families remained quite high until at least the end of the century. The data in tables 2–4 also suggest that postwar immigrants from Europe adopted the same political preferences as their coreligionists who had arrived earlier. The voting patterns of the 1880s and 1890s can be expected to show the same strong correlation between religious style and partisanship that appears in the data from the 1870s and that probably existed in the late 1850s. Indeed the correlation would be high even if religious issues did not enter into the political campaigns of the 1880s and 1890s, since the great majority of midwesterners undoubtedly maintained the same religious style and the same political affiliation their families had acquired three or four decades earlier. The Republican-pietistic and Democratic-liturgical pattern was also reinforced by postwar political issues of keen interest to the electorate.

The prohibition movement revived after the apparent triumph of radical reconstruction in 1868 freed pietistic energies from an obsession with Civil War issues. The Good Templars, a pietistic secret society with 400,000 members, created the Prohibition party in Michigan in 1869, and the Woman's Christian Temperance Union formed in Ohio in 1874 after a sudden, spontaneous outburst of antisaloon activity. Major efforts to submit prohibition amendments to state constitutions came in Iowa in 1880, Michigan and Wisconsin in 1881, and Illinois, Indiana, and Ohio in 1882. (The

13. The details for each state can be traced in *Cyclopedia of Temperance and Prohibition* (New York, 1891); *The Standard Encyclopedia of the Alcohol Problem*, 6 vols. (Westerville, Ohio, 1924–1930); and Ernest Cherrington, *The Evolution of Prohibition* (Westerville, Ohio, 1920). For the national scene see Joel Silbey, ed., *The Transformation of American Politics, 1840–1860* (Englewood Cliffs, 1967).

electorate actually voted on these proposals in Iowa [1882], Ohio [1883], and Michigan [1887].) Meanwhile the temperance advocates took advantage of "local option" laws that permitted counties, townships, and cities to banish the local saloon. The prohibition question was the paramount state or local issue, year in and year out, throughout most of the Midwest (and much of the rest of the country) in the 1880s. Invariably the Republican party favored dry solutions, while the Democrats were on the wet side.[14]

Superficially, the fundamental lines of cultural conflict in the Midwest paralleled the distinction between immigrants and old-stock Americans. The more perceptive participants in the heated campaigns of the 1880s realized that the prohibition issue tapped a deeper layer of values and beliefs than was represented by the old-stock versus immigrant cleavage. Eminent wet Democrats, for example, spoke for a large body of old Americans, while most of the Scandinavian immigrants, particularly the Swedes, were more resolutely dedicated to radical prohibition than even the Methodist Yankees. The systems of values and beliefs that the prohibition issue brought into open conflict were not peculiar to the Midwest. Everywhere in America, and in much of western Europe as well, the tensions existed. Since prohibition was the vehicle chosen by the more aggressive group, its goals and its ethos assumed great importance.

After Reconstruction the temperance crusade assumed a life of its own, transcending the revivalistic theology that had given it birth. Intemperance was not merely an impediment to successful revivals, it was the root of all social evil in America. All Christians, the reformers said, had a duty to free society from this curse. Moderate drinkers endangered their bodies and souls, set a horrible example to others, and sabotaged the onward march of godly reform. They sinned by drinking. The primary goal of the movement had become the moral reform of society, beginning with the extirpation of the root of corruption, the saloon.

The raw, unsettled condition of the frontier had once provided a hospitable environment for heavy drinking, but now, the drys proclaimed, the progress of civilization demanded an end to intemperance. The ideal was a middle-class society, free from the

---

14. See the compendia cited in note 13, and D. Leigh Colvin, *Prohibition in the United States* (New York, 1926).

evils spawned by excesses of wealth and poverty. Thrift, industry, temperance, and piety were the cardinal virtues, and the saloon mocked those virtues, substituting for them improvidence, sloth, drunkenness, crime, and political corruption. Where not so long ago slavery had constituted an imminent threat to the existence of a free, progressive, Christian society, now demon rum was the remaining obstacle to the advance of civilization.

The drys expended considerable effort and statistical ingenuity in gathering and disseminating information that purported to expose the baneful effects of liquor. For the drinker, alcohol was a poison, a debilitating instrument of physical, mental, and moral degeneration. Economically, the liquor traffic was a parasite on society, draining away valuable human and physical resources from socially useful purposes. The farmer, laborer, mechanic, or clerk, the propaganda asserted, threatened the well-being of himself, his wife and children, his coworkers, and his fellow citizens by dissipating his wages on drink. Socially, the effects of drinking were disastrous. Intemperance, the standard argument went, incites the base instinct of destructiveness, weakens the inhibiting ability of moral judgment, deadens the sense of self-respect and shame, tempts to idleness, neutralizes the drive for achievement, and begets illiteracy, poverty, and vice. Ignorance and poverty, the drys maintained, did not in themselves lead to crime; demon rum was the essential ingredient.

The saloon was at once the father of vice and the root enemy of all social, religious, or political efforts to combat vice and social evil generally. The well organized, lavishly financed, single-minded liquor power, with its hundreds of thousands of besotted or befuddled minions, was the cancer gnawing at the soul of America, said the drys. The Midwest, with just pride in its educational achievements, its middle-class society, and its low rates of pauperism, crime, and corruption, could maintain its purity and its nobleness of achievement only if it resisted the blandishments of King Alcohol. America must be dry.[15]

15. This synthesis of dry ideology is based primarily upon the items cited in notes 13 and 14 and the periodical literature, especially the *New York Voice* (weekly organ of the Prohibitionist party), and the *National Temperance Advocate,* the monthly magazine of the National Temperance Society.

Save perhaps in the raw new towns in western Iowa and northern Michigan, the saloons were placid affairs; the naked eye could hardly see the corruption that logic required of them. Usually it just saw a few bearded Germans sipping their lager and a ruddy-faced Irishman drinking his whiskey, with, perhaps, a poker game in the corner that kibitzers found more exciting than the players. No matter; the saloon was evil incarnate, and should the bystander need evidence, the minister had a shelf full of magazines and books that uncovered the whole lurid truth. The drys did not need that evidence, for opposition to the evils of alcohol was a tenet of religious belief, as vital a part of dry Christianity as the existence of hell. In 1888 the Methodist church proclaimed the witness of the drys clearly:

> The liquor traffic is so pernicious in all its bearings, so inimical to the interests of honest trade, so repugnant to the moral sense, so injurious to the peace and order of society, so hurtful to the homes, to the church and to the body politic, and so utterly antagonistic to all that is precious in life, that the only proper attitude toward it for Christians is that of relentless hostility. It can never be legalized without sin.[16]

The other pietistic denominations pulled abreast of the Methodists in the 1880s. The Presbyterians in 1883 officially denounced the liquor traffic as "the principal cause of . . . drunkenness and its consequent pauperism, crime, taxation, lamentations, war, and ruin to the bodies and souls of men," and advised their members to "persevere in vigorous efforts" for total prohibition.[17] Various religious assemblies increasingly called for members to ignore the strong ties of party and vote for none but supporters of strict dry laws. The small Reformed Presbyterian Church, U.S.A., which was so alienated from the "godless" American constitution that its adherents were not permitted to vote, even relaxed its extreme position to allow voting for prohibition. The overwhelming opinion of ministers and, probably, of laymen in the pietistic denominations favored total prohibition. Many ministers joined the Prohibition party and coaxed their congregations to follow, especially Methodists, Quakers, United Brethren, Free Methodists, Freewill

16. *Cyclopedia of Temperance,* p. 426.
17. Ibid., p. 494.

Baptists, United Presbyterians, Winebrennerians (Church of God), and General Synod Lutherans.[18]

Opposed to the pietists were the majority of the communicants of the liturgical churches. In politics, the most significant opposition to the drive for prohibition came from the Episcopalians, the Roman Catholics, the German Lutherans, and some of the Calvinistic Presbyterians and Baptists. Unfortunately, the opponents of prohibition among the nonchurch members were so diverse, scattered, or anonymous that generalization about their cultural attitudes and beliefs becomes impossible. The moderate and wet influence among the church members, however, was only one mode of expression of a broad set of attitudes, beliefs, values, and way of life.

The Catholic church in the Midwest still was in the brick and mortar stage in the late nineteenth century. The problems of providing adequate religious care for the Irish and German laborers and farmers who kept pouring into the Midwest absorbed most of the energies of the priests and bishops. The Catholics labored under the twin disabilities of poverty and prejudice. A sense of devotion to "Holy Mother Church," often as a substitute for loyalty to the village or province back in the old country, stimulated the Catholics to immense financial sacrifices as they built thousands of churches, parochial schools, and charitable institutions. The hostility of the Protestants could not so easily be overcome. The American Protective Association, an anti-Catholic hate group, sprang up in Iowa in 1887 and rapidly spread across the Midwest in the next five or six years. A variety of other anti-Catholic groups flourished, but generally were of more importance in other parts of the country. The APA, which became an important political issue in 1894, was merely a symptom of the tensions between Catholics and Protestants. In scattered localities, riots broke out between Catholics and Methodists; in the coal-mining centers, the interreligious conflict raged, as we shall see later. Meanwhile the respected leaders of the Protestant community warned darkly of the "Romanist Peril."[19]

18. *Ann. Cycl. 1889:* 716; *New York Voice,* September 6, 27, October 4, 25, 1888; *Cyclopedia of Temperance,* p. 186; *One Hundred Years of Temperance* (New York, 1886), pp. 96, 98, 344, 351, 414, 423.

19. Josiah Strong, *Our Country* (New York, 1885), pp. 46–59; *Ann. Cycl.*

A church comprised largely of poor workers, led by men of the cloth concerned with saving souls and erecting buildings, could not aspire to lofty cultural or intellectual achievements. Even the devotional activities of Catholics seldom went beyond Sunday mass and occasional rosaries. Nevertheless a quasi-pietistic movement, akin to French Jansenism, flourished among Irish priests and numerous converts from Protestantism. Led by John Ireland, the vigorous and controversial archbishop of Saint Paul, it advocated evangelistic fervor in missionary work and demanded strict standards of personal morality among Catholics. Ireland, with support from the pope and fellow bishops, led the Catholic temperance movement and secured official condemnations of saloons. Although Ireland was a founder of the Anti-Saloon League, neither he nor any other prominent Catholic advocated total prohibition. Personal temperance, if not total abstinence, coupled with local option and high annual licenses for saloons, were his goals. Ireland scandalized conservative Catholics by his search for a compromise with the Protestants on the explosive parochial school question. Making the Jansenist pattern congruent with the pietistic, Ireland enthusiastically supported the Republican party. Republican efforts to woo the Irish vote seemed, indeed, to have focused on the Jansenists like Ireland.[20]

"To an unusual degree," the historian of the Catholic Total Abstinence Union found, the union "accepted the point of view of respectable, Protestant America."[21] Any Methodist Prohibi-

---

1893: 519–20; *New York Times,* November 1, 1889. The APA will be examined in chapter 8.

20. Kenneth Scott Latourette, *Christianity in a Revolutionary Age* (New York, 1961), 3: 71–72; *Cyclopedia of Temperance,* pp. 68, 181–82, 597–600; *One Hundred Years of Temperance,* pp. 556–60, 594–99, 654; John T. Ellis, *American Catholicism* (Chicago, 1956), p. 134; Aaron Abell, *American Catholicism and Social Action* (Garden City, 1960), pp. 40–44, 91–98, 104–5, 127–31; John Kane, *Catholic-Protestant Conflicts in America* (Chicago, 1955), p. 43; Cross, *Liberal Catholicism.* The leading "Jansenists" included bishops John Spalding of Peoria, John Keane of Dubuque, and James Cardinal Gibbons of Baltimore. The Paulist order spearheaded the movement; see Joan Bland, *The Hibernian Crusade* (Washington, 1951), pp. 70, 269, 271.

21. Bland, *Hibernian Crusade,* p. 267. A careful Boston observer found that Catholic retreats, conducted by Jansenists, "in purpose and method closely resemble [Protestant] revival meetings and protracted services." Robert Woods, ed., *The City Wilderness* (Boston, 1898), p. 202.

tionist would have cheered Bishop Spalding's declaration that "there is still left in the mass of the people a deep moral earnestness, which, if it can be called into action, may lift the whole nation to higher and purer life. Our two great parties are the principal obstacle in the way of such a movement." Conduct, the Peoria bishop felt, "is three-fourths of life."[22] Cardinal Gibbons, in one election sermon, admonished his flock that:

> Political life is to be gauged by the standards of domestic life. What would it profit you to be esteemed in public as a free and honorable citizen . . . if in the sanctuary of your home you were a slave of anger, lust or intemperance?

To help God "save our country from the moral decay and corruption which befell the Roman Empire," Gibbons instructed Catholics to "give your suffrages to men of clean hands and hearts, who are above the taint of corruption and who are conspicuous for integrity of character."[23]

The German Catholics, on the other hand, saw nothing wrong in drinking beer, and occasionally produced an articulate wet spokesman to flay the fanaticism and supposed hypocrisy of the drys. A leading Cincinnati priest in 1889 displayed this animus against pietists (and indicated a certain distaste for Irishmen):

> The American nationality . . . is often the hotbed of fanaticism, intolerance, and radical, ultra views on matters of politics and religion. All the vagaries of spiritualism, Mormonism, free-loveism, prohibition, infidelity and materialism generally breed in the American nationality. While the Irishman will get drunk and engage in an open street fight, and the German drink his beer in a public beergarden, the American, pretending to be a total abstainer, takes his strong drink secretly and sleeps it off on a sofa or in a clubroom.[24]

The Germans, equal in number to the Irish but far weaker in influence, demanded more liturgicalism in the Catholic church.

22. Quoted in Thomas McAvoy, "Bishop John Lancaster Spalding and the Catholic Minority," in Matthew Fitzsimons et al., eds., *The Image of Man* (Notre Dame, 1959), pp. 399, 402.
23. *Chicago Herald,* November 7, 1892.
24. Anton Walburg, *The Question of Nationality* (Cincinnati, 1889), in Robert Cross, ed., *The Church and the City* (Indianapolis, 1967), p. 118.

Theologically, they repudiated Jansenism (without using the term), asking:

> Are not the supernatural virtues of Faith, Hope, and Charity enough? Do not these supernatural virtues necessarily establish temperance? Is there any holiness that cannot be found in the Catholic supernatural life? Are not the administration of the sacraments by the clergy and their devout reception by the people, attendance at Mass, and hearing the word of God—are not these enough to secure the attainment of any virtue?[25]

More concretely, the Germans resented the Irish hegemony in the American hierarchy and wanted to use the parochial schools to inculcate in their children the language and the culture of the fatherland. Archbishop Ireland wanted to use the parochial schools to Americanize the Catholics and to teach the Jansenistic virtues. The Germans were fond of their customs, their relaxed Sundays, and their native language. Bishop Ireland, they charged, was a "Puritan" Republican set out to Protestantize the church. A good many Irish laymen probably agreed with the Germans; most of the Irish at least regarded "the temperance swindle as an outflow of Puritan bigotry." Other Catholic immigrant groups, the Poles especially, resented the Irish control of the American church, and went as far as schism. The Germans protested to Rome, and the 1890s witnessed the great crisis in the Catholic church, technically revolving around the charges of the existence of an "Americanist" heresy. A tacit compromise emerged. The Jansenistic priests relaxed their temperance work, and focused their demands for stringent morals on sexual matters, Mass on Sunday, fish on Friday, and unquestioned obedience to the bishop. The Germans accepted the new emphasis, and drank their beer unmolested; they continued their parochial schools, but the rising number of second generation parents gradually spelled the demise of the German language.[26]

25. Bland, *Hibernian Crusade,* p. 160, quoting the Paulist Walter Elliot's 1890 summary of the liturgical Catholic position. Elliot replied that the development of supernatural virtues presupposes the natural ones, "especially self-restraint or temperance." The dry Protestant pietists, on the other hand, argued that drinking was a sin in itself.

26. Quote from Carl Wittke, *The German Language Press in America* (Lexington, 1957), p. 134, and his *The Irish In America* (Baton Rouge,

The Protestant Episcopal church had opposed the prohibition movement from its beginning. The Church Temperance Society, imported from Britain in 1881, promoted "union and co-operation on perfectly equal terms" among total abstainers and moderate drinkers. Coffee houses and $1,000 annual licenses were its answer to the saloon menace. The society favored a "broad, tolerant, and scriptural" approach to the liquor question, as did most of the high-church wing of the denomination. Apparently, the only radical drys among the Episcopalians belonged to the minority low-church wing.[27]

The dignity and maturity of the Episcopalian denomination proved amenable to the tastes of upper-class American society. Its strength among the social elite of the larger cities (where half its adherents lived) constituted the major obstacle to the pietistic claim that all the "best" people were dry. In Chicago in 1911, for example, only Presbyterians outnumbered Episcopalians among the business and professional elite.[28] Most of the Episcopalians in

---

1956), pp. 49–51. On the German-Irish tension, see Coleman Barry, *The Catholic Church and German Americans* (Washington, 1953), esp. pp. 17–19, 84, 192–93, 250–76, and 305–6; and Philip Gleason, *The Conservative Reformers: German-American Catholics and the Social Order,* (Notre Dame, 1968), pp. 29–45. In Detroit in the 1950s the "devotional" (Jansenistic) Catholics considered moderate drinking to be wrong more often than the "orthodox" (liturgical) Catholics; Gerhard Lenski, *The Religious Factor* (Garden City, 1963), pp. 207–8, 310. On the compromise, see Zane L. Miller, *Boss Cox's Cincinnati* (New York, 1968), pp. 136–38, and Louis Putz, ed., *The Catholic Church U.S.A.* (Chicago, 1956), pp. xviii, 14–17, 375–93.

27. *One Hundred Years of Temperance,* pp. 379–84; *Standard Encyclopedia of the Alcohol Problem,* 2: 614–15; *Cyclopedia of Temperance,* pp. 81, 216; *Ann. Cycl. 1882:* 709; Church Temperance Society, *Prohibition as We See It* (New York, 1928), pp. 13–14; *Papers, Addresses and Discourses at the Fifteenth Church Congress* (New York, 1893), pp. 12–36; and, generally, E. Clowes Chorley, *Men and Movements in the American Episcopal Church* (New York, 1946).

28. A random sample of 10 percent of the 7,500 men in A. N. Marquis, ed., *The Book of Chicagoans* (Chicago, 1911), a directory of the city's business and professional leaders, gave 310 men who specified denominational affiliation. Of these, 57 were Episcopalian; 107, Presbyterian or Congregationalist; 32, Methodist; 30, Catholic; 23, Baptist; 20, Jewish; 15, Unitarian; 14, Lutheran; and 12, other denominations. See Richard Jensen, "Quantitative Collective Biography: An Application to Metropolitan Elites,"

the Midwest were high-church liturgicals, and probably shared the annoyance expressed by William Perry, bishop of Iowa, with "the disappointments and disasters, the illiberal fanaticism and unwarranted license, of the so-called temperance reform."[29] Bishop Charles Grafton of Fond du Lac, Wisconsin, explained the liturgical position clearly:

> All Christians feel the need of strength against temptations to intemperance, and lessening them. Sectarianism in its Puritan spirit [pietism] strives to do this by force, or law, or prohibition. It is a judicial mode of dealing with a moral problem. The Church looks rather to the aid of moral restraint, and to the aid of grace. . . . For great as is the evil of any fleshy sin, it often, by the shame it brings, leads to repentance . . . while on the other hand the spiritual sins of pride, self-sufficiency, etc., are more deadly because unsuspected and more lasting in their effects.[30]

Episcopalians residing outside the large cities endured a surprising amount of hostility from pietists. Bishop Grafton lamented in 1891:

> There are indeed those who bear the name of Christian who, under the influences of jealousies resulting from an unhappy divided Christendom, in small ways seek to persecute us. It is quietly made known to persons about to join our communion that if they do so, it will be to their pecuniary or social disadvantage.[31]

The sources of the animosity included liturgicalism, support of the Democratic party, and opposition to prohibition. Bishop Grafton complained that "designing mischief makers . . . repeat the silly cuckoo cry of Romanism," and expressed amazement that because of "our deepened spiritual life developed by use of our Sacraments,

---

in Robert Swierenga, ed., *Quantification in American History* (New York, 1970), pp 389–405, for further detail. Note that most of the adults in Chicago in 1911 were Catholics.

29. *29th Annual Convention, Diocese of Iowa* (Davenport, 1882), pp. 33, 56–57.

30. B. Talbot Rogers, ed., *The Works of the Rt. Rev. Charles C. Grafton* (New York, 1914), 7: 324–25.

31. Ibid., 7: 17–18.

our members have been thought worldly minded and undevout."[32] In 1869 a leading Unitarian minister warned that in the midwestern cities "Catholicism and copperhead Episcopacy rear their heads in insolent pretension," probably alluding to the lukewarm support given by high-church Episcopalians to the Union war effort. One observer recalled that in Indianapolis "in the war time Christ Church was one of the few where a Democrat could worship without being hit periodically with a religio-political brick," and that Republicans had dubbed it "The Church of the Holy Rebellion." The anonymity of large cities protected most Episcopalians, for there were few large concentrations in rural areas. One colony of Englishmen in Le Mars, in northwest Iowa, scandalized the pietists by their support of elegant saloons. One, the "House of Lords," featured imported liquor, good English ale, and a private locker room for tippling young British gentlemen. The "unsavory reputation" and "flagrant violation of all law" at the House of Lords led to scuffles and headlines about a "War between the Races." The British, annoyed by the efforts of the natives to close the pubs, voted Democratic.[33]

The Calvinistic Presbyterians in the Midwest played only a minor role in the temperance controversy after their reunion with the pietists in 1869. The outstanding wet Presbyterian minister was Howard Crosby of New York, who frequently explained that the New Testament sanctioned drinking (in moderation, of course) and that absolute prohibition would never work.[34] The most out-

32. Ibid., 7: 93, 155, quotes dated 1896 and 1900. On the epithet "Romanism" applied to high-church Episcopalians, see A. A. Barton, ed., *The Church Cyclopedia* (New York, 1883), p. 665.
33. A. D. Mayo, "Religious Tendencies in the United States," *Christian Examiner* (1869) 87: 49; Jacob P. Dunn, *Greater Indianapolis* (Chicago, 1910), 1: 612; Jacob Van Der Zee, *The British in Iowa* (Iowa City, 1922), pp. 210–16. See also Alexander Allen, *Life and Letters of Phillips Brooks* (New York, 1890), 1: 425. On low-church support for Lincoln, see James B. Bell, "Charles P. McIlvaine," in Kenneth Wheeler, ed., *For the Union: Ohio Leaders in the Civil War* (Columbus, 1968), pp. 252–56. On the bitter high–low factionalism, see A. T. Andreas, *History of Chicago* (Chicago, 1885), 2:413 and 3:779–85; and George Smythe, *A History of the Diocese of Ohio Until the Year 1918* (Cleveland, 1931), pp. 325–39, 367–70.
34. *Standard Encyclopedia of the Alcohol Problem*, 2: 734–35; *National Temperance Advocate* (July, 1886) 21: 125. Donald K. Gorrell, "Presbyterianism in the Ohio Temperance Movement of the 1850's," *Ohio Archaeological and Historical Quarterly* (1951) 60: 292–96, notes that Old

standing wet Presbyterian layman was Grover Cleveland, who as a beer-drinking bon vivant offered a sharp contrast to the prim, pietistic Presbyterian, Benjamin Harrison. Cleveland issued a quiet warning to the radical prohibitionists at the 1888 Presbyterian convention by pointing out that "the church which is most tolerant and conservative, without loss of spiritual strength, will soonest find the way to the hearts and affections of the people."[35]

The Calvinistic Baptists were a minority in the Midwest, and not a vocal one at that. They failed to keep their state conventions from adopting dry resolutions, although they did have support from a few widely read Baptist magazines.[36]

The position taken by the elite wet Episcopalians and Presbyterians reduced the possibility of prohibition merely expressing a kind of nativism. The patterns of the immigrant voters destroyed that possibility. The Swedish Lutherans were staunch Republicans and radical drys. Their Lutheranism was not, however, a liturgical transplant from the Church of Sweden; far from it. The great majority of Swedish immigrants, and nearly all their pastors, had been pietistic dissenters within the Church of Sweden. Their break with the rote Christendom practiced by the established church, derived in part from their firm convictions on temperance and in part from the encouragement of evangelistic American missionaries, was directed against the horrible addiction of the Swedes to strong liquor. The main religious body of the Swedish immigrants, the Augustana Lutheran Synod, in 1880 declared it the duty of the Christian citizen "to cast his vote against the manufacture and sale, as a beverage, of all intoxicating drinks." Like the pietistic

---

School Presbyterians abandoned temperance reform by 1855. For the Calvinistic Presbyterians' conservative reaction to social problems, see Elwyn A. Smith, *The Presbyterian Ministry in American Culture* (Philadelphia, 1962), pp. 225–34, and Lewis Van der Velde, *The Presbyterian Churches and the Federal Union, 1861–69* (Cambridge, 1932). The intellectual leader of Calvinism in America, Charles Hodge of Princeton, made eloquent appeals for more liturgy, while furiously denouncing prohibition; *Discussions in Church Polity* (New York, 1878), pp. 157–67, 224–31. On liturgicalism see Thompson, *Presbyterian Churches,* pp. 231–36.

35. George Parker, ed., *The Writing and Speeches of Grover Cleveland* (New York, 1892), p. 188.

36. The prestigious *Baptist Quarterly Review* was staggered by hostile reaction to its cautious support of high license; see (1890) 12: 351, and *National Temperance Advocate* (January 1891) 26: 7.

Norwegian Lutherans of the Hauge Synod and the United Norwegian Church, the hard-working Swedes often "out-Puritaned the Puritanism of the New Englanders."[37]

Most of the Norwegians in the Midwest belonged to pietistic Lutheran groups, particularly the United Norwegian Lutheran Church. A minority of about 30 percent belonged to the predominantly liturgical Lutheran group, the Norwegian Synod. One stronghold of the latter was in Winneshiek County, Iowa, and an analysis of three Norwegian farming communities there reveals their divergence from their pietistic brethren. The towns of Pleasant, Glenwood, and Madison were 93 percent Republican in 1881, but gave a prohibition amendment the next summer only 45 percent of their votes. The cross-pressures at work, on the one hand historic Republicanism and on the other opposition to the legal regulation of morality, led to a drop in turnout in the three towns at the special election, while the other Norwegian communities in Iowa increased their turnout and overwhelmingly supported the prohibition amendment. The Republican inclinations of the liturgical Norwegians weakened during the continued temperance agitation of the 1880s. In 1885 the Republican vote of this group slipped to 77 percent; in 1891 it plunged to 60 percent. After the satisfactory resolution of the liquor issue by the Republican party in 1893, the vote shot up to 76 percent, and reached 80 percent in 1894. The dilemma of the liturgical Norwegians had been resolved, and they returned to the Republican fold.[38]

37. On the Swedish support for prohibition, *Iowa State Register,* June 23, 1882, and O. Fritiof Ander, "The Swedish-American Press and the Election of 1892," *Mississippi Valley Historical Review* (1937) 23: 539. On the religious patterns see George M. Stephenson, *The Religious Aspects of Swedish Immigration* (Minneapolis, 1932), pp. 16–32, 123–30, 139–43, 373–74, 404, 433–44, and his "The Mind of the Scandinavian Immigrant," in *Norwegian-American Studies* (1929) 4: 49–71; Latourette, *Christianity,* 2: 167–87. For quotes, Theodore C. Blegen, *Norwegian Migration to America* (Northfield, Minnesota, 1940), 2: 223; and Abdel Wentz, *A Basic History of Lutheranism in America* (Philadelphia, 1964), p. 320.

38. On the religious tensions among Norwegians, see Blegen, *Norwegian Migration,* 2: 204–06, 221–23; *Ann. Cycl. 1890:* 511; Marcus Hansen, *The Immigrant in American History* (Cambridge, 1940), pp. 113–21, and Latourette, *Christianity,* 2: 154–66. On the prohibition campaign in Winneshiek county, *Iowa State Register,* June 16, 1882. On the persistence of Norwegian pietism, see W. Lloyd Warner, ed., *Democracy in Jonesville* (New York, 1949).

The million and a half Protestant Germans in the Midwest, although divided into numerous feuding denominations, equalled the German Catholics in numbers and represented the most aggressive and articulate bastion of liturgicalism. About a million were intensely liturgical Lutherans, belonging to the independent Missouri, Joint Ohio, Wisconsin, Iowa, or Michigan synods. Another fifth belonged to the Reformed church or the Evangelical Synod, both of which split along liturgical-pietistic lines. The remainder affiliated with pietistic bodies, chiefly the United Brethren, the Evangelical Association, and the Methodist Church (all of which merged in 1968). In addition there were German Baptists of various sorts, a small but extremely articulate and powerful band of wet freethinkers (the "Forty-Eighters"), and about sixty thousand Reform Jews. In general, the Germans of the Midwest were much more religious and liturgical than the population of the old country. Probably many families immigrated to America in part to secure more latitude for their religious practice.[39]

Significantly, the churches of the eighteenth-century German immigrants (the "Pennsylvania Dutch") held very little attraction for nineteenth-century immigrants. The pietistic Lutheran bodies, the United Brethren, and the Evangelical Association were too "puritan" for the newcomers. The Missouri Synod repeatedly excluded the Pennsylvania-based General Synod from its conception of Lutheranism. (It was "a composite of Methodistic Presbyterianism with the Lutheran name added.")[40]

The fact that theology, rather than language, customs, or heritage, was the foundation of cultural and political subgroups in America was nowhere better illustrated than among the Germans.

---

39. Statistics derived from Carroll, *Religious Forces;* Erwin Lueker, ed., *Lutheran Cyclopedia* (Saint Louis, 1954), was especially helpful in untangling the various synods and theologies. Also useful were Henry Jacobs and John Haas, *The Lutheran Encyclopedia* (New York, 1899), Julius Bodensieck, ed., *The Encyclopedia of the Lutheran Church*, 3 vols. (Minneapolis, 1965), and Philip Schaff, *America* (New York, 1855), pp. 176–205.

40. *Lutheran Witness* (November 21, 1889) 8:93. In reply the pietists ridiculed the Missouri Synod as too "Dutch" and "crankish"; ibid., (December 7, 1889) 8:100. On the German Methodists, see Carl Wittke, *William Nast, Patriarch of German Methodism* (Detroit, 1959), pp. 70–71, *Iowa State Register*, June 3, 1882, and Paul F. Douglas, *The Story of German Methodism* (New York, 1939).

The German freethinkers, Catholics, pietists, and Lutherans cordially hated each other. The pietists were closely allied with their Yankee counterparts in the Republican party; the freethinkers, led by Carl Schurz, shuttled back and forth between high positions in the two parties; the Catholics and Lutherans, with much mutual recrimination, were both in the Democratic camp. The Missouri Synod, largest of the Lutheran bodies, denounced theologically suspect Lutheran synods in sarcastic terms, but considered the Catholic church to be the embodiment of the Antichrist. While pietists hailed Archbishop Ireland, the liturgicals denounced him for "exciting in silly, incredulous mortals the belief that by such influences [Jansenism] Rome may be freed from its superstitions and idolatries and atrocities, and its subjects rendered the free and enlightened people which the Lutheran Reformation has made the citizens of these United States."[41] Politics made strange bedfellows in those days—the German Catholics and Lutherans found in each other their best allies in the emotion wracked campaign of 1890.

The Missouri Synod never endorsed the saloon; indeed, said the synod, it "wages a war against the saloon, and disciplines such members as, after warning, continue to engage in such a mode of obtaining a livelihood."[42] However, the synod showed more concern with the dangers and basic "immorality" of social dancing than with liquor. After careful theological investigation, it decided that temperate drinking was perfectly moral. "The real principle involved in prohibition," it decided, "is directly adverse to the spirit, the method and the aim of Christian morals." The trouble with the reformer was that, "instead of relying on God's spirit," he "puts his trust in fallible legislators. Instead of using spiritual influence, he resorts to the tricks and treacheries of politicians."[43] Actually, the reformers were equally repulsed by such "tricks and treacheries." Nonetheless the Missouri Synod became the most

---

41. *Columbus Theological Magazine* (February 1893) 13:184–85; this was the organ of the liturgical Ohio Synod, a smaller German Lutheran body; Allbeck, *Lutherans in Ohio,* pp. 150–90, 221–58, 287–97. "The Army of Antichrist" was the headline of a typical Missouri Synod report on Catholic growth; *Lutheran Witness* (June 7, 1886) 5:21; cf. Lueker, *Lutheran Cyclopedia,* pp. 37–38.

42. Jacobs and Haas, *Lutheran Encyclopedia,* p. 488.

43. *Lutheran Witness* (February 7, 1889) 7: 131; and see the series of articles by Rev. W. Lewereng, ibid., October 21, 1887, to January 21, 1888.

thoroughly wet denomination in America, or in the world, for that matter. The Lutheran Synodical Conference, controlled by Missouri, resolved in 1888 that, "We as a church cannot participate in the present ecclesiastical political temperance movement." This was, first, "because [the movement] does not discriminate between secular and ecclesiastical action . . . [and] it is the duty of the church to save men by faith in Christ from committing sin," and, second, because moderate drinking is not itself evil.[44]

Despite its wet stance, the Missouri Synod was deeply disturbed about the nation's moral health, and in 1886 it expressed cataclysmic fears of the extent of moral decay in American society:

> Unbridled covetousness and usury, the open and unpunished teaching of atheism, prevalent perjury and profanity, riotous and lewd life, secret and open murders, and gross neglect of the gospel-means of education, all these have brought the free people of this glorious country to the brink of ruin.[45]

This deeply alienated spirit aligned the Missouri Synod with the premillenial pessimists of other denominations who, in the twentieth century, would flock to the fundamentalist crusades and the Jehovah's Witnesses.[46] In the context of the 1880s and 1890s, furthermore, this bitterly pessimistic view of society meant that the synod would not be likely to trust established political parties. Remarkably few American politicians ever emerged from the Missouri Synod, despite its size, intelligence and wealth. Party loyalty, to the extent that it signified loyalty to the forces that were in league with the devil, would never be palatable to these Lutherans.

Both the German Evangelical Synod and the (German) Reformed Church in the United States (they merged in 1934 and in 1957 entered the United Church of Christ, with the Congregationalists) were unable to adopt a uniform policy on temperance. Pietists struggled with liturgicals for control, leading to regional animosities and tensions inside individual congregations. Sometimes a devout pietistic minister tried to reorient the moral prin-

---

44. *Illinois Staats-Zeitung* (Chicago), June 21, 1888.
45. *Lutheran Witness* (June 7, 1886) 5: 28.
46. Cf. Milton Rudnick, *Fundamentalism and the Missouri Synod* (Saint Louis, 1966); Kleppner, *Cross of Culture*, pp. 79–83; and Rodney Stark and Charles Glock, *American Piety* (Berkeley, 1968).

ciples of his flock; more often, the congregation was more pietistic than its bookish or "worldly" liturgical minister. In Lincoln, Illinois, some years after the interviews with its inhabitants included in table 4 were conducted, one such confrontation took place. Shocked by their pastor's sons playing tennis on Sunday afternoons, a delegation of pious elders from the Evangelical Synod congregation paid a solemn visit to the Reverend Gustav Niebuhr. The minister listened to the grave charges, but permitted the boys to continue their fun. The elders may have shaken their heads sadly when one of the boys later became a Marxist in Detroit. Of course the Niebuhr brothers, Richard and Reinhold, eventually turned out well, but the tensions persisted and the Evangelical Synod redoubled its efforts to establish parochial schools "in order to stop the anglicizing process going on everywhere."[47]

The relative numbers of pietists and liturgicals in the Midwest cannot be known exactly, but they can be estimated for 1890. The problem of estimating involves finding a way to translate the membership figures tabulated by each denomination into comparable population statistics. Although the federal census never inquired into the religious preferences of individuals (it asked church officials for data), the Iowa state census of 1895 did ask each person over ten years of age to state his religious preference (not necessarily membership, which was much more restricted).[48] The results appear in table 5, column 2. For each denomination the ratio of people expressing a preference to recorded members is

47. *Ann. Cycl. 1889:* 366; June Bingham, *The Courage to Be* (New York, 1961), pp. 57–59, for the Niebuhr incident; see also Hansen, *Immigrant in American History,* pp. 113–21; *Cyclopedia of Temperance,* pp. 187, 411; *One Hundred Years of Temperance,* p. 458; and Kleppner, *Cross of Culture,* pp. 49–51, 83. The Dutch Reformed groups were also divided sharply along theological lines. Henry Lucas, *Netherlanders in America* (Ann Arbor, 1955), pp. 471–72, 544, 564; Cyrenus Cole, *I Remember, I Remember* (Iowa City, 1936), pp. 48–53, 99; *One Hundred Years of Temperance,* pp. 448–449; Robert Swierenga, "The Ethnic Voter and the First Lincoln Election," *Civil War History* (1965) 11:27–43; Schaff, *America,* pp. 146–52; and Kleppner, *Cross of Culture,* pp. 59–61.

48. *Census of Iowa for 1895* (Des Moines, 1895), pp. 435–36; Bureau of the Census, *Report on Statistics of Churches . . . Eleventh Census: 1890* (Washington, 1896), pp. xxi, 435–82; Carroll, *Religious Forces,* p. xxxiv, used different multipliers, based on the Canadian census.

shown in column 3. By assuming the ratios were about the same for the same denomination in other midwestern states (a fairly strong assumption, especially when dealing with cities) it becomes possible to estimate the results of a hypothetical survey (in 1890) asking each person over the age of ten to state his religious "preference."

Table 5

Approximate Distribution of Religious Affiliation in Iowa, 1895 (Age Ten and Above)

Denominational groupings	Number of formal church members	Number acknowledging affiliation or preference	Ratio of affiliated to members
Methodists	132,000	265,000	2.01
Catholics	152,000	192,000	1.26
Lutherans (total)	69,000	189,000	2.72
German	29,000	79,000	
English	2,600	7,100	
Swedish	9,000	24,500	
Norwegian	26,000	70,000	
Danish	2,800	7,600	
Presbyterians	47,000	85,000	1.82
Disciples and Christians	31,000	74,000	2.35
Baptists	34,000	69,000	2.04
Congregationalists	30,000	49,000	1.62
United Brethren	10,000	19,000	1.94
Evangelical Synod	12,000	19,000	1.59
Episcopalian	7,000	17,000	2.42
Reformed (Dutch and German)	7,100	16,000	2.32
Friends	8,100	12,000	1.43
Jewish	920	3,500	3.86
Smaller denominations and miscellaneous	22,000	51,500	2.3
Not given, "Protestant," or none (estimated)	—	428,000	
Total	562,000	1,488,000	

The results of the calculations (using the 1890 census data on formal church members as a base) indicate that the Midwest contained:

2,000,000 Roman Catholics (17%)
1,800,000 Methodists (15%)
1,500,000 Lutherans (13%)
  690,000 Baptists (6%)
  560,000 Presbyterians (5%)
  550,000 Disciples and Christians (5%)
  480,000 Evangelical and Reformed (4%)
  260,000 United Brethren (2%)
  220,000 Congregationalists (2%)
  190,000 Episcopalians (2%)
  390,000 other Protestant denominations, and Jews (3%)
3,200,000 no preference (27%)

To estimate the number of pietists and liturgicals, it is necessary to hazard some guess as to the relative strength of the two factions in each denomination. Table 6 is based on the classification as liturgical of 90 percent of the Catholics, German Lutherans, Episcopalians, and Orthodox Jews, together with half the Presbyterians, Evangelical Synod, Reformed, and Norwegian Synod adherents, one-fourth of the Baptists, and 10 percent of all other denominations. The classification is, of course, guesswork, but a variation of the different proportions in doubtful cases makes only a very small difference in the overall pattern state by state.

Regionally the pietists compromised 41 percent of the population, and liturgicals only 32 percent. There was considerable variation from state to state. In Indiana and Ohio, the pietists had about double the strength of the liturgicals. In Illinois and Michigan they were equally matched, and in Wisconsin the liturgicals held a wide lead. The large cities were overwhelmingly liturgical, especially Chicago. The distribution in Iowa was quite similar to the Midwest as a whole, suggesting that the religious dimension of politics in that state, the subject of the following chapter, may be representative of the patterns of the entire region.

Table 6

Estimated Division of Midwestern Population by Religious Outlook, 1890

	Pietist	Nonmember	Liturgical	Total population age 10 and above (= 100%)
Illinois	36%	28%	35%	2,900,000
Indiana	55	23	21	1,700,000
Iowa	40	31	29	1,400,000
Michigan	31	38	31	1,600,000
Ohio	49	24	27	2,900,000
Wisconsin	33	19	48	1,300,000
Total Midwest	41	27	32	11,800,000
Chicago	18	29	53	880,000
13 other cities over 40,000	32	16	51	1,240,000
Downstate Illinois	45	27	28	2,000,000

4

Iowa, Wet or Dry?
Prohibition and the Fall of the GOP

Iowa will go Democratic when
hell goes Methodist.

J. P. Dolliver, 1883[1]

In 1888 the Midwest remained a Republican stronghold. The GOP controlled all six governorships and five of the congressional delegations; only Indiana was at all doubtful. Imminent success for the Democrats in any of the states would have seemed absurd. Yet all of the governors and congressional delegations elected in 1889 and 1890 would be Democratic—it would be one of the most spectacular, and short-lived, political reversals in American history. For many years there had been lurking an issue capable of shaking the loyalty of enough Republicans to defeat that party, and in 1889 it came to a head, defeating overconfident Republicans in four midwestern states and pointing the way to the Democratic landslide of 1890.

The issue was the tension between the pietistic and liturgical world views, and in 1889 it emerged in the guise of the prohibition of the liquor traffic. Indeed, for most of the last third of the century, the liquor question, throughout the Midwest, was the major factor activating the latent tensions and leading to changes in voting patterns. Other issues blazed into prominence from time to time, subsiding as quickly as they ignited, and leaving little impress on voting patterns. But cultural tension was important year in and year out, thanks to a large, articulate, dedicated band of pietistic temperance advocates, and an equally determined body of liturgical opponents. A review of the role of the prohibition question in Iowa from 1855 through 1891 will suggest the contours of the issue, while detailed discussion of the elections of 1889 in Iowa, Ohio, Chicago, and Indianapolis will show its critical importance.

In 1888 Iowa carried high the banner of midwestern Republicanism. Not since the organization of their party had the Republicans lost control of Iowa's electoral votes, its statehouse, its congressional delegation, or its legislature. Leading the GOP were three men of national stature. Senator William Boyd Allison, a

1. Thomas R. Ross, *Jonathan Prentiss Dolliver* (Iowa City, 1958), p. 65.

serious aspirant to the White House and a power in Congress, enjoyed the deference due the outstanding citizen of Iowa. James Clarkson, editor of the Des Moines *Iowa State Register,* the voice of Iowa Republicanism, was a power in the GOP national committee and directed the national campaigns against Cleveland in 1888 and 1892. The other triumvir, Colonel David Henderson, represented the Dubuque district in Congress, and in 1899 became Speaker of the House. Long years of secure power, however, had rusted the fighting gear of the GOP. Overconfident and carelessly organized, the Republicans relied heavily upon party loyalty of the Iowans who cherished the memory of Lincoln and who endorsed the sound, conservative Republican administration of state and national affairs.[2]

The Democratic party, by contrast, was a motley coalition of losers. The Bourbons sat on top. They were old stock businessmen, editors, or wealthy farmers with an emotional and intellectual attachment to the principles of the Democrats: tariff for revenue only, strong presidents (Cleveland was their hero) and weak congresses, deep fear of corruption, conciliation toward the white South, frugal government, and opposition to radical crusaders, whether abolitionist, socialist, or prohibitionist. In a Republican stronghold, the Bourbons more often got the prestige of an important nomination than the office itself. Cleveland's entry into the White House stirred their hopes for federal patronage; but the president knew which state parties were important, and in four years gave Iowa only the minor sop of commissioner of patents, and that only after half the term had expired. The Democrats did win local offices in many of the heavily immigrant counties along the Mississippi River, but the Germans and Irish, not the Bourbons, got these plums. Thousands of old Jacksonian Democrats, mostly poor farmers of southern heritage, clung to the party of their fathers without hope or want of patronage. Their aggregate vote was important, but their opinions vague and unheeded.[3]

2. Leland Sage, *William Boyd Allison* (Iowa City, 1956), pp. 205–39; Cyrenus Cole, *I Remember, I Remember* (Iowa City, 1936), pp. 138–50, 176.

3. Horace Merrill, *Bourbon Democracy in the Middle West: 1865–1896* (Baton Rouge, 1963); Benjamin F. Gue, *History of Iowa* (New York, 1903), 3:1–4, 14, 61, 96–97, 137. Robert Kelley, *Transatlantic Persuasion*

So bankrupt was the Democratic party after the war that it groped desperately for fusion or submersion into any popular movement that showed even a glimmer of electoral hope. John P. Irish, Iowa Democratic state chairman, in 1873 pronounced his party dead: it was "hopelessly bankrupt," having "outlived its day and its usefulness." He urged Democrats to join the new Anti-Monopoly party. That strategem proved no more successful than had fusion with the Liberal Republicans in 1872, with the Green-backers sporadically from 1878 to 1886, or with the odd "Union Anti-Negro Suffrage party" in 1865. The Republicans merely flayed the Democrats, even in disguise, as Copperheads, ridiculed their platforms (after extracting any especially popular ideas in them), drew upon their reservoir of party loyalty, and triumphed every time.[4]

In 1889 the Democratic prospects suddenly were not so bleak. Mobilizing its respectable Bourbon candidates and the full voting strength of its rank and file, the party made a new appeal to luke-warm Republicans and independents. Democrats sensed confusion and disarray among the opposition, and vigor and harmony in their own ranks. They had come upon a new stone for their old sling, and now set about to slay Goliath upon the battlefield of the ene-my's choosing. The Republican leaders, to their own amazement, found themselves helpless to avoid this deadly conflict, for the bat-tlefield was the cultural and religious values of the people, and the issue was the morality of drinking.

In 1855 the Whig party of Iowa secured passage of a constitu-tional amendment to prohibit the manufacture and sale of alcoholic beverages within the state, and then promptly expired. Its succes-sor, the Republican party, concentrating its crusading fervor against slavery, quickly exempted beer and wine, permitted towns the local option of licensing saloons, and neglected to enforce prohibition in counties that did not want it. The beer-drinking liturgical Germans pouring into Iowa, not to mention the whiskey-

---

(New York, 1969), without mentioning Iowa, analyzes the Bourbon outlook brilliantly.

4. Mildred Thorne, "The Liberal Party in Iowa, 1872," *Iowa Journal of History* (1955) 53:121–52, and "The Anti-Monopoly Party in Iowa, 1873–1874," ibid. (1954) 52:289–326.

guzzling unchurched old Americans, must not be alienated, the ambitious Republicans decided.[5]

The Republicans' refusal to enforce prohibition frustrated both the Democrats, who hungered for a viable issue, and also the reformers, who considered intemperance to be the greatest evil in Iowa. After the Civil War, three distinct positions emerged on the liquor question. Most zealous were the pietistic drys, the total abstainers who considered even moderate drinking to be sinful and properly subject to legislative prohibition. At the other pole the liturgical and unchurched wets, men not adverse to a drink now and then, or perhaps more often, wanted their saloons. Even the liquor dealers among them did not always oppose a little regulation or taxation of the trade—high tavern licenses, after all, might cut down competition. All the wets bitterly denounced any attempt to abolish the saloon as an infringement of personal liberty and constitutional rights. In between came the moderates, who, whatever their own drinking habits, viewed the question not in the stark tones of the wets and drys, but in the gray zone of matters of practical public policy.

The Democrats, their party machinery largely housed and greased by the saloon and powered by its patrons, naturally championed the wet cause. They seldom missed an opportunity to decry "sumptuary laws," as they always called prohibition laws, or to denounce the GOP as "the tool of fanatical preachers," a "Holy Alliance of . . . abolitionists, Whigs, Know Nothings, Sunday and Cold Water Fanatics." Yet no matter how hard they tried, whether they pitched high or low, the Democrats could make little headway on the issue before the Republicans helped them out in the late 1870s and early 1880s.[6]

During the Grant administration, the drys, animated by the good ladies of the Woman's Christian Temperance Union, and muscled

5. Louis Pelzer, "The History and Principles of the Democratic Party of Iowa: 1846–1857," *Iowa Journal of History* (1908) 6:211, 237; Dan Elbert Clark, "The History of Liquor Legislation in Iowa," ibid. 6:67–68, 80–87; *The Cyclopedia of Temperance and Prohibition* (New York, 1891), pp. 148–49, 587–89; David Sparks, "The Decline of the Democratic Party in Iowa, 1850–60," *Iowa Journal of History* (1955) 53:17–18.

6. Quote from Carl Wittke, *The German Language Press in America* (Lexington, 1957) p. 140. Merrill, *Bourbon Democracy,* pp. 58–60; *Cyclopedia of Temperance,* pp. 148–53, 559–67; *Dubuque Herald,* October 31, 1882.

by their husbands' votes, formed a Prohibition party. They garnered more scorn than votes, and seemed, at first, ludicrously unimportant and old-fashioned in the Gilded Age. But the shocking excesses of the age—the Whiskey Ring scandals, for example—led many sober drys into the ranks of the crusaders. In Iowa, and across the Midwest, the WCTU prospered and spread, the Sons of Temperance revived, the Order of Good Templars reorganized its teetotaling brothers. Most important, the leading pietistic ministers, headed by Methodists, rekindled their traditional support for prohibition and entered the political fray. Organized into the Iowa State Temperance Alliance, the dry crusaders constituted an unmeasured power of disquieting magnitude to the nervous Republican leaders. Slowly the Republicans edged toward the dry camp. New, more stringent licensing and local option laws in 1868, 1870, 1872, 1873, and 1874 carried Republican endorsement, but failed to satisfy the drys. At the Republican convention of 1875 the drys, in coalition with the soft-money men, almost won the gubernatorial nomination for their champion, General James B. Weaver, only to meet sudden defeat at the hands of desperate moderates and conservatives.[7]

The threatening growth of the dry and inflationist Greenback party after Weaver's defection to it in 1877, coupled with the rising militancy of the dry crusaders, forced the issue. In 1879 the Republicans resolved in favor of submitting to the vote of the people a prohibition amendment to the state constitution that would join Iowa with Kansas and Maine as the driest states in America. The Prohibition party collapsed in 1879, as its adherents rushed to endorse the new Republican pledges. True to the party's platform, the Republican legislatures of 1880 and 1882 passed the necessary legislation for submission, and in anticipation of the outcome curtailed the sale of liquor by druggists.

The special election of June 27, 1882, climaxed the long and bitter struggle for constitutional prohibition in Iowa. In every county of the state, and in nearly every township and school district, the Temperance Alliance mobilized its men and, especially, its

7. Clark, "Liquor Legislation" 6:342–64; Fred Haynes, *James Baird Weaver* (Iowa City, 1919), pp. 80–83; David Brandt, "Political Sketches," *Iowa Journal of History* (1955) 53:341–65; *Cyclopedia of Temperance*, pp. 589–91.

women, who could not vote but who had ways of influencing their menfolk. Prohibition of liquor—and this time beer and wine as well—the drys insisted, was merely the natural advance after the legal prohibition of murder, thievery, prostitution, gambling, and political corruption; indeed, they said, it was the best way to banish all those practices from Iowa. The achievement of a higher stage of American civilization and Christian morality, they concluded, rested on the outcome of the vote.[8]

The opposition, mobilized by the Brewers' Association, perforce fought on a narrower field. Funded by a $6000 assessment on beer sales, and with some help from friends in Saint Louis, Chicago, and Milwaukee, the liquor interests worked through local saloons and local Democratic organizations. Denouncing the "puritanical" fanaticism of the drys, the wets hit "sumptuary" laws as alien to the American genius of personal liberty, and the wisdom of the German and Irish liturgical culture. Prohibition, they argued, was not only legally and politically unsound, but was impossible of enforcement, unjust to the honest businessmen of the trade, and a threat to the economic well-being of Iowa.[9]

One of Herbert Hoover's most memorable boyhood experiences was that of a hot June day when his mother, a Quaker spiritual leader, brought him along to the polls "where the women were massed in an effort to make the men vote themselves dry." The pietistic Quakers prided themselves on a long record of strong opposition to social evils. The liquor traffic, no less than slavery, appeared to them an abominable curse, which society had to extirpate. Springdale, the prosperous Quaker township in Cedar County that embraced Hoover's village of West Branch, was a Republican stronghold; but even more it was a temperance stronghold—the village Democrat doubled as the village drunk. The townspeople had sheltered John Brown twenty-five years before, and now were equally serious. They endorsed the amendment by a convincing 342 to 29 vote.[10]

8. Clark, "Liquor Legislation" 6:368–73, 503–19; Brandt, "Sketches" 53: 347–50. The Des Moines *Iowa State Register* (Republican) and the *Dubuque Herald* (Democratic) carried full accounts of the campaign.

9. Clark, "Liquor Legislation" 6:519–24; T. C. Leggett in *Advance* (August 10, 1882), p. 518.

10. Quote from Eugene Lyons, *Herbert Hoover* (Garden City, 1964), pp. 4, 16; Herbert Hoover, *Memoirs* (New York, 1951), 1:9; see letter from

A few miles east of West Branch lay another prosperous community of farmers and villagers, Farmington Township. Not less religious than their Quaker neighbors, nor less hard working nor less devoted to the ideals of liberty were the men of Farmington. Yet they were different, for they were German immigrants and liturgical Lutherans. The temperance crusade of the Quakers, the Methodists, and the other pietists struck anxiety into the hearts of the Germans, for they felt they were the target of the new laws; it was their fondness for beer that seemed to call down the wrath of the God-fearing Yankees. The Germans did not appreciate their prospective role as outlaws. Narrowly Republican in 1875, Farmington moved towards the Democrats as the Republicans endorsed more and more dry programs. The amendment failed in the township 25 to 189, and the general elections that fall saw the Democratic share of the vote jump to 78 percent, 21 points higher than in 1881.[11]

The amendment did pass, but not overwhelmingly. The final returns showed 155,436 (55.3 percent) for, and 125,677 against. To a large degree, the vote followed party lines. The Republicans supported the amendment, except for the Germans and scattered other groups. Most of the Democrats voted no, but the efforts of the Temperance Alliance and the churches to woo dry Democrats probably were not entirely futile. The correlation of the vote with party loyalties did not necessarily imply that partisanship *determined* the vote. True, - the amendment might have failed had not the Republicans urged moderates and wets in their ranks to support the measure for the good of the party. But for most of the people, support or opposition to prohibition rested on the

---

Laurie Tatum, of Springdale, to *Friends' Review* (July 1, 1882) 35:758–59; *Iowa Census of 1880* (Des Moines, 1883), p. 618, giving township returns for the referendum and for the general elections of 1881 and 1882. *The History of Cedar County, Iowa* (Chicago, 1878), chronicles the stories of West Branch and Farmington.

11. By 1888 the Democrats had consolidated their hold on Farmington and polled 83 percent of its vote for Grover Cleveland. *History of Cedar County*, p. 618; William Harsha, *The Story of Iowa* (Omaha, 1890), p. 155; *Iowa State Register*, October 1, 1889; Frank Hickenlooper, *An Illustrated History of Monroe Co., Iowa* (Albia, Iowa, 1896), pp. 188–89.

same pietistic-liturgical basis as support or opposition for the Republican party itself.[12]

Many Republican state leaders, including Allison, Clarkson, Henderson, former Governor Samuel Kirkwood, and State Senator William Larrabee, grew worried when the amendment campaign stirred beliefs and prejudices stronger and more basic than party loyalty. Devoted liturgical Republicans might abandon their party on the issue; thousands did. The practical politicians, seeking to keep the Republican party open to men of all religious persuasions, wanted to banish the temperance issue from partisan politics, and hoped that the passage of the amendment would kill the issue. Their premonitions of danger proved to be solidly grounded.[13]

The anger of the liturgical Germans, directed at the Republicans, led to a plunge in the strength of the GOP in German strongholds. The fourteen most German counties in Iowa, with about a third of their voting population German-born (and many others the sons of immigrants), had produced Republican pluralities of 3,500 in 1876 and 6,400 in 1880. They turned in a majority of 9,320 against the amendment, and in the 1884 presidential election gave Cleveland a plurality of 5,200 votes. The German counties before the referendum were two to four percentage points less Republican than the remainder of the state; after the referendum they were eight to thirteen points less Republican. Only in 1896 did the Republicans recapture the German vote, as table 7 suggests.[14]

Some of the fine points of the movements between parties appeared in the heavily Catholic city of Dubuque, and may be inspected in table 8.

12. Harsha, *Iowa,* pp. 325–34; Truman O. Douglas, *The Pilgrims of Iowa* (Boston, 1911), pp. 230–31; Samuel P. Hays, "History as Human Behavior," *Iowa Journal of History* (1960) 58:196–97.

13. Sage, *Allison,* pp. 188–93; Brandt, "Sketches" 53:351–52; Johnson Brigham, *James Harlan* (Iowa City, 1913), pp. 290–93, tells of the driest Republican politician.

14. The election returns are based on *The Iowa Official Register* (Des Moines, 1889–1897), *The Iowa Census of 1885* (Des Moines, 1885), *The Iowa Census of 1880* (Des Moines 1883), and the *Iowa Census of 1875* (Des Moines, 1875). The fourteen German counties were Bremer, Butler, Carroll, Clayton, Clinton, Crawford, Dubuque, Grundy, Ida, Lyon, O'Brien, Osceola, Plymouth, and Scott. In each, more than 10 percent of the 1900 population was German-born.

Table 7

Voting Patterns in Fourteen Predominantly German Iowa Counties, 1876–1896

	1876	1880	1882 referendum	1884	1888
Percent Republican	55	56	39 (% dry)	44	44
Plurality and party	3500 R	6400 R	9300 wet	5200 D	7000 D

	1889	1890	1891	1892	1893	1896
Percent Republican	36	36	37	41	42	52
Plurality and party	15,100 D	12,800 D	15,700 D	10,600 D	8300 D	3500 R

Table 8

Ward Voting Patterns in Dubuque, 1875–1885[15]

Ward*	1875 %GOP	1881 %GOP	1882 %dry	1882 %GOP	1881–82 %GOP loss	1885 %GOP
1	24	23	12	16	— 7.5	19
2	30	41	14	30	—11.0	37
3	41	51	10	23	—27.8	33
4	60	62	33	51	—10.7	58
5	40	63	6	22	—40.8	36
..	..	..	..	..	..	..
City	41	50	15	28	—21.5	38
Total vote	2,906	3,528	4,003	3,937	———	4,359

*Ward 1 was predominantly Irish; Wards 3 and 5, German; Ward 2, mixed; Ward 4, the silk-stocking home of wealthy Germans, Yankees, and others.

15. *Dubuque Herald,* and sources cited in note 14.

The demolition of the gains the Republicans had made among liturgical German farmers and workers, especially in the larger cities like Dubuque, would not, by itself, be sufficient to cost the GOP control of the state. The amendment, after all, had passed by 30,000 votes; the GOP kept above the 50 percent line. But fate took nasty turns in Iowa politics. The prohibition issue was far from dead. In January 1883 the state supreme court stunned the people and the politicians of Iowa by declaring that a trivial error in the enactment procedure rendered the amendment invalid.[16]

The Republicans dared not resubmit the prohibition amendment, for another temperance crusade might spell disaster. Yet they had to mollify the angry drys and the moderates who recognized that a majority of the population wanted prohibition. The election campaigns of 1883, 1884, and 1885 focused largely on Republican promises to enact prohibitory legislation. The Democrats used the opportunity to solidfy their hold on the German vote, but the Republicans won anyway. The Republican drys rammed through one of the three stiffest prohibition laws in America at the 1884 session of the Iowa legislature; its consequences took a decade to unfold.[17]

The brewers and saloon-keepers, and their patrons and employees, did not explode many firecrackers on July 4, 1884. That day the new prohibition laws took effect. In hundreds of towns, villages, and crossroad hamlets where dry sentiment was strong, the saloons closed, reluctantly, and not without some rioting. In the larger towns and cities the law was often flaunted, even openly, sometimes with the approval of local officials. The new governor, William Larrabee, formerly a foe of prohibition, suddenly found it expedient to become its most ardent champion. Before Larrabee became governor, the liquor laws had been poorly enforced, except in the more pietistic rural townships. Some 1,800 saloons had flourished before prohibition; in 1885, eighteen months after the laws took effect, perhaps 2,200 regular outlets served the drinkers of Iowa. In the two dozen largest cities there had been 865 saloons paying $290,000 annually in license fees. In 1885, however, no

16. Clark, "Liquor Legislation" 6:529–35.
17. Ibid., 538–41; *Cyclopedia of Temperance,* pp. 109, 104–5, 296–302, 307–9, 502–13.

license fees were collected, but more than 1,400 holes-in-the-wall flourished. Larrabee was disturbed by this situation, and initiated strict enforcement of the original laws, which were augmented by new statutes in 1886. During his first administration he forced the saloons to retreat from the fifty-nine counties they had served in 1885, into just twenty-two counties in 1887. No town of more than 1,500 nor any German settlement remained wholly without some facilities for the drinking man, but in the Larrabee years liquor became harder and harder to get in ninety of Iowa's ninety-nine counties. Anyone dying of thirst, however, could obtain a "prescription" from a friendly doctor, and fill it at a friendly "pharmacy"— or he could hunt out a rumshop in the nearest large city; some men preferred to cross the state line, or to import cases of liquor (in the original package) by mail. Everywhere in Iowa the people added a new noun to their vocabulary: "bootlegger."[18]

The assassination of a dry leader in 1886 enraged the temperance men, but opposition to the enforcement of the laws rapidly built up. New laws imposed unusually severe restrictions on druggists, many of whom were ex-saloonkeepers, and the legitimate pharmacists of Iowa angrily demanded relief. Their pleas were answered by further restrictive laws in 1888. Eager prosecutors and informers rushed to obtain the bonuses for uncovering illicit liquor sales; they raided the homes of respectable men suspected of harboring illegal bottles of bourbon or champagne. By 1889 all of Iowa was caught up in the furor over prohibition. The Republicans, however, had seemingly mobilized just enough support to frustrate the drinkers and the Democrats.[19]

There is much ruin in a ruling party. Not content with their radical temperance position, the Republicans devised other programs to enhance the progress of Iowa and test the loyalty of the rank and file. With the strong backing of the party organization, Senator Allison led the opposition to President Cleveland's proposals to lower the tariff. Allison's revisions of the House-passed

18. Clark, "Liquor Legislation" 6:541–63; Brandt, "Sketches" 53:354, 358; see *New York Voice*, March 12, 26, 1885, and *Ann. Cycl. 1885:* 499 for details of enforcement.
19. Clark, "Liquor Legislation" 6:558–568; Gue, *Iowa*, 3:138–39; *Cyclopedia of Temperance*, pp. 201–2, 517; *New York Times*, July 27, 1889.

Mills bill stymied all efforts at tariff reform on the eve of the 1888 election. The farmers of Iowa, most of whom were paying off mortgages, had been growing restless under the mounting burden of debt and did not always appreciate the logic of the protectionists; they wanted higher prices for their land and products, not for their purchases. Led by Clarkson, the protectionists sought to build Iowa into an industrial state; a high protective tariff was needed to nurture the infant industries of the state. "The policy of the Republican party," Allison reassured the farmers, "is to diversify employment and industries and thus find a market constant and sure at our own doors and in our own country for farm products." Allison had a grand dream, the farmers agreed, but some wondered if it was not too long-range, too neglectful of the immediate needs of Iowa agriculture.[20]

Next to prohibition and the tariff, the most talked about issue in Iowa was the regulation of railroad freight rates. Iowa's Granger laws, among the first to regulate rates, had proved unsatisfactory, and had been repealed as soon as the momentum of the Granger movement was spent. Difficult times for the farmers, coupled with animosity toward Eastern stockholders, fueled an undercurrent of hostility toward the roads in the 1880s. The adjustment of rates following the Interstate Commerce Act of 1887 hurt the competitive position of Iowa jobbers and wholesalers vis-à-vis Chicago, and added an articulate, although small, force to the antirailroad coalition. Larrabee himself had played an important, cautious role in regulation legislation before he became governor, but no one expected the bombshell contained in his second inaugural address in January, 1888.[21]

20. *Iowa State Register,* October 9, 1889; Cole, *I Remember,* p. 145; *Third Annual Report of the [Iowa] Bureau of Labor Statistics* (Des Moines, 1889), pp. 111–23, for the views of farmers.

21. J. Brooke Workman, "Governor William Larrabee and Railroad Reform," *Iowa Journal of History* (1959) 57:239–54; William Larrabee, *The Railroad Question* (Chicago, 1893), p. 337; Frank H. Dixon, *State Railroad Control* (New York, 1896), pp. 135–38; Benjamin F. Shambaugh, ed., *The Messages and Proclamations of the Governors of Iowa* (Iowa City, 1904) 6:17–18, 73–75; Brandt, "Sketches" 53:358–60. In his unsuccessful bid for the GOP gubernatorial nomination in 1881, Larrabee had the support of the railroads and the wets, but failed to crack the opposition of the reformers. Brandt, ibid., 53:176, 353–59.

"New ideas, born of the spirit of progress," Larrabee told the legislature, "constantly battle with the musty conceptions of conservatism, prejudice and tradition; and gigantic interests, the creation of our inventive age, are constantly striving to usurp illegitimate, as well as to assert legitimate right." It was tempting for him "to make a truce with the enemy," but "solemn obligation makes the conflict an imperative duty." Larrabee thus declared war on the railroads. After sketching the dastardly record of the railroads in Iowa, the crusading governor denounced their high and unfair rates, and their low wages. Comparing the companies with the cruel British landlords in Ireland, and even with Greek pirates who once "ravaged villages and plundered unfortified places," Larrabee demanded an end to their "usurping unlawful powers and invading public rights." The reform-minded Republican legislature quickly and unanimously enacted a strong bill giving extensive powers to control rates and police the companies to the Board of Railroad Commissioners, which was to become an elective body. The board promptly cut rates 20 percent. The railroads fought back vigorously in the courts and at the polls. A compromise eventually resolved the rate dispute, but not before a new issue further enlivened Iowa politics.[22]

Cleveland and Harrison battled vigorously for the doubtful states in 1888, but Iowa was not among them. Disappointment mingled with pride in the summer of 1888 when Senator Allison failed in his bid for the presidential nomination. The ostensible issue in Iowa was the tariff, but the real excitement came from the railroad issue. Both parties endorsed the principles of regulation. The Republicans endorsed the actions of Larrabee, the legislature, and the regulatory board. The Democrats, however, coyly played on both sides of the fence. The Democratic nominees for railroad commissioner included Peter Dey, who was an incumbent appointed by Larrabee, and Herman Wills. Wills was a nationally prominent leader of the Brotherhood of Locomotive Engineers, which had led the fight *against* regulation. Both Dey and Wills received strong labor union support, and Dey's candidacy

22. Shambaugh, *Messages* 6:91–107; Workman, "Larrabee" 57:254–61; Sage, *Allison,* p. 211; Gue, *Iowa,* 3:142–52; *Ann. Cycl. 1888:* 444–46; *1889:* 448–49.

pleased the jobbers, wholesalers, and other antirailroad groups as well. The shippers, most of them wealthy Republicans, joined with Henry Wallace's influential farm paper, *Iowa Homestead,* the Farmers' Alliance, and the remnants of the Union Labor party to elect Dey. Meanwhile the railroads rallied their employees, most of them Democrats anyway, to defeat Dey's opponent, John Mahin, who favored both stiff rate regulation and absolute prohibition.[23]

The count of the ballots gave Iowa's thirteen electoral votes to Harrison, his reward for a plurality of 31,000 in the state. The rest of the Republican ticket swept into office, save for Mahin, who polled 200,075 votes to 201,265 for Dey. Peter Dey thus became the first Democrat to carry the state in a third of a century. In the fourteen German counties, at least one Republican in six split his ticket to vote for Dey; elsewhere, only one Republican in twenty-four cut Mahin's name, mostly Republican businessmen whose defection to Dey was only an affirmation of confidence in the incumbents on the Board of Railroad Commissioners. The Democrats could hardly expect this silk-stocking vote to come their way again. Much more significant was the large defection of German Republicans to Dey. Mahin contended that he was sacrificed because of his radically dry stance on prohibition. Many of those German Republicans who had not defected to the Democrats in 1882, or who had since returned to the GOP, were restless. If the Democrats were to carry Iowa, it could only be with the capture of their votes, and the issue had to be prohibition.[24]

By 1889 public opinion in Iowa reached a turning point. The

23. *Ann. Cycl. 1888:* 446–47; *Dubuque Herald,* October 26, 27, November 7, 18, 28, 1888; *Chicago Herald,* September 9, 1888; Merrill, *Bourbon Democracy,* pp. 203–204; Cole, *I Remember,* pp. 166–68; J. Irwin, "Is Iowa A Doubtful State?" *Forum* (April, 1892) 13:259–61; Sage, *Allison,* pp. 223–32. Pietist ministers also seem to have been unhappy that year with Benjamin Harrison's failure to endorse prohibition. A poll of all the Methodist clergy at the annual convention of the northwest Iowa district showed forty-four favored Clinton Fisk, the Prohibition party candidate, thirty-three supported Harrison, ten were undecided, and one intrepid circuit rider admitted favoring Cleveland. The year before, the ministers had nearly all voted Republican. *New York Voice,* October 25, 1888.
24. *Dubuque Herald,* November 7, 18, 20, 28, 1888.

enthusiasm of the drys, unchecked for five years, began to flag. The mysterious postponement of the dawn of a new stage in civilization, and the curious interlude of massive disrespect for the law, led the bitter prohibitionists to demand more laws, stricter enforcement, harsher punishment. Calmer men began to question the wisdom of absolute prohibition in a state with such different religious and cultural values as the Yankees and the Germans represented. A large portion of the upright citizenry clearly rejected the harsh laws—but were they not a minority and ought not the majority rule? While moderates debated these points, other worries abounded in Iowa.

The economic health of the state came into question. The commercial growth of Iowa depended upon an adequate railroad network, but the roads claimed that the new regulated rates stifled the development and extension of their lines. Construction of new mileage abruptly halted in mid-1888; several small lines closed; railroad spokesmen warned of further regression. Urban promoters not only found the railroad situation disturbing, but noted a sharp downturn in the rate of construction and population growth. The value of new private and public construction in Des Moines, for example, had grown rapidly up to 1883, when the city collected $1,200 annual license fees from each of fifty-two saloons. Opponents of prohibition pointed out that with the coming of prohibition and the official closing of the city's saloons, the construction industry slumped. The 1883 level of building activity was reached only once in the next fourteen years.

Iowa was uneasy; the questions the people asked were hard ones. Did the regulation of railroads impede economic growth? Had prohibition slowed the influx of hard-working, beer-drinking German mechanics and farmers? Could the financial crises of the larger cities be resolved from revenues from saloon licenses? Would the manufacture of beer and whiskey in Iowa raise the demand for the state's corn and barley crops? Had cranks and radicals taken control of the Republican party? Did prohibition prohibit? The intense resentment of the Germans and Irish against prohibition, the obvious failure of the noble experiment, the threatening stagnation of commerce, transportation, construction, and agriculture, coupled with the seemingly blind abandon of the ruling party, readied Iowa for a political revolution. The only ingredient still lacking was firm leadership.[25]

Peter Dey's election made the Democrats confident that they could carry Iowa. The spring mayoralty election in Keokuk gave them a blueprint for the 1889 gubernatorial campaign. Keokuk with its large German and Irish population was wet, but still Republican, even though the city had rejected the prohibition amendment 62 percent to 38 percent. The mayor in 1888 was a dry Republican who enlisted the pietistic churches, some of the businessmen, and the police in a crackdown on the city's many saloons. With resentment high, the Democrats nominated John Craig for mayor in late March, 1889. Craig was a distinguished Bourbon legislator, a good Protestant, a teetotaler, and an advocate of high license fees. A brief, bitter campaign, centering on the saloon issue, ended with a Democratic landslide. Democrats across the state watched the Keokuk race with keen interest—did Craig have the secret, they asked, that would carry Iowa?[26]

Horace Boies, although not widely known outside Waterloo, was the perfect candidate for governor. The Republican commitment to prohibition and protective tariffs had forced him to switch to the Democratic party in 1884. Boies, like Dey and Craig, was a man of unblemished character; he was a teetotaler (his only lodge was the Good Templars), and possessed a totally honest "affidavit face." He articulately opposed paternal government, centralized power, radical prohibition, high tariffs, and intrusions against private property. He favored high license fees, ballot reform, moderate regulation of railroads, harmony between capital and labor and between the diverse cultural groups of Iowa. A Bourbon to the quick, Boies was the hope of Iowa Democrats. At

25. Will Porter, *Annals of Polk County, Iowa* (Des Moines, 1898), pp. 470–97; Cole, *I Remember*, pp. 154–56, 164–65; Irwin, "Iowa," pp. 262–64; Gue, *Iowa*, 3:147; *Iowa State Register*, November, 9, 10, 1889; *Dubuque Herald*, July 12, November 10, 1889; *New York Times*, August 12, 16, 1889; Harsha, *Iowa*, pp. 337–38. For the doubts of Iowa bankers, see *New York Voice*, July 23, 30, August 13, 1888.

26. *Chicago Tribune*, March 30, April 2, 1889; Clark, "Liquor Legislation" 6:562; *Ann. Cycl. 1890*, pp. 133–34; *Cyclopedia of Temperance*, p. 517; *New York Voice*, October 18, 1888.

the September state convention he outpolled Mayor Craig 502–161 and became the Democratic nominee for governor.[27]

The Republican leaders realized the dangers in 1889, but the party was out of their control. Allison, Henderson, and Clarkson were in Washington, attending to the critical legislation of the Fifty-first Congress, and to important national party problems. The governing body of the Iowa GOP, the state convention, consisted of delegates elected at county conventions, which in turn were largely packed by radically dry or antirailroad political amateurs. Only men committed to railroad reform and strict enforcement of the liquor laws could win the nominations of many local conventions. The crusading pietists in some counties even demanded that all candidates be teetotalers—had that policy been adopted generally, the Republican party of Iowa would have sunk without a bubble. The local lieutenants of the moderate top leadership resisted the trend; but the amateurs, thoroughly organized, controlled the state convention in August, and nominated Joseph Hutchison, a wholesale grocer and a dry who was supposedly a strong friend of rate regulation, to oppose Boies.

Prohibition, the convention declared, "has become the settled policy of the State . . . there should be no backward step. We stand for the complete enforcement of the law." In opening his campaign, Hutchison rejected the idea that prohibition was an experiment that ought to be evaluated pragmatically. It was, rather, a "fixed institution of our progressive state." Every recent election, he noted, had affirmed the will of the majority for strict liquor laws. Iowa, dry Iowa, "has made a struggle for morality, for the reduction of corruption, debauchery, and crime, for the true elevation of the human race, for self-respect, for decency, for manhood, for the wife and family, for the sacred virtue and honor of the home." Dry Iowa, he continued, "has triumphed against the saloon and its thousand attendant evils," yet the Democratic party had just "resolved in favor of this cursed barnacle, which modern civilization, as constituted in Iowa, is determined to destroy." "And today," he affirmed, to the thunderous applause

27. Cole, *I Remember,* pp. 172–74; Jean B. Kern, "The Political Career of Horace Boies," *Iowa Journal of History* (1949) 47:215–19; *Dubuque Herald,* July 12, September 28, 1889; *Chicago Times,* August 24, 1893.

of his parched audience, "by the goodness of God and the continued virtue of our people, we proclaim to the civilized world that we shall maintain the stand we have taken."[28]

The Republican orators and workhorses dutifully rallied to the dry crusade. Hutchison himself had a facility for boring a red-hot audience by droning monotonously through a well-written speech. Occasionally he was eloquent, as when he sternly lectured the German voters at Postville for half an hour on the evils of indulgence in beer and on the need to obey the voice of the majority and stop drinking. Fortunately he escaped the auditorium before precipitating a riot.

The temperance forces enthusiastically rallied to Hutchison. The WCTU dropped the nearly forgotten Prohibition party and worked for the GOP. The pietistic churches did their part, too. The Des Moines Methodist Conference a year before had declared "uncompromising hostility to the liquor traffic," and demanded its "unconditional surrender." Now, only a month before the election, the Upper Iowa Conference resolved that "no Methodist voter should permit himself to be controlled by party organizations which are managed in the interests of the liquor traffic." For the benefit of any slow-witted Methodist who thought that high licenses and local option might harmonize the interests of church and state, the conference reaffirmed its "uncompromising hostility to license high and low," and for good measure went on to denounce "desecration of the Sabbath" by baseball games, Sunday newspapers and railroad service. The Good Templars ditched their brother Boies and announced for Hutchison on October 17. The next day the state Baptist convention, meeting in Des Moines, protested "against any movement looking toward the repeal of the prohibitory laws of Iowa." The Baptists further demanded new laws that would effectively dry up "the few remaining rebellious cities in the state." Two days later the Iowa Synod of the Presbyterian church advised its members to "resist, by every legitimate means, every effort to restore this saloon iniquity under any li-

---

28. Hutchison quotes in *Iowa State Register*, October 1, 1889; platform in *Ann. Cycl. 1889:* 449–50. The turmoil in the GOP was recorded by the *Iowa State Register,* see especially October 2, 6, 12, 13, November 10, 1889; *New York Times,* August 12, 16, 1889; *Chicago Tribune,* July 1, 21, 1889; October 28, 1891; and Brandt, "Sketches" 53:362–64.

cense, high or low."[29] The target of the pietistic scorn, of course, was Horace Boies.

The Democrats concentrated their efforts on Boies' campaign. The other state offices were unimportant; control of the legislature seemed impossible. Boies and his Bourbon managers realized that a winning coalition had to consist of the full traditional Democratic vote, supplemented by wet and moderate Republicans, discontented independents, and any other stray votes available. The German Republicans, it was expected, would provide thousands of votes, as they had for Dey a year before. The Union Labor party, the vehicle of the disintegrating Knights of Labor, might yield up its German voters. Moderate nonpietistic Yankees were to get a reasonable compromise on the liquor issue; radical prohibitionists were to be ridiculed and repudiated. Discontented farmers, many of whom were drys, had to be won over, or at least cross-pressured into staying at home, by a frontal attack on the Harrison administration and the protective tariff. Shippers had to be mollified by an endorsement of the principle of railroad regulation, but railroad workers and officials, and their sympathizers, would be wooed by promises of reasonable, profitable rate levels. Other discontented groups would get special treatment too. Horace Boies would be the articulate champion of all the aggrieved classes of Iowa.[30]

The Democrats' most successful strategem was their appeal to opponents of prohibition. "In the interest of true temperance," the platform read, "we demand the passage of a carefully guarded license tax law . . . of $500 [to] be paid into the county treasury." Each township would have the option of permitting or prohibiting saloons, and could keep for itself all license fees above $500. Boies made his opposition to the existing laws clear; his proposals for local option and high saloon licenses were acceptable to the wets, and strongly appealed to most of the moderates.

Generally Boies avoided direct appeals to the ethnic loyalties of the German and Irish voters. That task could be left to local

---

29. For the Methodists, see *The Political Prohibitionist for 1889* (New York, 1889), p. 76 and *Iowa State Register,* October 9, 1889; for the Baptists, ibid., October 25, 1889; Brandt, "Sketches" 53:362–64; for the Presbyterians, see minutes of the *Eighth Annual Meeting of the [Presbyterian] Synod of Iowa, Oct. 17–21, 1889* (Mt. Pleasant, Iowa, 1889), p. 222.

30. *Iowa State Register,* November 17, 1889 (editorial).

spokesmen. Boies, in countercrusading style, did condemn Know-Nothingism and intolerance. He saw "no material difference in the intelligence, morality or respect for ordinary laws [among] our people. There is and always will be," he added, "a wide difference in their social habits, depending largely upon the customs of their fathers, the influence of education and the surroundings in which they live."[31]

Boies' endorsement of a pluralistic society in Iowa differed sharply from the Republican vision, which saw the pietistic old stock, whether Yankee, Southerner, or Pennsylvania Dutch, as the "leaven" that would transform the immigrants into true Americans. "Where the American leaven was not smothered beyond impressing or absorbing capacity all is well," the leading Republican newspaper editorialized. But, it continued, "Here and there it has not had time to accomplish its task and in these spots the Democrats propose to offer the temptation of the saloon."[32]

It was not the return of the saloon, but the repeal of absolute prohibition that Boies sought. He eloquently defended the right of the local community, not the state, to establish local practices. Local option would preserve prohibition in those areas that wanted it. High licenses would curb all the evils of the saloon without infringing personal liberty, and would also restore needed revenues to the hard-pressed cities. The destruction of the state's brewing and distillery business in 1885 had been an unjust confiscation of private property, he asserted, and the reopening of those manufactures would create a welcome new demand for the corn and barley crops.[33]

Boies had to tread cautiously on the liquor issue. To meet the intense criticism of the pietists, he had to assure the people that Iowa would not become another Chicago, clogged with saloons, vice, and corruption. Most of the factory and railroad managers strongly urged temperance for their men. The more secure ranks of mechanics thought prohibition to be a "good thing for the wage-workers," according to a poll taken a few months before the election. Even the unskilled laborers considered prohibition to be desir-

31. For the Democratic platform, see *Ann. Cycl. 1889:* 450. For Boies' speeches, see *Dubuque Herald,* October 6, and November 10, 1889.

32. *Iowa State Register,* October 6, 1889 (editorial).

33. *Dubuque Herald,* November 10, 1889, and Kern, "Boies" 47:219–22.

able; the coal miners approved prohibition three to one. As the additional remarks of these workers made clear, they were endorsing prohibition for *other* wage workers; they did not, furthermore, think that Iowa had prohibition. Everyone could see that the state had plenty of liquor. Probably the workers felt that prohibition would be good for thrift, industry, and virtue; in their own cases, most may have felt a policy of moderation would serve the best of two worlds.[34]

To keep the Republicans on the defensive, Boies barnstormed the rural areas denouncing the protective tariff. Answering Allison's promise that American industry would provide a home market for American crops, Boies warned that Iowa's farmers "are not going to wait for a home market to grow up around them." The vital international market, he continued, would be closed by a high tariff. Strong support for the Democratic position came from the Farmers' Alliance and former Grangers. The threat of higher prices for manufactured commodities, along with depressed land and commodity prices and ever-present mortgages, weakened the party loyalty of Republican farmers and strengthened the resolve of the Democrats. The virtual bankruptcy of the GOP on the tariff issue became clear when the *Iowa State Register* began to urge farmers to burn their corn in place of coal, thus saving money and forcing up prices. The GOP soon discovered that burning corn-cobs make a very hot and unpleasant fire.[35]

The confusion of the Republican campaign permitted Boies to run away with the railroad issue. Hutchison strongly defended the new railroad laws as beneficial to manufacturers, farmers, wholesalers, and the railroads themselves. The Democrats undermined his stand by demonstrating that he and his running mate had pro-railroad records in the legislature. Boies, however, actually won the support of the railroads. He endorsed the principle of regulation, but promised fair administration and fair profits. The man-

34. Iowa B.L.S. *Third Report* (1889), pp. 25, 47, 62–63, 131–34, 226–31, *Second Report* (1887), pp. 151–52, 204–11.
35. Kern, "Boies" 47:219–27; *Chicago Tribune,* October 28, 1889; *New York Times,* November 4, 5, 7, 1889; *Iowa State Register,* October 11, November 5, 11, 1889, and January 24, 1890; *Dubuque Herald,* July 12, September 1, 6, 28, October 6, 11, November 2, 10, 12, 1889. On the farmers' price situation, see Herman Nixon, "The Economic Basis of the Populist Movement in Iowa," *Iowa Journal of History* (1923) 21:387–88.

agers and their men threw their political resources behind Boies, while the guilt of association with railroad lobbyists clung to Hutchison.[36]

The Democrats picked up discontented groups wherever they could be found. The Des Moines Negro community, usually strongly Republican, found the Democrats seeking their votes on the liquor issue.[37] An agreement with James Sovereign, Iowa Knights of Labor leader, apparently gave Boies hundreds of votes that otherwise would have gone to the Union Labor or Republican tickets.[38] The disgruntled pharmacists of Iowa had been ignored by the Democrats in 1888, but now Boies promised them relief from the $1,000 bonds and humiliating affidavits of rectitude required by the latest prohibition laws. The Linn County druggists formally endorsed the Democratic platform, and doubtless many of the state's 1,800 pharmacists voted Democratic for the first time in 1889.[39]

The success of a campaign is seen in the vote. The GOP plurality of 32,000 in 1888 withered to 1,600 for lieutenant governor. The Republicans lost eighteen seats in the legislature, but all their statewide candidates squeaked through. All, that is, save Hutchison. Boies ran 5,000 votes ahead of his ticket, and bested his adversary by 6,564 votes out of 360,945 cast. Boies captured 49.9 percent of the vote, Hutchison 48.1 percent, the Union Laborite 1.6 percent, and the Prohibitionist only 0.4 percent. Boies carried five of Iowa's eleven congressional districts, all but one of which had Republican representatives, and lost three other Repub-

36. *Cedar Rapids Gazette,* October 23, 28, 1889; *Iowa State Register,* October 15, 16, 24, 27, November 9, 10, 16, 1889; Kern, "Boies" 47:220; Brandt, "Sketches" 53:356–65; Shambaugh, *Messages,* 6:277–80; *New York Times,* August 12, 16, October 5, 12, 14, 18, November 4, 5, 1889; *Dubuque Herald,* September 11, 1888, July 12, August 18, September 3, 28, October 6, 29, 1889.

37. *Iowa State Register,* October 17, 1889; *Chicago Tribune,* September 17, 1890.

38. Fred Haynes, *Third Party Movements* (Iowa City, 1916), p. 334; *Dubuque Herald,* October 26, 1888, August 4, September 6, October 5, 26, 29, 1889.

39. *Dubuque Herald,* September 7, 8, October 6, 1889; cf. October 5, 1888; Shambaugh, *Messages,* 6:30, 55–56, 285. Nearly $10,000 in fines had already been exacted from seventy-five "pharmacists" convicted of selling liquor in 1887 alone.

lican districts by a total of only 562 votes. Only in two predominantly pietistic old-stock congressional districts did Hutchison hold the 1888 GOP share of the vote.

The excitement of the campaign was seemingly belied by the relatively low turnout. About 78 percent of the eligible men voted, the lowest turnout in any year from 1883 through 1897, except in 1887 when 77 percent had voted. In 1888 less than 50,000 eligible citizens did not vote; in 1889 about 100,000 stayed away from the polls. Republicans by the thousands were disappointed with their party. Some—the Germans, especially—voted Democratic; thousands more registered their unhappiness by staying home. Boies' vote actually exceeded Cleveland's the year before by 243, while Hutchison lagged behind Harrison's total by 38,000. In the fourteen German counties, Boies almost exactly matched Cleveland's vote, but the Republican vote fell from 27,200 to 19,200.

The disaster hit the GOP hardest in the large cities. The nine cities in the state with 14,000 or more population had been a close battlefield in 1888. Cleveland carried only the four most German cities, Dubuque, Davenport, Burlington, and Council Bluffs, garnering 51.8 percent of the two-party vote in the nine. Boies swept all nine, with a phenomenal 64.4 percent of the vote. Even Des Moines, the pride of Iowa Republicanism, fell into Boies' column by a bare 85 votes. Harrison had accumulated a Republican plurality of 33,200 outside the nine cities; Boies' reduced that 90 percent to a mere 3,246. It was Boies' plurality of 9,810 votes in the nine cities that put him in the Iowa statehouse, as table 9 shows.[40]

The immigrants who were pleased with Boies on the liquor issue, especially those in the cities, decided the outcome. Table 10 presents some of the fine detail of culture-group voting patterns.[41]

40. The nine cities, and their 1890 population, were Des Moines (50,000), Sioux City (37,000), Dubuque (30,000), Davenport (27,000), Burlington (23,000), Council Bluffs (22,000), Cedar Rapids (18,000), Keokuk (14,000), and Ottumwa (14,000). As usual, the *Iowa Official Register* provided the election data.

41. The data represents sample counties, towns, wards, and townships with the most homogenous populations, and only approximates the voting patterns of individual Germans, Irish, and others. Compare chapter 8, note 52, and chapter 10, note 56.

111

Even without the liquor issue, the Republicans suffered reverses. As table 10 suggests, Hutchison lost 2 to 3 percent of the vote in the dry Republican Yankee and Norwegian strongholds. The cam-

Table 9

Two-Party Vote in Iowa, 1888 (President) and 1889 (Governor)

| | President 1888 | | Governor 1889 | |
	GOP	Dem	GOP	Dem
Nine largest Cities	19,114	20,675	12,261	22,071
Rest of state	192,394	159,202	161,295	158,049
Total for state	211,508	179,877	173,556	180,120

Table 10

Republican Share of Total Vote, 1888 (President) and 1889 (Governor), by Ethnic Groups in Iowa*

Predominantly Liturgical Groups

	Entire state	14 German counties	9 German city wards	9 Irish wards and townships	7 Bohemian wards and townships
GOP 1888	52.4%	44%	28%	20%	20%
GOP 1889	48.1	36	15	15	16
Loss	−4.2	−7.8	−12.8	−5.4	−4.5

Predominantly Pietistic Groups

	31 old stock counties	39 old-stock small towns	11 rural Norwegian townships	6 rural Swedish townships
GOP 1888	53%	59%	77%	73%
GOP 1889	51	57	74	68
Loss	−1.8	−2.3	−2.6	−5.2

*All figures represent Republican percentage of the total vote cast, including the small minor-party vote.

112

paign involved many issues, and any parcelling out of losses among them would be simplistic. Businessmen, for example, found Boies' candidacy attractive—in Burlington, Dubuque, Council Bluffs, Davenport, and Sioux City he carried the traditionally Republican upper-class wards. Did the more sophisticated businessmen admire Boies' style more than his free-trade ideology? Perhaps, but one cannot be sure. One can be sure that it could have been worse for the GOP. The Lee County chairman reported that hundreds of staunch Republicans bolted because "they were tired of free saloons on every street" and liked Boies' high license proposals. More than a third of those Republicans who did vote for Hutchison, the chairman continued, strained party loyalty to do so; again they preferred Boies' stand on prohibition. The low Republican turnout did not represent apathy. On the contrary, it represented one solution to the dilemma of the loyal Republican who could not support his party's nominee or platform in 1889.[42]

If the situation could be made worse, the moralists would find a way. The drys still controlled the legislature, though by sharply reduced margins. The laws regulating druggists were relaxed slightly, and provision was made to provide guardians for habitual drunkards. The legislature could not agree on any basic changes in the prohibition laws, although it did pass a stiffer railroad regulation law that stirred up new legal strife. The Republican legislators defiantly refused to accept Boies' proposals; there would be no "backward step" on Iowa's march toward civilization, they proclaimed.[43]

The Democrats entered the 1890 campaign with unaccustomed confidence. Boies had been unable to legalize liquor, but that meant the initiative on the issue still rested with the Democrats. Boies did downplay the enforcement of the existing laws. His pharmacy commissioner, for example, was a lazy soul with little interest in tracking down errant druggists. Unfortunately, the quality of Boies' other appointments to high state positions also tended to be restricted by the demands of his patronage-hungry party. The fall campaign for minor state offices and congressmen was

42. *Iowa State Register,* November 23, 28, 1889; *Dubuque Herald,* November 12, 1889; *New York Times,* November 7, 1889.
43. *Ann. Cycl. 1890:* 445–48; Clark, "Liquor Legislation" 6:575–59.

quiet: the Democrats had too little money, the Republicans too little enthusiasm, to generate much excitement. The liquor issue still sparked most of the arguments, but the new McKinley tariff came in for considerable discussion, too. The election saw the Republicans narrowly salvage the state offices, but for the first time since the formation of the GOP the Democrats gained an edge in the congressional delegation, six to five. The new People's party displayed strength only in the wheat counties along the Nebraska border. Everyone agreed, however, that the Democrats had achieved parity with the Republican party in Iowa. Impish Democrats consoled their proud Republican friends with the thought that, after all, Senator Allison's chances for the GOP presidential nomination in 1892 were enhanced, now that he came from a doubtful state.[44]

Prohibition, complained the angry Republican leaders, certainly does not stop drinking, but it does seem to prohibit Republican victories! Professional Republican politicians had sensed the disaster inherent in a party endorsement of absolute prohibition. The leaders themselves generally were moderate drinkers; no GOP presidential candidate had been an abstainer; few of the men of Congress or other high offices were unfamiliar with strong liquor. Only the fervent moral demands of the politically less experienced dry element—or, more likely, their threat of retribution at the conventions and the polls—forced the party leadership to go along with the prohibition planks. Throughout the 1880s the conflict between wets and drys and moderates raged within the Iowa GOP. A dry challenge to Senator Allison's reelection bid failed in early 1890, but the drys had their way at the state convention the next summer.

At the 1891 convention the outnumbered wets urged the Republicans to at least adopt an ambiguous stand on the liquor issue. The drys would hear none of it; they felt the 1889 loss of the governorship was due more to the tariff than to the liquor issue, and shouted down a local-option plank 951 to 107. Two amateur politicians, both prominent farmers, received the top nominations to oppose the Democratic ticket, which Boies again headed. The main issue

44. Clark, "Liquor Legislation" 6:581–83; Brandt, "Sketches" 55:353–58; *Dubuque Herald,* September 17, October 4, 5, 18, 19, 23, 28, 30, November 14, 1890.

again was prohibition, but the Democrats, becoming more confident, endorsed free silver, denounced the McKinley tariff, and called for high licenses. The Republican platform charged that "that outlaw"—the saloon— "has the patronage, council and protection of the Democratic party." The real issue, it insisted, "is law against defiance of law, subordination against insubordination, and the State of Iowa against the Democratic party." Obviously the drys were losing their composure. The people let their opinions be known at the polls: the entire Democratic slate swept to victory. Boies' plurality was 8,200 out of 420,000 votes; his running mates secured margins varying from 829 to 7,946. The distribution of votes repeated and reinforced the patterns set in 1889. But this time turnout soared to 88 percent, the highest in any gubernatorial campaign in Iowa history. Those frustrated Republicans who sat home in 1889 came out in 1891, and most of them voted Democratic. If the Republicans hoped to save Iowa's thirteen electoral votes in 1892, some way had to be found to shake the albatross of dry platforms.[45]

The struggle over prohibition in Ohio closely resembled the pattern in Iowa, and suggests that the liquor issue was not an ephemeral affair in one state, but the indication of conflict between massive forces. While it had never been a dry state, doubtless because of the power of the Cincinnati German community, Ohio did experiment with a variety of licensing laws. The drys got the Republicans to submit a constitutional amendment for prohibition in 1883; the amendment got a plurality, but not the necessary majority of all the votes cast for governor. The Republican gubernatorial candidate, Joseph B. Foraker discovered that the temperance agitation cost him even a plurality of the votes in his race. Foraker did win the 1885 election, however, and tried to avoid antagoniz-

45. For platform see *Iowa Official Register 1892:* pp. 162–70, *Ann. Cycl. 1891:* 383–84. Brandt, "Sketches" 55:358–61; Clark, "Liquor Legislation" 6:584–87; Cyrenus Cole, *A History of the People of Iowa* (Cedar Rapids, 1921), pp. 477–81; Kern, "Boies" 47:221–26; Haynes, *Third Parties,* pp. 304–20; Sage, *Allison,* pp. 248–49. *New York Times,* January 28, July 9, 13, 27, September 21, November 12, December 11, 1891, August 18, 1893. *Chicago Tribune,* July 2, October 20, 28, 1891. The Democrats estimated that they lost only 2,000 of their pietistic supporters to the dry Republican appeal in 1891. *Chicago Herald,* November 3, 1892.

ing the German Republicans by insisting that the liquor question "is so related to personal habits and private morals as to render it impossible to make it a political question in the ordinary sense." However the drys were able to pass laws levying an annual statewide tax of $250 on liquor dealers and, more radically, requiring that all saloons close on Sundays.[46]

The temperance issue exploded in 1889 over the Sunday closing laws. In the spring local elections, the Democrats scored major gains in cities across the state. In Cincinnati, the Evangelical Association, a group of public-minded pietistic ministers, demanded enforcement of the hitherto neglected Sunday laws. Working through a Committee of Five Hundred, silk-stocking moralists ran a full slate of independent candidates in the city elections. They swept all the offices, except the crucial post of mayor, which went to John Mosby, a lackey in George Cox's corrupt Republican machine. Mosby slipped into office by promising the Germans continued nonenforcement of the closing laws.

Angered by the barrage of abuse hurled by the ministers and the moralists, the saloon-keepers decided to force the issue. They demanded that Mayor Mosby enforce *all* the ordinances prohibiting common labor on Sunday. For two Sundays in July the nonessential shops of the city remained closed. Tension soared and violence threatened; the city remembered the bloody riots it had experienced a few years before and prepared for the worst. On July 25 the saloon-keepers, organized into the League for the Preservation of Citizens' Rights, called for a showdown. Three hundred German saloon-keepers formally resolved to openly do business all day on Sundays. A defense fund, bonds, and competent defense attorney stood by in readiness.[47]

46. *Cyclopedia of Temperance*, pp. 106–8, 143–45, 152, 651, 335; *Ann. Cycl. 1883:* 607–9, *1886:* 731. Joseph Foraker, *Notes of a Busy Life* (Cincinnati, 1917), 1:128.

47. The *Cincinnati-Gazette* and the *Cincinnati Enquirer* provided full coverage. See also *Chicago Tribune*, March 20, 26, April 1–3, 1889. Foraker, *Notes,* 1:412–14; *Cyclopedia of Temperance*, pp. 268–70. In 1884, 54 men died and 200 suffered injuries in five days of rioting against state militia in the backlash of a thwarted lynching. *Ann. Cycl. 1884:* 630–31; Zane L. Miller, *Boss Cox's Cincinnati* (New York, 1968), pp. 59–64, 79–81. For a similar episode in Madison, Wisconsin, in 1884, without the political repercussions, see David Thelen, "LaFollette and the Temperance Crusade," *Wisconsin Magazine of History* (1964) 47:293–99.

Governor Foraker, just renominated for his third term, shot off a letter to Mosby:

> Do not tolerate any defiance of law. No man is worthy to enjoy the free institutions of America who rebels against a duly enacted statute and defies the authorities charged with its enforcement. Smite every manifestation of such a spirit with a swift and heavy hand.[48]

The beer-loving Germans of Cincinnati were not about to be smitten. Briefly, massive rioting threatened. Quickly, however, the saloon-keepers' League realized that the conflict could best be won at the fall elections. Armed with heavy assessments from saloons, brewers, distributors, and friends of "Personal Liberty," the League attacked Foraker and called for a massive repudiation of him at the polls. The drys defended the governor vigorously, and the attention of the state focused on the gubernatorial contest.

Foraker carried many weaknesses into the campaign of 1889. His dynamic opponent, Congressman James Campbell, attacked the Republicans' support of high tariffs, denounced Foraker's bid for a third consecutive term, and hurled charges of dictatorial control, fiscal waste, and administrative mismanagement at the governor. Seldom had a midwestern campaign descended to the level of personal abuse that marked this one. At the climax, shortly before the election, Foraker revealed the existence of documents implicating Campbell in a scheme to defraud the state. The chief Republican newspaper, the *Cincinnati Commercial-Gazette,* reproduced the documents, but omitted the signatures of John Sherman, William McKinley, and other Republican leaders apparently equally guilty. Campbell, stunned momentarily, proved that the documents were total forgeries. Foraker and Murat Halstead, the editor of the *Commercial-Gazette,* apologized a few days before the election, but their doom was imminent.[49]

Campbell swept into office by a plurality of 11,000 votes out of 280,000 cast. The remainder of his ticket lost by small margins—

48. Foraker, *Notes,* 1:414; cf. *Cyclopedia of Temperance,* pp. 269–70.

49. The *Cincinnati Commercial-Gazette,* blushing, gives the details. Foraker, *Notes,* 1:402–11; Everett Walters, *Joseph Benson Foraker* (Columbus, Ohio, 1948), pp. 91–97; John Sherman, *Recollections of Forty Years* (Chicago, 1895), 2:1053. *Ann. Cycl. 1889:* 674–75.

twenty-two votes, in the case of the lieutenant governor—but the Democratic legislature reversed those margins the next year. Foraker suffered small losses across the state, and massive ones in Hamilton County (Cincinnati), where he ran far behind his ticket. In Hamliton, Campbell picked up 3,100 more votes than Cleveland's total in 1888, while Foraker ran 8,000 behind Harrison. The Republicans, racked by intraparty feuds, starved for patronage by President Harrison, and confused and humiliated by Foraker's actions, were in disarray. The Germans rightly claimed credit for the upset, and exulted in their prowess.[50]

"Even the faintest concession to the 'muckers' and law-and-order fanatics," the *Cincinnati Freie-Presse* had warned in September, "would be a nail in the coffin of Republican chances of victory." To the German eye, Foraker and his party conceded too much. The *Cincinnati Times-Star,* spokesman for the Committee of Five Hundred, had rallied the moralists with advocacy of $1,000 saloon licenses and effective Sunday laws should the GOP win. "The Germans waxed wroth at this," snorted the *Cincinnati Volksblatt,* "and the Germans, being mad, they knocked the Republican party into smithereens." "The Germans," the *Volksblatt* added, "thought that a Legislature should pass laws for the people and not against the people."[51]

The year 1889 was an ominous one for the GOP across the Midwest. In Chicago the Democrats waged a vigorous campaign to recapture city hall in the April elections. Pietistic clergymen criticized Mayor John Roche, a Republican, for tolerating widespread violation of the Sunday closing laws; Catholics grew angry when they discovered that Roche belonged to a secret anti-Catholic society. The Democrats won over the numerous trade union members with promises of more municipal ownership, and darkly warned that the Republicans were moving toward prohibition for the city. The latter charge gained credence from the heated campaign in the industrial suburb of Hyde Park. There the Republicans de-

50. *Cincinnati Commercial-Gazette,* September 8, 10, 16, November 8, 1889; Foraker, *Notes,* 1:416–21.

51. *Cincinnati Freie Presse,* September 16, 1889; *Cincinnati Volksblatt,* November 8, 1889, quoted in *Cincinnati Commercial-Gazette,* September 17, and November 9, 1889.

clared for enforcement of Sunday closing laws and talked of $1,000 saloon licenses. The Germans of the township reacted vigorously. The Republican vote plunged from 55 percent in November, 1888, to 44 percent the next April. In Chicago the Democrats reclaimed city hall with 55 percent of the vote, their best showing in six years.[52] The fall elections for Cook County offices saw the Republicans again hurt by the Sunday closing issue. An interdenominational association of pietistic ministers, including several Jansenistic Catholic priests, demanded the enforcement of the laws. That was enough to spark another Democratic sweep.[53]

The unkindest blow to President Harrison, hardly settled in the White House, came in the October city elections in his home, Indianapolis. There a group of reformers, mostly wealthy Republicans and pietistic ministers, had organized the High-License League of Indiana, and determined to raise the city's low $100 license fee. The Republican city council raised the licenses to $250, and the Democrats promptly charted their course, as proclaimed by the *Indianapolis Sentinel*:

> Local option . . . contemplates the exercise by the majority of the power to dictate to the minority in matters of personal right. The democratic theory of government is certainly in conflict with this policy. Democrats believe in the largest measure of individual liberty consistent with social order and the public security. They do not believe the state should usurp the function of private conscience.[54]

The Republicans, handicapped by the removal of their ablest leaders to Washington, attempted to mobilize the support of the pietistic reformers. They declared that "the city must control the saloon —not the saloon the city." Indeed, said Charles Fairbanks, later Theodore Roosevelt's vice president, "It is purely and solely a

---

52. Bessie Pierce, *A History of Chicago* (New York, 1957), 3:364–66; *Chicago Tribune*, March 17, 18, 22, 25, April 5, 1889.

53. *Chicago Tribune*, September 15, 27, 30, October 21, 28, 1889. Aaron Abell, *American Catholicism and Social Action* (Garden City, 1960), p. 91; for the Jansenistic Irish Catholic involvement in the Sunday closing movement, see M. Sevina Pahorezki, *The Social and Political Activities of William James Onahan* (Washington, 1942), pp. 47, 65–68.

54. Quote from *Indianapolis Sentinel*, June 29, 1889 (editorial); *Indianapolis Journal*, April 15, June 5, 18, 1889.

question of whether the honest, conservative, law-abiding elements shall prevail, or whether a premium shall be placed upon law-breaking." The Democrats had the Keokuk example of how to handle such a situation; so they nominated an outstanding reformer, denounced corruption in the city government, and appealed to the Germans to protect their personal rights.[55]

For the first time in a dozen years the Democrats triumphed in Indianapolis. Disappointed patronage-seekers had refused to work for the Republican ticket. Conservative businessmen, liberal Mugwumps, and personal-liberty Germans all moved toward the Democratic camp. The antisaloon crusade of the ministers was "good morals but bad politics," commented the expert *Cincinnati Commercial-Gazette,* "and as is invariably the case when the preachers step from theology into politics they make a mess of it."[56]

The unpleasant experiences of 1889 troubled thoughtful Republican leaders and led to a reorientation of the party. In Iowa the party professionals ousted the amateur drys in 1893, and buried the liquor issue for another decade with an ingenius "mulcting" plan. In Ohio, the ruling coalition of McKinley, Hanna, and Sherman refused to let the GOP become embroiled in further efforts to enforce the Sunday laws; the party relied on its own mulcting scheme to resolve the tension between drys, moderates, and wets. In Chicago, the drys concentrated their fury, with some success, on an effort to close the World's Fair on Sundays. In Washington, the experiences led to new caution. Finding that President Harrison was ready to propose Sunday laws for the District of Columbia, Secretary of State Blaine warned of trouble. If the relaxed "continental Sunday" enjoyed by the Germans were disturbed, he wrote Harrison, it would "widely and severely affect our party by driving the Germans from us." Harrison dropped the proposal.[57]

55. Quote from *Indianapolis Journal,* September 15; also July 20, September 16, 18, 26, 1889. *Indianapolis Sentinel,* September 30, October 8, 1889.
56. Quote from *Cincinnati Commercial-Gazette,* October 17, 1891. *Nation* (October 22, 1891) 53:306; *New York Times,* October 8, 28, 1889; *Indianapolis Sentinel,* October 9, 11, November 26 (for election returns), 1889. *Minutes of the [Presbyterian] Synod of Indiana* (Indianapolis, 1887), p. 31; ibid. (1888), pp. 27–28.
57. Blaine to Harrison, November 30, 1889, in A.T. Volwiler, ed., *The Correspondence Between Benjamin Harrison and James G. Blaine* (Philadelphia, 1940), pp. 90–91; *Ann. Cycl. 1890:* 178, cf. *Ann. Cycl. 1889:* 193.

The Republicans had played with firewater, and were burned. The politicians of the day never fully understood why innocent laws advocated by nearly all their upright constituents had such sweeping and disastrous aftermaths at the polls. Without quite realizing it, they had assumed that the pietistic ethic was unchallenged in their constituencies. Their opposition came not so much from liquor dealers or frequenters of saloons as from thoroughly respectable liturgical voters who saw prohibition as a threat to their own ethic. Thanks to the closely matched, fully mobilized political system of the Midwest, the grievances of a portion of the population were immediately translated into smashing defeats for the offending party.

The temperance question involved not just liquor but also, and more importantly, the basic religious, cultural, and political values of the people. In the half century since the pietists began to crusade for a single standard of American morality, the lines of antagonism had hardened. The same basic pattern of religious, cultural and political conflict, if exposed suddenly without planning or warning, and if brought to the arena of partisan politics before the professionals had an opportunity to formulate a reasonable compromise, could explode even more forcefully and fearfully than in Iowa in 1889. In Wisconsin in 1890 the tinder was dry and the pietists struck a spark that led to the downfall of the dominant party; seldom in American history, and only once before in midwestern history (in Ohio in 1863) was a political battle so bitterly fought or so decisively won.

5

Education, the Tariff, and the Melting Pot:
Culture Conflict and the Democratic Landslide of 1890

> The defeat was inevitable. The
> school law did it—a silly, senti-
> mental and damned useless
> abstraction, foisted upon us by a
> self-righteous demagogue.

Senator John Spooner[1]

Wisconsin contained the ingredients for a severe conflict between the opposing religious outlooks. The Germans and Irish outnumbered the pietistic and unaffiliated Yankees, Scandinavians, and British. The Germans, however, were divided into four bitterly antagonistic groups: Catholics (liturgical), Lutherans (liturgical), other Protestants (pietistic), and anticlerical freethinkers. The old-stock Yankees dominated the leadership of both parties, but any political issue that united the liturgical groups against the pietists could lead to a political upheaval.

Only in Wisconsin did an immigrant group outnumber the Yankees. Among the 462,000 eligible voters in 1890, only 22 percent were old stock (mostly New Englanders and New Yorkers); 39 percent were Germans, 13 percent were Scandinavians (mostly Norwegians), 9 percent were British, almost 9 percent were Irish, and another 9 percent acknowledged diverse heritages, Polish and French mostly. By uniting the Yankees, the British, and the Scandinavians with a substantial minority of the Germans, the Republicans controlled the state, with but one interruption since 1855.[2]

As might be expected, the only Republican defeat came on the liquor issue. In 1872 the Republicans enacted a stiff saloon licensing law, and made it even more obnoxious in 1873. The Germans protested, and handed the government to the Democrats, who bungled their opportunity. The Republicans, in 1875, nominated the mayor of Milwaukee who refused to enforce licensing laws, and swept back to power. Several times in the next dozen years

1. Spooner to H.M. Kutchin, November 18, 1890; in Spooner MSS, Library of Congress.
2. Bureau of the Census, *Report on Population . . . Eleventh Census 1890:* (Washington, 1897), pt. 2, pp. 100, 348, 490–91; see Frederick J. Turner, *The Frontier in American History* (New York, 1920), pp. 227–36.

fracases erupted between liturgicals and pietists over Sunday closing of beerhalls, support of the public schools, and local option, but the firm leadership of "Boss" Elisha Keyes and Philetus Sawyer refused to allow the Republican party to again ensnarl itself in disastrous conflicts.[3]

In 1889 the new Republican governor, William Hoard, recommended major reforms in Wisconsin's child labor and compulsory education laws. The old attendance law, requiring all private schools to be taught in English, had never been enforced. State senator Levi Pond introduced a bill requiring statistical reports from all private schools to enable the state to judge whether sufficient English instruction was provided. A barrage of tens of thousands of signatures protesting the Pond bill convinced the legislature that the scheme was unwise.[4]

The legislature then passed, without opposition and without debate, a new bill introduced by Michael Bennett, a young Catholic representative from Pine Knot. Bennett had consulted with educational leaders in Chicago, both Germans and Yankees, Protestants and Democrats, who had drafted a model law to assure compulsory education of young people and to banish child labor. In Illinois, a similar bill, known as the Edwards law, passed the legislature with only token opposition in May, 1889. Bennett merely copied the model law, discussed it with a few interested men, sent three hundred copies to Wisconsin educators, and pushed it through the legislature. The Bennett and Edwards laws contained nearly identical provisions requiring that English be the predominant language used in every school. Section five of the Bennett law provided:

3. Herman Deutsch, "Yankee-Teuton Rivalry in Wisconsin Politics of the Seventies," *Wisconsin Magazine of History* (1931) 14:262–82, 403–18, narrates the manifestations of the basic tensions; see also idem, "Disintegrating Forces in Wisconsin Politics of the Early Seventies," ibid. (1932) 15:168–81, 282–96, 391–411; David Thelen, "LaFollette and the Temperance Crusade," ibid. (1964) 47:291–300; and Horace Merrill, *Bourbon Democracy of the Middle West: 1865–1896* (Baton Rouge, 1953), pp. 85–90, 106.

4. J. Mapel, "The Repeal of the Compulsory Education Laws in Wisconsin and Illinois," *Educational Review* (1891) 1:52–53; William Whyte, "The Bennett Law Campaign in Wisconsin," *Wisconsin Magazine of History* (1927) 10:377–78, a participant's account; Deutsch, "Wisconsin Politics" 14:406–9; M. Justille McDonald, *History of the Irish in Wisconsin* (Washington, 1954), p. 169; and Robert J. Ulrich, "The Bennett Law of 1889," (Ph.D. diss., University of Wisconsin, 1965), pp. 154–64.

> No school shall be regarded as a school under this act unless there shall be taught therein, as part of the elementary education of children, reading, writing, arithmetic and United States history in the English language.

Both laws gave the local boards of education, not the parents, final authority over the education of all children.[5]

In late June, two months after Governor Hoard proudly signed the Bennett act, the Wisconsin Synod met, a conservative Lutheran denomination with 45,000 communicants in three hundred Wisconsin parishes. The synod was affiliated with the other liturgically-oriented German Lutherans in the Synodical Conference, and educated about 9,000 Wisconsin children in 164 parochial schools, a third of which used German exclusively. Two vigorous spokesmen, A. F. Ernst, the president of Northwestern College in Watertown, and Christian Koerner, an editor of *Germania,* Milwaukee's Lutheran weekly, put the synod in the fore of the opposition to the Bennett law. It declared the law to be "tyrannical and unjust," because "it jeopardises the permanency of our loyal parochial schools . . . permits unjustified encroachment upon parental rights and family life," and "is a contradiction of the spirit of our free institutions." The synod demanded repeal or drastic modification of the law, and threatened "recourse to the courts or to the ballot box."[6]

Wisconsin's 160,000 Lutheran communicants belonged to nine

5. The legislative history of the Bennett and Edwards laws was much debated in 1890. Compare the texts of the two laws in the *Chicago Daily News Almanac for 1891* (Chicago, 1891), pp. 66–67. On the passage see Whyte, "Bennett Campaign" 10:377; William F. Vilas, "The 'Bennett Law' in Wisconsin," *Forum* (1891) 12:198–99; *Oshkosh Daily Northwestern* (GOP), March 31, 1890; *Chicago Tribune,* March 13, April 7, 8, 10, 21, May 20, 1890, November 7, 1892; Walter Beck, *Lutheran Elementary Schools in the United States* (St. Louis, 1939), pp. 227–29; and Louise Kellogg, "The Bennett Law in Wisconsin," *Wisconsin Magazine of History* (1918) 2:4–5. For Bennett's own version see his letter in the *Milwaukee Journal,* October 28, 1889.

6. Roy A. Suelflow, *Walking with Wise Men: A History of the South Wisconsin District of the Lutheran Church—Missouri Synod* (Milwaukee, 1967), pp. 128–29; *Lutheran Witness* (July 21, 1889) 8:29, (October 21, 1889) 8:80; Beck, *Lutheran Schools,* pp. 192, 205, 221, 229–31; and Bureau of the Census, *Report on Churches . . . Eleventh Census:1890* (Washington, 1894), p. 465.

hundred congregations divided among fifteen separate synods, representing Germans, Scandinavians, and old-stock Americans of numerous theological and cultural outlooks. One by one the liturgical forces among them discovered evil in the Bennett law. The Wisconsin district of the large, tight-knit, intensely conservative Missouri Synod, seeing a threat to its 136 German-language parochial schools, declared the law a "violation of the natural rights of parents and the Constitution." The Ohio, Iowa, Michigan, Minnesota, and Buffalo synods, each with struggling parochial schools, proclaimed their alliance with the larger German groups. The old-stock Lutherans, although few in number in the state, were pietistic in outlook and opposed to parochial schools. They favored the Bennett law, as for the moment did the Scandinavians.[7]

Of the 70,000 children in Wisconsin's parochial schools, 40,000 attended Roman Catholic institutions. The opinion of their fathers would weigh heavily in the dispute, but the attention of the Catholics had been preempted by an equally divisive controversy, Bible reading in the public schools. A large number of Catholic children, perhaps half, attended the common schools of the state, many of which required classroom readings from the King James Bible. The Catholics, supported from the sidelines by the other liturgical churches (except the Episcopalians), and also by the large German freethinker community in Milwaukee, appealed to the state supreme court to declare the practice unconstitutional, chiefly because it constituted sectarian instruction. The attorneys for the defendant school board heatedly retorted that the Roman church was a menace to the public school system. The unanimous

7. Beck, *Lutheran Schools*, pp. 221, 232, 237–40; *Lutheran Witness* (April 21, 1890) 8:175–76; Kellogg, "Bennett Law" 2:14–15; Ulrich, "Bennett Law," pp. 173–76. In 1890 the *Lutheran Witness* reported that half of the confirmands in the Missouri Synod were abandoning German-language churches in favor of English-language churches, or were converts to the Presbyterian or Episcopal denominations. Perhaps the elders of the German Lutheran communities were especially anxious over the effect the Bennett law might have on this alarming trend. "We know that our offspring will become Americanized," declared the President of the Missouri Synod, "but we ought not to be blamed when we try to make this change a gradual one." *Lutheran Witness* (September 7, 1889) 8:53–54; Carl S. Meyer, ed., *Moving Frontiers* (St. Louis, 1964), p. 359.

verdict of the court, delivered in March, 1890, upheld the Catholic position, much to the annoyance of the pietistic denominations.[8]

Following the Christmas festivities in 1889, the German Lutherans established a state committee to lead the growing opposition to the Bennett law.[9] The Democratic leadership noted the surging unrest among the German Lutherans, many of whom were staunch Republicans, but being uncertain how to harness it, talked in terms of waging the 1890 gubernatorial, legislative, and congressional campaigns on the tariff and charges of corruption in the state treasurer's office.[10] The Republicans, despite Governor Hoard's original intention of avoiding the dispute, landed in the thick of the school question in late January, when J. B. Thayer, the state superintendent of education, proclaimed that the Bennett law would "save the future citizens, reared within this commonwealth from the irreparable loss and disadvantage which will follow neglect or cupidity, in depriving children of their rightful heritage."[11]

The champions of the parochial schools protested that none of their children grew up unable to speak English; their adversaries, however, wanted the children to read and write English, too. In March the Catholic hierarchy of Wisconsin escalated the controversy with a formal manifesto. The three bishops, all Germans, found that the Bennett law interfered "with the rights of the Church and of the parent." Believing that the true object of the law was "to place the parochial and private schools under the control of the state," the bishops perceived "the further object of entirely eliminating the parochial schools."[12] Wisconsin's 100,000 Catholic

8. Bureau of the Census, *Report on Population*, pt. 2, pp. 113–15; for different estimates, see *Milwaukee Journal*, April 10, 1890, *Chicago Tribune*, September 2, 1890, and Ulrich, "Bennett Law," pp. 309–11. On the Bible case, J. B. Thayer, *Biennial Report of the State Superintendent of . . . Wisconsin for . . . 1890* (Madison, 1890), pp. 29–31; *Ann. Cycl. 1890:* 855; Kellogg, "Bennett Law" 2:20. On Catholic hostility to public schools in the 1880s, see John Evans, "Catholics and the Blair Education Bill," *Catholic Historical Review* (1960) 46:273–96.
9. Beck, *Lutheran Schools*, p. 233; Kellogg, "Bennett Law" 2:18–19; *Milwaukee Sentinel*, December 30, 1889.
10. Horace Merrill, *William Freeman Vilas* (Madison, 1954), pp. 162–63; *Milwaukee Journal*, January 18, 1890; Ulrich, "Bennett Law," pp. 180–86.
11. *Milwaukee Journal*, January 29, 1890; Kellogg, "Bennett Law" 2:17–18.
12. *Milwaukee Journal*, March 12, 1890; see Whyte, "Bennett Campaign" 10:378–82, and Ulrich, "Bennett Law," pp. 213–20.

voters were mostly Democrats, but that massive bloc could scarcely be ignored by the GOP.

Republican state chairman Henry Payne, of Milwaukee, feared that the Bennett furor would cost the party dearly in the upcoming local elections, and recommended that the Germans be conciliated. But Hoard insisted that the German Republican vote was small and inconsequential, and that, anyway, a vigorous defense of the law would attract old-stock Democrats and anticlerical Germans, and thus more than make good any losses. The Democrats calculated otherwise. One week before the April elections, the Milwaukee Democrats named George ("Bad Boy") Peck, a Yankee humorist, journalist, and amateur politician as its mayoralty candidate. Peck's platform declared "the so-called Bennett law wholly uncalled for—its provisions uselessly harsh and unjust, infringing on the natural liberty of conscience and on the natural right of paternal control."[13]

The GOP's expected allies, the anticlerical Germans in the Turnerverein and trade unions, did, indeed, defend the Bennett law; but they also voted the Citizens Labor ticket, the remnant of the labor party that had swept Milwaukee four years before, and the harbinger of the Socialist party that would eventually dominate the city. Payne and the leading Republican newspaper, the *Milwaukee Sentinel,* tried to soothe the fears of the German Lutherans and Catholics, but their party was popularly identified with the obnoxious law.

For the first time in a decade and a half the Democrats captured a majority of the Milwaukee vote. Affable George Peck, running several hundred votes ahead of his ticket, polled 16,416 (53 percent) to only 9,451 (30 percent) for the incumbent Republican and 5,261 (17 percent) for the labor candidate. Turnout was down slightly from the 1888 city election, and down 6,000 from the presidential vote seventeen months before. The Democrats gained everywhere, especially in the precincts teeming with recent immigrants, and more in the German wards than in the heterogeneous wards elsewhere in Milwaukee, as table 11 shows. The *Germania* exulted over "the wonderful victory for Germandom over narrow-hearted nativism," and the *Milwaukee Seebote* rejoiced that "We

13. *Milwaukee Journal,* March 24, 1890; see also February 13, March 4, 22, 1890; Ulrich, "Bennett Law," pp. 227–65.

will not be robbed of the dear speech in which our mothers taught us our first songs."[14]

Elsewhere in Wisconsin, the Bennett law eclipsed the prohibition (local option) issue, and increased the tension between wets and drys, liturgicals and pietists. In Hoard's home city, Fort Atkinson, the school issue swept the Germans into a victorious Democratic coalition. In Madison, Oshkosh, and Racine, Eau Claire and Wausau and Ripon, and many smaller communities the

Table 11

Milwaukee Popular Vote by Ward Groups, 1886–1896[15]

| Ward groups | Party | Percent of total vote | | | | | | |
		1886 Cong.	1888 Pres.	1890 Mayor	1890 Gov.	1892 Pres.	1894 Gov.	1896 Pres.
11	GOP	31	52	34	46	52	48	59
German	Dem	25	36	49	51	44	27	37
wards	Labor	45	11	18	3	3	23	1
7	GOP	29	37	24	33	38	42	44
other	Dem	27	49	60	64	59	39	54
wards	Labor	44	13	15	2	2	17	1
Entire	GOP	30	47	30	41	47	46	54
city	Dem	25	40	53	55	49	31	43
	Labor	45	12	7	3	3	21	1
Turnout X 1000		26	37	31	38	45	43	56

14. Translated in Whyte, "Bennett Campaign" 10:21–22.
15. Except in the 1890 elections, the Prohibition party secured about 1 percent of the vote in both groups of wards. Returns from *Milwaukee Journal*, April 2, 1890, and the *Blue Book . . . Wisconsin* (Madison, 1887–1897, biennial). Wards 1,2,5,6,8–10,13,15–17, and (after 1895) 19 to 21 were predominantly German, with the recent immigrants concentrated in wards 2,5,9,10,13, and 19–21. See Bureau of the Census, *Report on Vital and Social Statistics . . . Eleventh Census: 1890* (Washington, 1896), pt. 2, pp. 370–71; and Wisconsin Secretary of State, *Tabular Statement of the [Wisconsin] Census* (Madison, 1895, 1905).

wet voters declared for the licensing of the liquor traffic, Sunday opening of saloons, and weekday opening of the parochial schools. The invincible Wisconsin GOP was in serious trouble, and it shared its misery with Republicans in Indiana, Michigan, Illinois, and Iowa, who likewise tasted spring defeat in local elections waged chiefly on the liquor issue.[16]

The elections shocked every Republican in Wisconsin. Governor Hoard, speaking the following day to a meeting of public school teachers, railed against the "unprogressive elements" who "deliberately enter into a conspiracy against poor, ignorant and defenseless children." Expressing his concern for the "poor German boys" in the clutches of such dark forces (their parents and pastors), Hoard proclaimed that their intellectual salvation lay in "that unrivalled, that invaluable political and moral institution—our own blessing and the glory of our fathers—the New England system of free schools."[17]

Hoard combined the pietistic morals of a New Englander with the enthusiasm of a political amateur. The governorship was his first public office, and he had won it by overwhelming the regular party organization. Hoard had pioneered the development of modern dairy farming ("Speak to a cow as you would to a lady," was his slogan), and had founded the Wisconsin Dairymen's Association in 1872. Through his two weekly newspapers, and his hundreds of appearances before local farmers' institutes, he had developed a grass-roots support that surprised and impressed the professionals at the 1888 state convention. Convinced of the soundness of his insights, Hoard brushed aside the wisdom of the professionals, an action that would cost him dearly.[18]

Although an amateur in politics, Hoard did realize that elections were won by majorities. He claimed that the Lutheran ministers were systematically misleading their flock, and produced letters from German farmers endorsing his stand. The fifty thousand people at the sixty farmers' institutes that winter, he argued, had expressed their approval of the Bennett law, and he was dedicated to

16. *Milwaukee Journal,* April 3, 1890; *Wisconsin State Journal* (Madison), April 2, 1890; *Chicago Tribune,* April 9, 14, May 7, 1890.
17. *Wisconsin State Journal,* April 3, 1890, for full text.
18. *Blue Book 1889,* pp. 459, 490; Whyte, "Bennett Campaign" 10:368, 387; Ulrich, "Bennett Law," pp. 134–37.

their mandate. Anyway, he explained to worried party leaders, not one German Lutheran in five was a Republican, and almost no Catholics were. The pietistic elements, he felt, supported the Bennett law. "The German Methodists, Baptists, Presbyterians, Scandinavian Lutherans and all that great body of English speaking Protestants can see no danger to religion or the rights of religious worship in the law. Are they so stupid," Hoard asked, "that they do not know when religion is attacked?" Furthermore, he contended, the Irish Catholics "are quite generally in favor of the law." "Have they suddenly become blind to the great danger that threatens their religious existence and integrity?"[19]

The Republican professionals listened to Hoard with dismay. H. A. Taylor, the former state chairman and editor of the influential Madison *Wisconsin State Journal,* rejected Hoard's exclusionary policy. "The republican party," he editorialized, "is to-day, as it has ever been, friendly to every people and every class. It is liberal and progressive." Taylor ridiculed the "well-meaning but fanatical men who think they see in the opposition of the Catholic priests to the public schools as places of learning a great menace to our liberties."[20] More concretely, Taylor joined Payne, Secretary of Agriculture Jeremiah Rusk, Senators Philetus Sawyer and John Spooner, and other leaders to head the party toward a pluralistic outlook. The professionals could not rebut Hoard's glib analysis of the religious forces at work, but instinctively they knew that his course would yield disaster.[21]

Senator Sawyer, the strong man of the party, wanted to conciliate the Germans. "Denunciations of the anti-Bennett-lawites will accomplish no good for the Republican party," he argued, but he conceded that any attempt to block Hoard's renomination would tear the party apart.[22] Spooner, whose reelection to the Senate depended on the election of a Republican legislature in 1890, and several of the congressional delegation struggled to get Hoard to

19. *Wisconsin State Journal,* April 3, 1890; *Chicago Tribune,* April 5, 1890.
20. *Wisconsin State Journal,* April 12, June 26, 1890.
21. *Chicago Tribune,* May 1, August 1, 1890; Dorothy Fowler, *John Coit Spooner* (New York, 1961), pp. 146–48; Whyte, "Bennett Campaign" 10: 381, 386, 390; cf. Belle and Fola LaFollette, *Robert M. LaFollette* (New York, 1953), 1:87.
22. *Chicago Tribune,* April 25, 1890.

promise to amend the law. "Some of my colleagues," Congressman Nils Haugen wrote Superintendent Thayer, "lost all courage at the first volley and were ready to resign—no, I will not accuse them of that, but they wanted to compromise."[23] Confident that Haugen's support meant the Scandinavians would be solid, Hoard remained obdurate: "There will be no compromise on the Bennett law."[24]

Payne and Spooner, however, finally reached an agreement with Hoard. The full resources of the party would be thrown into the campaign, but the party platform would promise to amend the Bennett law to acknowledge the educational rights of parents. To save themselves, the Republicans had to be united, and they could only unite on the governor's terms. Much as they wanted to dump Hoard as a candidate for reelection, the GOP high command refused to split the party in the hour of crisis. The convention in August was routine. The critics sat silently as the Wisconsin GOP pledged opposition to repeal of the "wise and humane" Bennett law. "We are unalterably opposed," the platform announced, "to any union of church and state. . . . We repudiate as a gross misrepresentation of our purposes, the suggestion, come whence it may, that we will in any manner invade the domain of conscience, trample upon parental rights, or religious liberty."[25]

If those harsh words were designed to soothe the Germans, they failed. The Germans wanted repeal, and a wholly new law; only major concessions could mollify them now.[26] During the summer the Missouri Synod and the Synodical Conference organized methodically. Declaring that every member was "in conscience bound to combat each and every law which is directed, or may be used, to the detriment and damage of Lutheran parochial schools,"[27] Missouri and its allies briefed every pastor, set up committees in every parish, printed leaflets and posters, held rallies and passed resolutions, and readied their 100,000 Wisconsin com-

23. N. P. Haugen to J. B. Thayer, April 27, 1890, copy in Haugen Letterbooks, Wisconsin State Historical Society.

24. *Chicago Tribune,* August 1, 1890.

25. *Blue Book 1891,* p. 390; *Daily News Almanac 1891,* pp. 182–83; *Milwaukee Sentinel,* August 21, 1890; *Chicago Tribune,* August 20, 21, 1890.

26. Fowler, *Spooner,* pp. 148–50; *New York Times,* August 22, 1890.

27. Beck, *Lutheran Schools,* pp. 235–37; *Ann. Cycl. 1890:* 510; *Lutheran Witness* (July 7, 21, 1890) 9:21, 29.

municants (about 30,000 voters) for battle. In early June the German Lutherans and Catholics joined hands in Milwaukee, pledging cooperation to overthrow the Bennett law.[28]

To the faithful, the German priests and ministers emphasized the rights of parents and the church, and suggested that the true goal of the educational "reformers" was not the promotion of English, but the destruction of the "divisive" parochial schools, and, indeed, of all non-Yankee culture.[29] Bishop Katzer of the Catholic diocese of Green Bay maintained, "The Bennett law was conceived in the minds of free-thinkers and those opposed to the Catholic church and her schools." The Freemasons, he insinuated, were probably responsible for the agitation.[30] Forming committees in every parish, the German Catholics pledged themselves "irrespective of former party affiliations to support only such candidates who will advocate and vote for the repeal of the law."[31] Bishop Katzer, a former Republican, reportedly told his congregation that "personally and officially as Bishop of the diocese [I] should consider anyone who did not vote for the repeal of the law a traitor to the Catholic Church."[32]

But Hoard had already discounted the votes of the German Catholics and Lutherans. The Republicans figured there were at most 14,000 German Lutheran Republicans, and a smaller number of Catholics. Hoard's plurality in 1888 had been 20,000, and the school issue supposedly was good for 7,000 Prohibitionist and 10,000 Democratic defections. The GOP would not only win, but enhance its plurality, the calculators concluded.[33] But the folly of the amateur politician is the oversimplification of the complexity of political and cultural forces, and his ignorance of the

---

28. *Milwaukee Journal*, June 4, 1890; for the account of one active Lutheran, see Otto F. Hattstaedt, *History of the Southern Wisconsin District of the Evangelical Lutheran Synod of Missouri*, W.P.A. translation (Madison, 1941), p. 77.

29. Ulrich, "Bennett Law," pp. 435–38.

30. *Chicago Tribune*, May 28, 1890.

31. Ibid.

32. *New York Times*, October 28, 1890; on Katzer's Republicanism, *Milwaukee Journal*, June 2, 1890.

33. *Chicago Times*, October 25, 1890; *Milwaukee Journal*, October 24, 1890.

dynamics of elections. The campaign, unknown to the amateurs, would be fought on more than religious grounds.

Given the Republican determination to uphold the Bennett law, its opponents realized they had to forge a strange coalition to defeat it. First the Democratic party must pledge itself to repeal the law, and the German Lutherans and Catholics had to be fully mobilized. The winning margin, however, had to come from the normally Republican Scandinavians and non-Christian Germans, and there could be no large-scale defection of Yankees and Irish from the Democratic fold.

The organization of the German Catholics and Lutherans reached perfection by early June, and in late August the Democratic party swung into line. Led by the vigorous, methodical new state chairman, Edward Wall, and the brilliant, wealthy William Vilas, a holder of two portfolios in Cleveland's cabinet and later a senator, the Democrats endorsed the anti-Bennett position. The platform, written by Vilas, rang the changes on the theme of Republican paternalism and centralization. The protective tariff, the civil rights bill, Speaker Reed's rules, extravagant expenditures, all reflected obnoxious paternalism at the federal level. "The Bennett law," the platform then charged, "is a local manifestation of the settled republican policy of paternalism." Its underlying principle was "needless interference with paternal rights"; the plea of supporting the English language was a ploy "to mask this tyrannical invasion of individual and constitutional rights." The Democrats of Wisconsin, the platform concluded, "Denounce the law as unnecessary, unwise, unconstitutional, un-American and undemocratic, and demand its repeal."[34]

The political expertise of the Democratic party was now aligned against the Bennett law, and took charge of the campaign. To win the pietistic and non-Christian Germans, the Democrats invoked the glories of the German language and the monuments of the culture of Goethe and Schiller and Beethoven. "What is the difference," Vilas asked German audiences across the state, "if you say 'two and two make four,' or 'zwei und zwei machen vier?' "[35]

34. *Blue Book 1891*, p. 394; *Daily News Almanac 1891*, p. 183; *Chicago Tribune,* August 27, 28, 1890; Merrill, *Vilas*, pp. 162–67.
35. Merrill, *Vilas*, p. 168; Whyte, "Bennett Campaign" 10:386.

When the news arrived in late May that the Indianapolis school board, by a ruse, had sharply curtailed the teaching of German in the public schools, the opponents of the Bennett law claimed that a nationwide conspiracy was afoot to banish the German language. Even the anticlerical "forty-eighter" German newspaper editors rallied to the defense of their mother tongue.[36] The anticlerical Turnerverein reversed its earlier support of the Bennett law, and in national convention resolved "to protest against prohibition, puritanism, Sunday closing, and the attacks on the German language in the West."[37]

The parallel campaign in Illinois against the Edwards law reinforced the Wisconsin campaign, and drew sustenance from it. Koerner alerted his Lutheran colleagues to the south to the need for an aggressive defense of their parochial schools, and received aid from Chairman Wall in spreading his propaganda. A delegation of German Lutheran, Catholic, Evangelical, and Reformed laymen and ministers appeared before both the Illinois Democratic and Republican conventions to demand repeal of the law. The Democrats agreed, pledged repeal, and declared as a self-evident truth that, "To determine and direct the education of the child is a natural right of the parent."[38] For state superintendent of public instruction the Illinois Democrats nominated Henry Raab, a German noted for his opposition to the Edwards law.

The Illinois Republican convention rebuffed the German committee, although it did promise to strengthen parental control of education. The GOP platform came out strongly for the public school system (which no one was attacking), and endorsed "all

36. Whyte, "Bennett Campaign" 10:382–84; Kellogg, "Bennett Law" 2:10–14; Francis Ellis, "German Instruction in the Public Schools of Indianapolis, 1869–1919," *Indiana Magazine of History,* (1954) 52:265–75. In 1889 the Chicago School Board nearly dropped German language courses. *Illinois Staats-Zeitung* (Chicago), February 11, 1889. An attempt to pass legislation similar to the Bennett law failed in Nebraska in 1889 in the face of German opposition; Frederick Luebke, *Immigrants and Politics: The Germans of Nebraska, 1880–1900* (Lincoln, 1969), p. 143.

37. *Chicago Tribune,* June 25, 1890. On the earlier Turner support of the Bennett law, see *Milwaukee Journal,* April 7, 1890; Suelflow, *Walking with Wise Men,* p. 133; and Kellogg, "Bennett Law" 2:21; on the later opposition, see also *Chicago Tribune,* September 24, and October 24, 1890.

38. *Daily News Almanac 1891,* p. 164; *Chicago Tribune,* April 5, June 3, 5, 1890.

proper and practical methods for abating the evils of the liquor traffic."[39] With a whoop they renominated controversial Richard Edwards for superintendent, and to head the ticket named Fritz Amberg for state treasurer. Amberg, although born in Bavaria, made his attitude on the burning issue clear:

> I believe in compulsory education and in the English language. The first aim in the education of the youth of this country should be to spread that language. I also admire the German language; it is all right in its way, but I am against educating the children of this country in that language. If there is any danger of our children being injured in any way by neglect of English education, it is the duty of the state to protect them.[40]

With such friends the compulsory school laws needed few more enemies. But they acquired some more.

The Republican solidarity of the Scandinavians in both Illinois and Wisconsin proved remarkably easy to breach. In 1890 the Scandinavians grumbled that the GOP was taking their vote for granted and was refusing to give their leaders deserved patronage. Even more important was the question of assimilation. The Norwegian Lutherans in America had long quarreled over the role of parochial schools in their communities. The liturgical founders of the Norwegian Synod (The Norwegian Church in America) argued the necessity of establishing Norwegian language parochial schools to preserve the cultural and religious heritage of the homeland. While the pietistic Norwegians quietly sent their children to the public schools, anticlerical groups of intellectuals loudly demanded an end to the parochial system and an immediate integration of the Norwegians into American society.[41] Led by the Reverend H. A. Preuss, the liturgical element seized upon the Bennett agitation to join with their fellow immigrant Lutherans. The general con-

39. *Daily News Almanac 1891*, p. 164; cf. *Lutheran Witness* (July 21, 1890) 9:31.

40. *Chicago Tribune*, June 26, 1890, see also June 24 and 25, 1890. For the Lutherans' activity, see *Illinois Staats-Zeitung*, March 7, April 18, 1890; and Beck, *Lutheran Schools*, pp. 245–48.

41. Laurence Larson, *The Changing West* (Northfield, Minnesota, 1937), pp. 116–46. On the patronage issue, see *Chicago Skandinaven*, October 3, 1890 (editorial), in Chicago Foreign Language Press Survey, microfilm reel 45, code IF6.

vention of the Norwegian Synod not only rejected the compulsory education laws, but urged each congregation to begin at least part-time Norwegian instruction. Preuss, the synod's president, declared "the ill-famed Bennett law . . . contains features by which the political and religious rights of the people are trampled upon and whereby the liberty of conscience and religion given us by the state and country are deprived us." "Members of our Lutheran congregations ought," he felt, "to see that they cast their votes for the right men."[42]

The overenthusiastic friends of the school laws were unwittingly undermining the Republican loyalties of the Scandinavians. In September the Wisconsin Methodist Conference concluded, "It is a question of domestic or foreign domination. Shall there be one or many nationalities on our soil? Shall Roman Catholicism and Lutheranism maintain foreign ideas, customs and languages to the exclusion of what is distinctively American?"[43] The editor of a Scandinavian Methodist newspaper noted that the "state church" faction of older Norwegian Lutheran ministers was leading congregations into opposition to the school laws. In Rockford, Illinois, Democrats found that the Swedish Lutherans, pietistic and Republican to a man, but proud of their language and culture, wanted the Edwards law repealed.[44] The Republicans expected Congressman Haugen to hold the Norwegians in line, and he toured Wisconsin and subsidized *Amerika,* a Chicago Norwegian weekly, to help the cause. But *Amerika's* publisher told Haugen that "our stand on the Republican platform does not satisfy all the fire-eating Synod people. Some have already stopped the paper."[45]

42. *Amerika* (Madison), August 9, 1890, quoted in a campaign circular in the collection of the Wisconsin State Historical Society. See Beck, *Lutheran Schools,* pp. 240–41.

43. *Chicago Tribune,* September 30, 1890; *Lutheran Witness* (October 21, 1890) 9:77.

44. *Chicago Tribune,* April 5, October 23, 1890.

45. Kalheim to N. P. Haugen, October 8, 1890; see H. Payne to Haugen, October 5, 1890, both in Haugen MSS. On the Swedish newspaper opposition to the law, see O. Fritiof Ander, "The Swedish American Press and the Election of 1892," *Mississippi Valley Historical Review* (1937) 23:542–43, and also his "The Swedish American Press and the American Protective Association," *Church History* (1937) 6:167, 173–75.

Haugen, who had little contact with religious leaders, felt that "every child should be educated in the English language, and for its protection and future welfare the state should intervene in its behalf when the parent negligently or criminally fails in his duty."[46] Haugen conceded that "how far the foreign-born citizen should or ought to endeavor to perpetuate the national sentiments and language of his fatherland is a matter of individual choice," but, he argued, "it would be better to melt the question of nationality into one pot of loyal Americanism."[47] Reports from the grass roots revealed a different sentiment, especially among the least acculturated recent arrivals. "Those who have come here within the last ten years," LaFollette learned, "have not the affiliation for our party that the Norwegians of . . . [the] old counties have."[48] The new immigrants had not come to America to have their religion assailed and their language ridiculed; some loyalties were stronger than the bonds of party.

The challenge of holding the Jansenistic Irish Catholic and pietistic old-stock Yankee Democrats to their party proved more nettlesome. The Irish resentment of the German bishops, Hoard hoped, would win him their votes. The Irish generally avoided the parochial schools, few of which taught in English, and sent their children to Wisconsin's public schools. The Irish awaited the word of Archbishop Ireland; it came, but was somewhat ambiguous. Speaking to the National Educational Association, Ireland declared the compulsory school laws "objectionable in a few of their incidental clauses. These, I am confident, will readily be altered in approaching legislative sessions. With the body of the laws, and their general intent in the direction of hastening among us universal instruction I am most heartily in accord."[49] Nothing on the language controversy—was Ireland for or against the law? The Republicans claimed he was for, and distributed copies of his speech. On the other hand, Archbishop Feehan of Chicago, an Irishman, and the Illinois hierarchy considered the Edwards law "an insidious

46. Haugen to L. Jaeger, April 26, 1890, copy in Haugen Letterbooks.
47. Ibid.; Haugen to A. Johnson, September 8, 1894, Haugen Letterbooks. This was the first known use of the melting-pot metaphor.
48. J. Peterson to S. Harper, October 11, 1888, LaFollette MSS, Wisconsin State Historical Society.
49. *Chicago Tribune,* July 11, 1890.

and an unjust law."[50] The rumors, assiduously spread by the GOP, that Ireland endorsed Hoard, and that Bishop McGobrick of Duluth endorsed the law, proved ineffective in neutralizing the explicit pronouncements of the Wisconsin hierarchy.[51]

A substantial minority of the Democrats who publicly announced their support of the Bennett law were Irish (the majority were of old Yankee stock), but most of the Irish editors and all the priests in Milwaukee, German and non-German, reportedly favored repeal or radical modification of the law.[52] The normal Democratic allegiance of the Irish strengthened with the crescendo of vituperative attacks on the Catholic church from the Bennett supporters. The campaign exposed an undercurrent of anti-Catholicism, and gave bigots prestige and large new audiences. The head of the Good Templars wrote in the Prohibitionist paper, "You can find no minister or other person who opposes the Bennett law who preaches or practices total abstinence. The churches that oppose it are beer churches and supported by beer drinkers."[53] Pietistic Protestant pulpits in Wisconsin and Illinois rang with fierce denunciations of the Catholic church. A leading Chicago Presbyterian sermonized that the "Romanist" church "is in politics to stay until the public schools are made feeders to Catholicism—until Protestantism breaks if it will not bend." The minister further exhorted, "If any political candidate belongs to that church whose sole aim is to capture the country for the church he ought to be defeated, as he will be if the two-thirds of the people of Chicago not of that church will do their duty on election day."[54]

Even the Democratic Bennett Law League, which tried to woo Irish voters into the Republican camp, succumbed to anti-Catholicism. Its chairman protested that:

50. From a pastoral letter read September 11, 1892, in all Catholic parishes in Illinois, and signed by Archbishop Feehan and Bishops Spalding of Peoria, Janssen of Belleville, and Ryan of Alton. Spalding was a leading Jansenist. *New York Times,* September 13, 1892.
51. On Bishop McGobrick, *Chicago Tribune,* April 17, 1890; on the rumors, Whyte, "Bennett Campaign," 10:385.
52. McDonald, *Wisconsin Irish,* pp. 173–80.
53. Quoted, with glee, in *Milwaukee Journal,* March 29, 1890.
54. Sermon of Dr. John Withrow, reported in *Chicago Tribune,* November 3, 1890, and typical of many reported there, and in the issue of October 27, 1890. In 1896, Withrow became Moderator of the Presbyterian General Assembly.

This unholy crusade against the common schools is carried on by a coalition of priest, pettifogger, politician and poltroon. Some are inspired by hate. Some by love of gain. Some by hope of office. All are willing to sacrifice the common schools. Woe, woe the day when the fangs of the church clutch the throat of the common schools of Wisconsin.[55]

The leading Irish Catholic newspaper in Wisconsin lamented that "the Bennett law drew all the sectarian, bigoted, fanatical and crazy impurities in the Republican body (and some in the Democratic also) to a head and the consequent boil governs the Republican party rather than its brains."[56] The German Catholics exploited fully the anti-Catholicism in the enemy's camp. Observing that the burning school dispute in Boston was directed against the immigrant Irish, Bishop Katzer explained "They are all of a class, these laws, whether in Wisconsin, Illinois, or Massachusetts."[57] Hoard's plans to split the Catholics had disintegrated. The pastors in Milwaukee gave anti-Bennett sermons the Sunday before election, and on Tuesday the Polish priests lined up their parishioners and marched them to the polls. Monks who had never before voted emerged from their monasteries to register their protests.[58]

The greatest challenge to the Democrats was the problem of holding their old-stock American supporters. The Democratic Bennett Law League included numerous prominent Yankees. James Morgan, the Democratic gubernatorial nominee in 1888, repudiated the 1890 ticket. Several former legislators, gagging at the "un-Democratic, un-American, and unconstitutional" platform of their party, supported Hoard.[59] To attract the old-stock waverers, the Democrats nominated the cultured Yankee humorist, Mayor Peck, to oppose Hoard, and they stifled all dissent at the state convention. Colonel Charles Felker, an Oshkosh editor and the leader of the pro-Bennett Democrats, was not surprised:

55. Milwaukee speech of Colonel Charles Felker, full text in *Chicago Tribune*, October 19, 1890.
56. *Catholic Citizen* (Chippewa Falls), November 8, 1890, quoted in McDonald, *Wisconsin Irish*, p. 180.
57. *Chicago Tribune*, May 28, 1890.
58. Ibid., November 3, 5, 1890.
59. Ibid., September 4, 1890, quoting the *Milwaukee News* (GOP); see *Chicago Tribune*, September 5, 6, 8, 10, 13, 1890, and the *Milwaukee Sentinel* for the entire months of September and October.

> When kid and copperhead, Puritan and blackleg, German Lutheran and German Catholic join with the Democrats in assaulting the common schools of this country it is proper that the Democratic party be led by a clown.[60]

Hoard's rhetoric, meanwhile, degenerated into a defense of the public school system, which every one of his critics insisted was not under attack at all. His friends plastered Wisconsin with posters of a neat little red-frame building carrying the slogan, "The Little Schoolhouse: STAND BY IT!" The Democrats responded with pictures of the same schoolhouse and the slogan, "Peck and ALL the Schools!" Like Hutchison in Iowa the year before, Hoard kept falling back on the inexorable laws of history: "Ignorance," he said, "cannot control the destinies of our country; the question will be a menace to the progress of civilization and the perpetuity of our institutions."[61] The Prohibitionists refused to endorse Hoard, and ran their own ticket, but their leaders did add their mite to the cause:

> We are going to fight for a higher, purer, and grander civilization, and he who stands in the way of it is an enemy of his country and mankind. The Bennett law is the opening wedge to this higher civilization. Sustain this law and we have won our first great victory in Wisconsin for total abstinence and prohibition.[62]

To bolster their ranks and capture some Republican Yankees and Scandinavians, the Democrats hammered at Republican misuse of funds in the state treasury, and at the protective tariff. In early October President Harrison signed the McKinley tariff into law, and the Democrats slammed into the GOP. Already on the defensive for the blunders of the Harrison administration and the paternalism of the Fifty-first Congress, Republican morale dis-

---

60. *Chicago Tribune,* August 28, 1890; one eminent liturgically-oriented Philadelphia Presbyterian publicly *opposed* the Bennett law, *Lutheran Witness* (August 7, 1890) 9:40.

61. Whyte, "Bennett Campaign" 10:389, 385–86.

62. E. W. Chafin in Madison, *Western Good Templar* (Prohibitionist), quoted in the *Milwaukee Journal,* March 29, 1890; see *Chicago Tribune,* July 23, 1890. Accordingly the Blatz and Schlitz breweries in Milwaukee gave their employees extra time off on election day. *Milwaukee Herold,* November 5, 1890.

integrated under the burden of the tariff. LaFollette, who helped write the tariff law, vigorously justified the bill against the brilliant attacks of Vilas and the Texas tariff reformer Roger Q. Mills. The need to defend the tariff, to extol its benefits for Wisconsin, and rebut the misrepresentations of it spread by the Democrats, consumed much of the energy Hoard hoped the GOP would throw into the school fight.[63]

Never in its history did the GOP labor under such burdens as the 1890 campaign imposed. In nearly every northern state the Germans and Irish looked upon the Republicans as the sponsors of prohibition. In Wisconsin and Illinois, especially, the compulsory education issue incited the immigrant groups. Every consumer lamented the higher prices sparked by the McKinley tariff; every states-righter repudiated the force bill. Disappointed office-seekers and pension-seekers sulked together. The economical resented the billion-dollar spending extravaganza the GOP had conducted in Congress—and everywhere men looked in vain for the industrial utopia Harrison had promised them from his front porch.

Seldom has an incumbent major party been so unmistakably headed for disaster, and never more surely has disaster come. In the Congress that had produced more important legislation than any other from Lincoln's day to Wilson's, the slim Republican edge became a lopsided Democratic majority. The GOP risked 176 House seats at the polls, and salvaged 87. The Democrats began with 156 districts, and emerged with 236 House seats. The most brilliant and promising midwestern Republicans — McKinley, Spooner, Cannon, and LaFollette—carried their records to their constituents, and were retired from office. Although the GOP share of the vote declined only 2 percent in Illinois since 1888, 4.1 percent in Indiana, 3.3 percent in Iowa, 6.5 percent in Michigan, 0.5 percent in Ohio, and 5.8 percent in Wisconsin, the party lost seven House seats in Illinois, one in Indiana, four in Iowa, six in Michigan, nine in Ohio, and six in Wisconsin. Twenty-four midwestern Republican congressmen retained, and thirty-three lost,

63. C. Harper to S. A. Harper, September 18 and October 22, 1890, in LaFollette MSS; Nils P. Haugen, *Pioneer and Political Reminiscences* (Madison, 1929), pp. 94–95; Merrill, *Vilas*, pp. 168–69; Ander, "Swedish-American Press and 1892" 23:537–39.

their seats—the Midwest was now Democratic. The Democrats controlled nearly every large state, and Republican prospects for winning Congress or the White House in the foreseeable future were dismal.

In Wisconsin, every major office was lost, save the congressional seat held by Haugen. Governor Hoard ran an unusual 7,000 votes ahead of his ticket, thanks mostly to Prohibitionists and Laborites who split their ballots.[64] But his 1888 plurality of 20,000 became a deficit of 28,000. In not a single county did Hoard equal his first vote; he averaged only 75 percent of his 1888 vote, while Peck ran 3 percent *ahead* of Cleveland. It was not an off year for the Democrats; indeed, not until 1970 did any Democratic gubernatorial candidate in Wisconsin surpass Peck's 53.6 percent share of the total vote.

Everywhere in Wisconsin the Republicans slipped. Among the German Lutherans and Catholics the losses were, of course, heaviest. The Catholic Germans of Wheatland, in Kenosha County, had voted Democratic 124 to 83 in the last election; now they were for Peck 126 to 50, a jump from 60 percent to 72 percent. In nearby Randall the Catholic Germans moved from only 28 percent for Cleveland to 48 percent for Peck. The German Lutheran farmers in Lomira, Dodge County, had given Hoard 158 (44 percent) of their 358 votes the first time he ran; now they gave him only 80 (20 percent) of their increased (to 410) turnout. Table 12 displays the voting pattern of a sample of thirty-three rural townships settled by German immigrants who had long lived in America. About one in three Germans usually voted Republican, something Hoard never realized. In 1890 he got the votes of, at most, one in four of the German Catholics and one in five of the German Lutherans. Even the pietistic German groups showed sharp falloffs. Not until 1894 did the GOP fully recover from Hoard's impact.

The Norwegians expressed their pride in their cultural and religious heritage with striking effect. In Vernon County, in the

---

64. The Union Labor party nearly split over the school issue, and fielded weak candidates. See Thomas Gavett, *Development of the Labor Movement in Milwaukee* (Madison, 1965), pp. 76–77; *Chicago Tribune*, July 23, 1890, and *New York Times*, September 5, 6, 1890.

older Norwegian settlements, where party loyalty had deep roots, the Republican share of the vote slipped from 59 percent in 1888 to 55 percent. The newer immigrant settlements proved more volatile; there the Republican share of the vote plunged from 84

Table 12

Voting Patterns in Thirty-three Old, Rural German Settlements in Wisconsin, 1888–1896

| | | Percent of total vote | | | | |
	Party	1888 Pres.	1890 Gov.	1892 Pres.	1894 Gov.	1896 Pres.
21 Catholic townships[65]	GOP	33	25	30	40	49
	Dem.	63	72	67	56	48
Total vote		5,110	5,043	5,474	5,395	6,314
12 Lutheran townships[66]	GOP	35	21	29	37	49
	Dem.	63	78	70	61	47
Total vote		3,866	3,642	3,904	3,774	4,310

65. The Catholic townships (towns) sampled were Brillion, New Holstein and Woodville (Calumet County); Medina, Middleton, Roxbury and Springfield (Dane County); Lincoln (Eau Claire County); Forest and Ripon Town (Fond du Lac County); Ahnapee (Kewaunee County); Centerville, Eaton, and Two Rivers (Manitowoc County); Center and Cicero (Outagamie County); Saukville (Ozaukee County); Lisbon, New Berlin, and Muskego (Waukesha County), and Remington, (Wood County). The sample was based on a detailed study of the 1895 state census, county histories, and on Kate Levi, "Geographic Origin of German Immigration to Wisconsin," *Collections of the State Historical Society of Wisconsin* (Madison, 1898) 14: 341–93.

66. The Lutheran townships chosen were Herman and Lorima (Dodge County); Aztalan, Farmington, Jefferson (town and city), and Lake Mills (Jefferson County); Berlin, Hamburg, Stettin and Wausau (town) (Marathon County); Wolf River (Winnebago County); and Bloomfield (Waushara County). All the sample communities were overwhelmingly German, but the religious affiliations were sometimes diverse.

percent to 69 percent. In Dane County the Democrats enlarged their share of the vote in the newer settlements by 5 percent, and in the older by 6 percent. Actually, the number of Democratic votes stayed about the same, but the Republican total fell off sharply, indicating that unhappy Norwegians simply stayed home on election day. Table 13 shows the distribution of the Norwegian vote in Wisconsin, based on a sample of fourteen predominantly rural settlements.

Only in scattered localities did Hoard improve, or even match, his pluralities of 1888. In Richland County, the Yankee stronghold in an immigrant state, Hoard's vote dropped from 2,457 to

Table 13

Voting Patterns in Fourteen Norwegian Settlements in Wisconsin, 1888–1896[67]

		1888 Pres.	1890 Gov.	1892 Pres.	1894 Gov.	1896 Pres.
	Percent					
5 newer	GOP	73	66	66	75	81
settlements	Dem.	19	26	23	16	16
	Proh.	8	7	10	6	3
Total vote		2,116	1,582	2,204	2,202	2,322
9 older	GOP	64	60	59	66	69
settlements	Dem.	26	32	27	23	29
	Proh.	9	5	9	7	2
Total vote		2,592	1,988	2,519	2,599	2,870

67. The more recent settlements in Dane County were Christiana, Pleasant Springs and Staughton City; the older towns were Blue Mounds, Deerfield, Dunkirk, Perry, Primrose, and Rutland. In Vernon County, the newer settlements were Christiana and Coon, and the older, Jefferson, Franklin and Sterling. The remainder of the vote was Union Labor or Populist. For other analyses of German and Norwegian voting patterns in 1890, see Roger Wyman, "Wisconsin Ethnic Groups and the Election of 1890," *Wisconsin Magazine of History* (1968) 51:269–93, and Paul Kleppner, *The Cross of Culture* (New York, 1970), pp. 158–71.

1,874, and his share of the total slipped 3.5 percent, to just 51 percent.

Proudly maintaining that "I would rather be the humblest citizen and feel that I had done right than to be Governor of the State by refusing to meet a question of right and wrong," Hoard retired to Fort Atkinson to look after his two newspapers, six creameries, six acres of land, and one cow.[68] The professional politicians were left to pick up the shattered remnants of the party. Spooner, soon to be an ex-senator, pondered "how far a large body of Republicans have been permanently alienated from the party."[69] Chairman Payne thought the task of recovering the German vote "almost hopeless." Editor Horace Rublee, whose *Milwaukee Sentinel* had inflamed religious conflicts, agreed that the Republicans "need to cultivate harmony and cannot afford to quarrel over the past." Still Rublee felt he had been right, and refused "to conform my opinions to suit the voters that are controlled by German and Polack priests or German Lutheran ministers."[70] The once mighty Wisconsin Grand Old Party evidently had a great deal of rethinking and rebuilding to do.

Despite the earnest desire of most professional politicians in the Republican party to avoid a catastrophic contest pitting liturgicals against pietists, the Wisconsin situation reached a stage of no compromise in 1890. Hoard, it is true, forced his party into an extreme position during his reelection campaign, but by the spring of 1890 the Germans were in no mood to compromise anyway, and Hoard's provocative actions may have salvaged more votes than any conciliatory gestures could have done. Originally, the dispute was all a misunderstanding. When the Pond bill to inspect parochial schools came before the legislature in April, 1889, the Germans reacted with a barrage of hostile petitions that immediately killed the proposal; the Republican legislators proved themselves unwilling to antagonize the Germans. The Bennett law, however, slipped through without any hostile comment, despite Bennett's conscien-

68. Quote in *Chicago Tribune,* November 6, 1890. For Hoard's holdings, see Whyte, "Bennett Campaign" 10:370, and G. Steevens, *The Land of the Dollar* (New York, 1897), pp. 153–63.
69. Spooner to F. S. Bestow, November 18, 1890, copy in Spooner MSS.
70. Payne to J. Rusk, December 2, 1890, and Rublee to Rusk, December 2, 1890, quoted in Richard Current, *Pine Logs and Politics* (Madison, 1950), pp. 253–56.

tious efforts to inform educational leaders about his proposal. Bennett, himself a Catholic, did not recognize anything controversial in his proposal; nor did professional educators, all of whom remained remarkably silent throughout the entire dispute. Bennett apparently failed to consult liturgical church leaders. Probably most of the Germans he contacted were Americanizers in the legislature, and freethinkers outside who represented a small but extremely articulate anticlerical element in the German community. Not until the Lutheran churches noticed the new law did controversy begin. The politicians, therefore, were caught completely by surprise by the sudden involvement of a powerful new group in public affairs, the German priests and ministers.

The reaction of the Germans astounded the politicians by its ferocity, which exceeded even the antiprohibition reaction in the 1870s. Doubtless the temperance movement simmering beneath the surface of Wisconsin politics sensitized the liturgical elements to pietistic attacks on their way of life. But the Bennett law cut far deeper than the question of beer-drinking; it threatened the fundamental values of church, family, and language.[71] Unlike the prohibition battles, in which the liturgical churches never took *official* positions on public issues, the assault on the Bennett law enlisted the full and vigorous support of all the liturgical German church bodies. The liturgical churchmen for the first time in midwestern history assumed a role in public affairs that their pietistic counterparts had long played—they led their people to the ballot box arrayed in the armor of Christian wrath.[72]

Although the counterattack of the liturgical forces resembled

71. One long-run result of the battle was a determined effort by Lutherans to enlarge their English-language work, especially in their parochial schools. Suelflow, *Walking With Wise Men,* pp. 141–46; J. C. Jensen, "The Problem of Holding the Young, and How the United Norwegian Lutheran Church is Solving It," *Lutheran Church Review* (1897) 16:412–21.

72. One Lutheran paper noted, "Methodists, Presbyterians and Congregationalists ought to be the last ones to tender complaint at the supposed fact that the Lutheran Church has entered the field of politics. [They] have been in the field long before." *Lutheran Witness* (December 21, 1890) 9:106. A recent, sympathetic historian of the Missouri Synod has suggested the Bennett conflict "marks the coming out of by far the largest segment of Wisconsin Lutherans into the mainstream of American politics." Suelfow, *Walking With Wise Men,* p. 125. Nevertheless very few liturgical German Lutherans became regular politicians, then or later.

pietistic crusades in terms of organizational tactics, it differed radically from the crusading style. A crusade is basically a mobilization of moralistic (especially pietistic) common citizens, regardless of party, against a monstrous, nebulous, conspiratorial threat of corruption of power. Crusaders believe that evil men control the government, either openly or covertly, and must be exposed and destroyed by democracy's weapons—a free press, free assembly, and an independent vote. Although some German leaders sensed the existence of a nationwide nativistic conspiracy in 1889, they did not conduct their 1890 campaign as a crusade against evil Yankees. Indeed they threw their votes to a Democratic party dominated by Yankees like Vilas and Peck. And at no time did the Germans entertain plans to form a third party (crusaders always talk in terms of either starting a new party or taking over an old one). Crusaders, furthermore, devote special attention to the personal moral qualifications of the men they vote for. In 1890 the Germans almost completely avoided the personal qualifications of Hoard and Peck. Peck himself was in no way a crusader; he attended to the affairs of the Milwaukee city hall throughout the campaign and, although he was an accomplished orator, he did not even make campaign speeches in his own behalf.

The anti-Bennett campaign was not a crusade but a countercrusade. Hoard was the crusader—the amateur politician rallying the people in their righteousness to prevent the corruption of public education and smite the evil of priestly control of Wisconsin politics. Crusades have excited American elections ever since the Federalists attacked the Republicans in 1798 as secret allies of the French enemy. The Jeffersonian Republicans promptly counterattacked, charging in the Kentucky and Virginia Resolutions that the Federalists were dangerous men perverting the Constitution. Ever since, the best strategy for a countercrusade has been to attack the crusaders not as evil creatures but as reckless fanatics, as radicals who threaten to upset the tranquility of society by foolish panaceas and dangerous laws. Thus the Democrats attacked Frémont and Goldwater, and thus the Republicans attacked Greeley and Bryan. Such was the German strategy in 1890. They did not propose a panacea, or a moral cleansing of politics, or organize a permanent movement to change society. Rather they used a temporary expedient to repeal a single law and punish the party re-

147

sponsible so thoroughly that it would never again infringe upon their cultural rights. The Germans did not all switch to the Democratic party (which crusaders would have done), but they did abandon the GOP. The Republicans did learn their lesson, but a generation later a war between the German Empire and the United States would inexorably tear open old wounds and pit immigrant against American.

In Illinois the reaction to the Edwards law nearly equalled the Wisconsin maelstrom. The Democrats carried their ticket by 10,000 votes out of nearly 700,000 cast. Raab, benefiting from the split tickets of Germans, defeated Edwards by a plurality of 34,000. The contest had been clouded somewhat in Illinois, as in every midwestern state, by confusion over the mood of the organized farmers. Five farmers' associations claimed 62,000 members in 2,200 clubs in Illinois alone, and supposedly had their greatest strength in Michigan.[73] A local leader in Wisconsin explained to Congressman Haugen the mood of one group, the Farmers' Alliance:

> We feel that we are compelled to do something to protect ourselves as Farmers. The major part of Bussiness out side of ours are not only protecting their interests but are and have been forming Trusts and Combinations against the Farmer and our only remedy is the ballot-Box if we can Elect Representatives that will work for our interest we *will*. There has been to much Legeslation in favor of Capital and we will work hard to Elect men that will Rrepresent us.[74]

Were the farmers demanding an end to government by interest groups or were they asking for fairer representation of their own interests? No one was quite sure exactly what the farmers wanted, or the extent to which the exaggerated demands of various farm

73. To play the numbers game, see Robert V. Scott, *The Agrarian Movement in Illinois: 1880–1896* (Urbana, 1962), p. 61; cf. *Chicago Tribune,* October 21, 1891.

74. P. L. Scritsmier to N. P. Haugen, October 10, 1890, Haugen MSS. The author (who doesn't mention the Bennett law), was president of the eighty-one-member Sand Creek Farmers Alliance, Local No. 80. There were very few letters in this vein from farmers to politicians.

"leaders" and "spokesmen" represented the true mood of the agrarian Midwest. Bad weather conditions in 1890 produced poor crops and high prices, the latter absorbing many farmers' complaints. Prices had been considered relatively low for some years, but there was no upsurge of rural hardship, and foreclosures of mortgages were rare. What rural hardship existed in the nation was mostly concentrated in the wheat and cotton states, and there the Farmers' Alliances controlled the Populist movement, and usually formed coalitions with a major party. In the six midwestern states, the People's party appeared only on the Indiana ballot, but won less than 4 percent of the vote. The new Patrons of Industry party polled only 3 percent of the Michigan vote, but displayed impressive strength in the several pietistic Yankee areas. Elsewhere the proto-populists gained from 0.2 percent to 2.3 percent of the total vote, and in Illinois they did not even run a state ticket.[75]

Most of the farmers' groups maintained neutrality in 1890, but local clubs often endorsed candidates, and occasionally supported independents. In Illinois, major party candidates endorsed by local agrarian groups ran about even with their tickets, and the independents trailed even the Prohibitionist vote. The peculiarities of the Illinois system of multiple voting for assembly candidates did, however, result in the election of three Farmers' Mutual Benefit Association candidates who had garnered major party backing.

In the legislature these three held the balance of power between 101 Democrats and 100 Republicans, who were grappling to elect a United States senator. For weeks the backstage maneuvering continued, and the three FMBA men refused to join the Republicans in voting for the state president of their Association. They also resisted the efforts of a Cook County judge, John Altgeld,

75. The midwestern Populists were less significant and interesting than the Prohibitionists, but for sentimental reasons have attracted more scholarly attention. For Illinois, see Scott, *Agrarian Movement,* and Chester McA. Destler, *American Radicalism: 1865–1901* (New London, Conn., 1946); and his "The People's Party in Illinois: 1888–1896" (Ph.D. diss. University of Chicago, 1932); for Indiana, Ernest Stewart, "The Populist Party in Indiana," *Indiana Magazine of History* (1918) 14:332–67; for Iowa, Herman Nixon, "The Populist Movement in Iowa," *Iowa Journal of History* (1926) 24:3–107; and for Michigan, Sidney Glazer, "The Patrons of Industry in Michigan," *Mississippi Valley Historical Review* (1937) 24:185–94. Generally, see John Hicks, *The Populist Revolt* (Minneapolis, 1931), and Fred Haynes, *James Baird Weaver* (Iowa City, 1919).

to buy the Senate seat for himself. Finally, betraying the hopes and shattering the illusions of many farmers, two of the three voted with the Democrats to elect a conservative, John Palmer. The apparent perfidy of the three disgraced all the farmers' groups in Illinois, and they promptly disintegrated. Thus ended the most successful venture of the organized midwestern farmers in playing politics.[76]

The prevalence of "local" disturbing factors, education and prohibition, frustrated the GOP's attempt to wage the 1890 campaign on national issues. In Ohio, however, the Republicans had their opportunity to justify the tariff and the Harrison administration. The Democratic legislature had gerrymandered the congressional districts to guarantee a lopsided victory for them even if the Republicans carried the state. William McKinley's district, in the industrialized northeastern part of the state, came in for special attention. Holmes County, which had never gone Republican, replaced one of McKinley's old counties, and, with other clever changes, the new district was guaranteed for a 2,000 or 3,000 Democratic plurality; not since 1872 had the district displayed a Republican plurality.

William McKinley, chairman of the House Ways and Means Committee, was the Republican spokesman on the tariff, and a rising young star in the party. With no presidential race in 1890, his bid for reelection was the center of national attention. McKinley's friends, and his party, rallied to his aid. To his district flocked the statesmen and the hacks, the field marshalls and the privates. Speaker Reed came, and Secretary of State Blaine, and Senator Sherman; President Harrison himself made five speeches in the district.[77] From Birmingham, England, came Consul John Jarrett, the former head of the iron and steel workers' union, to plead with his friends that McKinleyism meant protection for the American worker. But most of all there was McKinley himself, the

76. On the confused activities of the farm groups in the 1890 campaign, Scott, *Agrarian Movement,* pp. 89–101; on the senatorial debacle, ibid., pp. 102–18; and Harry Barnard, *Eagle Forgotten* (New York, 1938), pp. 144–47; and *Chicago Tribune,* October 15–17, 1892.

77. Harrison made twenty-three appearances in early October in the Midwest. For his ostensibly "nonpolitical" speeches on the tour, see Charles Hedges, ed., *Speeches of Benjamin Harrison* (New York, 1892), pp. 234–86, esp. 280–86.

tireless campaigner. In a month of stumping he delivered fifty-one major speeches, traveled thousands of miles, seeing nearly every one of his district's 2,000 square miles and 40,000 voters. Praising their modern farms, luxurious flocks, rich coal mines and active mills, McKinley assured his constituents that the new tariff

> was framed for the people of the United States as a defense to their industries, as a protection to the labor of their hands, as a safeguard to the happy homes of American workmen, and as a security to their education, their wages and their investments. . . . It will bring to this country a prosperity unparalleled in our own history and unrivalled in the history of the world.[78]

The Ohio Democrats were determined to destroy McKinley, and they did not rely on gerrymandering alone. Into the district came Governor Hill of New York, Congressman Neal, Governor Campbell, and the workhorse of the party, Texas Congressman Roger Mills. Grover Cleveland, annoyed that his foe Hill was around, refused to come, but encouraged the voters to turn out their rabid protectionist.

To oppose McKinley the Democrats nominated the most distinguished man available, former lieutenant governor John Warwick, a rich capitalist and coal-mine operator. Warwick's speeches, ranging from 17 to 149 words long, went unnoticed, but he did not need oratory. The Democrats had supporters of the tariff on the defensive. Young party workers peddled wagonloads of tinware from house to house, asking fifty cents for twenty-five-cent items, and explained to dismayed housewives that McKinley's new tariff had doubled the price of tin. The Republicans, who long had hoped that a protective tariff on wool would woo the sheep farmers, countered by buying flocks of sheep at double their value.[79] But it was no use. The nation's importers, jobbers, wholesalers, local storekeepers, and legitimate pushcart peddlers exploited the passage of the new tariff law in early October to raise their prices across the board, even on goods not covered in the bill. One New

78. Speech August 26, 1890, at Orrville, in *Speeches and Addresses of William McKinley* (New York, 1893), p. 464. On the campaign, see *Chicago Tribune*, October 8, 9, November 4, 1890; *Cincinnati Enquirer*, October 27, 1890.
79. *Chicago Tribune*, November 10, 1890.

York merchant explained that the new, higher duties, "affect all classes of dry goods, and particularly the lower grades or cheaper qualities, such as the poorer classes require."[80] The sweetener in the bill, free sugar, would not go into effect for six more months; and, the Republicans suddenly realized, the long-term benefits to the economy would come long after the short-run disgust with higher prices. In the long run, they might all be politically dead.

Everywhere the Democrats explained that the price rises were tributes to the greedy monopolists benefited by the corrupt law, with the result, as Speaker Reed discovered:

> The Democracy has one great advantage. . . . The republican party does things; the Democratic party finds fault. It follows from the very necessity of achievement that the Republican party must take positive ground on some known spot of the earth. The Democrats are free then to skirmish through all creation. Of course that gives them during the early part of the conflict the appearance of occupying the earth.[81]

McKinley very nearly did the impossible. Election night showed him holding a narrow lead; only the late returns from rural German districts reversed the totals and gave Warwick the district by three hundred votes. Everywhere McKinley's impressive showing was hailed as a moral victory of the first magnitude (there not being any real Republican triumphs that year), and he became the obvious candidate for governor in 1891, and a major prospect for president in 1892 or 1896.[82] The McKinley campaign boosted the GOP back into power in Ohio. Although the gerrymander gave the Democrats fourteen of Ohio's twenty-one congressional districts, the GOP polled a statewide majority of 11,000, elected its state ticket, and made Cincinnati a Republican stronghold again. Not for twenty years would the Democrats carry Ohio.

Nationally, however, the elections of 1890 constituted a massive Republican debacle, and made the party an almost hopeless underdog in the 1892 presidential election. The sources of the landslide were complex. The record of the "billion-dollar" Congress was

80. Ibid., October 6, 18, 1890.
81. Chicago speech, text in *Chicago Tribune,* October 25, 1890.
82. See H. Wayne Morgan, *William McKinley and His America* (Syracuse, 1963), pp. 148–51.

a heavy burden, and the McKinley tariff a smashing blow. Yet in Ohio and Iowa, where the Republicans focused all their attention on the tariff and national issues, they recaptured ground lost in 1889, although still falling short of their 1888 achievement. The tariff issue gave the Democrats a psychological boost in the last month of the campaign; coupled with the disorganization of the Republican party machinery and Harrison's dreary image, it boxed the Republicans into a hopeless corner. Yet the basic weakness of the GOP was its shelter for the pietistic reformers who harped on divisive cultural issues. The party weakened all along the line, but especially among the immigrants. Only if the professionals could curb the moralistic crusading of the amateurs, or if sudden new issues would appear, could the GOP recover control of the Midwest and the nation.

6

From Battlefield to Marketplace:
Transition in Electioneering Style

> The Democratic Party is willing to
> trust the ordinary intelligence of
> our people for an understanding of
> its principles. . . . Therefore the
> labor of their education in the
> campaign has consisted in persuad-
> ing them to hear us; to examine
> the theories in party organizations
> and the ends to which they lead; to
> recall the promises of political
> leadership and the manner in which
> such promises have been redeemed;
> and to counsel with us as to the
> means by which their condition
> could be improved.
>
> Grover Cleveland[1]

The upheaval of 1890 taught the Republican leaders that the GOP needed restyling. Victory demanded the abandoning of losing positions, revamping the party organization, and developing more effective campaign techniques. In 1891 two midwestern gubernatorial campaigns attracted national attention as indicators of the dilemma and the hope of the Republican party. The Iowa GOP again marched behind the pure white banner of prohibition, and suffered the worst defeat in its history. In Ohio William McKinley was in command as the nominee for governor. Defeat would destroy his ambitions; victory would revitalize his party.

The Democratic incumbent, Governor James Campbell, was an able, ambitious, and ruthless politician; the national convention of 1892 might look favorably on the man who finally destroyed the prophet of the protective tariff. The canvass was the most thorough Ohio had known since 1875. Campbell did not shy from the attack. He ridiculed Republican claims that in six months the tariff of 1890 had fostered a great new tinplate industry, raised American wages and developed new jobs for American workingmen. Opening

---

1. George Parker, ed., *The Writings and Speeches of Grover Cleveland* (New York, 1892), p. 261, speech of December 23, 1890.

his debate with McKinley, Campbell warned that the American way of life was endangered by the protective tariff:

> With the enormous increase in living necessities, with the daily reductions in the wages of workingmen and women, with the yearly depreciation in agricultural lands, and the growing unprofitableness of farming . . . with the pallid wives and children of starving miners reduced to destitution that protection may be maintained and greater profits flow into the coffers of the coal barons, already wallowing in wealth . . . with those who are sometimes well termed rotten rich defying the people and seeking from a venal press to destroy the reputation and the honor of the estate of one that may wage war too vigorously in the cause of the people. . . . [We] protest against the crimes that are committed in the name of protection.[2]

Campbell thus opened a crusade against the corruption wrought by the tariff and its leading proponent. Futhermore, Campbell ridiculed the "imported Huns, Italians, Bohemians, usurping the places of American freemen." The McKinley tariff, he went on, while its author sat quietly on the same stage, had indeed benefited one domestic industry, the manufacture of window glass. "Go to Fosoria and Findlay," the Governor suggested, "and see who makes the window glass. Mostly Belgians, unnaturalized aliens, who come to Castle Garden, New York, without vex or hindrance." The fervent low-tariff man then pledged he would put "a prohibitive tariff . . . on all aliens who came here without the intention to become an American citizen."[3]

Campbell's crusading fervor probably upset McKinley but did not surprise him, for the Democrats had grown increasingly vituperative on the tariff issue since their defeat in 1888. McKinley, in countercrusading style, stressed the extremism of the opposition and the moderation of his own position: "I am not here to preach the gospel of dissatisfaction, discontent and despair. Thank God, the Republican party never taught such a doctrine. Ours is the

2. *Cincinnati Commercial-Gazette,* October 9, 1891.
3. Ibid. The Window Glass Workers union favored high tariffs, so Campbell was appealing to their fear of "invasion" by "the cheap labor of Europe." See the union leaders' remarks to McKinley in 1896, in Joseph Smith, ed., *McKinley, The People's Choice* (Canton, 1896), pp. 57–58.

doctrine of hope, and cheer." Crusading moralism would no longer be tolerated in the Ohio GOP, he implied, thus pointing the way to the reconstruction of the entire party. Moving to the tariff, he explained that it was a

> question of individual as well as of National prosperity. It is a question of whether we shall have industrial independence in this country, as one of the great manufacturing nations of the world, furnishing employment to labor and giving a home market for the products of our farms, or whether we shall rely solely for our manufacturing goods on foreign countries, and looking exclusively to foreign lands for a market for our surplus goods.[4]

McKinley rejected the counsel of the moralistic reformers but, to soothe their ire, appealed strongly to American nationalism and to the dream of a rich, self-sufficient America freed from the vicissitudes of Europe. McKinley was not dallying with nativism; he was welcoming the European immigrant to come and take part in America's destiny.

The next day, at Findlay, Ohio, McKinley carefully refuted Campbell's calumnies against the glass and pottery workers of the city. Ohio wage rates, he demonstrated, were three to six times higher than the wages for the same skills in Belgium; only 10 percent of the Findlay glass workers were Belgians, and nearly all had become citizens.[5] Tirelessly, McKinley stumped the state, expounding his vision of America's industrial future, and explaining the necessity of a protective tariff. He envisioned a pluralistic society in which all groups—ethnic, religious, occupational—could live together in harmony, cooperating for the common good under the benign protection of his tariff. Crusades against any segment of society were unnecessary and harmful. Throughout September and October he appeared before increasingly large and enthusiastic audiences of farmers, mechanics, businessmen, and tradesmen. McKinley brought his case to the people, and few prominent Democrats dared journey to Ohio to challenge him; one of the few was Roger Mills. The Republicans knew Mills well by now, and joked that "in his attempts to discourage the tariff sentiment in this state,

4. *Cincinnati Commercial-Gazette,* October 9, 1891.
5. Ibid., October 10, 1891.

[he] is working rather for the Mills of Texas than for the mills of Ohio."[6]

McKinley's enemies split on the currency issue. Over strong opposition Campbell defeated a resolution favoring "honest money" at the state convention, and injected into the platform a denunciation of the "Crime of '73" and a demand for the "free and unlimited coinage" of silver.[7] The Ohio Democrats had long been torn by the demands of the hard and soft money men, and McKinley himself had long supported bimetallism (although he never had declared for the free coinage of silver, and certainly not at sixteen to one). Reversing his stand, McKinley attacked Campbell's platform and called for sound money. "Sound money," then and in 1896 when the silver issue achieved paramount attention, did not preclude the coinage of silver, and it allowed for the establishment of bimetallism on an international basis; what it clearly emphasized was the primacy of gold as the backing for both specie and paper currency.[8]

The campaign of 1891 was unusually long and hard-fought. But the dirty tactics cherished by connoisseurs of Ohio politics remained unused. Like most state campaigns it was contested on national issues: tariffs and money. McKinley ran 13,000 votes ahead of his ticket, but so exciting was the gubernatorial campaign that Campbell ran 19,000 ahead of his. McKinley, the "Napoleon of protection," won by 21,500 votes, and reversed the narrow Democratic control of the legislature to a two-thirds Republican majority. The Republicans retained approximately the share of the vote they received in 1889 and 1890, while the Democrats lost about 3 points, largely to the Populists in rural areas. There were no dramatic realignments of voting patterns, but William McKinley was now the hero of the Grand Old Party, and was clearly destined for its presidential nomination.

6. Ibid., September 27, 1891 (editorial); on McKinley's tour, see October 7 and September 19, 1891. On the campaign generally, *Ann. Cycl. 1891*: 692–93; *Chicago Tribune*, October 3, 9, 10, 16, 25, 31, 1891; and Roger Van Bolt, "The Gubernatorial Campaign of 1891 in Ohio," (M.A. thesis, Ohio State Univ., 1946). For speeches, see *Speeches and Addresses of William McKinley* (New York, 1893), pp. 523–63; and John Sherman, *Recollections of Forty Years* (Chicago, 1895), 2:1108–40.

7. *Ann. Cycl. 1891*: 692–93.

8. *Nation* (September 24, 1891) 53:229; compare *McKinley Speeches*, pp. 454–55 with 525–27 and 538–44.

Ohio had to be the model for the 1892 Republican campaign. With Pennsylvania, it was the only major state where the Republicans had avoided or recovered from major electoral disaster, and McKinley had demonstrated the efficacy of a well-organized, tariff-centered campaign that avoided antagonizing immigrants and that successfully met the money issue. In Iowa, of course, Boies and the Democrats were piling up unprecedented margins and giving clear warning of the reefs that might again sink Republican hopes.

In 1892 the Iowa GOP learned, too. It reached a modus vivendi which postponed the showdown on prohibition and kept that divisive issue out of the 1892 campaign.[9] By avoiding dry talk (and avoiding trouble on compulsory education), the Republicans felt confident they could prevent further erosion of their German support. To win back lost German votes, a new issue was necessary; a glimmer of hope appeared in the issue of money. Every politician realized, though none could say precisely why, that the Germans, of every religious persuasion, staunchly opposed all inflationary schemes. The Germans "are naturally Republicans on the great financial questions whose principal proponent you are," Iowa GOP chairman James Blythe wrote Senator Sherman.[10] And out of Ohio politics came the specific issue the GOP hungered for.

Bank notes, the Democratic inflationists believed, were too scarce. Since the Civil War a prohibitive 10 percent federal tax on currency issued by state banks left only the national banks in the business of printing money. At the Democratic convention in 1892, at the recommendation of the Ohio delegation, a plank favoring the repeal of the 10 percent tax was written into the platform upon which Grover Cleveland again ran for president.[11] The GOP had its opportunity, and McKinley opened the assault. The seemingly innocuous proposal, thundered the new governor of Ohio, "would be a thousand times more harmful, more destructive to business and trade, more disastrous to every interest, than the free and unlimited coinage of silver—bad as that would be."[12] In Iowa the Repub-

9. See chapter 7 for details.

10. James Blythe to John Sherman, September 28, 1892, in Sherman MSS, Library of Congress.

11. George Knoles, *The Presidential Campaign and Election of 1892* (Stanford, 1942), p. 83; *Nation* (October 6, 1892) 55:253–54.

12. *McKinley Speeches*, p. 614, from Philadelphia speech of September 23, 1892.

licans shouted their awkward new slogan, "HONEST MONEY—must be saved next Tuesday or 'wildcat' will return to impoverish you!"[13]

"Hard-money" Cleveland, however, had no intention of yielding to the inflationists in his party. His letter of acceptance (his chief campaign statement) simply avoided the banknote tax and the unusually ambiguous currency plank also passed by the Democratic convention.[14] However, Cleveland's running mate, Adlai Stevenson of Illinois, an old inflationist, was considered unsound on the money issue. To divert the mounting Republican assault on the inflationist peril of the banknote tax repeal, Cleveland prepared Stevenson's letter of acceptance, which, "without reservation or qualification," committed the Illinois silverite to "sound, honest money."[15]

Success rewarded the Republican efforts in Iowa—Harrison captured the thirteen electoral votes with a handsome plurality of 24,000, and his party unseated five of the six Democratic congressmen. In Dubuque, the GOP increased its share of the German vote (in the Fifth Ward) to 37 percent, up sharply from 23 percent in 1891, and nearly matching the 40 percent obtained in 1875 before the prohibition battle. In the fourteen most German counties of Iowa, the GOP vote moved up from 37 percent in 1891 to 41 percent in 1892. In Wisconsin, too, the Republicans bounced back in German esteem, although they failed to erase all the losses of 1890. (See tables 11 and 12 in chapter five.)

The Wisconsin GOP wanted to bury the Bennett law imbroglio. Half the Republican legislators joined with the Democrats in 1891 to repeal the law. In 1892, two Republican state conventions de-

13. *Iowa State Register,* November 4, 1892; see also Sherman, *Recollections* 2:1171, 1173; Walter Nydegger, "The Election of 1892 in Iowa," *Iowa Journal of History* (1927) 25:429; *New York Tribune,* October 11, 19, 1892, for speeches of Sherman and Foraker.

14. Knoles, *1892 Election,* pp. 174–75; R. W. Gilder to Grover Cleveland, September 2, 1892, in Grover Cleveland papers, Library of Congress; Alfred D. Noyes, *Thirty Years of American Finance* (New York, 1902), pp. 177–78. For the text of Cleveland's letter see *Chicago Daily News Almanac for 1893* (Chicago, 1893), p. 164; *Literary Digest* (November 5, 1892) 6:22–24.

15. Knoles, *1892 Election,* pp. 213–15; George Parker, *Recollections of Grover Cleveland* (New York, 1909), pp. 169–71; *New York Times,* October 31, 1892.

clared the issue permanently settled, warned that further agitation would be harmful, and nominated an opponent of the law, former Senator John Spooner, for governor. Spooner tried to direct the attention of the Germans to the banknote tax, but his adversaries were not yet through with the German vote. Aided by generous contributions from Milwaukee breweries and two rich New York Germans, Henry Villard and Joseph Pulitzer, Democratic Chairman Edward Wall refueled his campaign against the "anti-foreigner Republicans."[16]

Wisconsin's German Lutherans squirmed restlessly in the small niche assigned to them in the Democratic party. Some complained that they were considered "only good enough to elect Irish and Polish Catholics to office."[17] Wall pressured Governor George Peck to appoint more Germans and Norwegians to lucrative patronage posts. But when Senator William Vilas, to keep the Lutherans happy, opposed the presentation of a statue of Pere Marquette to the national Capitol, Wall hastily intervened to avoid alienating the Catholics. The alleged anti-Catholicism shown by the Harrison administration's handling of missionary activities among western Indians further aided the Democrats, despite Harrison's choice of a Catholic as Republican national chairman in the summer of 1892. It was a trying challenge to yoke Lutherans and Catholics, but Wall and Vilas succeeded by harping on the dead Bennett law.[18]

As in Wisconsin, so too in Illinois did the school controversy rage in 1892. John Peter Altgeld, the Democratic nominee for governor, concentrated his campaign on the German Lutheran vote, with great success, thus establishing the Democratic model for 1894; but that story is best told in connection with the con-

16. *Daily News Almanac for 1893*, pp. 154–55; *Ann. Cycl. 1892:* 810; Horace Merrill, *William Freeman Vilas* (Madison, 1954), pp. 188–95; Dorothy Fowler, *John Coit Spooner* (New York, 1961), p. 165; *Milwaukee Sentinel,* November 2, 1892; *Chicago Herald,* November 2, 1892.
17. C. F. Huth to W. F. Vilas, February 6, 1893, in Vilas MSS, Wisconsin State Historical Society.
18. Merrill, *Vilas,* pp. 188–95; M. Justille McDonald, *History of the Irish in Wisconsin* (Washington, 1954), pp. 181–84; Donald Kinzer, *An Episode in Anti-Catholicism* (Seattle, 1964), pp. 66–67. On the Indian school question, see ibid., pp. 74–78, and Harry Sievers, "The Catholic Indian School Issue and the Presidential Election of 1892," *Catholic Historical Review* (1952) 38:129–55.

troversy over the nativist societies that achieved greatest notoriety in 1894.

In 1892 Altgeld won the governorship, and Cleveland became the first Democrat since Buchanan to receive Illinois' electoral votes (twenty years later, Woodrow Wilson would be the second). Rebounding from their defeat in 1890, downstate Republicans elected five congressmen, but lost control of the state senate. The major shift in voting patterns came in burgeoning Chicago. Harrison had barely carried Cook County in 1888, but in 1892, with 50 percent more votes cast there, Cleveland swept the county by 33,000 votes. In the seventeen most heavily German wards in Chicago, Harrison averaged only 36 percent of the vote, but even in the other wards he averaged only 49 percent. Mayor Washburne, a Republican, complained that his party would have regained the German vote if only it had successfully exploited the banknote issue. As it was, the powerful Chicago trade unions rallied the Germans to Altgeld and Cleveland. Another Republican suggested that the nomination of Whitelaw Reid for vice president antagonized many union leaders in Chicago and around the country. Furthermore, he noted, the agonies of the Homestead strike that summer convinced laborers that the protective tariff was not the panacea that they had once believed, at least not for the workingman.[19]

For the successful exploitation of cultural and religious tensions by some Democrats, the Republicans had only their moralistic adherents to blame. Increasingly the Democrats charged collusion between the GOP leadership and various nativistic and anti-Catholic groups. The accusations usually displayed more exaggeration than fairness, yet too often the cautious Republican professionals hesitated to repudiate the vicious slanders that lent credence to the Democratic charges. In 1894 the issue, under the "APA" banner, would come to a head; meanwhile the Democrats took full advantage of the Republican vulnerability.

The GOP, although whipped in 1890, was neither demolished nor blinded. With the presidency and many governorships still in their control, the Republicans restructured their party and revolu-

19. *Chicago Times,* November 7, 10, 1892.

tionized their thinking about elections. The restructuring process almost foundered in the struggle between Harrison and the national committee for control of the party. Secretary of State Blaine, Senator Quay of Pennsylvania, Senator Platt of New York, Clarkson of Iowa, McKinley, Hanna, and Foraker of Ohio, and many other state and county leaders discovered that their president exuded the warmth and charm of an iceberg. The professionals sympathized with Harrison's apparent goal of strengthening the professionals in the party organization at the expense of the amateurs, but distrusted the president's methods. Harrison's inability to establish cordial working relationships with his party's leaders did not in itself bring ruin; trouble came with the distribution of patronage.

The chief font of national patronage was the post office. Clarkson, as first assistant postmaster general, handled the chore of removing incumbents, and relied heavily on the recommendations of Republican congressmen for replacements. In the Midwest alone there were 820 presidential postmasterships in the larger towns and cities, carrying total salaries of nearly $1,400,000 annually. A survey of 437 removals, nationwide, showed 427 of the replacees were Democrats; of 513 new appointees, 510 were Republicans. Fully two-thirds of the new men had been active in the presidential campaign of 1888, especially as editors. The burden of refusing applicants for the postal plums troubled the local Republican congressmen, who found that careful recommendations would strengthen their control of the local party organization and simultaneously alienate enough disappointed men to weaken their reelection prospects. Happy, and rare, was the congressman battling for reelection unhindered by hometown factional squabbles.[20]

The blatant use of the postal service for party reorganization alienated most of those midwestern Mugwumps who had supported Cleveland in 1884 and switched to Harrison in 1888. They were noisy—Teddy Roosevelt spoke for them, although he was not one

20. *Tribune Almanac for 1891* (New York, 1891), p. 157; W. D. Foulke, "Fifth Report of the Special Committee of the National Civil Service Reform League," *Civil Service Chronicle* (1890) 1:75, 186. See also Stanley Hirshson, "James S. Clarkson and the Civil Service Reformers, 1889–1893," *Iowa Journal of History* (1959) 57:267–78; Dorothy Fowler, *The Cabinet Politician* (New York, 1943), pp. 213–18; and Frank Hickenlooper, *History of Monroe County, Iowa* (Albia, Iowa, 1898), pp. 163–64.

of their number—but they controlled few votes. Politically disastrous, however, was Harrison's handling of his other major patronage choices. Besieged by office-seekers in the traditional manner from the moment of his election, the new president begged for patience. "The Senators and Representatives," he grumbled, "appear to think that the President of the United States has nothing else to do but to fill the offices."[21] Actually, Harrison was keenly concerned with the problem, and devoted much of his time to it. But unable to assuage the discontent of the disappointed, and sometimes losing even the friendship of the men whose requests were granted, Harrison succeeded in factionalizing instead of unifying the party.

Patronage, Harrison felt, ought to be distributed equitably. Mathematical precision was his goal; lopsided imbalance the result. Indiana and New York, the two most doubtful states, received far more than their share of patronage, especially at the prestigious cabinet, subcabinet, ambassadorial, and consular levels. Harrison apparently wanted to equalize the ratios of each state's Republican vote to its share of the patronage (as measured by summing salaries). Harrison's friends did not make exorbitant demands (he did not have many friends). Rather he was using the patronage to weaken his enemies, who usually were the most talented leaders and organizers in the party. By putting his own men in power, the president sought to split enough local organizations away from the control of his enemies to guarantee himself renomination in 1892. Speaker Reed complained that he had only two political enemies in Maine; Harrison released one from the penitentiary, and appointed the other port collector at Portland. Harrison's strategy worked. At the 1892 convention, federal officeholders swarmed in unprecedented numbers, the president's enemies were overwhelmed, and Harrison was nominated on the first ballot. A clever strategy, but a greedy one, and Harrison paid dearly for it in November, 1892; his party paid in November of 1889, 1890, and 1891 as well.[22]

21. Interview with *Philadelphia Inquirer,* quoted in *Indianapolis Journal,* April 22, 1889.
22. On Harrison's precision, see his letter to George Steele, October 16, 1889, in Benjamin Harrison papers, Library of Congress (series 1, microfilm reel 23); J. Blaine to Harrison, April 21, 1892, in A. T. Volwiler, ed., *The Correspondence of Benjamin Harrison and James G. Blaine* (Philadel-

The Pension Office, too, threatened to become a grievous liability to the Republicans. The Fifty-first Congress did pass a pension bill in 1890, but the benefits were reserved for veterans over sixty and those unable to earn a living except by common labor. The stinginess did not suit thousands of expectant veterans, and their sulkiness did not help the GOP in the fall elections. The moral sensibilities of the reform-minded, moreover, cringed before the spectacle of Harrison's first pension commissioner, none other than Corporal ("God help the surplus!") Tanner. After six months Tanner was out (he joined the swelling GOP opposition), but his successor did not elevate the character of the office.[23]

The pension act of 1890 may not have satisfied the able-bodied veterans, but a great many men soon found themselves sufficiently "disabled" to obtain the $6 to $12 monthly checks. Fewer than 200,000 pensions went to the Midwest when Harrison entered the White House; by campaign time, 1892, the number approached a third of a million men and widows, collecting $50 million a year.[24] The beneficiaries of Republican largesse, and their families, agents, and attorneys, remembering how testily Cleveland had vetoed their succor, may not have been quite so hostile to candidate Harrison as their professional GOP neighbors.

Patronage and pensions were only supplementary to the 1892 campaign, but they presaged a revolution in the strategic thinking of the top professional leadership. In typical campaigns up through 1888, the candidates and their managers thought in military terms. The election was conceived as a great battle pitting the strength of two opposing armies and the genius of their generals, with the spoils of victory being patronage positions and the seats of power.

phia, 1940), pp. 261–69; *Chicago Tribune,* April 1, 3, 1889; and Harry Sievers, *Benjamin Harrison* (Indianapolis, 1968), 3:41–50, 174. On the 1892 Republican convention, see Knoles, *1892 Election,* pp. 34–73, esp. 68–70; Robert Marcus, *Grand Old Party: Political Structure in the Gilded Age, 1880–1896* (New York, 1971), pp. 159–74; Lucius Swift, "A Review of Two Administrations," *Forum* (1892) 14:208–15; and *Civil Service Chronicle* (1892) 1:334–48, 376–82, with lists of names.

23. Mary Dearing, *Veterans in Politics* (Baton Rouge, 1952), pp. 392–400, 422–23, 426–35; Sievers, *Harrison,* 3:41–50. Cf. interview with Congressman William D. Bynum in *Indianapolis Sentinel,* October 11, 1889.

24. *Daily News Almanac for 1893,* p. 234; *Tribune Almanac 1891, p.* 113; *1893,* pp. 131–33; *1895,* pp. 147–49.

The parties were army-like organizations, tightly knit, disciplined, united. All the voters, save for a few stragglers and mercenaries, belonged to one or the other army, and the challenge of the campaign was the mobilization of the full party strength at the polls on election day. To heighten the morale of the troops, the generals employed brass-band parades, with banners, badges, torches and uniforms. Chanting sloganized battle cries, waving placards and flags, the rank and file marched for hours before smiling, waving politicians, who invariably thought the men would appreciate a two-hour speech.

Harrison's first presidential campaign was the epitome of the "army" style of campaigning. During his administration, the rise of cultural issues, prohibition and language especially, forced a radical reassessment of the traditional style. The liturgical Germans, in particular, had emerged as a large, cohesive block of voters that could swing from one party to the other in reaction to party pledges and platforms, and to the policies of the men in power. The Germans were organized and united, but not controlled; their reaction was practically spontaneous, and could not be quenched with heavy doses of patronage or subsidies. Similarly, the drys and the moralists were coming to assume such an independent stance. Again and again they urged pietists to lay aside old party loyalties and participate as independent, crusading citizens. The politicians began to realize that when issues that tapped loyalties stronger than party affiliation were abroad, it was necessary to appeal to the voters on a higher plane than a colorful rally would permit. Thus the platforms and slogans of the parties became less of a army-style device to encourage morale and more of an intellectual appeal to the needs and wants of the voters supplemented by direct, tangible benefits like pensions. The symbolic features of the party slogans and platforms, indeed, remained for the benefit of the old party faithful, but the new emphasis was on the man who might be swayed by intelligent argument. A fresh approach to elections based on advertising, the "merchandising" style, emerged.

The new style of campaigning implicitly compared with the parties to two stores competing for customers. The analogy with oligopolistic business competition, inspired by Harrison's choice of John Wanamaker, the most prominent retail merchant in the country, for postmaster general,[25] was not completely valid, however, for when two large companies compete for the same market they tend to stabilize their respective shares of the market and thus avoid cutthroat competition. The parties, on the other hand, strive constantly for a larger share of the "market" (the popular vote), although they do impose self-restraints on the type and extent of promises they offer to the electorate, and when they already have an overwhelming majority, they rarely try to destroy the opposition altogether. Nevertheless, both the mercantile and the political entrepreneurs intend to remain in business permanently, and thus they both develop certain codes or standards of personal probity. Fly-by-night operations or fraudulent business practices are exactly as despicable among businessmen as party irregularity or demagoguery among politicians. Business-minded politicians no longer lavish patronage, like spoils of war, on their oldest workers; they distribute it scientifically to their most effective publicists, especially editors.

The actual transition from the army to the merchandising style had begun by 1888, but not until 1892 did observers realize the startling changes underway. The *New York Herald,* finding in 1892 an "exceptional calmness," and "an unprecedented absence of noisy demonstrations, popular excitement and that high pressure enthusiasm which used to find vent in brass bands, drum and trumpet fanfaronade, boisterous parades by day and torchlight processions by night, vociferous hurrahs, campaign songs, barbecues and what not," announced that the campaign "indicates the dawn of a new era in American politics."[26]

Dissatisfaction with the army style first appeared in the Democratic camp in 1888. Rallies and parades, explained William Vilas to the Wisconsin state chairman, "stir up the other side almost as much as their own. The trumpet that sounds the note of battle, not only inspirits its friends, but awakes its enemies." Observing the proselytizing success achieved by the crusading drys and the Grangers with the tactic of schoolhouse meetings and prolonged discussions, Vilas recommended a program of "school district

---

25. Herbert Gibbons, *John Wanamaker* (New York, 1926), 1:270–75.
26. *New York Herald,* October 26, 1892 (editorial); see Knoles, *Election of 1892,* pp. 203, 222, 247.

speaking." The "simple ingratiation of sound education," he argued, would "tell for the gain of more voters . . . than all the rest of the campaign work together. Indeed, all the rest is simply to 'dress the ranks.' "[27]

Even more important in the transition of style than the theorizing of Vilas was the opinion of his close friend, Grover Cleveland. President Cleveland proudly initiated a "campaign of education" in 1887 to explain to the people the meaning of tariff reform. In 1888 he sought to apply the principle to his reelection campaign, and in a public letter clearly expressed the new style:

> We have undertaken to teach the voters, as free, independent citizens, intelligent enough to see their rights, interested enough to insist upon being being treated justly, and patriotic enough to desire their country's welfare.

> Thus this campaign is one of information and organization. Every citizen should be regarded as a thoughtful, responsible voter, and he should be furnished the means of examining the issues involved in the pending canvass for himself.[28]

The new style required a substantial redistribution of party resources and rhetorical emphasis. In line with the new principles, the Michigan, Wisconsin, and Illinois Democratic leaders spent all their available extra funds to extend the circulation of party newspapers, and as early as April, 1888, the Midwest regional office of the national committee sought capable speakers "to take part in the discussion, at local meetings and debates in the villages, towns, and country school districts." The effort to shift from rallies to intensive discussions probably reflected an awareness of the success temperance crusaders had had with schoolhouse meetings. A new National Association of Democratic Clubs attempted to coordinate the work of 500,000 activists in 3,000 clubhouses across the country. The national committee itself distributed millions of speeches and supplied boiler plate to more than 3,000 party

27. W. F. Vilas to E. B. Usher, March 20, 1888, in Usher MSS, Wisconsin State Historical Society; see Horace Merrill, *Bourbon Democracy in the Middle West* (Baton Rouge, 1953), pp. 190–91, and his *Vilas*, pp. 154–55.
28. G. Cleveland to C. F. Black, September 14, 1888, in Allan Nevins, ed., *Letters of Grover Cleveland* (Boston, 1933), p. 189. See also the speech of December 23, 1890, in Parker, *Speeches of Cleveland*, pp. 258, 259.

organs.[29] However, the Democrats started too late and suffered from the weak leadership of a national chairman still wedded to the army-style organization. The month before election day, furthermore, was a poor time to sell new ideas. Cleveland realized later that "the noise and excitement of a campaign are not conducive to the accomplishment of missionary work or the effective dissemination of political truth."[30]

The Democratic party in 1888 was too used to the old style to change overnight. Defeat that year shocked it, and in 1889 Horace Boies in Iowa was conducting a systematic reeducation of the people on the meaning of prohibition and protective tariffs. In 1890, nearly all the midwestern Democrats were hammering at the theoretical difficulties of the tariff, and, of course, at the Republican "threat" to the integrity of various cultural groups in Wisconsin and Illinois. In 1892 the Democratic campaign was wholly in the merchandising style. The Minnesota state chairman described the typical approach:

> Our general canvass is an open and manly "campaign of education." The appeal is made in earnest, argumentative words to the intelligence, judgment and conscience of the voter. We have not a uniformed club in the state; we have no torches; few brass bands; but the campaign is one of earnest argument.[31]

While the Minnesota Democrats may have adopted the new style for lack of money, the Democratic National Committee had a very large sum, about $2.5 million to spend. The doubtful states (especially those in the South threatened by Populism) received much of the money, but most went for speakers, literature, and advertising. In Wisconsin, chairman Wall had $70,000 to work with, not counting local and national funds spent there. In the two years before the election, Wall allocated his money for "speak-

---

29. W. J. Mize to Usher, April 24, 1888, for quote; I. M. Weston to Usher, March 21, 1888, in Usher MSS; *St. Louis Republic*, October 6, 14, 17, 1888; Festus P. Summers, *William L. Wilson and Tariff Reform* (New Brunswick, 1953), pp. 107–8; Knoles, *Election of 1892*, pp. 134–35.

30. Speech of October 21, 1889, in Parker, *Speeches of Cleveland*, pp. 287–88; S. Richmond to Usher, October 28, 1888, Neal Brown to Usher, November 7, 1888, in Usher MSS; Nevins, *Cleveland*, pp. 415–17.

31. Lewis Baker to G. Cleveland, September 16, 1892, in Grover Cleveland Papers (series 2, microfilm reel 71).

ers, travelling expenses, postage, express, telegraph bills, circulation of [25,000] newspapers [per week] . . . the printing of an immense number of documents; the care of the Lutheran department and the expenditures of that department."[32] Significantly, nothing went for the old-fashioned paraphernalia.

The new style was universal among midwestern Democrats in 1892. In Ohio, the Democratic leadership

> concluded that the better way to carry Ohio this fall is to do it by a quiet and vigorous organization and active campaign work, and not with a bluster of brass horns and blazing torches, but by seeing that every voter . . . has placed in his hands such papers as the New York Weekly and other documents relating to Tariff Reform and your [Cleveland's] late administration.[33]

In Illinois, while Altgeld was personally educating his German Lutheran friends in the horrors of Republicanism, the western branch of the Democratic National Committee, under dapper Benjamin Cable, had 14,000 men working in the field. They distributed 1.9 million documents in twelve languages among the state's 900,000 voters, and mailed another 2 million to five nearby states. Cable's 7000 Chicago workers spent $30,000 in naturalizing 16,000 new voters, and an office staff of 75 clerks typed 100,000 letters in English and German encouraging party activists across the Midwest to hammer harder at the GOP. It was the most massive advertising effort ever conducted in the Midwest before 1896.[34] Congressional candidates further educated their constituencies. Julius Goldzier, Democratic candidate for Congress in northern Cook County, for one, distributed 85,000 pamphlets and 100,000 cards, fliers and leaflets to explain the issues of the day to the 75,000 voters in the district. Goldzier no longer had to worry about bribery, but, as in every political campaign, the "bummers, strikers, touchers" and hangers-on wanted money. They got little. Instead, the $20,000 or more he spent went to circulate posters, portraits, and, especially, documents; to charity;

32. E. C. Wall to W. Vilas, November 30, 1892, in Vilas MSS.

33. B. J. Wade to G. Cleveland, September 21, 1892, in Grover Cleveland Papers (series 2, reel 71).

34. *New York Times,* November 17, 1892; *Chicago Times,* November 7, 8, 12, 1892; *Chicago Tribune,* October 2, 1892.

to speakers and doorbell ringers; and to his office workers. Gold-zier's opponent worked just as hard, and both men talked tariff ad nauseam; it was a remarkably modern performance.[35]

The new style helped the Democrats to hold most of their gains from the landslide of 1890, as they swept to their most satisfying victory over the GOP in the nineteenth century. No significant realignments in voting patterns occurred in 1892 as compared to 1890—and the new Populist party cut a very small figure in the Midwest, failing to capture even 5 percent of the vote in any of the six states. Republicans recouped slightly, winning all the electoral votes in Iowa, all but one in Ohio, and half in Michigan. Illinois, Indiana, and Wisconsin remained solidly in the Democratic camp, providing more than an ample cushion for Cleveland's majority in the electoral college.[36] The Republicans apparently would have a long wait before returning to power unless they drastically changed their approach—or unexpected disaster befell the Democrats.

The Republican transition to the merchandising style took place after 1888, being delayed by Harrison's original commitment to the army style. In 1888 he had spoken of "a contest of great principles," but made it clear that he wanted it to be

> fought out upon the high plains of truths, and not the swamps of slander and defamation. Those who encamp their army in the swamp will abandon the victory to the army that is on the heights.[37]

Harrison, the former general, continued to talk like one when he referred to the Democrats who "have left their ambuscades and taken to the open field, and we are to have a decisive battle on this question"; or when he explained that the GOP of Kentucky was important, even though it always lost, because, "There is no better way that I know of to keep one detachment of an army from

---

35. *Chicago Herald,* November 13, 1892, for a very full description of the campaign; Goldzier held the anti-Edwards-law Germans and won.

36. For analysis of the votes, see W. Dean Burnham, *Presidential Ballots: 1836–1892* (Baltimore, 1955), pp. 145–56; Knoles, *1892 Election,* pp. 242–44; Paul Kleppner, *The Cross of Culture* (New York, 1970), pp. 130–78.

37. Speech, October 25, 1888, in Charles Hedges, ed., *The Speeches of Benjamin Harrison* (New York, 1892), pp. 183–84.

re-enforcing another than by giving that detachment all it can do in its own field."[38]

General Harrison's rhetoric typified the GOP leadership through the 1888 election. William McKinley, once described as being "as great and as successful . . . a gladiator in the political combats of the country as he was a hero on the battle-fields of the Republic,"[39] used the military analogy extensively in his speeches before 1892. In 1885, for example, he ridiculed "inoffensive Republicans" who

> are only useful to the enemy; they only retard the movement of our advancing columns; they are the stragglers moving with the baggage train—enrolled among us, but never ready for duty and always ready to surrender without resistance.[40]

In 1892, however, McKinley spoke only of the Democrats, and not of his GOP, in military terms. By 1893 he completely abandoned the military analogies and had adopted the merchandising approach.[41]

Although in 1888 the rich amateur politician John Wanamaker had already declared the old style of campaigning outworn, and had called for putting the campaign on a "business basis,"[42] it was James Clarkson who led the stylistic reorientation within the GOP. As party leader in Iowa for many years, chief of national patronage in 1889 and 1890, national chairman in 1891 and early 1892, and founder of the Republican National League, Clarkson developed the implications of the new strategy and had the power to

38. Ibid., pp. 180, 129, for speeches of October 22, and September 18, 1888. Nevertheless the Indiana GOP began sending boiler plate to one hundred papers in 1888, and the national committee scheduled appearances by nearly three hundred prominent speakers. *St. Louis Republic,* October 13, 17, 1888.

39. Speech by Joseph Foraker, nominating McKinley for governor in *Cincinnati Commercial-Gazette,* June 18, 1891.

40. Campaign speech, October 1, 1885, in *McKinley Speeches,* p. 179.

41. Ibid., pp. 575–78, 633, for speeches of May 17, 1892, and February 14, 1893.

42. Gibbons, *Wanamaker,* 1:257. Note that in 1892 the modern techniques of mass advertising were just emerging. Senator Chauncey Depew, one of the most popular Republican speakers and president of the New York Central Railroad, that year declared: "Every enterprise, every business, and I might add every institution must be advertised to be a success. To talk in any other strain would be madness." Quoted in *Printers' Ink, FiftyYears: 1888 to 1938* (New York, 1938), p. 26.

implement his ideas. The League he founded, the prototype of the Young Republican clubs, was designed to be a full-time advertising and educational force, superior in flexibility to the old party organizations. In Clarkson's plans the League would "go to every neighborhood in the land and open schools of investigation in every community, will invite everybody to come to its place of meeting and on the open floor discuss and comment on political questions." The League would also "establish a library in each farming community and village and give young men a chance to develop as speakers, workers and publicists."[43] The League would be a great school for political salesmen.

Clarkson's plans were not idle daydreams. In 1888 the GOP had organized a million voters into 6,500 clubs in every state. In 1892, under League auspices, two million members worked through some 20,000 clubs. Occasionally the old military style still pervaded local clubs, as in Davenport, Iowa. There the four hundred League members in 1892 were smartly uniformed, well drilled, and equipped with "all the paraphernalia of a hot campaign." Torchlight processions and flag-raising ceremonies were their specialty, and from the farms nearby rode cavalry companies of young Republicans, fully uniformed, carrying flags, banners, or torches, and eager to show their "hearty interest in the welfare of the Republican national ticket."[44] Outside Davenport, however, Republican clubs reoriented themselves to more productive activities.

The serious work of the League was polling voters, with the special aim of spotting independents or wavering partisans and soliciting names for cheap subscriptions to party newspapers. Clarkson, an editor himself, felt that the campaign of education in 1892 "could be won by one agency alone, that of the party press." Reading material was especially valuable in the wintertime, he added, because then the readers were influenced "by conviction and by their own interests, and not by prejudice or eloquence."[45]

43. Interview in *New York Mail and Express,* August 7, 1891, clipped in scrapbook No. 16, in Benjamin Harrison papers (microfilm reel 146).

44. *Ann. Cycl. 1888:* 780–81; *Chicago Tribune,* October 17, 25, November 3, 1892.

45. *New York Mail and Express,* August 7, 1891. Democratic Congressman Harter of Ohio suggested that the new campaign style implied sending Democratic newspapers primarily to Republicans and independents; Michael

Wall, the most imaginative campaign theorist in the Democratic party, agreed with Clarkson, but added that:

> There may be people who listen to eloquent orators, who have for a long time been anxious to change their political creed, whose thoughts have been turned that way by some quieter means, that are influenced to make public their secret thoughts that would not otherwise have done so.[46]

Oratory was not outmoded, but now had to focus on the wavering or uncertain voters, not on the party faithful. To spot these doubtful voters, each party polled every midwestern county at least once in 1892, "to get down to bed-rock facts on which to base our calculations and efforts," explained one leading Democrat,[47] and increased the frequency of small discussion sessions in schoolhouses and other gathering places. Far more pamphlets were distributed than there were readers, so that no one would be missed.

Indiana, which had been so demonstrative in 1888, appeared apathetic in 1892. Not really, the Republican state chairman explained. Although there was less "enthusiasm, red fire, processioning and noise," he pointed out that the GOP was working feverishly, and had planned eight to ten thousand educational meetings across the state in the last three weeks of the campaign alone.[48] The windows formerly filled with portraits of Harrison or Cleveland were no longer obscured, and the streets were no longer ablaze with torchlight parades every night. But in the last week of the Indiana canvass in 1892 five thousand audiences, of several dozen or several hundred citizens, sat patiently by the hour listening to speakers untangle the intricacies and implications of the tariff and money questions.[49]

An influential Wisconsin editor wondered whether a shortage of campaign funds had necessitated the transition to the merchandis-

---

Harter, "Campaign Committee: A Plan for More Effective Management," *Forum* (1892) 14:40.

46. Wall to Vilas, November 30, 1892, Vilas MSS.

47. Donald Dickinson interview, *New York Times,* September 7, 1892.

48. *New York Times,* October 13, 1892; *Chicago Tribune,* October 17, 1892. But cf. Marcus, *Grand Old Party,* pp. 188–90, for the weakness of the Indiana GOP.

49. *New York Herald,* November 6, 1892; *New York Times,* October 12–14, 1892; *Chicago Tribune,* October 17, 29, 1892.

ing style, but finally traced the change to the conviction of the party managers that

> they can put campaign funds to better uses than the purchase of uniforms, torches and banners, the hiring of brass bands and all the rest. They consider that not many votes are made in that way. . . . But the same amount of money used to notify persons by mail of the importance of registration and voting, to hire carriages and wagons to carry voters to the registration booths and polls, in short to perfect systematic arrangements for getting voters out, is believed to bring better and less uncertain results.[50]

The editor warned, however, that the "hurrah business" could easily be undervalued. Most men, he thought, tend to be politically apathetic unless stimulated. "The indifferent man," he explained, "is more likely to register and vote when his neighbors appear to be aroused and the only outward and visible sign of wakefulness is the hurrah."[51] The old pro Lyman Trumbull of Illinois grumbled that nowadays campaigns, "are not what they were in the fifties. There is an apparent lack of enthusiasm, feeling, fire."[52]

The critics had their point. The voters' reaction to the new-style educational campaigns was lethargic. In 1892 turnout in the northern states was the lowest in any presidential election since 1872.[53] Excluding Iowa, the midwestern states had averaged a 10 percent increase in total vote cast in each of the three preceding presidential elections, but in 1892 the increase was only 5.4 percent. (In Iowa, where the cross-pressures generated by the prohibition movement were in abeyance for the year, and so did not act to depress turnout, the turnout rate, 91 percent, was the highest ever known in the state.) Perhaps the voters who had no intention of changing parties, but who were not especially interested in politics anyhow, became bored by the lectures in 1892 and longed for the thrill of a colorful campaign. Education was dull in 1892, but it became

50. Editorial in *Milwaukee Sentinel,* October 16, 1892, apparently written by Horace Rublee, the editor and a former Republican state chairman.
51. Ibid.
52. *New York Times,* November 14, 1892.
53. W. Dean Burnham, "The Changing Shape of the American Political Universe," *American Political Science Review* (1965) 59:11; cf. Oscar Austin, "Presidential Canvass of 1896," *Ann. Cycl. 1896:* 673.

incredibly exciting four years later when Bryan and McKinley bid for the votes of every citizen in the land. By tailoring their appeal to independents and waverers at the expense of their dependable supporters in 1892, the two parties contributed further to the erosion of partisan loyalties. In another three or four decades campaigns would be routinely conducted on merchandising principles, often with heavy emphasis on simplistic mass media advertising, and less and less use of educational programs or party symbols. The result would be confusion and apathy, for the voter whose partisanship was weak could no longer understand public affairs by reference to a consistent set of party principles constantly reiterated by a captive press. These effects, though noticeable for the first time in 1892, took many years to unfold.

The most immediate effect of the transition in campaign styles was a shift in power inside the parties. The distribution of literature, newspapers, and speakers was very expensive, yet the old source of party finances, contributions from officeholders, began to dry up as civil service coverage became more widespread. The local organizations, which had been supreme when the basic strategy was to bring fully committed partisans to the polls, now lost power to the state and national leaders who could tap the business community for large contributions. Grover Cleveland and the Bourbons allied with him, by maintaining close ties with financial and business leaders, thus kept their control of the Democrats until after the 1894 elections, despite the unpopularity of these leaders at the grass roots. When the silverites finally displaced the Bourbons in 1895–96 they discovered they had no money to conduct a merchandising campaign, and so they introduced economical variations of the style. Similarly, power in the GOP after 1892 devolved upon William McKinley, whose manager, Mark Hanna, was the most skillful fund-raiser of the era.[54]

---

54. Marcus, *Grand Old Party*, argues persuasively that Republican finances became the pivot of power on the national level only in 1896, while Matthew Josephson, *The Politicos: 1865–1896* (New York, 1938), pp. 638–39, pushes the date back to 1888. As far as state-level politics are concerned, a date in between seems reasonable. On the importance of high finance to the Democrats, see Merrill, *Bourbon Democracy*.

As power drew upward in the GOP hierarchies, the professionals seized the opportunity to tackle the last remaining task before the Republican party would be ready for its comeback: the crusading moralists had to be purged. In Iowa, the scene of the moralists' greatest victories, the purge came in 1893. In Ohio, McKinley suppressed the moralists during his two terms as governor (1891–95). In 1895 ex-governor Foraker staged a dramatic comeback, taking complete control of the Ohio party. The crusading Foraker of 1883 and 1889 was gone, replaced by a shrewd politician with close ties to big business and the Cox machine in Cincinnati. Foraker was no longer a friend of prohibition—and Ohio stayed wet until the drys finally destroyed Senator Foraker in 1908.[55] In Michigan the chief moralist was Hazen Pingree, businessman-mayor of Detroit. The state Republican organization, led by Senator James McMillan, tried every maneuver to end Pingree's career, or at least minimize his threat to the party. The mayor, however, was no temperance man, and when it became clear that he was needed to carry the state for McKinley in 1896 he finally received the gubernatorial nomination. Whether necessary or not, McMillan's work effectively saved the Michigan Republican party from reacquiring the pietistic image it had won by supporting prohibition in the 1880s.[56] In Wisconsin, the leading moralist, ex-governor Hoard, attempted a comeback by promoting first Nils Haugen and later Robert LaFollette for govenor. LaFollette, formerly as regular a professional as the GOP could boast, had broken sharply with the party leadership in 1891 and was becoming more and more the crusading moralist. In a hard-fought series of contests the professionals defeated Haugen and LaFollette, and eliminated crusading from the Republican stylebook.[57] In Illinois and Indiana the moralists had never posed a serious threat to the professionals, and the GOP escaped acrimonious purges.

The success of the professionals in revamping both major parties was striking. The Democrats had solidified their control of

55. Marcus, *Grand Old Party*, pp. 215–19.

56. Melvyn G. Holli, *Reform in Detroit: Hazen S. Pingree and Urban Politics* (New York, 1969), pp. 139, 150, 188–195; cf. Kleppner, *Cross of Culture*, pp. 172–75, 210–14.

57. Richard Current, *Pine Logs and Politics: A Life of Philetus Sawyer* (Madison, 1950), pp. 269–90; Fowler, *John Coit Spooner*, pp. 175–80, 193–96; Kleppner, *Cross of Culture*, pp. 256, 366–67.

the nation by adopting a campaign style brilliantly suited to attracting disaffected Republicans. No longer would they have to rely primarily on half-forgotten Civil War memories. The themes of Republican corruption, paternalism and fanaticism, coupled with the Bourbon's low-tariff, hard-money stance, made excellent selling points. The change in style gave the party more flexibility than the Bourbons realized. A campaign of education could just as well be used to sell other ideas—free silver, for example. The silverites, laborites, and agrarians, who never much liked the Bourbons, were ready to install new leadership and move in new directions. In 1896 they had their opportunity.[58]

The transition in styles was a painful process for the GOP. By suppressing the amateurs, the professionals were primarily attempting to end the series of disasters wreaked by the uncompromising crusaders. The amateurs, however, were more representative of the pietistic grass roots of the party, and were not at all content to be squelched. They looked to McKinley in 1896 to save them from the bosses, but he only tightened the screws—and in the early twentieth century they gave their support willingly to anti-machine "Progressive" crusaders. To understand the tensions between the moralists and the professionals, it is necessary to explore their characteristics in more detail.

58. Marcus, *Grand Old Party,* pp. 192–95, has an insightful discussion of the tensions in the Democratic party. See also J. Rogers Hollingsworth, *The Whirligig of Democracy: The Democracy of Cleveland and Bryan* (Chicago, 1963).

7

Moralism, Professionalism and Reform:
The Social and Ideological Impact of Pietism

> There is something pathetic in
> the history of these endeavors.
> For it [prohibition] has been, to a
> large extent, a history of hope
> deferred; of the Promised Land
> ever approaching yet ever again
> receding; of strenuous efforts and
> sanguine expectations issuing in
> comparative failures and disap-
> pointments. Action has been
> followed by reaction, and an ebbing
> has always succeeded the flowing
> tide.
>
> Reformed minister[1]

The impact of religion upon political behavior did not cease with
the formation of partisan loyalties and the intrusion of ministers
into political campaigns. The tension between pietistic and liturgical outlooks sharpened the relationship of occupation to party,
sparked urban-rural and immigrant-old-stock conflicts, and alienated Republican politicians from their constituents.

Urbanization had long been underway in the Midwest by 1890.
Only 39 percent of the people were farmers that year; 17 percent
lived in the thirteen largest cities (over 45,000), 10 percent
lived in other cities over 10,000, 15 percent lived in towns over
1000, and 19 percent were nonfarmers living in villages or open
country.[2]

Urbanism affected political patterns in a variety of ways. The
ability of the largest cities to finance their party operations from
their own patronage resources permitted them to operate independently of the main currents of state and national politics. The attraction of medium and large industrial centers for newly arrived

1. Rev. J. Spangler Kieffer, "Prohibitory Temperance Legislation," *Reformed Quarterly Review* (1883) 30:146.
2. *Ann. Cycl. 1891:* 841. The number of families living in farm and nonfarm dwellings was used to estimate the proportion of farmers; Bureau of
Census, *Report on Farms and Homes: Proprietorship and Indebtedness . . .
Eleventh Census: 1890* (Washington, 1896), pp. 286, 325.

immigrants produced a predominantly liturgical, and hence Democratic, electorate. Cities and towns of all sizes differed sharply from rural areas in the extent of the division of labor. Even small towns displayed wide heterogeneity in occupation and life style. Occupation, or perhaps the social relationships and level of wealth, education, and income associated with occupations of different status, did have an effect upon partisanship, even among men of the same religious outlook. The businessmen, professionals, and skilled factory workers of the urban Midwest heavily favored the Republican party, while unskilled laborers and craftsmen concentrated in the Democratic fold. The tendency of pietistic old-stock youth to choose high status occupations, while liturgical boys had to settle for low-status jobs, added to the political distance between men living in the same community. The tendency toward neighborhood segregation on the basis of income and ethnicity in the cities may have further widened the political outlook of different occupational groups, and may have involved both residential and hiring discrimination against liturgicals and Democrats.[3] All these factors were "real" in the sense that they operated even if the actors did not pay attention to them continually. When they did pay attention, even more powerful attitudes and prejudices came into play.

The emotional dimension of urbanism was metrophobia, the rural and small town fear of the great metropolis. Some farmers distrusted the far-off grain exchanges and livestock markets; some local merchants worried about the competition from jobbers, who supposedly had secured privileged rates from the railroads; most of all the pietists feared the violence and vice that big city crime represented, and the corrupt machine politics that threatened the future of republican virtue and democratic government in their states. Potentially the antibusiness fears redounded to the credit of Democrats, for most brokers, railroad magnates, wholesalers, and other businessmen were Republicans.[4] Fear of corruption,

---

3. See appendix for details.
4. For farmers' views, see *Ann. Cycl. 1896:* 273, *1893:* 294; on the businessmen see Richard Jensen, "Quantitative Collective Biography: An Application to Metropolitan Elites," in Robert Swierenga, ed., *Quantification in American History* (New York, 1970), pp. 398–401; Paul Kleppner, *The Cross of Culture* (New York, 1970), pp. 307–14.

on the other hand, was an underlying issue that tended to favor the Republicans, since most criminals were identified with immigrant groups in the Democratic camp,[5] the most obnoxious machines were conspicuously, if loosely, affiliated with the Democratic party, and most of the antimachine crusaders were middle-class pietistic Republicans.[6] Furthermore the dry pietists repeatedly discovered that big city voters and legislators were all that prevented the passage of temperance legislation. In Michigan in 1887, for example, Detroit's wet plurality of 22,000 (augmented by heavy vote frauds) overwhelmed the outstate dry plurality of 18,000 votes and defeated a prohibition amendment to the state constitution.[7]

The danger was not that the pietists were threatened with a loss of social or economic status. In every state, in rural areas, metropolitan areas, and smaller cities, the old stock held a virtual monopoly on leadership positions in banking, finance, factory and railroad management, large mercantile establishments, newspapers, and the professions. True, the rich farmlands were gradually passing from the hands of pioneers to hard-working immigrants, but that was not a disturbing development. The bright young sons of the old-stock farmers moved to the nearby small towns, or occasionally even to the more distant cities, where white-collar opportunities provided security, comfort, status, and ever brighter opportunities for their children. In 1905, in the 165 small cities in Iowa having from 1,000 to 8,000 population, the old stock was a minority in only 29. This group constituted 56 percent of Iowa's rural population, 61 percent in towns of 1,000 to 2,000, and 67 percent in cities of 2,000 to 15,000—but only 52 percent in cities over 15,000. The old stock in Iowa in 1890 made up 52 percent of the total male work force, but 78 percent of the lawyers, 71 percent of the male teachers and professors, 66 percent of the female school teachers, 76 percent of the physicians, 68 percent of the government officials, 70 percent of the bankers, and 73 percent of the telegraph

5. On criminals, see *Chicago Daily News Almanac for 1891* (Chicago, 1891), p. 346; on reaction to criminals, Richard Sennett, "Middle Class Families and Urban Violence," in Stephan Thernstrom and Richard Sennett, eds., *Nineteenth-Century Cities* (New Haven, 1969), pp. 386–420.

6. A sense of antibossism among professional politicians appears in John Sherman, *Recollections of Forty Years* (Chicago, 1895), 2:1158–59.

7. *Cyclopedia of Temperance and Prohibition* (New York, 1891), p. 112.

operators.[8] Elsewhere in the Midwest the economic and social dominance of the old stock was equally secure, and hardly diminished between 1880 and 1910. "The ministers, church, Sunday schools, most of the public school teachers, professors in colleges, nearly all the women of the State, and most of the best people everywhere are against the saloon," boasted one Iowa minister.[9] Money, employment, culture, communications, and learning were theirs—but not control over morality.

In the smaller cities and towns, everyone knew nearly everyone else. The strict moral codes of the pietists could not be flouted openly without the transgressors eventually being discovered by their neighbors. In such an atmosphere gossip and the economic consequences of losing one's reputation effectively policed morality, though it remained true that personal standards were the best regulators of conduct. The minority liturgical populations, in low repute and concentrated on the wrong side of the railroad tracks, ignored the censures of the pietistic majority at the cost of social and economic immobility. The control of local government by the pietists meant that flouting of the Sunday laws or the liquor codes by saloon-keepers was dangerous or even impossible. In areas dried up by local option or state prohibition, an enterprising drinker could find "a few secret dives," and bootleggers enjoyed a profitable business, but open saloons were nonexistent, and the bootleggers had, in the absence of prostitutes, the meanest rank in society.[10]

8. Also 56 percent of the clergymen, 60 percent of the bookkeepers, and 59 percent of the merchants and peddlers. *Census of Iowa for 1905* (Des Moines, 1905), 686–89; Bureau of the Census, *Report on Population* . . . *Eleventh Census: 1890* (Washington, 1897), vol. 1, pt. 2, p. 556.

9. Open letter of Rev. J. H. Rhea (Methodist) to Horace Boies, October 17, 1891, in *Chicago Tribune,* October 20, 1891.

10. Quote from Hutchison campaign speech, *Iowa State Register,* October 1, 1889. On the moral atmosphere of the rural and small town Midwest see Newell Sims, *A Hoosier Village* (New York, 1912); Lewis Atherton, *Main Street on the Middle Border* (Bloomington, 1954); Edwin S. Todd, *A Sociological Study of Clark County, Ohio* (Springfield, Ohio, 1904), pp. 29–99; Thorstein Veblen, "The Country Town," in *Absentee Ownership and Business Enteprise in Recent Times* (New York, 1923), ch. 7; and, with caution, the novels of Sherwood Anderson, Sinclair Lewis, Herbert Quick and Brand Whitlock. Compare the reform movement in Kansas, Robert Dykstra, *The Cattle Towns* (New York, 1968), ch. 7. Inquisitive statisticians in Indiana in 1879 uncovered 374 houses of ill-fame, 2277 prostitutes,

The conditions that made the towns the citadels of pietistic morality were weak or inoperative in the larger cities. In the metropolis, the highest stations in business, finance, and the professions no longer were monopolized by churchgoing pietists; sophisticated wet Presbyterians and Episcopalians were too important, as were other men who paid little attention to religious concerns. In any case the pietists were unable to control the moral climate or the political structure of the metropolis. This failure was largely a matter of numbers. In Chicago, Cincinnati, Cleveland, and Detroit in 1900, fewer than one-fourth of the voters were old-stock whites. In Milwaukee the old-stock proportion was barely one in ten; nearly half the voters were German.[11] As table 6 in chapter 3 demonstrated, the cities were liturgical bastions. Political power, one observer of the rising metropolis emphasized, "is where the voters live and the ballots are cast . . . these heterogeneous masses hold the reins of government, fill the offices of trust and power, give character to the prevalent style of civilization, and control the sources of law and legislation."[12]

The city was too large, too anonymous, too subject to constant turnover of population, to permit the spontaneous moral oversight that pervaded the rural Midwest. There was no way to establish or enforce a morality the inhabitants did not accept. Despite their social prestige, the word of pietistic ministers was not heard by the greater part of the metropolis. Revivals directed at liturgical immigrants repeatedly failed to attract their attention. In tacit acknowledgment of failure, after 1878 the foremost revivalist of the time, Dwight Moody, shifted the emphasis of the metropolitan revival from conversion to a rekindling of the faith of old-stock urbanites with pietistic backgrounds. Thanks to the change-over,

---

3060 pimps, 4760 deadbeats, and 2895 drunkards, statewide. Indiana Department of Statistics and Geology, *First Annual Report: 1879* (Indianapolis, 1880), p. 442.

11. Bureau of Census, *Thirteenth Census . . . 1910: Abstract* Washington, 1913), p. 113.

12. D. C. Eddy, "The Sovereignty of Saloons in Cities," in *National Temperance Advocate* (December, 1893) 28:194. Eddy, a leading Baptist minister in Brooklyn, had served as the American party (Know-Nothing) speaker of the Massachusetts legislature in 1854.

revivals continued to flourish in the cities and helped maintain the demand for pietistic reform among the middle classes.[13]

The cities, in the judgment of the reformers, were cesspools of corruption, poverty, immorality, and beer-drinking. Chicago—"wicked, infidel, worldly, grasping Chicago"—mesmerized the temperance crusaders.[14] The great metropolis of the Midwest was the epitome of vice, the capital of the rum power, the center of baneful influences. The reformers had only slightly higher opinions of Milwaukee, Saint Louis, Detroit, Cincinnati, Cleveland, and Dubuque, but Chicago was the great bugaboo, the home, moreover, of the wicked commodity exchanges, and the heart of the threatening railroad octopus. Every reformer had either visited Chicago, or could confirm his suspicions by the firsthand testimony of an acquaintance who had been there. If any more evidence was wanted, the *Chicago Tribune* was replete with lurid details. Full of Catholics, anarchists, socialists, railroad barons, trust-builders, commodity speculators, grasping bankers, saloon-keepers, and houses of ill repute, Chicago symbolized the consequences of a relaxation of the moral imperatives of the pietistic ethic. Even worse, Chicago was rich and growing, and every booster in every Zenith wanted to emulate that city's success.

The rapid growth of the cities, particularly the larger metropolises, threatened to take political power out of the hands of the old-stock Americans. The stagnation of the rural population in the Midwest soured the optimism of the growing villages and towns. The small towns were not declining in economic vitality, but their moral leadership could be doomed by the influx of foreigners into the burgeoning cities. "Think of cities and large towns under the control of the organizations whose sole business is to make criminals and paupers," urged Hutchison in warning Iowans against his opponent Boies and the saloon power.[15]

The corruption of the cities posed an immediate threat to the

13. James Findlay, *Dwight L. Moody* (Chicago, 1969), pp. 303–5; William McLaughlin, *Modern Revivalism* (New York, 1959), pp. 267–71; Bernard Weisberger, *They Gathered at the River* (Boston, 1958), pp. 229–30.
14. Quote from *Northwestern Christian Advocate,* the leading Methodist magazine in the Midwest, itself edited in Chicago, in *National Temperance Advocate* (February 1886) 21:29.
15. *Iowa State Register,* October 1, 1889.

families of the pietists: their sons and daughters were abandoning rural life to seek their fortune in the towns and, more ominously, in the large cities too. Action was urgently needed to protect the "purity of the home" and shield young people from the attractions of vice. Governor Larrabee warned Iowa parents that "the gilded or so-called respectable saloon is a tenfold more dangerous allurement for our boys than the squalid outlawed whiskey den."[16] The result was a systematic effort, peaking in the late 1880s and early 1890s, to equip the children with firm moral standards and to inculcate in them an intense hatred of the saloon, coupled with a movement to develop institutions that would isolate them from the depraved metropolitan environment. The Young People's Christian Endeavor Societies expanded rapidly, attracting millions of young Presbyterians, Congregationalists, and Disciples of Christ. Similar societies for Methodist, Baptist, and pietistic Lutheran youth also flourished. Church activities expanded on college campuses, spearheaded by the YMCA. A strong interdenominational Sunday school program reached 12 million young pietists across the nation by 1896. The WCTU, eagerly cooperating with these movements, secured the adoption of required courses in temperance hygiene in the public schools of most states. The WCTU also organized its own youth affiliates. The 200,000 boys and girls of the Loyal Temperance Legion paraded gaudy badges warning, "Tremble, King Alcohol, we shall grow up!" The older girls advised the older boys, "Lips that touch wine shall never touch mine."[17]

The campaign to save the boys actually worked. Gubernatorial candidate Hutchison explained in 1889:

16. Message to the legislature, February 13, 1890, in Benjamin Shambaugh, ed., *Messages and Proclamations of the Governors of Iowa* (Iowa City, 1904), 6:186.

17. The sentiment, but not the exact phrasing of the second quote appears in *New York Tribune*, August 23, 1896. On the isolationism of the metropolitan middle classes, see Richard Sennett, *Families Against the City* (Cambridge, 1970). On youth activities, *Ann. Cycl. 1891:* 83, 814–18, *1894:* 135, *1896:* 720; *Cyclopedia of Temperance,* p. 410; Joseph Gusfield, *Symbolic Crusade* (Urbana, 1963), p. 85; *One Hundred Years of Temperance* (New York, 1886), pp. 170–76, 252–69, 303, 467–70, 524–29; C. Howard Hopkins, *History of the Y.M.C.A. in North America* (New York, 1951), pt. 2.

The object of prohibition [in Iowa] has been attained. The gaudy saloon with all its attractions has been largely driven off the streets. . . . It is the rising generation . . . that we desire to save from the corrupting influences of the saloon. *The boys are safe.*[18]

Middle-class pietistic youth were in rebellion against the corruption, crime, and duplicity they saw in American society. Their revolt took the form of intensified devotion to pietistic morality, coupled among many with a burning missionary zeal to convert the world. About two-thirds of the college students in the Midwest were full members of pietistic denominations; the majority joined the intensely moralistic YMCA. All the faculty and students at Iowa State College at Ames endorsed prohibition, while a straw poll of undergraduates at the University of Chicago in 1892 disclosed 3 supporters of James Weaver (Populist), 52 of Grover Cleveland, 151 of Benjamin Harrison, and an amazing plurality of 164 for John Bidwell, the candidate of the Prohibition party.[19]

The teenagers took their moral training to heart. As adults they voted the nation dry, and manned the ranks of the Progressive movement. As late as 1950 consumer purchasing surveys revealed that fewer than 20 percent of the families in pietistic small cities like Bloomington (Illinois), Grinnell (Iowa), Anna (Illinois), and Garrett (Indiana), bought hard liquor for home consumption. In larger, predominately pietistic cities like Indianapolis, Des Moines, and Evansville, the proportion which bought liquor still fell under 25 percent. By contrast, in liturgical strongholds, the rate for Chicago was 47 percent, Cleveland 63 percent, Cincinnati 38 percent, Youngstown 48 percent, Milwaukee 43 percent, and Madison 34 percent.[20] After a span of half a century the charges of hypocrisy so often raised against the pietists remained untenable.

18. *Iowa State Register,* October 1, 1889.

19. John R. Mott, *The Young Men's Christian Association* (New York, 1947), 3:131; Laurence Veysey, *The Emergence of the American University* (Chicago, 1965), p. 279 for Chicago; Cyrenus Cole, *I Remember, I Remember* (Iowa City, 1936), pp. 99–100; *Iowa State Register,* June 15, 1882, for Ames. At the more worldly University of Wisconsin, only 10 percent of the undergraduates supported Bidwell; *Wisconsin State Journal* (Madison), November 1, 1892.

20. Bureau of Labor Statistics and Wharton School, *Study of Consumer Expenditures Incomes and Savings* (Philadelphia, 1957), 12:2–4, 7. Families in pietistic towns also purchased less beer and wine, and spent less for

Protection of their families was only part of the challenge the pietists faced; the saloon threatened their whole universe, for "the purity of the American home, the preservation of the American Sabbath, and the maintenance of good government, especially in the cities, are all at stake."[21] By counting 250,000 liquor dealers, 50,000 distillery and brewery workers, 250,000 saloon employees, and adding some 850,000 other men whose votes were "absolutely at the disposal of the liquor traffickers," the drys tabulated 1,400,000 voters—or one-eighth of the nation's electorate—as minions of King Liquor and their sworn political enemies. Supposedly these degraded souls would vote as a bloc to stop reform, banish good men from public office, control party conventions, plunder the public treasury, ensconce themselves in power, and destroy the hope of democracy in America.[22] The metropolis provided the natural arena for such sinister activities. "As now, so ever will the cities rule the land," began one reformer. But who would rule the cities? Not the churches; not the press. "We find the sovereignty of the saloon in great cities to be almost supreme. . . . It has the money to bribe, votes to barter, offices to bestow."[23] The implications were terrible. "Too often important elections are carried by means fraudulent, intimidating, corrupting and disgraceful," wrote a pietistic Lutheran minister. "Especially in the hoodlum districts of our larger cities, the polls are the scenes

---

drinks in restaurants. However they were about as likely to use tobacco as families in other cities. Of the 99 families in the liturgical centers of Chicago, Cleveland, Cincinnati, and Milwaukee whose head was born between 1875 and 1885, 56 percent drank beer, wine, or liquor, in contrast to only 33 percent of the comparable elderly families in pietistic Indianapolis, Des Moines, and Evansville. Ibid. 3:34–40. Corroborative survey data appears in Don Cahalan et al., *American Drinking Practices* (New Brunswick, 1969). pp. 55–64; and Walter Muelder, *Methodism and Society in the Twentieth Century* (New York, 1961), pp. 339–40.

21. *National Temperance Advocate,* (August, 1891) 26:134.

22. *Cyclopedia of Temperance,* pp. 384–85, 489–90; *New York Voice,* September 26, 1889; for an excellent dry analysis of the liquor power see D. Leigh Colvin, *Prohibition in the United States* (New York, 1926), pp. 546–74.

23. Rev. D. C. Eddy in *National Temperance Advocate* (December 1893) 28:194.

of wild and drunken orgies, besotted savagery, and open appeals to the buyers of votes."[24]

Naturally some reformers panicked before the threat. The president of the Iowa Temperance Alliance prophesied in 1891:

> The most powerful and unscrupulous horde that was ever marshalled against a righteous cause since Satan and his hosts were hurled over the battlements of Paradise will be arrayed against us. The advocates of the liquor traffic are the most unscrupulous men on earth. There is nothing too villainous for them to resort to. There is no crime they will not commit to gain their end. They have no regard for human rights, and to honorable controversy they are strangers.[25]

The reformers obviously were not strangers to nasty rhetoric. This outburst came a few months before Hutchison declared the saloon dead in Iowa, thus leaving in limbo the identity of the "unscrupulous horde." Evidently believing the worst, the Presbyterian Synod of Iowa had already announced:

> The liquor power, with its thorough organization, its shrewd brains, and seemingly inexhaustible treasury wields an influence and control so pervasive and effectual that no force can secure its overthrow save God's church.[26]

The good divines of the Presbyterian Synod of Iowa were not in doubt as to which was God's church. The reformers had great difficulty in specifying exactly how the omnipotent saloon power exercised its power, for their exhaustive research disclosed few direct manifestations. The reformers came to realize that the power of the saloon rested not so much on its activities as on the spontaneous sympathy of the liturgical and unchurched drinkers, most of whom appeared to be immigrants. "The ranks of the drinking men are constantly recruited by the influx of bibulous and intemperate foreigners," reported the Presbyterian Synod of Indiana in 1887. "The great majority of these alien immigrants, now over

24. Rev. J. Wagner, "The Pulpit and the Problems of Modern Life," *Lutheran Quarterly* (1891) 21:413.

25. J. A. Harney, in *National Temperance Advocate* (February 1891) 26:30.

26. *Minutes of the Eighth Annual Meeting of the [Presbyterian] Synod of Iowa, Oct. 17–21, 1889* (Mt. Pleasant, Iowa, 1889), p. 222.

a half million annually, are addicted to the use of strong drinks, as well as steeped in ignorance and vice," it continued.[27] More pointedly, a national temperance leader in 1891 asked, "How much longer [will] the Republic . . . consent to have her soil a dumping ground for all Hungarian ruffians, Bohemian bruisers, and Italian cutthroats of every description?" The eminent clergymen predicted that "temperance reform and the Christian Sabbath and intelligent freedom will not survive if our land shall keep open doors for all the godlessness and all the crime and all the reckless pauperism of the whole wide world."[28]

Actually the "new" immigrants from southern and eastern Europe seldom tarried in Indiana, and few voted anywhere in the Midwest. (They lived in Chicago, Cleveland, a few other cities, and numerous mining areas; most had not acquired citizenship before 1896.) The reformers met defeat at the hands of Irishmen and Germans who had made their homes in the region for decades. Not many reformers, at least in the rank and file, could overcome the prejudice against all Catholics noted by H. K. Carroll, himself a distinguished reformer:

> This prejudice of ours, which we too often mistake for a righteous indignation, makes us quick to believe the worst reports respecting Catholics. . . . How rank is the prejudice with which thousands of Protestants are imbued—prejudice not confined to children, or even to the lay element, but fully developed in ministers, Methodist, Presbyterian, Baptist, Lutheran, etc.[29]

The "worst reports" were indeed widespread. The Indiana Presbyterians charged that liquor dealers systematically "subsidized these foreigners, and indeed all who love the intoxicating cup" to "vote as they direct, and to carry elections." Was there any hope of converting these misguided souls? Not much, for "on such men reason and religion are utterly lost—they are as pearls cast before swine." Some Methodists agreed that it was with

27. Rev. W. P. Koutz, "Report of the Committee on Temperance," in *Minutes of the [Presbyterian] Synod of Indiana* (Indianapolis, 1887), pp. 29–30.

28. Rev. T. W. Cuyler, President of the National Temperance Society, in *National Temperance Advocate* (June, 1891) 26:91.

29. H. K. Carroll, "Our Attitude Toward Roman Catholics," *Methodist Review* (1895) 77:238.

"foreigners that moral suasion utterly fails—There is no conscience to which you can appeal."[30]

The "Romanist Peril"—which included threats to public schools as well as to good government and public morality—became a leading theme of pietistic discussion in the late 1880s, with such sophisticated intellectuals as Josiah Strong according it top priority.[31] Most dry leaders, in their sober moments, recognized the invaluable aid contributed by their Jansenistic Catholic allies. These leaders secured well-known Catholic sponsors for their programs, while diverting the attack away from the Catholic church as such and toward usually unspecified hordes of "foreigners." Instead of devising ways to weaken the Catholic hierarchy, the reformers called for immigration restrictions. The Indiana Presbyterians found their only hope lay in thorough revision of the immigration and naturalization laws, while the National Temperance Convention in 1891 stressed the "evil of threatening proportions" posed by continued immigration. The Prohibition party, which as late as 1876 had favored a "friendly and liberal" immigration policy, in 1892 discovered that "foreign immigration has become a burden upon industry, one of the factors in depressing wages and causing discontent. . . ."[32] These sentiments became popular before the depression of 1893 constricted economic opportunities in the society. Although efforts to restrict immigration also won favor with labor unions and were partially endorsed in major party platforms, the eagerness of industrialists to obtain fresh labor supplies for the expansion of their operations prevented any significant restrictions from becoming law.

The pietistic political ethic was derived from the image of a united America, in which all elements of society cooperated in

30. Koutz, "Report," pp. 29–30, *Methodist Protestant* (September 27, 1884) 54:4, quoted in Richard Cameron, *Methodism and Society in Historical Perspective* (New York, 1961), p. 256; for a similar attitude among Baptists, see John Cady, *The Origin and Development of the Missionary Baptist Church in Indiana* (Franklin, Indiana, 1942), pp. 246–51.
31. Josiah Strong, *Our Country* (New York, 1886, 1891), chs. 4,5,6,8,11; this book was a best-seller and very influential.
32. Koutz, "Report," p. 30; *National Temperance Advocate* (August, 1891) 26:134; Kirk Porter and Donald Johnson, *National Party Platforms: 1840–1964* (Urbana, 1966), pp. 53, 92. See also John Higham, *Strangers in the Land* (New York, 1963), pp. 97–105.

Christian harmony. The natural equality of every good man would find its highest expression in political and social democracy, while the occasional wrongdoer would eventually be exposed. Evil, unable to attract much support, could not flourish in such a society. The realization that ignorant immigrants, irrepressible saloons, patronage-filled city governments, and office-hungry politicians frustrated the proper working of a society based on a consensus of values—of pietistic values—was a cruel blow. Grass-roots democracy, to the moralists, meant that the government ought to reflect the will of the people; but with the foreign factor included no consensus was possible. The moralists rejected the alternative concept of pluralistic democracy, whereby the parties and the interest groups bargained among each other to arrive at mutually tolerable programs. Bargaining was anathema. The political party, unless like the Prohibition party or the early Republican party it represented the Christian force in politics, was a dangerous institution; uncritical party loyalty was a doctrine subversive of true Christianity. The moralists saw politics as an arena pitting good against evil, and neither could they compromise with the enemy nor graciously concede defeat.[33]

Frances Willard, the energetic head of the WCTU and an influence in most of the reform movements of her day, expressed the antiparty spirit in 1887. Calling for a "New Politics," she found that:

> the curse had coiled itself up in every caucus, darted its venom into every county, district, state and national political convention in all the land and had thrown the two great political parties into such abject fright that the Kingdom of Christ . . . was effectively kept out and Satan was victoriously barred in.

Her vision was millenial:

> I firmly believe that the patient, steadfast work of Christian women will so react upon politics within the next generation that

33. Compare Stanley Schultz, "The Morality of Politics: The Muckrakers' Vision of Democracy," *Journal of American History* (1965) 52:527–47; Richard Hofstadter, *The Idea of a Party System* (Berkeley, 1969); Daniel Boorstin, *The Genius of American Democracy* (Chicago, 1953), pp. 8–35; Ronald Formisano, "Political Character, Antipartyism and the Second Party System," *American Quarterly* (1969) 21:683–709.

the party of God will be at the fore; ministers will preach it from their pulpits, and Christian men will be as much ashamed to say that they never go to the [Prohibition party] caucus as they would be now to use profane language or defame character; for there is just one question that every Christian ought to ask, "What is the relation of this party, this platform, this candidate to the setting up of Christ's kingdom on the earth?"[34]

The old politics—bargaining, compromising, evading, seeking patronage—had to be destroyed. The new politics, based on the full participation of all Christians, would usher in the millenium. H. K. Carroll, a dry Republican, was troubled by the new vision:

You [Prohibitionists] form a millenial party, adopt a millenial platform, vote a millenial ticket, and expect the millenial dawn. All who refuse to vote your millenial ticket are in league with Satan to delay the millenium.[35]

Despite the ridicule, the new politics gained momentum, exciting the Prohibitionist party, conquering the temperance movement, and infiltrating the Republican party—as in Iowa, where it captured control of the GOP at the grass roots. Any form of compromise, such as licensing of saloons, came under brutal attack. To recognize the "personal rights" of a moderate drinker, proclaimed philosopher John Bascom, "is to enable him to stand across the path of public progress, to check the movement of society, and so ultimately to destroy his own well-being as well as that of others."[36] The pietistic churches joined in the 1880s in declaring liquor licenses to be "contrary to the laws of God," and threw their resources into efforts to defeat programs of regulation that many politicians, moderates, and nonutopian temperance reformers advocated. "The Prohibitionists," concluded the moderate head of the Episcopalian temperance society, "are earnest, ex-

34. Colvin, *Prohibition,* pp. 286–87.
35. From debate October 30, 1888, with Dr. Samuel Dickie, the Prohibitionist national chairman, in *Independent* (November 1, 1888) 40:1398; also see James Timberlake, *Prohibition and the Progressive Movement* (Cambridge, 1963), pp. 34–38, 191–92, and sources cited there on millenarianism.
36. John Bascom, *Sociology* (New York, 1887), p. 197, written as a college text while the author was president of the University of Wisconsin; his time in office was tumultuous.

treme, narrow partisan men as a rule. They bow down to a creed of law as their Shibboleth and have made it their God."[37]

Apocalyptic visions of the millenium generated radicalism. The utopian belief in the efficacy of the new politics to bring about God's kingdom on earth marked the watershed between conscientious temperance reform buttressed by occasional crusading, and the fanaticism of true believers who were unable to abide gradual progress. The term "temperate" fell out of fashion; moralists prided themselves on their "radicalism." Convinced that their struggle constituted Armageddon, the frenzied moralists repelled moderates, thus losing the broad base of silent support they needed for success. "To be in earnest on this subject," lamented a learned dry,

> is, in many places, to subject one's self to the imputation of being "well-meaning but misguided," to be civilly patronized in such a way that . . . is more cutting than open insult; or to be dubiously watched as a chronic disturber of established order.[38]

One element in the transition to fanaticism was a shift of the dry artillery from hard liquor to beer. Since most metropolitan saloons were owned and leased by breweries, this new emphasis brought a more direct confrontation with the enemy—the Germans. The original outcry against drunkenness faded, for beer was hardly as intoxicating as whiskey. (The drys simply explained that beer-drinking inexorably led to stronger beverages, and thus to physical ruin.)[39] In their clamor against the saloon, some drys even lost sight of the evils of alcohol and narcotics.[40] The rapid

37. *Political Prohibitionist for 1889* (New York, 1889), p. 77, quoting the Ohio Methodist Conference of 1888; the latter quote is from Robert Graham in *Addresses and Discussions at the Fifteenth [Protestant Episcopal] Church Congress . . . 1893* (New York, 1893), p. 31; see Colvin, *Prohibition,* pp. 266–71.

38. Rev. James C. Fernald, "The Church and Temperance," *The Homiletic Review* (1893) 25:175. Fernald, a Harvard man, was a Baptist minister in Ohio before becoming an editor of Funk and Wagnalls dictionaries.

39. See Colvin, *Prohibition,* pp. 548–49; on the liquor and beer industries, see Timberlake, *Prohibition,* pp. 102–15.

40. Drys at first welcomed the South Carolina state-owned dispensary system that abolished saloons while maintaining the flow of alcoholic beverages; *Literary Digest* (April 22, 1893) 6:694–95. *The Northwestern Christian Advocate* pleaded, "If our German adopted citizens are bound to drink their beer, we wish they would use it at home, and join all classes of citizens

growth of drug abuse, not being linked to the saloon, went unnoticed. "Injurious as is opium-smoking," editorialized the leading temperance journal, "the whiskey and beer shops are the cause of immensely greater harm to the individual and the community."[41] The same journal subsequently attacked some bottled soft drinks when its chemists discovered traces of fermentation. Hires Root Beer was made to appear as vile as poisoned moonshine.[42]

Violence seemed the natural culmination of dry fanaticism. The prohibition crusades of the 1850s, especially in midwestern Quaker and Congregational settlements, occasionally sparked antisaloon riots in which perfectly legal establishments were ransacked and their proprietors threatened with bodily harm by leading citizens.[43] In 1874 outraged ladies throughout the region confronted saloon-keepers with pray-ins, stern admonitions, and sometimes Carrie-Nation-style axe-wielding. After the violent stage ended, the aroused women formed the WCTU to institutionalize the light of reason, the wrath of women, the displeasure of God and (through alliance with the Prohibition party) the voting power of their husbands.[44] In 1886 a New York liquor dealers' magazine reported "an occasional blowing-up of saloons by powder or dynamite, or the torch applied on behalf of temperance, Christianity, and law

---

to banish the public saloon." Quoted in *National Temperance Advocate* (September, 1886) 21:150.

41. *National Temperance Advocate* (September, 1886) 21:145. In 1896 the WCTU antinarcotics task force discovered that "even Christian Temperance women use headache medicine, soothing syrup, balsam, Perry Davis Pain Killer, and like drugs. These contain opium." Among the young people, "cocaine parties are one of the latest forms of amusement." Nevertheless cigarettes remained the main target after liquor and beer. *Report of the National Woman's Christian Temperance Union* (Chicago, 1896), p. 247.

42. *National Temperance Advocate* (August, 1893) 28:138; on Hires, which advertised itself as a temperance drink, see *Western Christian Advocate* (Cincinnati) (April 14, 1897) 64:451.

43. Arthur C. Cole, *Era of Civil War: 1848–1870* (Springfield, Ill., 1919), p. 211; *Standard Encyclopedia of the Alcohol Problem* (Westerville, Ohio, 1925–1930), 3:1306, 5:2049, 6:2902.

44. *Standard Encyclopedia of the Alcohol Problem*, 6:2902–5; *Cyclopedia of Temperance*, p. 145; Annie Wittenmyer, *History of the Woman's Temperance Crusade* (Boston, 1882); Ernest Bogart and Charles Thompson, *The Industrial State: 1870–1893* (Springfield, Ill., 1920), p. 49; Dan Clark, "The History of Liquor Legislation in Iowa," *Iowa Journal of History* (1908) 6:364.

and order."[45] The incidents, although scattered and causing no bodily harm, forced the Prohibitionist party organ in 1890 to disapprove of violent tactics:

> They are cowardly and calculated to precipitate a bloody solution to the saloon problem, which may be avoided, we believe, by straightforward, courageous and open means. At the same time we would have the saloon men understand that we mean business. . . . The contest is drawing very near the final struggle.[46]

Armageddon never came, for the drys largely repudiated strong-arm methods and had no wish to be identified with the "White Cap" terrorists who flourished in the late 1880s in the Ohio River valley.[47]

In fairness to the radical drys, the violence they perpetrated should not be exaggerated. Far more often drunken ruffians made them the victims of verbal abuse, physical attack, dynamiting, and even assassination.[48] The drys branded the saloon as the ally and source of most violence in American life. They seldom failed to correlate the number of saloons with the arrest rate and the prison population, and they sought prohibition as the only true path to domestic tranquility in America. They were instrumental in organizing law and order leagues in the larger cities to force police officials to do their duty toward illegal liquor and vice operations.[49]

To proclaim the millenium, the drys needed access to the communications media. The pulpits of the pietistic churches were usually open to them, as were the forums at other church functions and revival meetings. Large-circulation religious magazines printed

45. The *New York Retailer,* quoted in *National Temperance Advocate* (Supp. June, 1886) 21:107.

46. *New York Voice,* quoted in *Literary Digest* (1890) 2:109.

47. *National Temperance Advocate* (March, 1889) 24:33; *Standard Encyclopedia of the Alcohol Problem,* 2:555.

48. *Standard Encyclopedia of the Alcohol Problem,* 6:2618–20, for list of outrages, and also 2:715, 724, 779; Colvin, *Prohibition,* pp. 210–11; Clark, "Liquor Legislation," 6:543–48, 558.

49. *Standard Encyclopedia of the Alcohol Problem,* 6:1512–13. By 1885 there were more than 500 local Leagues, with 60,000 members, concentrated in New England, Michigan, Illinois, Wisconsin, and Pennsylvania. The national governing board included Archbishop Ireland, a Prohibitionist party leader, and assorted governors, generals, and senators. *New York Voice,* February 19, 26, 1885.

their appeals, and theological journals justified their programs. In the late 1880s temperance groups published two dozen weekly newspapers in the Midwest, and distributed about two million copies of other kinds of literature in the region annually. The WCTU was especially active in seeing that Sunday schools and youth groups received appropriate magazines, pamphlets, handbills, and songbooks.[50] One lively tune carried the refrain:

> Oh, he is a crank, ha ha,
> and he is a crank, ho ho;
> we are all of us cranks,
> Won't you come to our ranks,
> and laugh as we merrily go.[51]

For political guidance, however, the vast majority of the electorate relied upon general newspapers, which proved surprisingly unreceptive to the call for a dry millenium. The Democratic press, of course, was thoroughly hostile and largely ignored the crusade in its news columns, except to notice demonstrations of opposition. The Republican papers, while providing more news coverage, almost unanimously refused to advance beyond high license.[52] In prohibition drives in every state the reformers complained about the open hostility of the press. After the *New York Tribune* passed from the hands of ardent dry Horace Greeley to the more flexible Whitelaw Reid, Republican candidate for vice president in 1892, hardly a major newspaper could be found anywhere in America that endorsed total prohibition. Although most Republican and many business-oriented Democratic papers favored stricter regulation of saloons, the mystified drys charged that immense slush funds enabled the rum power to buy the press out.[53] The Prohibi-

50. *100 Years of Temperance*, pp. 447–57; 466–68; John N. Stearns, ed., *Temperance in All Nations* (New York, 1893), 1:25–32.
51. *New York Voice*, February 28, 1888 (advertisement).
52. See ibid., March 29, 1888, for a pioneer content analysis of the distribution of news space in the leading papers. The *Cincinnati Enquirer* (Dem.) devoted 0.3 percent of its news space over a typical four-day period to temperance news, while the *Cincinnati Commercial Gazette* (Rep.) gave 0.5 percent, the *Chicago Tribune* (Rep.) 2.0 percent, and the *Chicago Daily News* (Ind.) 2.3 percent.
53. "The plan of the liquor traffic, officially adopted and officially announced, is to work on public sentiment by subsidizing the press" (*New York Voice*, January 12, 1888)—a rather strong interpretation of an am-

tionists disclosed that brewers paid from $50 to $4,000 to Nebraska papers for advertisements and fake editorials endorsing the wet position in the referendum of 1890. They also charged that the enemy bought $20,000 of influential advertising in the leading Philadelphia papers in 1889. When informed that their own propoganda would have to pay the same advertising rates as those charged to the wets, the drys bellowed wrathfully and paid up.[54]

The leading midwestern newspapers were immune to the blandishments of wet money. Most refused to accept any beer or liquor ads. Although the drys diligently combed both the classified and the display advertisements for evidence in refutation of such policy, they discovered fewer than two items per issue in the leading Chicago and Cleveland papers; the worst offender, disappointingly, was the wet, Democratic *Cincinnati Enquirer,* which averaged thirteen small items per issue, mostly classified notices of sales of barroom fixtures.[55]

Pressed by the pietists to join the great moral crusade, the editors and publishers refused. That Democratic spokesmen should have mirrored the beliefs of their largely wet constituencies was not unexpected; that their Republican counterparts declined to adopt the millenial stance favored by many, if not most, of their readers yields a deep insight into the nature of democracy and representation in the Midwest.

The editors would not allow the drys to flood the communications channels of their parties, and thus jam or distort the chief mechanism for relaying ideas and opinions between politicians and the people. The extraordinarily articulate moralists sought to overwhelm the uncommitted or fainthearted by dazzling arrays of "scientific" statistics and torrents of abuse. Sober wets and moderates were damned daily—and, more important, denied the opportunity to present their arguments and beliefs in a fair manner. The drys tried to seize the moral high ground by force, but

biguous item in the *Brewer's Journal* pointing out the power of the press. See also Rev. W. W. Ramsay, "Newspaper Responsibility in Relation to Intemperance," *Methodist Review* (1895) 77:568–80.

54. *Cyclopedia of Temperance,* pp. 120–23, 446–47; Colvin, *Prohibition,* pp. 204–6.

55. *New York Voice,* May 3, 1888, gives detailed breakdowns for twenty-six leading papers.

the party press would not let them. Many editors and publishers personally advocated temperance, in both abstract and concrete forms. Often they gave strong support to Sunday observance; in Iowa, for example, every publisher gave his men Sunday off, and no papers appeared on Monday morning. Had any Republican newspaper raised the dry banner it could have expanded its circulation, but its usefulness as a party organ would have been compromised. Whatever the virtues of moderation, temperance, saloon restriction, and Sunday observance, the perils of radical prohibition were clear to the editors. They had watched the emergence of the new politics in the 1880s and realized that whenever moral suasion gave way to legal coercion the political reverberations were disastrous to the electoral hopes of the GOP.

In rejecting radical prohibition the Republican editors were acting in their role as spokesmen for the party apparatus. The professional politicians at the highest level of the GOP had balanced the demands of the moralists, the votes of the wets, and the wisdom of the moderates and had settled upon a policy of supporting high license, local option, and the removal of the prohibition issue from the partisan arena. "We don't want to alienate anybody," explained a Michigan leader.[56] National politicians avoided public comment on the issue, calling it purely a local matter; when prohibition propositions were on the ballot they refused to vote on them, even when they were candidates themselves.[57] Senator John Sherman expressed the wisdom of the professionals as early as 1873: "Questions based upon temperance, religion, morality, in all their multiplied forms, ought not to be the basis of politics."[58]

The new politics of the drys caught the GOP off guard for a while in the 1880s. At first the response was insistence upon tradi-

56. A poll of fifty delegates to a national Republican meeting disclosed only four willing to alienate the German vote; *New York Voice,* December 22, 1887, with quote. By contrast 71 of 88 members of the Democratic National Committee wanted their 1888 platform to specifically condemn "sumptuary laws." Ibid., March 1, 1888.

57. Joseph B. Foraker, *Notes of a Busy Life* (Cincinnati, 1916), 1:128–32; on the silence of Blaine in 1884, Harrison in 1888, and McKinley in 1896, see Colvin, *Prohibition,* pp. 560–61, and *Cyclopedia of Temperance,* p. 109.

58. *Cyclopedia of Temperance,* p. 593; Sherman, *Recollections,* 2:846–47, 859–61.

tional party loyalty. This played into the hands of the moralists who argued that blind partisanship was abhorrent to the individualism and personal responsibility of the Protestant ethos. An Iowa Methodist minister who converted to the third-party ranks complained:

> The party leaders are whipping the party followers into line. . . . Whenever any individual manifests any disposition to use freedom in the exercise of an independent judgment, straightway he is denounced as a traitor, a turn-coat, a dude, a pharisee, a mugwump. . . . Instead of argument there is slang and abuse. Instead of appeals to reason, mud-slinging.[59]

Two years after this sermon the minister was assassinated by saloon hangers-on, a martyr to tyrannical party loyalty in the eyes of the drys.

The Republicans struggled to escape their dilemma. For a while in 1886 a national "Anti-Saloon Republican" movement came into existence. The professionals deemed the organization irregular, sentimental, and irresponsible, and quickly suppressed it.[60] Senator Benjamin Harrison agonized over the loss of Republican votes to third parties and concluded high license was the only solution, although it would not satisfy the ultras:

> A good deal can be done by looking after the nominations and getting in every instance sober, intelligent and able men. But, even when that is done, experience shows that there will probably be a small body of fanatical prohibitionists who will rather aid indirectly to elect a saloon keeper than such a man.[61]

59. Frank Haddock, *The Life of Rev. George C. Haddock* (New York, 1887), pp. 325–26; *Standard Encyclopedia of the Alcohol Problem*, 3:1163–64.
60. *Standard Encyclopedia of the Alcohol Problem*, 4:1852–53; *National Temperance Advocate* (December, 1886) 21:196.
61. Benjamin Harrison to Louis Michener, February 7, 1885, and see also January 13, 1885, in Louis Michener Papers, Library of Congress. Murat Halstead, powerful Cincinnati editor, put the same sentiment in saltier terms when he blasted the "cranks and boodlers, fools and spite-workers and blatherous lunk-heads who feel that they are of importance because their unscrupulous and unseemly combination defeated Blaine." *New York Voice*, July 16, 1885. Most Prohibitionist party leaders were professional men. Of the fifty delegates from Michigan and Indiana to the 1888 national convention for whom occupations are known, twenty-five were ministers, lawyers,

Harrison chafed at the maneuvers of his fellow pietistic Presbyterians. Similarly Rutherford Hayes grumbled, "The Methodist Episcopal Church is losing its hold on the people by its greed for gold and for power in partisan politics. . . . During the war it drove out all Democrats and now it is expelling all Republicans."[62]

Obviously a chasm gaped between the moral outlook of the professional politicians and the moralists. The professionals, whether of high office or low, did not markedly differ from their nonpolitical relatives and friends except in the manner of their approach to men and issues. The thousands of politicians of the Midwest displayed as many idiosyncrasies as any large group of prominent men. Yet, thanks to years of apprenticeship in the routine work of the party organization, and their long association with the elders of the party, they approached the relationship of man and government from a unique viewpoint. A hint at the special style of the politicians comes from their drinking habits. Politicians followed the code of gentlemen, and were almost as quick to offer each other a drink as they were to shake hands. Many a voter recalled the warm feeling inside him after he met a politician in a saloon. Very few prominent Republican politicians were abstainers, a remarkable fact considering the high regard for abstinence generally maintained among their nonpolitical associates. The politicians were not less likely to be churchgoers (many voters, after all, attended church), but they had developed their own standards of personal morality. A pietistic politician had more in common with a liturgical, or even an atheistic politician, than he did with the elders of his congregation.[63]

physicians, or teachers; fifteen were in business; seven were temperance organizers or editors, and only one was a farmer. Only the New York state delegation contained more than a handful of farmers. *New York Voice,* May 24, 1888; for the profile of husbands of WCTU leaders, see Gusfield, *Symbolic Crusade,* p. 130, which also finds an absence of farmers.

62. Diary entry of December 7, 1889, in Charles Williams, ed., *Diary and Letters of Rutherford Burchard Hayes* (Columbus, Ohio, 1925), 4:529.

63. One of the foremost Methodist laymen was Congressman (later Senator) Jonathan P. Dolliver of Iowa. He opposed prohibition, and when asked about his drinking habits explained he was "abstinent, but not totally so!" Thomas Ross, *Jonathan Prentiss Dolliver* (Iowa City, 1958), pp. 109, 176, 238 (quote). The only teetotalers in the Senate in 1886 were Frye of Maine, Blair of New Hampshire, and Chace of Rhode Island; *National Temperance Advocate* (June, 1886) 21:86. On the personal style of professional politi-

The professionals consequently fared poorly in the eyes of the general public: they seemed to lack moral fibre. In 1893, for example, the national organ of the Congregational church lamented that the Iowa Republican platform exhibited "the language of a party more anxious to gain office than to maintain a principle." Sadly it reported that: "The party of moral ideas has succumbed to the lawless opposition of the liquor power, and beats an ignoble retreat from the heights of principle to the treacherous grounds of party policy."[64]

Noble martyrdom in the service of a just cause evidently was a higher ideal for the moralistic amateur than for the pragmatic professional.[65] Pragmatism was the ethos of the politician: one made the best arrangement possible, balancing the demands of all the constituents, but constrained by the needs of the party. Especially in legislatures, the professionals refused to damn their opponents for supporting "immoral" causes, such as opposition to prohibition. One worked with his colleagues, and voiced opposition in the formal roll call, not in informal dialogue. The first lesson every professional had to learn was: to get along, one must go along. The ministers and their congregations lived in a world of good and evil, of sin and salvation; they hardly sympathized with the men who lived in a world of Republicans and Democrats, of elections and coalitions, of successes and defeats.

In Iowa the Republicans groped for a resolution to their party's deep split. The drys, although controlling most local and county conventions, failed to capture complete control of the party after their losses to Horace Boies in 1889 and 1891. The professionals, led by the editors, the federal patronage holders, and the congressional delegation could no longer tolerate defeat in a state so long

cians, see the biographies and David Rothman, *Politics and Power: The United States Senate 1869–1901* (Cambridge, 1966), and Donald Matthews, *U.S. Senators and Their World* (Chapel Hill, 1960).

64. *Advance* (August 24, 1893) 27:633–34.

65. "General if I should vote for this bill it would lay me in my political grave," one Republican politician remonstrated to a prohibition leader. "Vote for it and die, then," was the earnest response, "and I will write on your tombstone, 'Blessed are the dead that die in the Lord.'" John Brooks, *The Life of Clinton Bowen Fisk* (New York, 1888), p. 190; Fisk himself told the anecdote at third-party rallies.

a Republican stronghold. Wet sentiment predominated in the legislature of 1892, and would have repealed prohibition save for the skillful maneuvering of the drys. A presidential election year was not the opportune time for a final confrontation, and in the spring of 1892 a modus vivendi was achieved. The wet element would get more recognition from Republican conventions, the professionals would supervise the campaign that year, and the liquor issue would be ignored. The Republicans felt that a campaign based entirely on national issues would revive enough of the old party loyalty to carry the state. The state Temperance Alliance, meanwhile, was falling into the hands of third-party Prohibitionists who were anathema to the Republican professionals. The compromise proved effective. Reinvigorated by the postponement of debate on prohibition, the Republicans carried Iowa for Harrison and elected ten of their eleven congressional candidates.[66]

In 1893, when a governor and legislature were to be elected, the denouement came. The Temperance Alliance, thanks to its militant millenialism, had discredited itself among loyal party workers and no longer reigned supreme in local conventions. In May the homes of three prominent opponents of saloons in Muscatine were destroyed by dynamite. Miraculously, no lives were lost; almost as surprising, the drys were unable to exploit the outrage in their desperate attempt to retain power in the GOP. The spring meeting of the GOP state committee decided the time had come to scuttle the party's dozen-year-old commitment to total prohibition, "in order to preserve the life of the party," and to salvage "what may be saved of real temperance prohibition even if political prohibition has to suffer in the operation." "Prohibition for prohibition's sake," the committee concluded, "has been the blighting curse of temperance in Iowa."[67]

The issue came to a head at the state convention in August, 1893, the most bitter and significant party gathering in decades. The battle focused on the thirteenth plank submitted by the wet

66. *Ann. Cycl. 1892:* 357–59; Clark "Liquor Legislation," 6:588–91; Fred Haynes, *Third Party Movements* (Iowa City, 1916), pp. 321–29; Walter Nydegger, "The Election of 1892 in Iowa," *Iowa Journal of History* (1927) 25:358–449, esp. 369–70, 398, 424–26; *New York Times,* July 24, 31, August 13, 16, 17, 19, October 24, 1892.
67. Clark, "Liquor Legislation," 6:590–92; *Ann. Cycl. 1893:* 408–9; *New York Times,* July 10, 1893.

and moderate majority of the resolutions committee. "Prohibition," it read, "is no test of Republicanism." The dry laws were pragmatic matters, subject to "retention, modification or repeal" by the legislature. The laws ought to be made more efficient in those areas that truly detested the saloon, while other localities ought to be given an opportunity to regulate the liquor traffic in such a manner "as will serve the cause of temperance and morality."[68]

Everyone understood the import of the guarded phrases. The Republicans were drawing the line between responsible temperance and control of the saloon on one hand, and irresponsible, millenarian prohibition, with its secret dives and bootleggers, on the other. The effect was to endorse local option and high license, which had been precisely the platform that won Iowa for Boies four years before. The moderate and wet forces pointed to the success achieved in Des Moines and other cities by ordinances that annually fined the still illegal saloons the equivalent of a high license, but otherwise tolerated their orderly operation. The river towns had no such ordinances, and there saloons abounded without regulation or taxation. A scheme of "mulcting" the irrepressible saloon would give the cities needed revenue and control and, more important, would recognize and tolerate the moral standards of the liturgicals. Since the main prohibition statutes would not be repealed, the dry areas of the state would remain dry, and the morals of the moderate pietists would not be offended.[69]

The dry forces, recognizing the doom of their utopia, moved to delete the obnoxious sections of plank thirteen. As tension mounted there appeared at the rostrum one of the great men in the history of Iowa, James Harlan. He recalled how he led the Free Soil forces into the newborn Republican party, how he had fought for Lincoln's ideals in the United States Senate in the crisis years of the 1850s, 1860s, and 1870s. "If I do not know what Republicanism is, who does?" he cried out, and the convention roared its agreement. Republicanism, the older statesman patiently explained, was a national and not a local faith; it must not and cannot be modified or proscribed by factions. "Are we not wise

68. *Ann. Cycl. 1893:* 409.

69. David Brandt, "Political Sketches," *Iowa Journal of History* (1957) 55:361–62; *Advance* (August 24, 1893) 27:633–34, 639, 851; *Chicago Tribune,* July 10, August 14, 1893.

enough," he implored, "to cast out from among us all apples of discord, reestablish harmony and concord in our ranks, stop fighting each other and once more turn our guns on the common enemy?"[70] Harlan's exhortation, coming from a venerated founder of the party, a devout Methodist, and for forty years an ardent temperance man, solidified the moderates. The dry amendment failed 590 to 613 and the original platform passed 612 to 603. A vigorous young moderate, Frank Jackson, secured the nomination for governor and tried to unify his party by attacking the Democrats on economic issues. Despite the anguish of the diehard moralists, the GOP had found the answer to its dilemma.

After more than three years in office Governor Boies had failed to install a reasonable system of saloon control in the state. The initiative passed to the Republicans, who had an attractive program for all parts of the state and enthusiastically set about to recapture lost and strayed voters. In a last feeble gesture the Temperance Alliance endorsed the Prohibitionist party candidate, who secured only 2.4 percent of the vote. Jackson won 49.8 percent in leading his party to a clean sweep. The Democratic vote plunged from 49.4 percent in 1891 to only 42.1 percent in 1893. In an era of close elections, that was a disaster. In four years Boies had captured the state of Iowa for the Democrats and then lost it again. The Germans responded as the Republicans hoped. Jackson took 42 percent of the vote in German counties, a sharp gain from the meagre 37 percent his party received in 1891. The groundwork for reconciliation between the cultural traditions of the people had been laid. When the Republicans carried out their platform promises and enacted a statewide mulct law the Germans moved closer to the GOP, and in 1896 furnished a critical plurality to William McKinley (see table 7, chapter 4). The Republican professionals had redeemed Iowa. Not for another four decades would another Democrat occupy the governor's mansion.[71]

70. *Iowa State Register*, August 17, 1893; Johnson Brigham, *John Harlan* (Iowa City, 1913), pp. 296–305, for text.
71. *The Iowa State Register* and *Dubuque Herald* provided detailed coverage; but see also Clark, "Liquor Legislation," 6:592–94; Brandt, "Sketches" 55:361–66; Cyrenus Cole, *A History of the People of Iowa* (Cedar Rapids, 1921), pp. 483–84; *Ann. Cycl. 1893: 409–10, 1897: 419–20; New York*

The moralists were outraged at the reversal of their victories. With "substantial unanimity" the pietistic ministers endured "with mortification and disgust the Mulct Law nullification brought on by political intrigue." Corruption surely was the source of defeat, they felt, and they denounced "the cabal of railroad and saloon politicians who . . . in secret conspiracy, formed a plot to stifle the conscience of the Republican Party of Iowa."[72]

The reality was not so corrupt or conspiratorial. The local organizations of the midwestern Republican party in the 1880s encouraged the fullest participation of the rank and file in the selection of convention delegates, thus allowing a well-coordinated movement like the prohibition crusaders to seize power at the grass roots and impose their will on the party. The precinct and township conventions were mass meetings, open to all self-declared Republicans. Usually the local chieftans presented a prearranged ticket of candidates for local office and delegates to higher conventions, and elected it without controversy. An organized group of amateur politicians could, however, caucus beforehand and try to pack the mass meeting with supporters, who would either demand specific pledges from candidates for delegates or select their own leaders as delegates.[73] The pietists possessed the nucleus of organized caucuses in their temperance societies and, especially, in their voluntary church groups.[74] Local politicians facing the mass of angry and determined drys, fearing the threat of defection or systematic boycotting of the party ticket, went along at first and sent drys or moderates pledged to vote only for dry candidates to county and state conventions. Since the crusaders rarely demanded a share of the patronage or the honorific positions sought

Times, August 16, 17, September 5, 6, October 11, 28, 31, November 6, 8, 1893; *Chicago Tribune,* August 12–19, 23, 25, 1893.

72. Truman O. Douglass, *The Pilgrims of Iowa* (Boston, 1911), p. 231, for first quote; *Des Moines News* quoted in *New York Times,* August 19, 1893.

73. At the dry-dominated 1891 Iowa Republican state convention, fewer than a tenth of the delegates were officeholders. *Cedar Rapids Gazette,* July 23, 1891, quoted in *Civil Service Chronicle* (August, 1891) 1:260.

74. On local church organizations see Washington Gladden, ed., *Parish Problems* (New York, 1887), pp. 247–360; Sims, *Hoosier Village,* pp. 67–69; and John Baer, "The Work of the Christian Endeavor Societies in Behalf of Better Citizenship" in *Proceedings of the . . . Third National Conference for Good City Government* (Philadelphia, 1895), pp. 517–23.

by the politicians, the local leaders were not inclined to unnecessarily antagonize the drys by counterorganizing their own supporters. When the disastrous statewide effects of the dry platforms became clear the counterreaction began not at the local level but at the highest state level. The top professionals' control over patronage permitted the mobilization of any recalcitrant editors (who still depended on lucrative printing contracts for financial solvency) and local leaders. The Iowa professionals worked closely with railroad leaders, especially since Governor Larrabee's crusading had united the antisaloon and antirailroad forces. The railroad directors wanted both prohibition and conservative Republican victory, only they wanted the latter more than the former. (The railroads frequently imposed severe restrictions on drinking by their employees.) In 1893 the scent of victory was in the air; Iowa and Ohio were the two states in the region holding major elections, and the Iowa Republicans were eager to make their comeback. For the first time, the township and county conventions became battlefields. The professionals won simply by bringing in more supporters than the drys, and refusing to compromise with the moralists one more time. The amateurs, who never compromised unless they knew they were losing, were astonished by the strange behavior of the professionals, who in the past had always compromised when they were winning.[75]

When professionals lost they regrouped to fight another day. When moralistic amateurs lost their crusade collapsed. Based on the crusaders' conviction that they represented the true will of the people, that they were ultimately invincible, the dry crusade revealed itself to be a hollow movement controlled by a handful of fanatics as soon as the professionals mounted a full-scale counteroffensive. After the shattering experience of the 1893 convention one Iowan asked plaintively:

> What has become of the temperance meetings and prayer meetings? The hallelujahs and songs that a few years ago made the State vocal with non-partisan Christian, gospel temperance,

75. Gleefully the leading Republican newspaper reported how the Polk County (Des Moines) convention "fought to a finish the issue between liberal and illiberal Republicanism," with the liberals winning. *Iowa State Register,* August 13, 1893; see also *Chicago Tribune,* October 28, 1893.

and that raised the temperature to white heat, making it possible to pass the present law? It has largely disappeared except in a perfunctory way.[76]

The millenarian dream faded not only in Iowa, but throughout the Midwest and the North generally. William Jennings Bryan led its last hurrah in 1896. Even Frances Willard abandoned her vision of a new politics and set about achieving piecemeal reforms, much to the dismay of her less flexible followers. Utopian reformers can survive one or two setbacks by calling them accidents, but not monotonous defeat in a series of Armageddons! The chief vehicles of the utopians, the WCTU and the Prohibition party, split in 1896 on the question of broad-gauge, multipurpose reform, in which the abolition of liquor would be a minor aspect, versus narrow-gauge concentration on the original issue; afterwards the party and the union never played a major role in midwestern politics.[77]

The pietistic churches changed too. Sunday observance, or at least Sunday closing of saloons replaced prohibition as an issue, won considerable liturgical support, and resulted in a major effort to close the 1893 Chicago World's Fair on Sundays. One by one the denominations softened their stand on prohibition, refusing to mortgage their prestige to another futile crusade. Several states outside the Midwest abolished prohibition, and Indiana followed Iowa's example when it regulated saloons by the Nicholson law in 1895. Iowa prohibited the sale or manufacture of cigarettes— total prohibition at last achieved without controversy!—and other states passed less stringent laws. The Cumberland Presbyterian church discovered the evils of the bicycle, while the YMCA pondered the immorality of college students studying on Sundays. With the passing of the divisive prohibition issue, it became possible for the Presbyterians and Congregationalists to seriously consider a merger with the Episcopalians. The old chasm between pietists and liturgicals was closing rapidly.[78]

76. Letter from ex-senator Clark quoted in *National Temperance Advocate* (November, 1893) 28:188.
77. Mary Earhart, *Frances Willard* (Chicago, 1944), p. 358; Colvin, *Prohibition,* pp. 255–61, 289–91.
78. On Sabbath observance, see *Ann. Cycl. 1893:* 150, 654, 666, 667, 732; *1894:* 676–77, 681, 692; *1895:* 672–73, 675; *1896:* 680; on church union,

The temperance movement was not dead; it shifted style from millenarianism to professionalism. The Anti-Saloon League formed in 1893 and rapidly spread across the country. Its purpose was to work with the professional politicians to achieve whatever legislation or enforcement was tolerable, and to pressure the politicians into supporting dry programs by promises of help and threats of retribution at the polls. Forgoing statewide prohibition at first, the league concentrated on local-option laws; only when its political power within the major parties was sufficient did it switch to total prohibition. Born and headquartered in Ohio, the state famous for skilled professional politicians, the league became the training camp for the most effective lobbyists of the twentieth century. It brought together all parties and all creeds (ubiquitous Archbishop Ireland was a vice president), and developed modern techniques of centralized planning, systematized financing, carefully designed advertising, grass-roots cooperation, and unswerving devotion to the single issue of controlling the liquor traffic.

Although many moralists and amateurs supported the league, and the pietistic churches (especially the Methodists) were its mainstay, its control was exclusively in the hands of full-time paid organizers. The league's professional staff determined its policy, and then enlisted support. The league invented pinpoint lobbying. It never told anyone how to behave; it only cared how he voted. Gradualism was its style; Armageddons it could do without. It triumphed totally within a quarter-century. Professional politicians discovered they could always talk with and work with the league; it never asked a legislator to ruin his career to further the cause. Many old Prohibitionists, instead of welcoming a new ally, bitterly hated the league and tried to sabotage its work. They bemoaned its lack of moralistic, millenial fervor; the league represented hypocrisy, corruption, a sellout to political professionalism.[79]

1894: 157–58, 675. On denominational nonsupport, see *1895:* 670, *1896:* 475, 659, 663; and Colvin, *Prohibition,* p. 274. On the students, see Mott, *Y.M.C.A.,* 3:149–50. For anticigarette laws, see *Ann. Cycl. 1891:* 867, *1893:* 590, *1894:* 381, *1896:* 361, *1897:* 413, 530, 826, *1898:* 328, *Cyclopedia of Temperance,* p. 630, and the WCTU annual *Rèport.* In 1897 Iowa softened its Sunday laws to legalize baseball, football, and fishing; *Ann. Cycl. 1897·* 419.

79. Colvin, *Prohibition,* p. 395; Peter Odegard, *Pressure Politics* (New York, 1928), is the classic study of the League; see also Timberlake, *Prohibition,* pp. 125–84.

The changing configurations of midwestern politics dictated the replacement of crusading amateurs with pragmatic professionals. The recognition of diverse cultural and moral belief systems among the electorate prevented the continuation of monolithic movements, whether pietistic or partisan. Both in the GOP and temperance movement the results were remarkably successful. The Democratic party, however, moved in the opposite direction, opting for a moralistic, millenarian crusade in 1896, and lost its hold on the Midwest. The professionals took control of the GOP and led it to round after round of smashing victories. The old army-style of running a party was too monolithic to withstand the changeover. The professionals in both major parties discovered that party loyalty no longer could be relied upon for electoral success, even in "safe" districts. New methods of appealing to voters—the merchandizing style—apparently had revolutionized midwestern politics in 1892. With the progressive weakening of party loyalty on the part of immigrant groups, however, and the alienation from professional politicians of old-stock pietists, the stability of the system had deteriorated badly. Any grave new crisis might upset all the old patterns. In 1893 the crisis arrived, in the form of a nationwide depression that left millions unemployed or in fear of destitution. The response of the parties and the voters to this calamity, as the country feared for its economic survival and its political sanity, was more intense and far-reaching than anything since the Civil War.

8

Republicans Triumphant:
Depression, Nativism, and the Downfall of the Democrats,
1893–1894

> We are on the eve of a very dark
> night, unless a return of commer-
> cial prosperity relieves popular
> discontent with what they believe
> Democratic incompetence to make
> laws, and consequently with
> Democratic Administrations
> anywhere and everywhere.
>
> Confidential advice to
> President Cleveland, October 1894[1]

The reorientation of the GOP during Harrison's administration
did not suffice to save the White House in 1892. The Democratic
landslide of 1890 encouraged the restructuring of the Republican
party, but the losses inflicted took more than two years to heal.
How long the Democrats might have retained their supremacy can
not be known, for in 1893 came disaster to the economy and to
the Democratic party. An unusually severe economic depression
began, and the people demanded relief and recovery from the
party in power. The Democrats could not give it. The Republicans
had prepared the nation with forebodings of disaster should the
Democrats win in 1892, and now their predictions were fulfilled
and their exile from power ended. Whose blunders were to blame
for the depression of 1893 generated much controversy; more important, both the GOP and the Populists sought to channel the
resulting unrest to their advantage, and the GOP succeeded. Confused and shaken, the Democrats returned to the issues of cultural
tension that had given them victory in 1890 and 1892. They
sought once more to unite the liturgical groups against the Republicans, this time with the bogey of a secret anti-Catholic society
known as the APA. The Republicans were newly wise, and avoided
the issue. Led by McKinley, they promised what the immigrants,
indeed all citizens wanted—prosperity; the Democrats seemingly

---

1. F. L. Stetson to Grover Cleveland, October 7, 1894, in Allan Nevins,
ed., *Letters of Grover Cleveland* (Boston, 1933), p. 369.

offered only confusion, fear, and anxiety. A broad sketch of the political developments in the Midwest during the first two years of the depression will illuminate the dilemma and the disaster of the Democrats.

Proud of his stewardship, Benjamin Harrison yielded the presidency to the Democrats gracefully. In his valedictory message to Congress, he boasted:

> The general conditions affecting the commercial and industrial interests of the United States are in the highest degree favorable. . . . so high a degree of prosperity and so general a diffusion of the comforts of life were never before enjoyed by our people.[2]

No one could miss the political implications of Harrison's claim, which Governor McKinley spelled out two weeks before Cleveland's inauguration:

> In a few days the country passes into the control of the Democratic party, in a condition of matchless prosperity in every department of industry. We do not leave them a legacy of hard times, idle industries, unproductive enterprises and unemployed labor. We turn over to them a country blessed with unprecedented activity in every avenue of human employment, with labor in active demand and better paid than in all history before; a Government with unparalleled resources and credit, and with no strain upon its honor. . . . Of this rich inheritance the Democratic party becomes the trustee for the people. It is my hope that it may suffer no loss or waste in their hands. I wish the country could be assured it would not. If it does, the trust will come back to us—and it will come back to us— with the doubly-renewed confidence of the people.[3]

The Republicans felt that the economy would inevitably falter under the threat of tariff reduction and unsound Democratic finance, and that the reaction of the people would restore the GOP and its principles to power. "We have but to hold fast," counseled McKinley, "abating nothing of conviction and yielding nothing of

2. James Richardson, ed., *A Compilation of the Messages and Papers of the Presidents* (Washington, 1910), 8:5741, Fourth Annual Message, December 6, 1892.
3. Speech of February 14, 1893, in *Speeches and Addresses of William McKinley* (New York, 1893), pp. 638–39.

our faith in the great doctrines which are destined to secure victories as signal as any which have gone before."[4]

The Republicans had not long to wait. In the spring of 1893 several large bankruptcies, the crash of the stock market, and the worsening drain on the Treasury's gold reserves heralded a financial panic. The summer brought a massive banking crisis; runs closed nearly two hundred midwestern banks and six hundred across the nation. Even highly trusted institutions foundered. In Milwaukee, for example, three large banks closed, including one, with $9 million in assets, controlled by the newly elected Democratic senator from Wisconsin,[5]

The financial disorder demolished business confidence and slashed the money supply, igniting a chain reaction of bankruptcies, shutdowns, layoffs, unemployment, reduced expenditures, and more panic. By late summer the flush of prosperity had vanished from the land, and the nation entered perhaps the severest depression it had ever experienced. Accurate estimates of the extent of the hardship have yet to be made. In Ohio, however, monthly reports from all factories showed a plunge from 99,000 men employed in the state in April, 1893, to 71,000 in October, a decline of 26 percent; in Cleveland, there was a 27 percent drop; in Columbus, 26 percent; Toledo, 17 percent; Dayton, 46 percent; Akron, a terrifying 58 percent. The five largest cities suffered a 26 percent drop in factory employment, the next forty-four largest cities a 33 percent decline, and the villages and smaller mill-towns a 20 percent falloff.[6]

Even in industrial Ohio, however, factories employed only a fourth of the nonfarm labor force, and accurate estimates of unemployment rates in other occupations were not made. Railroad employment, nationwide, fell 11 percent in the year beginning July

4. Ibid.
5. Bankruptcy data for first ten months of 1893 from Albert Stevens, "Analysis of the Phenomena of the Panic in the United States in 1893," *Quarterly Journal of Economics* (1894) 8:117–48, esp. 133; on Milwaukee, *Chicago Times*, July 23, 26, 1893; generally, see also *Ann. Cycl. 1893*: 294–306.
6. *Nineteenth Annual Report of the* [Ohio] *Bureau of Labor Statistics* (Columbus, 1896), pp. 290–305; and for a variety of estimates, see Carlos Closson, "The Unemployed in American Cities," *Quarterly Journal of Economics* (1894) 8: 185–86, 258, 501.

1, 1893.[7] The construction industry probably bore the heaviest burden as private building starts dropped precipitously. In Chicago, the fastest-growing metropolis in the world, the carpenters' union reported in September that 80 percent of its members were without work.[8] A careful police department survey in late September revealed that half of Chicago's factory workers had been laid off. Only skeleton crews remained at the largest factories: Illinois Steel employed 225 men, while full capacity was 3,600; Pullman Palace Car, 1,670 of 4,348; Deering Farm Implements, 600 of 3,000; McCormick Reaper, 440 of 2,000. The railroad freight yards had laid off 20 percent of their employees, and the great meat-packing firms had laid off 25 percent of their workers. Several smaller factories were entirely closed. The large wholesale houses had not, however, let out their work force. Few estimates of unemployment among the many retail stores were made, but among dry goods, grocery, and clothing shops the impact of the depression was not yet severe.[9] To a greater or lesser degree, distress in the larger cities of the Midwest followed the Chicago pattern.

Boom, bust, and disaster was the story of 1893. Farmers watched prices tumble, and postponed major purchases; merchants retrenched or went bankrupt; ship and rail companies saw their traffic dwindle; bankers, hoarding their dwindling reserves, reluctantly turned down urgent loan applications from their best customers. The depression inexorably spiralled downward. Immediately, the people turned to the government for relief. In Washington, the Democrats were in control of both the executive and legislative branches for the first time since Buchanan's administration. President Cleveland, however, proved no more imaginative, resilient, or effective than his predecessor had been, for he waited until August to summon a special session of Congress, and he left

7. Bureau of the Census, *Historical Statistics of the United States* (Washington, 1960), p. 437, series Q 141; Paul Douglas, *Real Wages in the United States: 1890–1926* (New York, 1930), pp. 440–41.

8. Closson, "Unemployed," 8:189; See also Charles Hoffman, "The Depression of the Nineties," *Journal of Economic History* (1956) 17:147–48.

9. For the police report, see *Chicago Times,* September 30, 1893; for a detailed review of business conditions in Chicago and the Midwest generally. during 1893, see *Chicago Daily News Almanac for 1894* (Chicago, 1894), pp. 360–74.

action to it. Tracing the blame for the "alarming and extraordinary business situation" to the Sherman Silver Purchase Act of 1890, Cleveland demanded that Congress repeal that measure immediately. The House, acting under the efficient Reed rules, overwhelmed the silverites (led by Congressman William Jennings Bryan), and voted for unconditional repeal on August 28. The nation's business community applauded, for it firmly believed the Sherman Act had produced the crisis. In the Senate, however, the silverites from the West filibustered, although John Sherman and the other Republican leaders supported repeal, and not until November could Cleveland sign the repeal[10] Business confidence perked up, and the tempo of the economy quickened slightly, but full recovery was four years away. Meanwhile the Treasury verged on bankruptcy, and only a series of extremely unpopular loans from private bankers saved the nation from total financial chaos.[11]

Washington was too slow, but local government displayed impressive energy and imagination in meeting the crisis of unemployment. In Chicago, the closing of the World's Fair stranded tens of thousands of jobless men in the stricken metropolis. Socialists and anarchists organized mass demonstrations, and sporadic rioting erupted in August.[12] The city's business and political community rose to the challenge. An emergency relief committee created construction jobs for thousands of men, newspapers and restaurants set up bread lines, churches and police stations sheltered thousands of lodgers, and the city distributed bread and coal to the poor.[13] Many cities organized special programs. In Detroit,

10. *Ann. Cycl. 1893*: 224–44, 298–305; for good accounts, see Allan Nevins, *Grover Cleveland* (New York, 1932), pp. 523–48, or James Barnes, *John G. Carlisle* (New York, 1931), pp. 250–86.
11. See Nevins, *Cleveland*, ch. 29, and Harold U. Faulkner, *Politics, Reform and Expansion: 1890–1900* (New York, 1959), pp. 151–57.
12. For the anarchists, see *Chicago Times*, August 21, 1893, *Chicago Tribune*, August 16, 1893; for the riots, *Chicago Times*, August 27, 29, 31, 1893, and Closson, "Unemployed," 8:190. Note that the *Chicago Times* was then strongly prolabor.
13. *Chicago Tribune*, August 18, 1893; *New York Times*, August 18, 1893; Leah Feder, *Unemployment Relief in Periods of Depression* (New York, 1936), pp. 95, 106–10; Closson, "Unemployment," 8:470; Chester Destler, *American Radicalism: 1865–1901* (New London, 1946), pp. 177–79.

Republican Mayor Hazen Pingree opened vacant land for the cultivation of potato patches, a dramatic but inadequate measure. Most important was the upsurge in local public works projects. The level of public building expenditures, nationwide, more than doubled from 1892 to 1893, but absorbed only part of the unemployment.[14]

Politics during the depression reflected the distress, bewilderment, and, sometimes, anger of the people. The fall elections brought a Republican landslide. In Ohio, Governor McKinley campaigned for reelection opposed by Lawrence Neal, a dedicated Democratic tariff reformer. Neal desperately wanted to defeat McKinley in order to "Forever expunge the foul blot of protection from the fair escutcheon of our grand and mighty Republic."[15] Both candidates demanded repeal of the Sherman Act (Sherman wanted it repealed too), but McKinley arraigned the failure of the Cleveland administration to reverse the gold drain, stop the contraction of the money supply, and restore business confidence. Neal insisted that the McKinley tariff was equally as culpable as the silver purchases in causing the depression. McKinley answered that any attempt to lower the tariff would disrupt business and lead to further unemployment. The governor warned that even more foreboding than "evils apprehended" were "evils which are yet to come, evils which are threatened, evils which, it is believed, will follow the executed decrees of the last Democratic national platform."[16]

McKinley won again, by 81,000 votes (out of a total of 836,000 cast), the largest plurality in Ohio in thirty years. The Republicans took another 5 percent of the total vote away from the Democrats, while the minor parties remained static. The Republican gains tended to be uniform in all the rural, small-town, and urban counties, whether old-stock or immigrant, except for Cuyahoga County (Cleveland), where the Republican share of the vote jumped nine points. Every group in Ohio became more

14. Feder, *Unemployment Relief,* pp. 158–61, 186–88; Hoffmann, "Depression," 16:147–48.
15. *New York Times,* September 13, 1893.
16. Ibid. See also June 8 and September 15, 1893; *Chicago Tribune,* September 13, October 27, 28, 30, 1893; *Ann. Cycl. 1893:* 590–91.

Republican. The prophet of the protective tariff at last saw his enemies discredited and his warnings vindicated. McKinley became the man to beat for the presidency in 1896. Sound money and high tariffs were what the nation needed and wanted, so the happy Republicans claimed.

In Chicago the 1893 elections were unusually bitter. As unemployment soared above 100,000, recriminations raged over Governor Altgeld's pardoning of three anarchists convicted of inciting the Haymarket bombing of 1886. The Democrats refused to renominate the much-abused trial judge, Joseph Gary. The Republicans, realizing Gary's wide popularity among the middle classes, put him at the head of their judicial ticket, and charged Altgeld with condoning anarchism. Late in October, as unemployment reached a peak and the World's Fair closed, a demented office-seeker assassinated Carter Harrison, the city's popular Democratic mayor. Amidst the confusion and the rioting (not in the streets, but among the city's aldermen), the Republicans swept to a narrow victory behind Gary. In December, the Democrats pulled together, nominated John Hopkins for mayor, and defeated the interim Republican mayor by less than one-half percent of the vote.[17]

In Iowa the impact of the depression was less severe. The versatile corn belt system of agriculture proved resistant to falling prices, and unemployment among the small service-businesses dependent upon the farm trade was slight.[18] Even so, the bankers and businessmen were afraid, and they retrenched their operations. The Democrats, who renominated Governor Boies for a third term, set out to exploit the prohibition issue once more, but the Republicans, who had just settled the issue among themselves, concentrated their campaign on the failure of the Democrats to cope with the depression. "The spirit of distrust and uncertainty which today permeates and controls every part of our

17. Bessie Pierce, *A History of Chicago* (New York, 1957), 3:377–79; *Ann. Cycl. 1893:* 398–99.
18. Closson, "Unemployed," 8:205, 259, 475; Fred Shannon, *The Farmer's Last Frontier* (New York, 1945), pp. 165–69, 293–94; Herman Nixon, "The Populist Movement in Iowa," *Iowa Journal of History* (1926) 24:68–70, 107; John Bowman, "An Economic Analysis of Midwestern Farm Land Values and Farm Land Income, 1860–1900," *Yale Economic Essays* (1965) 5:338–41.

commercial and national life," charged the chairman of the Republican state convention, "is the logical sequence of the recent success of the Democratic party." Capital, fearing that the Democrats would lower the tariff and ruin home industries, "commenced to fortify itself, withdrawing from many enterprises and refusing its aid to others until failure follows failure and the laborer becomes a tramp."[19] Senator William Allison called for the immediate repeal of the Sherman Act, and suggested that "overtrading, overspeculation, and undue expansion of credits have been potential elements in producing the recent panic."[20]

Boies talked prohibition, and repudiated rising demands for free silver. Thereby he slowed the return of the Germans to the Republican fold, but he also alienated many dry Democratic farmers who wanted an inflated currency and continued silver purchases. Twice a day Boies explained to small audiences that if he were in the Senate he would fight for repeal of the McKinley tariff and vote for the repeal of the Sherman Act. Outmaneuvered by the GOP and exhausted by his desperate campaigning, he collapsed on October 30.

The Republican share of the Iowa vote held at 49.8 percent, nearly the same as in 1892. The Democratic vote, however, fell from 49.4 percent in 1891, to 44.6 percent in 1892, to only 42.0 percent in 1893. The Prohibitionists took advantage of the Republican abandonment of strict dry laws, but only gained 1 percent more of the vote. The Populist vote edged up from 21,000 in 1892 (4.7 percent) to 24,000 (5.5 percent). The bulk of the Populist vote came from old-stock wheat farmers, especially Yankees unable to match the hard work of their immigrant neighbors, coupled with some trade union supporters, particularly coal miners. General James B. Weaver and his corps of three dozen Populist orators (mostly outsiders) apparently failed to excite the interest of Iowa in their panaceas. The Populists failed to carry a precinct in the state, and the great majority of farmers of all backgrounds supported the major parties, even though the price of wheat hit the lowest levels in memory.[21]

19. *Chicago Tribune,* August 17, 1893.
20. Ibid., October 24, 1893.
21. *Chicago Tribune,* October 31, 1893; Nixon, "Populist Movement in Iowa," 24:71–75; for monthly average spot prices of spring wheat

The elections of 1893 gave the Democrats a painful setback; those of 1894 ruined the party in the Midwest for a generation. Spring thawed the economic distress somewhat, yet recovery was still not in sight. By April of 1894, factory employment in Ohio recovered to 84 percent of its peak level twelve months before, and in the villages employment was back to 95 percent.[22] The local elections in the spring showed unprecedented Republican gains everywhere. In Indiana the GOP for the first time carried the cities of Seymour and Decatur, and swept the Democratic citadel of Fort Wayne, a predominantly German city. The Democrats salvaged only five of the fifty-five Indiana city halls. The rapidly industrializing "gas belt" area round Muncie, especially hard hit by unemployment, gave the largest Republican landslides.[23]

The ineptness of the Democratic Congress further embarrassed the party. Despite the Republican warnings of the dangers of tampering with the tariff, Cleveland and his men in Congress were determined to slash the McKinley tariff. The House Ways and Means Committee forged a bill pleasing to the president, even though it contained an income tax to neutralize the loss of custom revenues and to help balance the budget. In the Senate, however, Arthur Pue Gorman of Maryland and other Democrats gutted the bill, jettisoned free coal and iron (leaving free sugar and wool), and hiked import duties to please special groups of manufacturers. Furthermore, the Senate debated the bill from February to August, leaving the nation's business community in doubt and confusion. Prompt action would have helped a little; interminable delay was a disaster. Trade faltered as everyone awaited the final outcome. At last a compromise was reached, but it sickened every friend of tariff reform. Cleveland, lashing out at the "communism of pelf" that frustrated his campaign promises, finally allowed the new tariff to become law without his signature.[24]

---

in Chicago, 1885–1900, see *Report of the Industrial Commission* (Washington, 1910), 6:192; see also Thorstein Veblen, "The Price of Wheat Since 1867," *Journal of Political Economy* (1892) 1:68–103; *Daily News Almanac 1896*, p. 369; *1897*, p. 454.

22. *19th Report Ohio BLS, pp.* 290–321.

23. *Chicago Tribune*, April 4, 5, May 2, 1894; *Detroit News*, April 3, 1894.

24. Nevins, *Cleveland*, ch. 31, sadly recounts the tragedy of the tariff of 1894; for more detail, see Festus P. Summers, *William L. Wilson and*

No Democrat could point with much pride to the climax of seven years of promises of tariff reform. In the Midwest, and even more in the South and West, the Democrats suffered the wrath of the silverites against Cleveland's hard-money policies. In March, 1894, the president vetoed a silver coinage bill, and in the spring he had to appeal again to Wall Street for gold to maintain the Treasury reserves. In July a boycott against Pullman cars closed nearly every railroad west of Indiana. Cleveland sent troops to Chicago and dozens of lesser rail centers, breaking the strike but sparking bloody riots. The heavy-handed action tore the Democrats asunder, pushing trade union members into the Populist or Republican ranks.

Many of the men without jobs during the depression were recent immigrants. Employers generally kept the highly skilled old-stock workers on the payroll and cut the unskilled immigrants. Return to Europe became more desirable, but more difficult. Without sufficient financial reserves to return home, or to weather the depression in America, the immigrants often suffered grievously. The sensitivity of immigration to the business cycle demonstrated the close relationship between jobs in America and the attitudes of the common laborers from Germany and Ireland and other countries. The trend of male immigration closely followed the business cycle, with a lag of a couple of months. Total male immigration plunged from 308,000 in 1893 to only 141,000 in 1894, the most precipitous decline recorded before 1906. Since the Catholic immigrants tended to be less skilled than the Protestant, the depression afflicted most heavily the Catholic communities concentrated in the larger cities.[25]

The loss of Catholic immigrant support doomed the midwestern Democrats. To salvage that vote from the Populists (who had strong support among recent immigrants), the Democrats harped

---

Tariff Reform (New Brunswick, 1953), pp. 152–208; For editorial comment on the progress of the bill, and indications of the anxieties of the business community, see *Literary Digest* (1894) 9:3, 64, 94, 121–24, 183–84, 211–12, 242–43, 277, 306–07, 361–63, 393–95, 482–86, 547–48, and especially 511–13.

25. Harry Jerome, *Migration and Business Cycles* (New York, 1926), pp. 97, 245–47; see also Brinley Thomas, *Migration and Economic Growth* (Cambridge, England, 1954), pp. 282–86.

on the incompatibility of Catholicism and the socialist elements of Populism. But the third party was hardly as serious a threat as the GOP, and to head off Republican gains the Democrats needed a desperate tactic.

The panicky Democrats sought to repeat their victories of 1890 and 1892 by focusing on the same issue that had worked so well then, the charge of nativism in the Republican party. They hoped the old issue of culture conflict could be revived and used to make liturgical voters overlook the hardships of catastrophic depression. Since the Republicans had not been so foolish as to support new Bennett laws or prohibition after 1891, a new slant was necessary to revive culture conflict. John Peter Altgeld had discovered such a new approach in Illinois in 1892, and used it to win the state house for the Democrats. Since Altgeld's approach provided a model for the Democrats of the Midwest and indeed the East as well, a return to that 1892 campaign is necessary for a full appreciation of the election of 1894.

The Illinois gubernatorial contest of 1892 was especially bitter. The incumbent Republican governor, Joseph Fifer, had responded to the Democratic landslide of 1890 by supporting efforts to repeal the Edwards school law. In Springfield, however, both parties jockeyed for the credit of repeal, and frustrated each other, leaving the obnoxious law on the statute books. The 1892 Republican state convention made the party position clear. Declaring the need for a compulsory education law, the GOP pledged that parents would be "absolutely free" to choose their children's schools and that "in no case" would civil authorities be authorized "to interfere with private or parochial schools." Finally and unequivocally the Republicans pledged the repeal of the Edwards law.[26] Governor Fifer, nominated for a second term, resolved to explain his commitment to the Illinois German community in person, and spoke to hundreds of German gatherings across the state, reaffirming the platform pledges. To the pietistic Prohibitionists the GOP's actions were "cowardly and unpatriotic," but the Illinois Republicans had learned the lesson of 1890.[27]

26. *Ann. Cycl. 1892*: 343; *Daily News Almanac 1893*, p. 138 for text. See also *Chicago Tribune*, May 4, 5, October 5, 1892.
27. *Daily News Almanac 1893*, p. 140, quoting the Prohibitionist state platform.

The Illinois Democrats, however, intended to keep the 1890 issues alive. Their nominee was John Altgeld, whose wealth, vigor, and ties with trade unions gave them the best chance in decades of capturing the statehouse. He charged that the Republicans were captives of nativists, and that their pledge to repeal the Edwards law would "do them no good:"

> It will deceive nobody; it will be insincere and will be regarded as a mere vote-catching maneuver. The spirit which enacted the alien and sedition laws, the spirit which actuated the "Know-nothing" party, the spirit which is forever carping about the foreign-born citizen and trying to abridge his privileges, is too deeply seated in the party. The aristocratic and know-nothing principle has been circulating in its system so long that it will require more than one somersault to shake the poison out of its bones.[28]

Altgeld let the national party handle the organizational problems of the campaign, while he conducted an exhausting handshaking tour of Illinois. Born in Germany of Lutheran parents, he concentrated his efforts on his Illinois kinsmen. Altgeld's speeches blended intemperate charges of administrative corruption with the issues of class conflict, lower tariffs, states rights (for whites only), and religious freedom (for Lutherans). He did not mention silver or the Haymarket anarchists, about whom he had much to say in the next four years.[29]

While observant Democratic leaders complained that "Altgeld is running a brass band campaign and simply trying to elect himself," the candidate drove home the allegation that Fifer was "secretly aligned with nativist societies, whose help he hopes to win."[30] Noting that the "Patriotic Sons of America" had declared their opposition to the repeal of the Edwards law, Altgeld charged that "those [patriotic] orders are to-day fighting the battle of the

28. John Altgeld, *Live Questions* (Chicago, 1899), p. 228, from his acceptance speech at the Democratic convention, April 27, 1892.

29. Ibid., p. 298, on states rights, and pp. 238, 248–51, on class conflict. Altgeld was not himself a Lutheran; he seems to have inclined more to Methodism. Harry Barnard, *Eagle Forgotten* (New York, 1938), p. 17.

30. E. C. Wall to W. F. Vilas, July 20, 1892, in Vilas MSS, Wisconsin State Historical Society; second quote from *Illinois Staats-Zeitung,* (Chicago), November 4, 1892.

Republican party." The voters must beware, he added, because these orders "do not march directly under the Republican banner."[31] Henry Raab, the Democrat who upset Richard Edwards in the 1890 election for school superintendent, echoed Altgeld, suggesting that if the GOP remained in power, "We [Germans] soon would have a prohibition law, besides the Edwards law, to enslave us."[32] In Raab's view, "This campaign is a matter of life and death to the German-Americans. The Germans of all parties should unite in order to fight the nativistic prohibition-fanatics and the bigoted Sunday-closers more effectively."[33]

The Democratic stance was extreme and disingenuous. Altgeld was introduced at a rally of French Canadians with the warning, "If a Frenchman wanted to teach his children how to be Catholic he should not be interfered with . . . [but] these rights the republicans would take away from them."[34] Altgeld, furthermore, pitched his appeal to the Lutherans, not the Catholics; the latter he considered partly responsible for the nativistic movement because "they have, in cases, been offensively aggressive, especially in the matter of securing and holding public offices, and also, perhaps, in not repudiating the sentiments of some of the priests who openly assail our public school system. The American people believe in the public schools, and are quick to resent any attack upon them."[35] On the eve of the election, too late to do any good, the Republicans discovered with amazement that Altgeld had read and approved the original draft of the hated Edwards bill, and perhaps even helped to write it. The candidate shrugged off the evidence and led the Democrats to an historic triumph the next day.[36]

31. Speech of September 13, 1892, in Altgeld, *Live Questions,* pp. 276–77.
32. *Illinois Staats-Zeitung,* November 4, 1892.
33. Ibid. See *Chicago Times,* November 6, 1892, for an elaborate attempt to link Fifer with the APA.
34. *Chicago Herald,* November 1, 1892.
35. Letter of January 11, 1893, in Altgeld, *Live Questions,* p. 408. Altgeld generally did not mention Catholics in a favorable way, or Lutherans in an unfavorable light. See pp. 224–25, 278.
36. *Chicago Tribune,* November 7, 8, 1892. Altgeld's friendly biographers considered his use of the Edwards law issue "unfair" and "unprincipled opportunism." Barnard, *Eagle Forgotten,* p. 160, and Ray Ginger, *Altgeld's America* (New York, 1958), p. 73.

Democratic smear tactics were probably unnecessary in 1892, but by 1894 the party was desperate for some means to stop the exodus of Catholics and other liturgical voters from their ranks. In Wisconsin, furthermore, the coalition of Lutherans and Catholics was weakening. E. C. Wall, the Democratic chairman, decided to "over-come prejudice by prejudice"; to hold the alliance together in 1894, he injected the nativist issue into Wisconsin politics. Aided by a staff of sixty German Lutherans, Wall spread the wholly untrue story that the American Protective Association, a new, avowedly anti-Catholic secret order, had been responsible for the notorious Bennett school law. The Democrats further charged that the Republican candidate for governor in 1894 was the nativist candidate, and that bigots controlled the GOP in Wisconsin. The APA in Wisconsin was in fact a small noisy group that had threatened in a few scattered towns to engulf the regular GOP organization. Led by ex-Senator John Spooner and other worried leaders, the GOP worked vigilantly to purge all the APA's members from official positions in the party.[37]

In Illinois, in 1894, the APA issue waxed fiercest in Chicago. The continuation of the depression made a Republican victory likely in that metropolis, which in 1892 had seemingly been a Democratic stronghold. The failure of Governor Altgeld and Mayor Hopkins to act during the railroad strike (both men favored the strikers) alienated conservative Democrats, while President Cleveland's use of troops to break the strike alienated labor. The fusion of Populists, trade unions, and various radical groups threatened further Democratic losses. As in Wisconsin the Democrats grasped at the APA issue.

Warning that the APA controlled 60,000 votes in downstate Illinois and another 40,000 in Chicago, the Democratic news-

---

37. Wall to Vilas, May 12, 1893, in Vilas MSS: Donald Kinzer, *An Episode in Anti-Catholicism: The American Protective Association* (Seattle, 1964), pp. 126–27, 151–54; Horace Merrill, *William Freeman Vilas* (Madison, 1954), pp. 219–23; Dorothy Fowler, *John Coit Spooner* (New York, 1961), pp. 178–79, for background. On the details of the APA operations in Wisconsin, see *Chicago Herald,* October 27, 1894, and *Chicago Times,* June 30, 1894. For a denial of the allegations, *Milwaukee Sentinel,* October 31, 1894; on Wall's efforts, *Chicago Tribune,* October 31, 1894. The revival of culture conflict in Wisconsin backfired, since it tended to pit Lutheran Democrats against Catholic Democrats. See also Paul Kleppner, *The Cross of Culture* (New York, 1970), pp. 251–67.

papers charged that the APA state president, one Clarence Johnson, was attempting to swing those 100,000 votes to the GOP. The secret order itself, however, was complaining that its machinations at the Republican state convention had been a ludicrous failure. [38] Nevertheless, the Democratic press and soap boxes rang with accusations and insinuations, all grounded not in fact but in panic. The smugly confident Republicans hardly bothered to refute them.

The Illinois APA was in fact bitterly divided in 1894. Discovering that the Chicago chapters were supporting not the GOP but a new "Independent American Citizens" ticket, Johnson attempted to purge the Chicago chapters. He failed when the national president, William Traynor, expressed his pleasure with the idea of supporting "patriotic" third parties. Late in October the treasurer of the Independent Citizens party, a former state president of the APA, resigned and turned his books over to the GOP. The Republican newspapers quickly published the records, which revealed that the bulk of the new party's funds came from a prominent leader of Chicago's Democratic machine, a close ally of Mayor Hopkins. Evidently the Democrats hoped both to drain Republican votes into the splinter party and to keep anti-Catholic agitation active in the city in order to forestall Republican victories in local elections. [39]

In every midwestern state, and in several eastern states as well (New York especially), the Democrats exploited the APA issue in 1894. Party conventions in each state denounced the APA either by name or by unmistakable reference. [40] In Michigan, the issue backfired and, combined with bitter factional struggles, helped to ruin the Democratic party in the state for forty years.

The internecine warfare among Michigan Democrats came to a head in the spring of 1893 when President Cleveland decided to distribute patronage in the state through his close friend and former postmaster general Donald Dickinson. Dickinson set up

---

38. *Chicago Times,* September 15, 1894.

39. Ibid., September 15, 23, 26, 27, October 2, 5, 7, 12, 1894; *Chicago Tribune,* October 28, 1894, for the exposé; *Ann. Cycl. 1894:* 686; Kinzer, *Anti-Catholicism,* p. 118.

40. For the platforms, *Daily News Almanac 1895,* pp. 184, 187, 190, 192, 205; and *Ann. Cycl. 1894:* 627.

secret panels of "referees" to nominate postmasters and other federal officeholders in the seven congressional districts represented by the Republicans. Dickinson's action insulted Daniel Campau, the state chairman and national committeeman, who because of his offices would ordinarily have had control of the patronage. Campau fumed that "the direction of Michigan's political affairs" had been given over "to private persons holding no official status," and demanded that Cleveland rescind his decision. Cleveland, never one to allow political compromise to challenge the generosity of personal friendship, refused.[41]

The referee dispute simmered throughout Cleveland's second term. In the Detroit mayoralty election of November, 1893, the antireferee (or "Snapper") and referee factions briefly combined and raised the APA issue against the popular incumbent Republican, Hazen Pingree, to no avail.[42] By 1894 the Michigan Democrats were in a hopeless shambles. The referees controlled the state convention, but Dickinson attempted to unite the party by giving the gubernatorial nomination to Spencer Fisher, who was acceptable to Campau. The Snappers still sulked, despite Dickinson's lure of a promise of a share of federal patronage.[43] The Democratic convention endorsed the national administration, but in defiance of Cleveland's policies declared strongly for the free and unlimited coinage of silver. The Snappers, who controlled the local organizations in the western half of the state, had demanded a silver plank, so the platform constituted another sop to them. Every leading Snapper nursed his own particular grievance against Cleveland, however, and unity was not easily achieved. Campau wanted to fuse with the Populists, recalling the fusion with the Greenbackers fifteen years before that had proven successful. Free silver was bad enough, but fusion with the Populists would have

41. *Detroit News,* May 19, 1893, for quote. On the controversy in 1893, see ibid., April 11, May 11, 27, June 26, 1893; *New York Times,* May 21, 23, 1893; and Robert Bolt, "A Biography of Donald M. Dickinson" (Ph.D. diss., Michigan State University, 1963), pp. 217–26.
42. Bolt, "Dickinson," p. 230; *Detroit Patriotic American* (the APA weekly), November 4, 1893; cf. Kinzer, *Anti-Catholicism,* pp. 60, 149, 173, 246. In his first mayoralty race in 1889, Pingree specially wooed Catholic support; *Detroit News,* November 2, 4, 1889. See also Melvin Holli, *Reform in Detroit* (New York, 1969), pp. 134–44.
43. Bolt, "Dickinson", pp. 231–32; *Detroit News,* September 6, 7, 1894.

been an intolerable affront to Cleveland, and his referees torpedoed the idea.[44]

The Republicans renominated Governor John Rich, whose prompt measures to aid destitute mining areas in the upper peninsula and decisive action against the perpetrators of the vote frauds won wide approval. Rich was not as popular among the trade unionists as Mayor Pingree, but his handling of the railway strike in July had prevented the rioting that inflamed Illinois, Indiana, Iowa, and Ohio. To mollify ex-greenbackers and other inflationists, the Republican platform pledged "to restore silver to its historic position in the United States as a money metal." This was bimetallism, a stance more inflationist than Cleveland's but shy of the free silver demands. Serenely confident, the GOP set out to demolish the Democrats.[45]

To hold the Catholics, the Democrats resorted to the APA issue; this time they could be a little more specific. They charged that Republican congressman William Linton of Saginaw, was an APA member and the chief spokesman for that society in Congress. While Linton was not in fact a member, he had made speeches in Congress that were commended by the anti-Catholics, and he had appeared before the APA national convention of 1892.[46] The Democrats also distributed a pronouncement of the small Michigan district of the Missouri Synod Lutherans condemning the APA as a secret society; the Republicans pointed out that the same Lutheran statement also condemned the Catholic Church. The Democratic nominee for attorney general, James O'Hara, warned his fellow Catholics that the Republican endorsement of a proposed constitutional amendment limiting suffrage in Michigan to fully naturalized citizens meant that "the Republican party has yielded to the A.P.A. hatred of foreigners and would

44. An astute reporter summarized the intricate factionalism of Michigan politics in the *Detroit News*, June 2, 1894. See also *Detroit News*, May 25, 1894, and *Chicago Times*, June 29, 1894; for the platforms, see *Daily News Almanac 1895*, pp. 191–95.

45. *Daily News Almanac 1895*, p. 191; see *Detroit News*, June 2, 1894, on the GOP infighting. See also *Nation* (August 9, 1894) 59:94. On Rich's effort to help the distressed miners, *Detroit News*, February 3, 1894.

46. Kinzer, *Anti-Catholicism*, pp. 60, 61, 99, 135–37, 150, 162, 210; on the APA in the spring elections, see *Chicago Tribune*, April 4, 1894.

sacrifice the latter's vote to keep the former."[47] The next day disaster struck O'Hara's party.

On October 6, one of the leading Snappers resigned from the Democratic state committee and released a letter from a former Democratic congressman charging that Fisher, the Democratic gubernatorial candidate, was "in affiliation" with the APA. Specifically, Fisher was charged with promoting the candidacy of an APA supporter, with opposing the appointment of Catholics to office, and, most damning, with having met with the state and national leaders of the association to obtain its bloc vote. Fisher admitted the minor charges, but denied that he had ever dealt with the APA leaders. The association itself vehemently denied the story.[48]

Michigan Democratic unity immediately disintegrated. An eyewitness attested to the fact of the alleged meeting. The nominee for lieutenant governor denounced Fisher and the APA, resigned from the ticket in disgust, and announced that he was thereafter a Republican. Several Snapper members of the state committee resigned, nominee O'Hara threatened to resign his candidacy, Campau and his followers refused to support the state ticket, and Catholic Democratic leaders switched to the Snapper faction. In Saginaw, the APA reacted by throwing its support behind Cleveland's referees, whereupon, in the final irony, thousands of Democratic Catholics voted for Linton and the Republican slate.[49]

The election was a rout. Rich whipped Fisher by 106,000 votes, the largest plurality Michigan had ever known. The Democrats salvaged a mere 31 percent of the vote, lost every congressional district, and elected exactly one member of the state legislature, which they had controlled only two years before. The Democrats suffered their worst drubbing in 1894, not only in Michigan, but in the remainder of the region and the nation as well. The new Fifty-fourth Congress would contain 245 Republicans (an increase of 121, the largest gain ever made), 204 Democrats (an

47. *Detroit News,* October 5, 1894, for quote; *Chicago Tribune,* October 31, 1894.

48. *Detroit News,* October 6, 8, 1894; *Detroit Patriotic American,* October 27, 1894.

49. *Detroit News,* October 6, 9, 12, 15, 1894; *Chicago Tribune,* November 2, 1894; Bolt, "Dickinson," p. 233; *Nation* (October 18, 1894) 59:278.

incredible loss of 118) and 7 Populists (a loss of 1). The Democrats elected 1 congressman from Illinois and 2 from Ohio; the other 86 representatives from the Midwest were Republicans. (In the Fifty-third Congress, elected in 1892, the Midwest had sent 45 Democrats and 44 Republicans.) The Midwest was now firmly Republican.

The roots of the upheaval were clear to everyone. Foremost came the depression itself, which made the contrast with the prosperity of the Harrison administration most embarrassing to the Democrats. A careful survey of 5,600 Michigan farm laborers in June, 1894, revealed the sensitivity of unskilled workers to changing conditions. Sixty percent of the men reported a decline in wage rates in the last year, and nearly half had difficulty finding work over the winter. Overwhelmingly (82 percent) the men declared that "times were worse" now than a year before, and indeed were worse than five years before. Although half the men were themselves immigrants, 62 percent claimed that further immigration would hurt them economically.[50] No wonder the people of Michigan voted 4 to 1 in 1894 to discourage further immigration by requiring full citizenship of voters.

A questionnaire survey of 935 farm owners in Michigan, also taken in June, 1894, suggested the outline of the farmers' opinions during the depression. Eighty percent said that in general farming was profitable, yielding an annual return of about five percent on the invested capital. Most agreed, however, that more money could be made in other businesses; they specified banking, politics, and shopkeeping as particularly remunerative. Even so, the farmers pointed out the advantages of healthy outdoor work, self-sufficiency, personal control of their own work, and lack of anxiety about becoming unemployed. None complained about the danger of mortgage foreclosure, but several mentioned the unfavorable effects of contracting currency (which led many Yankee farmers to vote for the Populists in 1894, and most to vote for Bryan in 1896). Only a handful thought that, in general, federal legislation would help them, but there was one major exception. Two-thirds of the farmers raised sheep, and to a man they com-

50. *Twelfth Annual Report of the Bureau of Labor and Industrial Statistics of Michigan* (Lansing, 1895), pp. 230–35.

plained of low prices for mutton and wool. They felt that the provisions of the new Democratic tariff that took the import duty off wool was injurious to the sheep industry. The McKinley tariff had levied a high tax on imported wool, and the farmers resented the loss of protection.[51]

Other groups in Michigan had their complaints against the Democrats also. The lumbering regions of the northern parts of the state hoped that Congress would continue the duties on imported lumber levied by the McKinley tariff. Their hopes were squelched, for the new bill put lumber on the free trade list. The iron and copper mining areas of the upper peninsula feared the same fate for their products; Cleveland in fact worked hard to remove the tariff on the ores, but he was unsuccessful. Nevertheless the depression and uncertainty in the iron and steel industry had led to the closing of most of the iron mines. With no other work available, the condition of the miners verged on starvation. Several relief commissions partially relieved their distress, and probably helped pull the predominantly Catholic miners away from Populism and the Democrats into the Republican ranks. In 1892 the lumbering and mining counties of the upper peninsula, as table 14 shows, had voted only 50 percent Republican, but in 1894 they became 64 percent Republican and moved up to 69 percent in 1896.

Table 14

Voting Patterns in Michigan's Upper Peninsula, by Party Percentages, 1888–1896

Party	1888	1890	1892	1894	1896
Republican	55	50	50	64	69
Democratic	42	45	43	24	30
Populist	—	—	3	9	—
Prohibitionist	3	5	5	3	1
Vote cast X 1000	33	29	40	33	43

51. Ibid., pp. 343–451; Frank Taussig, *The Tariff History of the United States* (New York, 1931), pp. 291–96, 328–32.

Not only in the upper peninsula, but in farming areas, mill towns, and, especially, in the larger cities the midwestern Catholics moved toward the Republican column, although a majority in 1894 still voted Democratic. Indeed the Republicans scored their greatest gains among Catholics, despite the APA issue. In Wisconsin, rural German Catholic settlements moved from 30 percent Republican in 1892 to 40 percent in 1894. From 1888 to 1894 the Republican gain in those settlements was 7.4 percent (that is, from 33 to 40 percent), while the corresponding gain in comparable Lutheran settlements was only 1.5 percent (from 35 to 37 percent), and the statewide gain was only 3.2 percent (from 50 to 53 percent). In Iowa nine mixed Catholic and Lutheran German city wards leaped from 28 percent Republican in 1888 to 38 percent in 1894, although the statewide Republican gain was only 2 percent.[52] In Detroit the Spearman rank-order coefficient of correlation between the Republican gains from 1892 to 1894 and the Catholic population was a high +.74.

The elections of 1894 constituted more of a decline for the Democrats than a great advance for the GOP. Regionally, the total vote cast declined only 4.5 percent (from 3.56 million to 3.40 million), an unusually small fall-off from the previous presidential election. The Republican total vote increased 8.6 percent (from 1.672 million to 1.82 million), while the Democratic vote plunged 24.6 percent (from 1.670 million to 1.26 million). The minor parties fared quite differently. The Prohibitionist vote fell 14.0 percent (from 106,250 to 91,370), while the Populist vote more than doubled (from 111,760 to 229,130, an increase of 105 percent). Although the Populists gained chiefly from the Democrats, they still won less than 7 percent of the regional vote, ranging from 5.2 percent in Indiana to 8.3 percent in Iowa. Probably most of the Populist vote came from trade union members, especially those who had engaged in the railroad and coal strikes. Only among the poorer Yankee farmers in scattered

52. For the Wisconsin data, see chapter five, table 12, above. The Iowa wards were Burlington (no. 1), Clinton (no. 4), Lyon (nos. 3 and 4), Davenport (nos. 1, 2, 3), Dubuque (no. 5) and Fort Madison (no. 4); in 39 old-stock Iowa towns the Republican vote edged up to 60.2 percent, the Democrats plunged to 29.1 percent, and the Populists swelled to 8.1 percent; cf. table 10 in chapter four, above.

townships in southern Michigan and western Iowa did the Populists attract even a fifth of the farmers' votes.

The depression and the loss of many Catholic voters aggravated the worsening cleavages within the Democratic party. In 1894 supporters of President Cleveland controlled the conventions in each midwestern state, and angered the pro-union and pro-Populist factions. On the money question, the conventions ranged from hostility to silver in Wisconsin, to cautious bimetallism in Indiana, Iowa, and Illinois, to free and unlimited coinage in Michigan and Ohio. Even when the Democrats offered platforms pleasing to the silverites, they lost ground on the issue to the Republicans, who endorsed bimetallism and pointed to Cleveland's unremitting work for the gold standard. The spectacle of the tariff travesty in the Senate led to demands for the direct election of senators in the Democratic platforms in Illinois, Indiana, Iowa, and Ohio. That did not satisfy the enemies of Cleveland, who sulked during the campaign, biding their time, working with the 1896 election in mind.[53]

After the November debacle, the Cleveland supporters in the Midwest were in disgrace; their enemies were vindicated, and now eagerly espoused the cause of free silver. In 1895 the silverites gained control of the Illinois and Michigan parties, and exerted considerable power in Ohio, Indiana, and Iowa. Only in Wisconsin were the Cleveland and gold men in firm control.[54]

The gubernatorial campaigns of 1895 were dull affairs. In Iowa the gold men narrowly defeated the silverites at the Democratic convention. Attempting to resurrect the liquor issue, the Iowa Bourbons ran a desultory campaign and were overwhelmed again by the Republicans.[55] In Ohio former governor James Campbell controlled the Democratic convention and now favored a moderate sort of bimetallism, virtually indistinguishable from Governor

53. For platforms, *Daily News Almanac 1895*, pp. 183–93, 205–6; *Ann. Cycl. 1894:* 627; Stanley Jones, *The Presidential Election of 1896* (Madison, 1964), pp. 47–48.

54. *Detroit News,* December 8, 1894, February 28, March 1, 1895, on Michigan; Merrill, *Vilas*, pp. 224–27, on Wisconsin; Jones, *1896 Election,* pp. 52–54, Barnard, *Eagle Forgotten,* pp. 351–53, on Illinois; on Iowa, Nixon, "Populist Movement in Iowa," 24:82–100.

55. *Ann. Cycl. 1895:* 368–70; Nixon, "Populist Movement in Iowa," 24: 78–82.

McKinley's. An effort to endorse free silver at 16 to 1 met a 2 to 1 defeat at the convention, so the Ohio silverites went over to Jacob Coxey, the Populist nominee for governor and the head of a famous army of tramps the year before. The Republican candidate to succeed McKinley (an ally of Joseph Foraker, not of McKinley) won easily.[56]

In Indiana the Democrats were sharply divided between gold and silver. In his one notable use of the patronage powers of the presidency, Cleveland had won Senator Daniel Voorhees to the sound money cause in 1893, and although an old inflationist, Voorhees, as chairman of the Finance Committee, carried the repeal of the Sherman Act through the Senate. Voorhees was unable to gain full control of the Indiana party, however, and it remained neutral on the currency issue until Bryan's nomination, when the gold leaders were purged, many joining the Gold Democrats.[57]

In early 1896 Cleveland realized that the silverites were gaining control of his party. Although loathe to intervene in state politics, he appealed to Donald Dickinson to recapture the Michigan party. Eager to depose Campau, Dickinson acted vigorously. Employing the full resources of the referee system (expanded to cover the entire state now that all the major officeholders in Michigan were Republicans), and aided by the sound money Germans, he swept the Wayne County (Detroit) convention among others, and easily controlled the state convention. The Michigan delegation to the Democratic national convention in Chicago was made up of thirteen gold men and eleven silverites, but was bound by the unit rule to cast all of its votes for the majority faction. With Wisconsin, Michigan was the only midwestern delegation supporting Cleveland and gold at Chicago.[58]

Campau was battered but not beaten by Dickinson. At Chicago he had his revenge, and initiated a move to replace four of Michigan's gold delegates with silverites. The silverites had a majority

56. *Ann. Cycl. 1895:* 624–25; Nevins, *Cleveland,* p. 683.

57. *Indianapolis Sentinel,* September 10, 1896; *Ann. Cycl. 1896:* 358; Nevins, *Cleveland,* pp. 541–42, 608, 691, 703; Jones, *1896 Election,* pp. 54, 62.

58. Nevins, ed., *Cleveland Letters,* pp. 429–40; Bolt, "Dickinson," pp. 237–46.

of the votes on the convention floor, but needed Michigan's 24 votes to obtain the two-thirds majority required to nominate a candidate. After a heated battle, the silverites took the seats, and switched 24 votes to the Bryan cause, materially aiding his nomination. Campau regained his power, and for the next dozen years was the virtual dictator of the Michigan Democrats. Dickinson and many of his gold-minded friends bolted the Chicago ticket, and lived thereafter in political exile. Campau's final victory proved hollow—the Republicans won every statewide election in the next twelve years. Depression, disunion, and defections had ruined the Michigan Democrats.[59]

Before discarding the APA on the trash heap of unsuccessful hate groups, it is necessary to consider more fully the validity of the Democrats' charge that it worked closely with the GOP and perhaps controlled elements of the party. And it would be well to consider the relationship of the society to the pietistic reformers, especially the prohibitionists.

The APA existed on two levels. In grandiose fashion its spokesmen claimed the leadership of all "patriotic" societies in America, but only the APA clubs proper played any role in politics. The society itself was a loose-knit coalition of local clubs, few of which ever did anything more than sponsor lectures on the "Romanist peril." Anti-Catholicism was its only unifying force, and the members were mostly common folk, inarticulate, and perhaps frustrated by lack of identification with the major elements of American society. Unlike the Know-Nothing movement of the 1850s, which supplied many Republican leaders and emphasized not so much anti-Catholicism as opposition to the supposed corruption of American politics by immigrant voters, the APA was not nativistic. Indeed many, if not most, of its members were foreign-born; Protestant Irish ("Orangemen"), Britons, and Scandinavian Lutherans were predominant in the Midwest. Wil-

59. *Detroit Free Press,* July 6, August 14, 26, September 6, 1896; *Ann. Cycl. 1896:* 485; *Official Proceedings of the Democratic National Convention* (Logansport, Indiana, 1896), pp. 136–67; Bolt, "Dickinson," pp. 252–53; Earl Babst and Lewis Vander Velde, eds., *Michigan and the Cleveland Era* (Ann Arbor, 1948), pp. 125–26, 221, 243, 259, 284. On Campau, see also John Lederle and Rita Aid, "Michigan State Party Chairman: 1882–1956," *Michigan History* (1957), 41: 264–68.

liam Traynor, head of the APA from 1893 to 1896, had been born in Canada and was a leader of the Loyal Orange Institutions (Orange Lodges).[60] The leaders of the APA never exercised real influence over the rank and file. They made ludicrous claims of gigantic "membership" totals; these claims reached two or three million by the mid-nineties, and even more after the order had virtually disappeared. In some states, the APA claimed a larger membership than the number of adult males. Considering its perpetually empty treasury, it seems generous to credit the society with 100,000 dues-paying members, nationwide, at its peak. Of course, both the APA and its enemies (especially the Democratic politicians) found it convenient to exaggerate the size, influence, and malevolence of the order. Some high-minded citizens, such as the prominent Ohio minister Washington Gladden, panicked and reported bigots under every bed. Ex-President Harrison, asked in 1894 about APA strength in Indiana, replied, "I have not heard of any in our state, except as our Democratic friends talk of it. I do not think there is any."[61]

In Marinette, Wisconsin, in the lumbering region, the APA was active among Swedes and Canadians in 1894. Shortly before the fall elections, the Democrats stole and published the records of the chapter. Evidently the club had not only talked about boycotting Catholic merchants and ousting Catholic officeholders, but had tried to do something about it. One night in the spring of 1894, the members invaded the Republican city convention and named the Republican ticket (although no APA members were chosen). By fall, however, the Republican professionals managed to split the APA and destroy its influence. With the exposure of its records, the chapter fell apart, and prominent citizens charged by the Democrats with membership vehemently denied that they had ever belonged to or sympathized with the APA. Similarly, in Michigan, the Republicans neutralized the order by playing its leaders against each other.[62]

60. Kinzer, *Anti-Catholicism,* for the best description of the APA.

61. Ibid., pp. 70, 84, 97, 131, 148; *New York Times,* October 25, 1894, for quote.

62. For the records, see the long story in the *Chicago Herald,* October 27, 1894; Kinzer, *Anti-Catholicism,* pp. 149–50.

The greatest success appropriated by the APA in the Midwest was the Republican landslide in Michigan in 1894. The order claimed the support of all twelve congressmen and a majority of the legislature. President Traynor was much in evidence in Lansing when the legislature convened in 1895, and he supported a bill that put Catholic parish property in the hands of the congregation instead of the bishop. A battery of witnesses denounced the bill in committee, recalling that in 1887 some 10,000 Catholics had signed petitions protesting a similar measure. The embarrassed sponsor backed down, claiming that he had drafted the bill in response to the supposed wishes of his Catholic constituents. The bill, and the entire APA boast, died a deserved death.[63]

The APA fed upon the conflicts between Catholics and Protestants, but it is unclear whether the movement also fed upon economic discontent. The Democrats worried the voters about this straw man in proportion as their electoral prospects worsened, and so they talked about it more in 1894 than previously. However, in Michigan the society was rapidly losing members early in 1894. The previously mentioned survey of 5,600 Michigan farm laborers in June, 1894, found only eighteen men who acknowledged affiliation with the APA, although over eight hundred belonged to other fraternal societies and clubs.[64] By the spring of 1894 the Michigan association had a bankrupt treasury, and disgruntled leaders complained that the membership had fallen to under 5,000—mostly semiliterate Protestants. One former official maintained that the Michigan leaders had approached all the candidates in 1894, offering to sell the order's vote for a few hundred dollars (an indirect substantiation of the charges against Democrat Fisher). Indeed, the APA, while still boasting of hundreds of thousands of members in Michigan, was unable

63. *Detroit News,* January 10, February 1, March 20, 25, 28, 1895. Kinzer, *Anti-Catholicism,* pp. 163–64, however, says the bill passed the state senate by a 26 to 1 margin, but failed in the lower house; probably another bill was involved, for the newspapers reported that the original measure failed ignominiously. The legislature did, however, vote unanimously to incorporate the Orange Lodges—a routine, noncontroversial action.

64. *Twelfth Report Michigan B.L.S.,* pp. 4–229: cf. Kinzer, *Anti-Catholicism,* p. 176.

to even pay transportation for its officers, who were easily dismissed by politicians with $30 and $150 bribes.[65] In Illinois the candidates supported by the Chicago APA chapter polled less than half of 1 percent of the vote. The APA was the phantom bogeyman of midwestern politics.

The Orange Lodges were not especially strong either. Although Michigan had one of the largest Canadian and British populations in the region, only sixteen of those farm laborers claimed membership in an Orange Lodge. In any case the order was usually nonpolitical, and more pro-Britain and anti-Irish than anti-Catholic. The scramble by the most distinguished politicians for the Irish Catholic vote annoyed the Orangemen. Yet they were powerless to act, since most of the American citizens among them were staunch Republicans, and in no single constituency did they constitute a significant proportion of the voters. Various British societies also harbored anti-Catholic attitudes from time to time, but there is little evidence that they were of any importance in American politics.[66]

The relationship between the APA types and the pietistic reformers usually was simple. The society perceived the latent anti-Catholic strain among the pietists and sought to exploit it, but was overwhelmingly rebuffed. Traynor attempted to forge an alliance with the Prohibition party in Detroit. The drys refused to follow Traynor, a heavy drinker and a former saloon-keeper (he was known as "Whiskey Bill"). The Michigan APA thereafter advised its members against voting for the Prohibitionist

---

65. *Detroit News,* March 5, 12–14, 1894; Kinzer, *Anti-Catholicism,* p. 172.

66. Rowland Berthoff, *British Immigrants in Industrial America* (Cambridge, 1953), pp. 189–201; on the lack of political clannishness among the British, see also *Detroit News,* September 13, 1891; on the Orangemen, see also *Chicago Herald,* October 22, 1894; Kinzer, *Anti-Catholicism,* pp. 34, 114, 132, 187; John Higham, *Strangers in the Land* (New York, 1963), pp. 61–62, 83. Note that the APA flourished for a while among Illinois coal miners. The mining town of Spring Valley had the largest APA chapter in the nation in 1893, and in nearby Grundy County, also a mining area, the Republicans exploited the APA to win political power. But the APA strength was only a manifestation of more important conflicts that will be discussed in the next chapter. *Chicago Times,* October 24, 1892; W. Lloyd Warner, ed., *Democracy in Jonesville* (New York, 1949), pp. 165, 215–17 and Joseph Rosenstein, "Small-Town Party Politics" (Ph.D. dissertation, University of Chicago, 1950), pp. 57–58, 126–27, 172.

ticket. In Illinois the APA claimed that some Prohibitionist candidates were members of the society, but still refused to endorse them. Since the APA never took a stand on prohibition, or even endorsed abstinence, the drys had no use for it, and did not want to antagonize their important Jansenistic Catholic supporters by being associated with the bigots.[67]

Among some of the liturgically oriented Catholics, especially the Poles, the APA became a bugaboo, associated with both "nativistic" Republicans and advocates of prohibition.[68] In Wisconsin, however, the German Catholics seemed to enjoy the fact that the society concentrated its venom on their rivals, the Irish Catholics.[69] The Jansenists feared that the reaction of the Irish to the fulminations of the APA would sabotage their efforts in favor of temperance and the Republican party. Archbishop John Ireland denounced the APA, and denied strongly that the order had any influence within the GOP.[70] The Jansenists and the pietistic reformers recognized their implicit alliance, and refused to let an unimportant flash in the pan interrupt it. Perhaps the wisest observation came from Bishop John Keane, the Jansenist rector of the Catholic University:

> The whole movement, now known as that of the A.P.A., is simply the outcome of imported British Orangeism, in alliance with the smaller lingering element of ultra New England puritanism, in which the intolerance of the former has fused with the worst forms of the superstition of the latter.[71]

The movement, Keane added, was ephemeral and Catholics ought not to be terrified by it.

67. *Detroit Patriotic American,* November 5, 1892, October 20, 1894.

68. See *Dziennik Chicagoski* (Chicago Democratic Polish daily), November 3, 1894, March 26, May 16, 1895, as translated in the Chicago Foreign Language Press Survey, microfilm reel 50, Chicago Public Library.

69. M. Justille McDonald, *History of the Irish in Wisconsin* (Washington, 1954), pp. 185–186.

70. Kinzer, *Anti-Catholicism,* p. 158; *Chicago Tribune,* November 4, 1894.

71. *Chicago Times,* December 21, 1894; see also, M. Sevina Pahoreski, *The Social and Political Activities of William James Onahan* (Washington, 1942), p. 174, on the Chicago Jansenist who was confident that "so unworthy and so unreasonable an outbreak of bigotry must soon run its course."

By 1895 the APA was burnt-out in the Midwest, and anti-Catholicism was in eclipse. The society lingered a while longer, making more and more outrageous claims, and played a minor role in the 1896 campaign, when both Bryan and McKinley took pains to dissociate themselves from the society and any tinge of anti-Catholicism.[72]

The inability of the APA to exploit the suspicions existing between Catholics and Protestants suggests that ethnic divisions and the conflict between pietists and liturgicals, who were both found in all major denominations, were more important than interdenominational conflicts. What support the APA did obtain in the Midwest stemmed more from the hostility between the British and Irish than anything else. The existence of anti-Catholicism as a latent attitude among many midwestern Protestants apart from the liturgical-pietistic tension cannot be denied; but it did not have important political ramifications. Nor was nativism or hostility to foreigners the critical factor; the APA was not opposed to immigration, and the impetus for immigration restriction came more from the East and from organized labor than from pietistic groups. Conflict between ethnic and cultural groups was not unusual in the Midwest, and it sometimes engendered hatred and violence. Perhaps the best approach to an understanding of the impact on voting behavior of the interaction of cultural conflict and economic distress would be an analysis of the conditions among midwestern coal miners.

72. Jones, *1896 Election,* pp. 142–44, 169–70, 290, 346, 373–74; Kinzer, *Anti-Catholicism,* pp. 213–30.

9

Conflict in Coal:
Labor Militancy and the Politics of Hardship

> We'll combine, the union join,
> And work eight hours a day;
> And keep the market clear of coal
> And then they'll raise our pay.
>
> From the miners' ballad, "Pat Mullay"[1]

Nowhere in the Midwest did ethnic, cultural, and economic conflict rage as fiercely as among the coal-mine workers. A large body of hard-bitten men, suffering severe economic and psychological hardship, and isolated from tempering influences, they struggled bitterly against their fate. What superficially appeared as a classic example of the ruthless exploitation of hapless men by wealthy predators actually represented, in stark and exaggerated form, the readjustments to depression and social change taking place in every industry. The reaction of the miners, at the polls and elsewhere, reflected the complex interplay of party and ethnic loyalties, of political possibility and economic necessity. The behavior of the miners, and of the railroad workers in 1894, illustrates the unfortunate aspects of the depression better than the behavior of any other group of industrial workers.

The coal industry boomed in the Midwest during the 1880s, although not quite as dramatically as in adjacent regions. Nationwide, coal output tripled in the 1880s, and then doubled again in the next decade. The various midwestern coal fields did not share equally in this growth, of course. Older seams ran low, exhausted mines closed down, new transportation facilities opened new markets, but always the incessant demands of burgeoning, industrializing America called for more and more energy, more and more coal. And the coal industry in the Midwest was huge. By 1894 some 84,000 midwesterners mined and loaded coal, as table 15 shows. Tens of thousands of other men operated the trains, stores, and saloons needed to move 40 million tons of coal annually.

.1. George Korson, *Minstrels of the Mine Patch* (Philadelphia, 1938), p. 232.

Table 15

Number of Midwestern Coal Miners, 1889–1896[2]

Year	Illinois	Indiana	Iowa	Ohio	Total
1889	30,100	6,450	9,250	19,300	65,100
1892	34,600	6,440	8,170	22,600	71,800
1894	38,500	8,600	10,000	27,100	84,200
1896	33,100	8,800	9,870	25,500	77,000

In good times, the work of the miner was hard, dirty, and dangerous. One miner in twelve met his death underground; more than a third were injured during their years in the mines. A heavier burden was imposed by falling wages and rising insecurity. New mines, new competition, new machinery, new immigrant workmen pulled down the price of coal and the wages of the miners. In the span of Harrison's administration, the selling price of coal in Illinois plunged 47 percent and more. If an Illinois miner earned 97 cents per ton in 1889, by 1893 his wage fell to 89 cents, and in 1895 and 1896 to only 80 cents. The mines were open only seven or eight months in good times, and only six during depressions.[3] The rapid fluctuations in prices and wages spawned uncertainty, confusion, and anxiety. The pattern of national averages (table 16) tells the story of the midwestern miner's income.

Real annual earnings of the miners remained fairly steady from 1889 through 1893, save for the unusual prosperity of 1890, then plunged sharply. The disparity between the income of miners and factory workers grew from 11 percent to 32 percent in the course of the Harrison and Cleveland administrations. Most of the gap emerged at the nadir of the depression, when manufac-

2. U.S. Geological Survey, *Mineral Resources of the U.S.: 1900* (Washington, 1901), pp. 378–79, 381, 386, 416.
3. Accident rates computed from the data preserved in Ernest L. Bogart and Charles M. Thompson, *The Industrial State* (Springfield, Ill., 1920), pp. 512–13. The average annual rate from 1883 to 1897 was projected onto a forty-year average work span. Prices and wage rates computed from ibid. and *Mineral Resources: 1900*, pp. 276, 378–79, 381, 386, 416.

Table 16

National Average Annual Earnings in Bituminous Coal, 1889–1897[4]

	1889	1890	1891	1892	1893	1894	1895	1896	1897
a) $ earnings[5]	$379	406	377	393	383	292	307	282	270
b) Index of (a)	93	100	93	96	94	72	76	69	67
c) Douglas index of real earnings		100	95	99	98	77	81	73	69
d) NBER index of real earnings	93	100	93	97	95	76	81	75	73
e) (a) as percent of factory workers' earnings	89	94	86	88	91	75	72	68	64

turers met the reduction in demand by laying off their workers and the mine operators cut wages and spread the work thin.

The immobility of human capital increased the economic insecurity of the miners. Hand mining was an exacting art. Skills were cherished, and passed from father to son. When to blast, when to undercut a seam, how to minimize waste and avoid rockfalls—these things the miner had to know, and his training was long and expensive. Experienced miners were loath to forfeit the value of their skills by abandoning the industry; their sons were freer, and after 1890 those who could escape the coal fields did so. But if the men were bound to the industry, they were at least not shackled to one mine; extensive migration between fields tended to equalize working conditions and enhance a sense of labor solidarity and uniformity of opinion.

However far a miner might migrate for better wages, he found himself in familiar surroundings. Coal camps consisted of flimsy,

4. Paul Douglas, *Real Wages in the United States: 1890–1926* (Boston, 1930) pp. 223, 350, 353; Albert Rees, *Real Wages in Manufacturing: 1890–1914* (New York, 1961), p. 74, gives the National Bureau of Economic Research data.

5. Douglas, *Real Wages*, p. 350, based on Illinois and Ohio data. For a slightly different, less reliable series, see *Report of the Industrial Commission* (Washington, 1901), 12:677.

unpainted shacks clustered around the minehead, the railway depot, and the company store. Isolated from the cities, with their offerings of diversity, opportunity, and anonymity, the miners acquired a homogeneity of views and a dependence on the caprice of a single industry unknown elsewhere in the Midwest. The faces around the bar grew monotonous, and so did the talk. But monotony could not soften the passionate damning of misfortune. The company stores, not everywhere compulsory, yet everywhere condemned, exchanged exorbitant prices for burning hatred. As the night and the liquor called forth grievance after grievance from every miner present, the talk would turn to wages—low enough in good days, they now kept falling and falling. The restless miners puzzled over how to support their families on such a pittance. What could be done to stay the torrent of reduction? What could be done to save the dignity of an honorable trade?

On May Day, 1889, the men struck fifty-nine large mines at LaSalle, Streator, Braidwood and other points in northern Illinois. The latest 12 percent slash was intolerable. The day before, the huge Spring Valley Coal Company had locked out its 1,300 recalcitrant men. The 7,000 strikers stayed out 138 days, days that would have been good for over a million dollars in wages. The men at Spring Valley, harrassed, threatened, half-starved, finally accepted the company's modified terms after 197 days, after losing some $400,000 in wages. The widespread hardship, if not actual starvation of the men and their families, elicited the compassion of sensitive men across the nation.[6]

"Strike!" was the call that filled the mine shafts. From 1887 through 1897, 116 major coal strikes shut down Illinois mines for an aggregate of 47,800 workdays. In all, the 78,000 strikers—many going out several times—sustained $6,000,000 in lost wages, while inflicting $1,600,000 in lost profit on the operators. Thirty-two times, Indiana miners walked out, closing the mines for 20,500 workdays, and foregoing $2,000,000 in wages. Only eight coal strikes occurred in Iowa, but the picket lines swallowed

6. Cf. Henry D. Lloyd, *A Strike of Millionaires Against Miners* (Chicago, 1890), for the original "exploitation"-type story of Spring Valley. See also *10th Annual Report U.S. Commissioner of Labor: 1894* (Washington 1898), pp. 186–89, 1282–85; Chris Evans, *History of the United Mine Workers of America* (Indianapolis, 1900?), 1:464–65, 474–77; *Ann. Cycl. 1889:* 419.

Table 17

Midwestern Coal Strikes, 1887–1894[7]

	Illinois strikes	Illinois lockouts	Indiana strikes	Iowa strikes	Ohio strikes	Totals
Number of strikes	116	4	32	8	111	271
Percent called by unions	67%	0	91	100	50	63%
Number establishments closed	1224	5	396	233	620	2478
Percent where strike failed	47%	40	44	90	60	54%
Aggregate days closed	47,800	626	20,500	12,700	24,500	106,100
Average days closed per establishment	39	125	52	55	40	43
Number of strikers	77,800	1400	28,700	13,400	70,700	192,000
Estimated wage loss X $100,000	$60.0	$4.0	$19.0	$6.1	$22.0	$111.0
Estimated profit loss X $100,000	$16.0	$0.5	$4.0	$1.1	$5.6	$27.0
Number of strikebreakers	1300	0	80	180	200	1760

7. *10th U.S. Labor Report: 1894*, 2: 1452–59, 1480–83, 1608–11. Rounding the data avoids some of the pretense of perfect accuracy. Data originally furnished by participants, and very approximate.

up 12,700 workdays and $614,000 in wages. In Ohio, 111 strikes cost 24,500 workdays and $2,000,000 in wages. Table 17 summarizes the extent of midwestern coal strikes from 1887 through the summer of 1894.

Every state, every field, nearly every mine and miner experienced strikes. The operator watched his capital sit idle, guarded by hostile pickets, and saw his competitors grab his market. The miners, deprived of outside employment, fell back on their meagre savings, and often had to rely on scanty charity to feed and clothe their families. Generally, the coal towns sympathized with the strikers, castigated the intransigence of the operators, and refused the use of local police to guard the operators' interests when violence flared. As grievance soured to hatred and tension escalated into violence, the tranquility of the mining towns, never very secure, collapsed. Both sides recognized the viciousness of the strike, as a joint union-management manifesto issued in the wake of the bloody Hocking Valley, Ohio, strike of 1884 made clear:

> [Strikes and lockouts] have become evils of the greatest magnitude, not only to those immediately concerned in them, but also to the general society, being fruitful sources of public disturbance, riot and bloodshed. . . . They engender bitter feelings of prejudice and enmity and enkindle the destructive passions of hate and revenge, bearing in their train the curse of widespread misery and wretchedness.[8]

Realization of the horrors of strikes did not prevent them. The miners' grievances ran strong and deep; union organization was not necessary to spark a walkout. While 70 percent of the strikes in all other industries were union-led, only 60 percent were so in coal. Nationally, 29 percent of the coal strikes demanded increased wages, 25 percent protested wage cuts, 21 percent sought adoption of a new wage scale, another 7 percent sympathized with fellow strikers elsewhere, and only 18 percent were due to other issues. The pressure of steadily falling income, not the militancy or agitation of unions, led to the spate of strikes in the coal industry. The sense of need for organization to con-

8. "Operators' and Miners' First Joint Circular," October 17, 1885, in Evans, *History UMW*, 1:148.

duct strikes stimulated the formation of miners' unions. The collapse of the industry-wide strike of 1876, coupled with internecine warfare between the Knights of Labor and the independent miners' unions impeded the development of a stable, effective national union. Finally, in 1890, the rival unions combined into the United Mine Workers of America, and dual unionism ceased to plague the coal miners.

The UMW was too small and weak to improve decisively its members' condition. Table 16 traces the decline of the miners' annual earnings from $406 in 1890 to $393 in 1892; the impact of the depression came late in 1893, and made the wages of three years before seem munificent. A wave of wage reductions, beginning in the Pittsburgh district, drove the miners to desperation. The UMW, with only 20,000 members, called a strike of all bituminous coal miners for April 21, 1894. Virtually all the midwestern and Pennsylvania miners quit their work, some 170,000 in all. The great coal strike of 1894 is now but a forgotten preliminary to the Pullman and railroad strikes of June and July 1894, but it assumed fearful proportions and deserves careful attention. As the flow of coal diminished, factories and businesses that had managed to stay solvent were forced to close down. Railroads curtailed service, cities faced an energy famine, a blackout that threatened their very survival. The strike ended in June, before disaster could ruin the cities, but not before pent-up tension in the coal fields exploded into violence. For ten days pandemonium raged in the Illinois coal fields. Mobs threatened defiant miners, ignited shafts, dynamited coal trains from the South, shot at trainmen, burned bridges, and defied three dozen companies of state militia. In Ohio attempts to destroy railroad bridges were foiled by Governor McKinley's swift but impartial use of militia. Two men died, others barely escaped, in Indiana riots. The strike, having lost the support of public opinion, rapidly collapsed. As the miners grumbled at the terms accepted by the UMW, union membership, which had soared to 80,000 at the peak of the strike, collapsed to 20,000. The men resolved to shift their protest to the polls.[9]

9. The best sources for the strike are the *Chicago Tribune; Chicago Times* (prolabor); *Chicago Daily News Almanac for 1895*, pp. 77–78, 400;

In the aftermath of a strike that cost the nation's economy perhaps twenty million dollars, and the mine workers one-fourth that in lost wages, resentment was high. Many miners reacted against the party in power, and voted Republican, but the militancy of the strike period encouraged the efforts of third-party forces in weaning miners away from their traditional party loyalties. Thousands of miners repudiated both the Republicanism of the operators and the Democratic policies of Cleveland, and voted Populist in 1894. Of the dozen Illinois precincts carried by the Populists in that year, half were coal camps, led by Spring Valley, whose 54 percent Populist support was one of the highest in the Midwest.

Despite the general economic upturn, the fortunes of the miners sank lower and lower, as table 16 shows. The index of real annual income slipped from 77 in 1894 to 73 in 1896, and then sank to 69 in 1897, probably the lowest level from the Civil War to the present day. Threatened by yet another wage cut, the UMW called a general strike for the Fourth of July, 1897. Across the nation 150,000 nearly destitute men dropped their picks and shovels, some 75,000 midwesterners among them. Union President Ratchford voiced their mood:

> Our suspension is not a choice but . . . is the voice of an enslaved class urged to action by cruel and unbearable conditions, the protest of an overworked, underpaid people against longer continuing a semi-starved existence.
>
> This movement is nothing less than a spontaneous uprising of an enslaved people.[10]

Ann. Cycl. 1894: 362, 372, 380; *Bradstreet's* (1894) 19: 258, 322, 338, 357, 370–71, 386; Evans, *History UMW,* 2: 352–64; Illinois Bureau of Labor Statistics, *Coal in Illinois: 1894* (Springfield, 1894), Appendix. On the UMW membership, see the interview with John McBride, head of both the UMW and the AFL, *Chicago Times,* December 24, 1894. The strike in Alabama is covered in Robert Ward and William Rogers, *Labor Revolt in Alabama* (University, Ala., 1965). For Ohio, see Paul Kleppner, *The Cross of Culture* (New York, 1970), pp. 234–49.

10. Statement of July 19, 1897, in *Daily News Almanac for 1898,* p. 242. See also J. E. George, "The Coal Miners' Strike of 1897," *Quarterly Journal of Economics* (1898) 12: 186–208.

Thus far the plight of the coal miners resembles the classical picture of an "over-worked, underpaid" laboring class struggling under the exploitation of ruthless capitalists in a materialistic society. Yet the closing words of President Ratchford's statement give pause to such a routine interpretation:

> It should be said, in justice to a large majority of employers, that they are not responsible for this condition. It is due to the actions of a few who have cut prices far below the demands of the market, thus demoralizing trade and cutting wages indiscriminately, until a point is reached where men can no longer live by thrift and industry.[11]

Not only did the union leaders absolve the large majority of operators, but both the general public and the operators themselves at first sympathized with, and supported the strikes of 1894 and 1897. The hostility of the public and the operators in 1894 came only after violence began. The Illinois Labor Commission in 1894 found a "universal sentiment of sympathy and kindness among the operators for the ultimate success of the movement." Similar reports came from Indiana and Ohio. Operators and union leaders, furthermore, had been holding regular amicable joint meetings since 1885. Powerful businessmen and politicians, notably Mark Hanna, himself a leading mine owner, William McKinley, and Governor Tanner of Illinois, proved to be staunch friends of the miners, and received both the confidence and the votes of the miners.[12]

If relations between capital and labor were so friendly, what caused the strikes and the violence? Why, indeed, did the operators approve some strikes and try to crush others? Why did so many miners vote Populist, and what were the general political implications of all this? A routine "exploitation of labor" theory cannot resolve the paradoxes of the coal miners. Understanding

11. *Daily News Almanac for 1898*, p. 243. Cf. Almont Lindsey, *The Pullman Strike* (Chicago, 1942), ch. 1, or Harold U. Faulkner, *Politics, Reform and Expansion* (New York, 1959), ch. 8.

12. *Ill. BLS Rept. 1894*, Appendix, p. 6; George, "1897 Strike," 12:200; Andrew Roy, *A History of the Coal Miners of the United States* (Columbus, Ohio, 1906), pp. 163–64, 173; Evans, *History UMW*, 1:145–6, 171–86; *Indiana 5th Report Department of Statistics* (Indianapolis, 1894), pp. 236–37.

must rest on a deeper analysis of the economics of the coal industry, the sociology of the mining camps, and the psychology of the men involved.

The true villain was the inadequate mechanism to adjust supply to demand in the coal industry. The operators were unable to control or even predict the demand for their product. Demand for coal to fuel the engines of an accelerating economy, to warm homes, stores, and factories varied with the business cycle and the weather. Since bituminous coal was used mainly by railroads and heavy industry, the demand for coal was an exaggeration of the demand for manufactures and transportation, both of which varied erratically. The unpredictable weather had a considerable effect on the demand for coal used in heating; as one operator noted, "The coal industry . . . is very sensitive to the mercury; it goes up and down with the thermometer." The 1880s and 1890s were generally cool in the Midwest, but 1889 and, especially, 1894 were warm. The coal operators could control their production, but being ignorant of what the demand would be, could not rationally adjust to the optimum output. Worst of all, output capacity was geared to peak demand; when depression came, so many operators were unwilling to shut down their expensive mines that the market could be cleared of the overproduction only by a drastic cut in prices. In other industries, such conditions would lead to the formation of pools or trusts to stabilize profits. Coal was different. The rapid growth of new fields, the fragmentation of the industry into thousands of mines scattered across broad areas, and the very size of the $100,000,000 industry frustrated all attempts at effective consolidation.[13]

Uncertainty ruled coal, and uncertainty fed upon itself. Storage of coal was so expensive that small market fluctuations were rapidly transmitted to the mines. The operators in a depression could not divert their capital investment to other uses. The midwestern mine fields offered little alternate employment to the miners, and they were reluctant to leave for distant cities. Unlike Pennsylvania, the midwestern fields had no textile or comparable industry to provide jobs for the women and thus smooth out fluctuations in family income. A coal town relied heavily on one

13. *Rept. Indstl. Com.*, 12:12, 8, 10.

basic source of income, and groaned under the anxiety and frustration generated by an unstable industry.

Coal cried out for rationalization. With capital consolidation impossible, only one mechanism could fill the need: adjustment of the labor supply. The miners and operators met regularly in an effort to equalize competitive advantages among fields by fixing a pattern of wage rates. Since two-thirds of the price of coal went for wages, the outcome sought was a stable price structure for the central competitive region of the industry, the Midwest and adjacent states. A drop in demand was met either by a sliding scale of wages or by the uniform cutback of mine output. However, the operators in the expanding new fields resisted the freezing of supply quotas implicit in standardized regional wages. One firm in particular, the New York and Cleveland Gas Coal Company, wanted more of the market, and broke the delicate wage-scale mechanism in 1894 and again in 1897, thereby demoralizing the industry and forcing the general strikes. Bilateral agreements could not succeed unless the miners' union was strong enough to hold every major firm to the terms. After the successful strike of 1897, the UMW enrolled nearly all the midwestern miners, and so was able to police the industry.[14]

The failure of bilateral agreements left one other system for controlling the supply of labor: the strike. The industry was so demoralized by the downward spiral of depression and cutthroat competition in 1894 and 1897 that the UMW call for a general strike won immediate acceptance from both the miners and the operators. John Mitchell, UMW president, explained the system in 1899:

> A general strike is only resorted to when the coal market becomes so demoralized and chaotic that it is absolutely necessary to curtail production, so that prices of coal may be restored and it is possible for employers to pay a higher rate of wages.[15]

In the spring of 1894 the market was glutted with large stores of coal ordered when more factories had been operating and the weather was colder. A general strike was necessary to stop further glutting, raise prices and wages, and save the industry from

14. Ibid., 12:173, 60–61, 73, 30–32, cxxiii–cxlii.
15. Ibid., 12:37.

the threat of bankruptcy. Ten weeks after the miners quit, the *Chicago Tribune* finally understood their goal. The coal strike, it charged,

> is not so much a strike of miners against employers for higher wages as of miners and mine-owners against the consumer to get higher wages for the one and larger profits for the other.[16]

The Illinois Commissioners of Labor found that "many of the operators expressed themselves frankly and freely as willing to make the matter a common cause with the miners that an advance in wages might thereby be assured." But a few operators revolted at the idea that labor, not management, should rationalize *their* industry, and shut down their mines just when the strike was forcing a sharp rise in prices.[17] Some big operators, it was said, tried to continue the strike so that some of their smaller competitors would go bankrupt. Some of the miners were so impoverished that they went to work at the few mines that refused to close. In most strikes, the strikers encourage competitors to operate at full capacity so as to force the struck employers to settle quickly; however the target of the general coal strike was the market, not the employers. All production or transportation of coal in the Midwest had to cease. The strikers used persuasion where possible, but some hotheads thought violence more persuasive.

16. *Chicago Tribune*, June 5, 1894 (editorial). See letter of John McBride in *Bradstreet's* (April 28, 1894) 19: 258.
17. *Ill. BLS. Coal in Illinois: 1894,* Appendix, p. 6. In Indiana, the operators sympathized with the strike, even continuing credit at the company stores. The men reported no grievances against the operators, but claimed they struck in sympathy with their Ohio and Pennsylvania brothers. *Indiana 5th Statistical Report*, p. 237. Ohio operators also were sympathetic, at least before the rioting. *Nation* (May 24, 1894) 58: 381. E. Bemis, "The Coal-Miners' Strike," *The Outlook* (May 12, 1894) 49: 822–23. John Altgeld, *Live Questions* (Chicago, 1899), p. 762. On the individualism of the operators, see letter to editor of *The Outlook* (1894) 49: 1048, and W. J. Ashley, *The Adjustment of Wages* (London, 1903), pp. 103–4; *Rept. Indstl. Com.*, 12:77, 119, 122; and Rowland Berthoff, "The 'Freedom to Control' in American Business History," in *A Festschrift for Frederick B. Artz* (Durham, 1964) pp. 158–80. Midwestern miners' wages failed to rise after the strike because huge quantities of southern coal flooded the midwestern markets for the first time. *Daily News Almanac for 1895*, p. 400.

The success of a general strike depended on economic conditions. Hardship among the miners increased the number of strikers, but reduced their capacity for endurance. An economy-wide depression, as in 1894, increased the need for a strike, but lessened the likelihood of its success and the favor of public opinion. The frustration arising from sustained hardship led to aggression and violence, which weakened the support of public opinion. In any case, the miners had to work together.

A strong union could impose the necessary discipline to carry a strike to a successful conclusion, as the later history of the UMW proves. But a strong union had to be founded on a good strike record, which the UMW lacked before 1897. Before then, the miners, with or without unions, had been unusually unsuccessful at winning strikes. In all industries, 47 percent of the strikes were successful; in coal the percentage was a dismal 19 percent. While only 25 percent of the strikes among the militant building tradesmen, and 41 percent of strikes in other industries focused on low wages, fully 75 percent of the coal strikes represented demands for better wages. Pathetically, only 15 percent of the coal strikes involving these gut issues succeeded. The operators sympathized with demands of their men for higher wages—they did not want to see their good workers impoverished. But the operators were in a bind; in a competitive industry they had no control over the price of coal. As it was, they did increase the share of the gross coal receipts going to the workers, from 54 percent in 1883 to 71 percent in 1891. Beyond that they could not go, for their margin per ton plunged from 68 cents in 1883 to 36 cents in 1891 to an abysmal 34 cents in 1894. No wonder the operators welcomed a general freeze on further production during slack periods.[18]

The strike mechanism for adjusting the supply of labor did not require unions; it was automatic. Whenever demand fell, operators began to close down their mines temporarily—even in good years they never worked full time. Always, some operators proposed to their men that a wage reduction would increase their competitive advantage and permit reopening. In cases of a temporary slack, this adjustment mechanism worked well. But when

18. Data for 1887–94, from *10th U.S. Labor Report: 1894,* pp. 1564–65, 1836–37; Ill. BLS, *Coal in Illinois: 1894,* xxxii.

falling demand for coal was general, the acceptance of lower wages poured cheap coal on the market and further squeezed the other operators. As the vicious cycle spiralled downward, the miners felt impelled to strike against further wage cuts.

The system of local strikes against reductions rationalized the industry as well as a general strike, but at a fearsome human cost. Since a localized stoppage raised the demand for coal in other areas, the wages of nonstriking miners rose, and the miners in the aggregate lost nothing. The statistics of "wages lost" in coal strikes, therefore, are misleading: other miners got the money. The miners seemed to have enough sense of solidarity to accept the local strike mechanism.[19] The operators were more individualistic. Although a local strike meant higher profits elsewhere, it meant losses to the struck operators, and might also mean a permanent loss of market. The human capital embodied in mining skills may have been sufficiently mobile to follow geographical shifts in production, but each operator's mine was firmly rooted in the ground. So the struck operators fought back. Some operators avoided necessary wage cuts by tampering with the weighing screens or overcharging at the company stores; such practices, of course, only multiplied grievances. Others resorted to reasoned appeals, concessions, blacklisting, or, in extreme cases, strikebreakers. The miners did not sit idly by while their strike was being beaten. They fought back, with persuasion, public pressure, and, sometimes, violence or the threat of violence.[20]

19. Testimony of Mitchell, *Rept. Industl. Com.*, 12:36–37, also 126–27, 213–14, 246–47; McBride interview, *Chicago Times*, December 24, 1894.
20. Testimony of Mitchell, *Rept. Indstl. Com.*, 12: cxxiv. After Italians were brought to Spring Valley following the 1889 lockout, the use of strikebreakers lost favor. The operators discovered, much to their horror, that the supposedly docile new immigrants were far more hostile to capital than the old miners. Attempts to replace the Italians and Slavs at Spring Valley, Pana, and Virden with Negroes in 1895 and 1898 led to bloody race riots. *New York Times*, August 5–9, 1895; *Rept. Indstl. Com.*, 12: 52–53, 118, 178–80; Victor Hicken, "The Virden and Pana Mine Wars of 1898," *Journal of the Illinois State Historical Society* (1959) 52:263–79. On the earlier use of strikebreakers, particularly Negroes and Scandinavians, see Herbert Gutman, "The Braidwood Lockout of 1874," in ibid. (1960) 53:5–28, and his "Reconstruction in Ohio," *Labor History* (1962) 3:243–64; Frank Hickenlooper, *An Illustrated History of Monroe County, Iowa* (Albia, Ia., 1896), p. 187; *Ill. 4th BLS Report 1886*, p. 401; *3rd U.S. Labor Report: 1888*, pp. 1100, 1103–4.

The success of a local strike depended on numerous factors. Regardless of the state of the market, a local strike hurt the men involved. The settlement process involved a wide range of techniques, from amicable collective bargaining to sheer economic and social warfare. The attitudes and financial balance sheets of the operators, as well as the discipline and attitudes of the miners, were key considerations. Our ultimate concern, however, is with the political behavior of the miners, so we must turn to an analysis of the changing social and psychological characteristics of this group.

From the Civil War to about 1890, the British and Irish dominated the midwestern coal fields. Thousands of English, Scottish, Welsh, and Irish miners, plus a smaller number from Germany and elsewhere, established the midwestern mining industry. The British found American wage scales attractive, but working conditions too harsh. They introduced British-style unions, with a high respect for union leadership, to cope with American conditions. The Irish brought a heritage of Anglophobia, but also a very high caliber of leadership. The conflict between the British and the Irish, with side-clashes involving Germans, Negroes, and Scandinavians, characterized mining up to the mid-1880s. But by 1890 those conflicts died away in the face of a vastly more serious threat to all the older, established miners—the "invasion" from eastern and southern Europe.[21]

Beginning slowly in the 1880s, the flow of the "new" immigrants became a tide in the 1890s,[22] causing immense economic, social,

21. See Rowland Berthoff, *British Immigrants in Industrial America,* (Cambridge, 1953), pp. 52–54; Clifton Yearley, *Britons in American Labor* (Baltimore, 1957), pp. 123–41, 168–83; Wayne Broehl, *The Molly Maguires* (Cambridge, 1964).

22. The "new" immigrants include, in descending order of importance in the coal industry, North Italians, Lithuanians, Poles, Slovaks, Magyars, South Italians, Russians, Bohemians, Croatians, and Belgians (who, though from western Europe, fit the "new" patterns). "Old" immigrants include the English, Scotch, Welsh, Irish, Germans, and Swedes, both first and second generations. The native born of native parents are grouped with the old immigrants, and the Negroes with the new. The French occupied an ambiguous position, comparable to the Belgians. Other groups were numerically unimportant in the midwestern coalfields. *Reports of the Immigration Commission* (Washington 1911), vol. 5, and especially vol. 6,

psychological, and political upheavals among the miners. From 1890 to 1900, the total number of miners in Ohio grew from 24,000 to 33,000, but the number of new immigrants among them jumped from 700 to 3,500. The most dramatic shift came in Illinois. Of 22,200 miners in 1890, only 3,180 (14.4 percent) were new immigrants. In 1900, the state had 38,200 workers, of whom 9,350 (24.4 percent) were new immigrants. These statistics partially conceal the depth of anxiety generated among the old miners, for thousands of the miners coming to the Midwest in the 1890s were old-immigration "refugees" from the earlier Slavic invasion of the Pennsylvania fields.[23]

The distribution of new immigrants was not uniform; the largest impact came in northern Illinois. From 1890 to 1893, some 900 Italians poured into Coal City, a town of only 2,500 people, displacing an equal number of old-immigration miners and families. In 1886, in Spring Valley, perhaps a dozen of the town's 4,000 inhabitants were Italian or Polish. By 1893, at least half of the miners were Italian or Polish; by 1900, over 80 percent of the miners were new immigrants. The pattern repeated over and over. A survey of 2,300 miners in northern and central Illinois in 1893 found that only 20 percent were American-born, while fully 43 percent were new immigrants, chiefly Slavs and Italians.[24]

The new immigrants could not directly influence midwestern politics during the 1890s since they did not vote. Many spoke no English; few met the citizenship requirements for suffrage.[25] Many

---

"Immigrants in Industries, Part 1, Bituminous Coal Mining" pp. 13, 578. The commission's scheme, although faulty in many technical ways, is appropriate for our purposes. The commission's research in the coal fields was quite extensive, and correlates closely with other source data.

23. Ibid. 6: 582–85, 253–55; data based on 1890 and 1900 censuses. Indiana saw an increase from 6,500 to 12,600 miners, but only from 280 to 990 new immigrants; Iowa gained from a base of 7,700 to a total of 11,100 from 1890 to 1900. Only 220 and 850, respectively, were new immigrants. Note that the 1890 data represent only foreign-born new immigrants, but the 1900 data also include a very small number from the second generation.

24. *Rept. Immig. Com.*, 6:592–94; *Ill. BLS, Coal in Illinois: 1893*, p. 120.

25. Throughout the period, suffrage in Illinois, Iowa, and Ohio required full citizenship, which meant at least five years' residence. Indiana, Michigan, and Wisconsin required only the filing of a declaration of intent,

were "birds of passage," intending only to amass enough money to make them rich in their home villages. They intended their stay in America to be brief, so even if they never did go back, they at first paid little attention to American politics. Fresh arrivals from northern and western Europe were no more quickly naturalized, nor any more committed to permanent settlement. In sharp contrast to the old immigrants, however, the new immigrants did not have a heritage of peaceful settlement of disputes or union membership. They were slow to join unions, uncertain in routine membership, and uncontrollably violent during a strike.[26]

If the votes of the new immigrants did not influence elections, their behavior certainly did. The newcomers were mostly unskilled peasants unfamiliar with the broad outlines, let alone the nuances, of the delicate tissue of human and industrial relations that had evolved in the coalfields.[27] For the newcomer, a strike was simply like a war. The rhetoric of the miners was couched in terms of struggle, grievances, hardship, and the need for action. Strike leaders fired up enthusiasm by singling out specific grievances, particularly those, like wage cuts, that translated well. But in Italian translation the call for a temporary walkout to enhance a bargaining position must have sounded like the call to battle against the oppressor. The new immigrants willingly fought a strike, and they used the most natural weapon: violence.

Up to the 1894 strike, the old miners generally were able to suppress the violent threats of the new immigrants, although a number of bloody episodes disgraced the Pennsylvania fields. In 1894, tension was much higher, violence was closer to the surface, as the record of bloodshed in strikes and riots across the country —indeed, across the world—proved. The Slavic, Italian, and Belgian miners were restless in 1894. The severity of the depression

---

plus a short state residency. In 1894 Michigan restricted its suffrage to full citizens. *Daily News Almanac for 1894*, p. 126.

26. *Rept. Indstl. Com.*, 12: 38, 51, 72, 84, 95; *Rept. Immig. Com.*, 6: 654–56.

27. A small number of newcomers had mining experience in Belgium, Italy, or the Austro-Hungarian Empire. Coal miners in those countries frequently staged massive strikes, attended by considerable violence and brutal suppression by the army. *Ann. Cycl. 1889*: 77–78; *1890*: 55, 71; *1891*: 68, 309; *1893*: 65, 76, 328, 286, 415; *1894*: 66, 321–22. *Rept. Immig. Com.*, 6: 45; *Rept. Indstl. Com.*, 12: 51, 71–72, 655.

came as a shock; many found their plans to return home frustrated. How much stranded immigrants contributed to the record of mob action across the country in 1894 is unclear; probably they constituted the bulk of the rioters, for example, in the Chicago railroad yards in July. At Spring Valley and vicinity, exiled Italian anarchists gained leadership of the Italian and Slavic strikers, and incited rioting and other incidents opposed by the old miners. In one case, a mine fired by arsonists burnt up because the new immigrants prevented the old miners from extinguishing the blaze. The Slavic miners overcame the resistance of the older men and acted on their own to close the few open mines, particularly those at Pana, Illinois, and to impede the movement of southern coal that was flowing into the midwestern market vacuum.[28]

Most strikes began with the support of public opinion, which was essential to forestall consumer demands for repression. The degeneration of the 1894 strike into violence quickly drained the reservoir of public approval and sharply lowered the prestige of the miners. Even Governor Altgeld was forced to call up the state militia to guard against mobs and violence to trains (but he refused to let the militia guard mines from arson).[29] The older miners deplored the violence and turned their resentment against the new immigrants. Very little was needed to stir the antagonism of desperate men.

The new immigrants seemed obnoxious to the old miners. Unskilled or unsophisticated in the art of mining, the former caused many accidents. Willing to work harder and longer for less pay, they drove wages down. Their availability prevented wages from rising in an expanding industry and permitted the introduction of machinery that obviated the need for many traditional skills. Above all, their language, religion, ignorance, and mode of living shocked and disgusted the more acculturated British, Irish, Germans, and Americans. Yet the economics of the industry dictated their employment.

28. *Daily News Almanac 1895,* pp. 77–78; *Ann. Cycl. 1894:* 362, 372; *Chicago Tribune,* May 2, 24, 26–30, June 1–3, 5, 9–15, 1894; Evans, *History UMW,* 2: 352–53, 361; *Ill. BLS 1894,* p. 56; *Ohio Annual Reports for 1894* (Columbus, 1895), 2: 488, 492, 494.

29. See the newspaper editorials in *Literary Digest* 9:153, 246; *Chicago Tribune,* May 26, 1894; on Altgeld, see Harry Barnard, *Eagle Forgotten* (New York, 1938), pp. 276–79.

The reaction of the old miners was complex. Large numbers moved west—the Pennsylvanians came to the Midwest. The midwesterners had less opportunity to escape to new fields, for the foreigners were already well established in western mines. Many reluctantly abandoned their mining skills, and sought low-paying jobs in the cities. Young men refused to follow their fathers' trade. Two classes remained in the mines after the "invasion." A disreputable, despised class were willing to work side by side with the Italians and Slavs. Highly skilled veterans moved up to supervisory, managerial, or very specialized positions. Except for these veterans, the old-stock miners suffered heavily from the coming of the southern and eastern Europeans.[30]

The immediate reaction to new immigrants in the field ranged from cruel "Polish jokes" and needling songs[31] to political action. Beginning in 1889, the Pennsylvania legislature built a system of licensing designed to exclude the Slavs from the mines. Illinois followed suit, but the plan backfired; it delayed the entry of the Slavs for a year or two, but effectively cut off the flow of "desirable" miners from northern and western Europe.[32] Probably more than any other large group in the country, the old miners advocated restriction of undesirable immigration. The problem was touchy, since the great majority of the old miners were first- or second-generation immigrants themselves, usually with relatives back in the old country who might want to come to America. Their resolution was to attack the further immigration of "paupers," "illiterates," "undesirables," "contract labor," or "unassimilable

30. The entire thrust of *Rept. Immig. Com.*, vols. 6 and 7, points up this tension; whether the charges against the new immigrants were solidly based on fact is irrelevant here; the charges were widely believed. See especially ibid. 6:423–27, 661–70. For further evidence, see *Ill. BLS. Coal in Illinois: 1893*, p. 119–21, 133–34; *Rept. Indstl. Com.*, 12: cxlvii, 38, 46, 50–51, 71–72, 83–84, 100, 140–41, 655, 671; Berthoff, *British Immigrants*, pp. 54–58; Roy, *History Coal Miners*, pp. 314–15; Evans, *History UMW*, 2: 348; Hicken, "Virden and Pana Mine Wars," 52:268; Peter Roberts, *Anthracite Coal Communities* (Philadelphia, 1904), pp. 22–38; Frank J. Warne, *The Slav Invasion and the Mine Workers* (Philadelphia, 1904); Jeremiah Jenks and W. Jett Lauck, *The Immigration Problem* (New York, 1926), pp. 194–208; Victor R. Greene, *The Slavic Community on Strike* (Notre Dame, 1968), esp. chaps. 2, 3, 6.
31. Korson, *Minstrels of the Mine Patch*, pp. 125–38.
32. Warne, *Slav Invasion*, pp. 87–88; *Rept. Immig. Com.*, 6:655–56.

classes." A poll of 400 Iowa coal miners showed that although half were foreign-born, 70 percent opposed immigration. The UMW reflected the sentiment of its preponderantly old-immigration membership by demanding in 1896 congressional protection from the "demoralizing effects" of immigration. The farsighted UMW leadership realized, however, that its future success demanded the membership of the new immigrants, and it worked hard to soften the internal conflict between nationalities that raged in the coal fields.[33]

The most interesting reaction came at the polls. Table 18 shows the approximate pattern of voting in Illinois coal camps.

Beginning with approximate parity in 1888, the Republicans slipped slightly in the coal towns, as the Democrats absorbed the Union Labor vote in 1890. In 1892 the Republicans fell consid-

Table 18

Illinois Coal-Town Voting, 1888–1896 (in percentages)[34]

	1888	1890	1892	1894	1896
Republican	48	47	44	51	52
Democratic	47	53	52	33	48
"Union Labor" or Populist	4	—	4	17	—

33. *3rd Rept. Iowa B.L.S. 1888–9* (Des Moines, 1889), pp. 126–34; 113 of 413 miners replying said immigration did not hurt them—but most of the 113 were themselves immigrants. *Rept. Indstl. Com.*, 12:50–51, cxlviii; Evans, *History UMW*, 2: 257, 269–70, 331, 423; Springfield, *Illinois State Journal*, July 5, 1894 (editorial). As early as 1888 the leading German newspaper of the Midwest demanded an end to Italian immigration. *Illinois Staats-Zeitung*, August 11, 1888 (editorial).

34. Based on the vote of Spring Valley, Streator, Girard, Virden, Mt. Olive, Braceville, Coal City, Braidwood, Percy, and Murphysboro—with the last two weighted double to give a better representation to southern Illinois. The total vote represented—the Prohibitionists and other minor parties excluded—ranged from 8,800 in 1890 to 13,500 in 1896. The miners who lived in larger cities, such as Springfield, may well have voted differently, but they cannot be isolated statistically. Probably two-thirds of the votes represented were cast by old-immigration miners, the remainder coming from tradesmen in coal camps and a few neighboring farmers.

erably behind their rivals, and appeared to be fixed in a minority status in the coal towns. The reaction against the depression pulled the Republicans up seven points in 1894, as the Democrats polled less than a third of the coal-town vote, compared to their 38.5 percent statewide showing. The Populists claimed one voter in six. In 1896, despite the fusion between Democrats and Populists, and despite the support given free silver by the UMW leadership, the Republicans gained another 2 percent of the vote and held a clear edge on the Democrats.[35]

The strength of the Populist vote among the miners in 1894 represented a continuation of the strikers' spirit of determination, defiance, and solidarity. UMW President McBride had formed a labor-Populist coalition in Ohio in August, and supported a similar coalition in Illinois. Two prominent UMW leaders ran for Congress on the Populist ticket in Illinois and Ohio, but between them they carried only one precinct and won only 6 percent of the vote. Probably they garnered the support only of those miners who were still union members in November.[36] The phenomenon of the loosening of party loyalty following a bitter, union-led strike was common among midwesterners. In 1889, for example, the strikers at the Streator and Braidwood mines, after having strongly supported Benjamin Harrison the previous fall, elected Democratic mayors in a landslide.[37]

The sharp Republican gains in the mining towns in 1894 indicated that disaffected Democrats, reacting against Cleveland's breaking of the railroad strike and perhaps Altgeld's use of the

35. The GOP vote rose from 50.5 percent in 1894 to 52.4 percent in 1896. On the politics of the UMW leaders, see Evans, *History UMW,* 2: 412; John R. Commons, et al., *History of Labour in the United States* (New York, 1918), 2: 513–14; William J. Bryan, *The First Battle* (Chicago, 1896), pp. 166–67. The 1895 UMW national convention tendered thanks to Governor McKinley for his mobilization of aid to destitute miners; the 1896 convention thanked Governor Altgeld for pardoning several miners convicted of rioting. Evans, *History UMW,* 2: 384–85, 418–19.

36. *Chicago Tribune,* August 16, 17, October 5, 8, 1894; *Illinois State Register* (Springfield), August 10, 1894 (editorial); *Illinois State Journal,* July 6, 1894; Chester Destler, *American Radicalism: 1865–1901* (New London, 1946), pp. 169–71, 179, 206–7.

37. *New York Times,* July 27, 1889; *Chicago Tribune,* October 31, 1889 (editorial); in Spring Valley the company and the UMW fought bitterly for control of local government. *Chicago Tribune,* October 14, 1894.

militia in their own strike, bolted their party in protest. In Indiana, however, the Democrats made a strong appeal to the miners to forgive the Democratic governor for his use of the militia and not to desert the party that was their true friend. The appeal was fairly successful.[38]

In the six coal counties in Illinois where new immigrants posed a real threat, holding a fourth of the mine jobs by 1899, the Populists polled 17 percent of the vote, and a much higher share among just the coal miners. But in the twelve coal counties where less than 15 percent of the miners were new immigrants by 1899, the Populist vote came to only 6 percent, slightly below its statewide average. The largest Populist vote in Illinois came in Spring Valley, where the rioting Italians had proved so obnoxious—and where the celebration of McKinley's assassination among organized anarchists led to a movement to expel the foreigners in 1901.[39] Meanwhile, the Indiana miners of Clay County, who were not affected by the new immigration, showed only a small gain for the Populists in 1894. But while Illinois miners moved toward McKinley, the Indiana miners moved sharply toward Bryan in 1896.

The old miners might have been protesting the coming of the new immigrants by their votes for the Populists and McKinley. One of the Populist resolutions adopted at Omaha in 1892 condemned

> the fallacy of protecting American labor under the present system, which opens our ports to the paupers and criminal classes of the world, and crowds out wage earners; [we demand] the further restriction of undesirable immigration.[40]

In 1894 the Illinois Populists reaffirmed the Omaha platform; the major parties chose to remain silent on the immigration issue. Although the Republicans, beginning in Pennsylvania in 1886, had toyed with immigration restriction planks, the GOP was trying to capture the foreign vote in the Midwest and still had not

---

38. *Chicago Tribune,* August 16, October 31, 1894; *Chicago Times,* August 16, September 23, and, especially, November 5, 1894.

39. *Chicago Tribune,* June 1, July 10, 1894, September 16, 22, 1901; *New York Times,* September 23, 25, 1901; cf. *Chicago Times,* August 17, 18, 21, 1894.

40. John Hicks, *The Populist Revolt* (Minneapolis, 1931), pp. 444 and 436.

fully shaken the "nativist" label thrown at it by the Democrats. The Republicans found silence wisdom. The Populists adopted the Omaha restriction resolution at the behest of labor unions; it was their response to industrial America. In Indiana, where the Democrats held up so well in 1894 and 1896 among the miners, they had stolen the Populist thunder. The 1894 Indiana Democratic platform, for example, denounced anarchy, dissociated it from legitimate labor movements, and demanded the exclusion of "the pauper and vicious classes" who "furnish a standing menace to the order and prosperity of our land." To make the point perfectly clear, the Democrats went on to laud their legislative achievements, including the abolition of mine hazards, blacklisting, company stores, and "importation of alien or foreign labor." The Iowa Republicans in 1894, for the first time, took a stand strongly approved by the miners regarding immigration. The Iowa Democrats, having worked so hard at establishing an image of liberalism toward immigrants on the liquor issue, were torn asunder in the mining towns by the Republicans and Populists. In Ohio, where both major parties had favored immigration restriction since 1887, the implications of the issue were less clearcut, but probably accumulated in Republican favor—McKinley, after all, kept emphasizing the need for "protection" of American workingmen from cheap foreign labor.[41]

In 1896 the GOP national platform avoided antagonizing the old immigrant voters by endorsing a literacy test that would have practically no effect on arrivals from Britain, Ireland, Scandinavia, and Germany, but would bar others, thus protecting "the quality of our American citizenship, and . . . the wages of our workingmen against the fatal competition of low priced labor." Immigration itself, Republican orators stressed, was not at all bad for industrial America; as one of their slogans had it, "Immigration follows high wages—high wages follow the tariff."[42]

---

41. *Daily News Almanac 1895*, pp. 183–89, *1888, pp.* 60–61; *Ann. Cycl. 1894:* 382. For miners' voting in Ohio, see Kleppner, *Cross of Culture*, pp. 29–31, 238, 247–49, 296–97.
42. Kirk Porter and Donald Johnson, *National Party Platforms: 1840–1964* (Urbana, 1966), p. 109, but note that "equality" has been incorrectly substituted for "quality." Republican National Committee, "The Coal Miner's Vote!" (Chicago, 1896, Pamphlet R); *Republican Campaign Text-*

The Democrats in 1896 went further in attacking immigration. The national platform even asserted, "The most efficient way of protecting American labor is to prevent the importation of foreign pauper labor to compete with it." Of course, nobody favored letting paupers in, but the Democratic campaign textbook, the bible of all stump speakers, flayed away at all immigration:

> While the manufacturers of the country have been "protected" by a tariff . . . the laboring part of our population were for a long time unprotected from the danger of being superseded by underpaid and underfed laborers, imported from overstocked hives of industry in the Old World.[43]

Noting the steep decline in arrivals since 1893, the Democrats proudly claimed it was "unquestionably due to a great extent to the strict inspection of immigrants insisted upon by the Democratic administration in lieu of the lax methods of their predecessors." Furthermore, the Bryanites noted, their policy was the one endorsed by the labor unions.[44] Bryan won the overwhelming support of union officials, in part on the basis of his party's clear promise to stop the inflow of all those troublesome new immigrants from eastern and southern Europe.

The tale of the coal miners is sad yet instructive. Buffeted by wave after wave of disaster, hardship, and disappointment, the old miners watched their dreams and their old way of life disintegrate. Some became embittered radicals as they traveled westward, adding a new hatred to life in the mining camps at Cripple Creek or Coeur D'Alene. It is a wonder that the miners' party loyalty held up as well as it did in those years when party and government seemed to fail them. No one was happy about the fate of the old miners, least of all the new immigrants, who found themselves entering a world of surprising animosity.

---

book: 1896 (Washington, 1896), p. 170 for slogan, pp. 168–70 for details of the literacy test. See also John Higham, Strangers in the Land (New York, 1963), pp. 56, 72–74, 103–5.

43. Porter and Johnson, National Platforms, p. 99; Democratic Campaign Book (Washington, 1896), p. 184.

44. Democratic Campaign Book, pp. 187, 188.

Coal did not typify American industry in the 1890s. The peculiar economics of supply and demand, as well as the isolation of coal's production points, guaranteed that. But the reactions of the miners serve as a model for understanding other workers in comparable situations. The miners were the first large group of skilled workers to be seriously affected by the influx of the strange new immigrants from the south and east of Europe. Urban workers who considered themselves inundated by Poles or Hungarians or Italians may well have shared the attitudes of the miners. True, the political environment of the large city opened a different set of possible reaction patterns, and the economic size and growth of the city afforded some protection from the newcomers. But the coal fields were growing rapidly, too. That did not halt the fall of wages, the influx of immigrants, or the growing bitterness of spirit. Finally, the vast amount of data available on the lives, fortunes, and votes of the midwestern miners—virtually all untouched by historical research—can yield insights into the life patterns of the large mass of workers whose heritage to posterity does not include such convenient records. Nevertheless, the urban workers played a larger role than the miners in the politics of the depression years, and for a full picture of the 1894 upheaval, we must also consider the most spectacular strike of 1894, perhaps the most famous incident in the history of American labor, the Pullman strike.

The Pullman strike of 1894 has attracted far more attention than the 1894 coal strike. Although three times as many midwestern miners struck as railroad workers, and for a longer period, the dramatic clashes between George Pullman and Eugene Debs, Governor Altgeld and President Cleveland, the railroad managers and the union, the troops and the mobs, fill the histories of the nineties. The strike against the Pullman company proper was unimportant compared with the consequent strike of the American Railway Union (the ARU) against the Chicago railroads, and the latter episode casts further light on the relationship between strikes and voting patterns.

In the spring of 1894 the year-old ARU reluctantly organized a strike against bad working conditions at the Pullman factory in Chicago, the manufacturer of the famous railroad cars. Realizing the strike was about to fail, and sensing the need for cooperation with the striking coal miners, the ARU determined to force Pullman to the bargaining table by calling a boycott against all trains carrying Pullman cars. The railroads, however, considered this secondary boycott to be an illegitimate strike and resolved to break it. The ARU had no specific grievances against the railroads (which were bound by contract to carry the Pullman cars), had made no demands, and had not even talked to the managers. But the ARU, under the bold, irresponsible leadership of Eugene Debs, then struck all the railroads operating out of Chicago, whether they used Pullman cars or not.[45]

By the end of June, the entire membership of the ARU (claimed to be 150,000) was on strike. Although the leaders of the older, established railroad brotherhoods refused to support the strike, many of their members also belonged to the new union and joined the walkout. Only a tenth of all railroad employees in the Midwest were actually on strike, but picket lines, threats and deeds of violence, and the withdrawal of specialized technicians effectively tied up nearly every line west of Cincinnati. ARU men and their sympathizers struck in each midwestern state, but Illinois was by far the hardest hit. Regionally, of 215,000 railroad employees, about 24,000 struck and another 40,000 were unable to work. The walkouts happened in different places at different times, beginning between June 26 and July 9 and ending from July 3 to 26.[46]

In Chicago the tie-up was complete. Railroads constituted the main system of transportation in the Midwest for all movements of more than a few miles, and, in Chicago at least, one man, Eugene Debs, could decide who could and who could not travel. The

45. U.S. Strike Commission, *Report on the Chicago Strike* (Washington, 1895), remains the basic record. See also Lindsey, *Pullman Strike;* Ray Ginger, *The Bending Cross: A Biography of Eugene Victor Debs* (New Brunswick, 1949); Barnard, *Eagle Forgotten,* pp. 280–317; and *Ann. Cycl. 1894:* 728–31; and *Railway Age* (Chicago, 1894), 19:361–65, 375–79, 390–95, 405, 407–8, 418–19, for the managers' viewpoint. The leading Chicago newspapers were not especially useful, and no careful study of the strike outside that metropolis has been undertaken. On the connection between the coal and rail strikes, see Ward and Rogers, *Alabama Labor Revolt,* pp. 103–6; Strike Commission, *Report,* pp. 170–71, 218; Lindsey, *Pullman Strike,* pp. 127, 135, 223; *Bradstreet's* (June 2, 1894) 19:338.

46. *10th U.S. Labor Report 1894,* pp. 254–57, 1018–21; *12th Rept. Michigan B.L.S.* (Lansing, 1895), pp. 514–31.

situation represented an intolerable assumption of unjustified power by an arrogant individual. The President acted, ostensibly to assure free movement for the mails. On July 2 the federal courts enjoined the ARU from interfering with mail trains. The injunction (a "Gatling gun on paper," the *New York Times* called it), enforced by federal troops, broke the strike, despite a flurry of sympathy strikes by other unions in Chicago. The arrival of the troops incited bloody rioting in Chicago, in Hammond, Indiana, and in railroad centers in the West and South. Perhaps two dozen men died in Illinois, Indiana, and Iowa; scores more were wounded or injured.[47]

The damage was great. In Illinois, Indiana, Michigan, and Ohio, railroad employees lost $1.5 million in wages, and some 16,000 strikebreakers replaced most of the 20,000 strikers in those four states. The companies suffered heavy physical destruction, and lost $5 million in business. Organized labor inevitably had to bear the blame for the violence.[48]

The strikers reacted at the polls. The railroad men, fretted a prominent Iowa Republican, "are still smarting under the strike and want to hit somebody, and it looks as though they would drift strongly towards the Populist."[49] Debs led the ARU into fusion with the Populists, but encountered difficulties. In Illinois the agrarian Populists feuded with the socialistic labor element, while in Indiana the AFL unions refused to cooperate politically with the ARU and the UMW if it meant supporting the Populists. Nevertheless, in the fall elections the Populist vote was noticeable in every railroad center, and usually exceeded the number of strikers. Beaten in July, the ARU lost again in November, as the Populists failed to win a single office of any importance in the Midwest. The friction among the various unions and the suspicions of the agrarians had frustrated the attempt to launch a farmer-labor coalition in midwestern politics; not for a quarter-century would another serious attempt be made.[50]

47. On fatalities, *Ann. Cycl. 1894:* 372, 380, 728–30; Lindsey, *Pullman Strike,* pp. 209, 214, 258–60, and, for quote, p. 162.
48. *10th U.S. Labor Report 1894,* pp. 250–61, 1018–21; Strike Commission, *Report,* pp. xviii–xix; Lindsey, *Pullman Strike,* pp. 308–38.
49. David B. Henderson to Nils P. Haugen, October 28, 1894, in Haugen MSS, Wisconsin State Historical Society.
50. Destler, *American Radicalism,* pp. 162–254; *Ann. Cycl. 1894:* 372–73.

The final verdict on the failure of the strikers to exert politcal muscle in 1894 must take into account the previous record of labor movements in the Midwest. Under what circumstances had significant movements begun, and when if ever had they been successful? The record indicates that trade unions had not always failed in the difficult task of creating a new political force in the face of the strong traditional partisanship of the rank and file. As recently as 1886 and 1887, years of prosperity, they made much better showings than in 1894, and even won pluralities in several large cities. Success at the polls, however, always followed in the wake of successful organizing drives or strikes that mobilized labor solidarity and bestowed prestige on aggressive leaders.

In 1886 the Knights of Labor, a conglomeration of established trade unions and new organizations, had achieved a membership of many thousands in the Midwest, including 35,000 in Illinois. On May Day, 1886, the Knights made their decisive move, calling a nationwide strike for the eight-hour day. In Chicago, 80,000 men struck, in Cincinnati 32,000, in Milwaukee 7,000, and in Detroit 3,000. Despite some successes, the killing of eight policemen at an Anarchist meeting in Chicago's Haymarket Square disgraced the movement.[51]

The Knights were doomed, not only by undeserved bad publicity but by weak organization; yet they did not immediately drift into oblivion. Instead they organized labor party tickets under a variety of names in at least sixty cities, especially in the Midwest. In the fall elections of 1886 the laborites scored a sweeping victory in Milwaukee, electing a full slate of county officers and a congressman. The new party had won the support of the Poles, the German socialists, and most union members, as well as others angry with the Republican governor for having used the militia to suppress the May Day riots in that city. Elsewhere, the laborites showed scattered strength, winning local offices in Clinton, Iowa, Eau Claire, LaCrosse and Watertown, Wisconsin, and nearly electing a congressman in Chicago.[52]

51. Commons, *History of Labour,* 2:375–94; *4th Report Illinois B.L.S.: 1885–1886,* pp. 145–63, 221–43.
52. *Milwaukee Sentinel,* October 16 (editorial), 18 (editorial), 26, November 4, 1886; Thomas Gavett, *Development of the Labor Movement in Milwaukee* (Madison, 1965), pp. 56–71.

In 1887, although the membership of the Knights was plunging, the laborites formed a national party, dubbing it the Union Labor party. They were unable to forge a working coalition of union members, greenbackers, socialists, single-taxers, and other radical elements who seemed ripe for combination. The major parties reacted in many cities by fusing behind "citizens" tickets for local offices and denouncing the attempt to inject class conflict into American politics. Only in Kenosha, Wisconsin, and several mining towns in the upper peninsula of Michigan were the laborites able to overcome fusion tickets. In Chicago the Democrats split between the Republican and the labor tickets, but the GOP polled 68 percent of the vote and destroyed the labor party. In Milwaukee, fusion only narrowly defeated the laborites, and they would return in a decade under the socialist label to control the city for much of the early twentieth century. In Cincinnati, an exciting three-way race saw the Republicans nip the labor candidates by only 600 votes, with the Democrats trailing far behind. In Eau Claire, Watertown, Clinton, and elsewhere, the laborites were unable to repeat their earlier victories, and vanished from politics. Only in Dubuque did labor win in 1887 in a three-way race. The city had long been a Democratic stronghold, and after a year of incompetent rule the labor party completely disappeared.[53]

In the presidential election of 1888, the Union Labor party, and a rival group, the United Labor party, fielded tickets, but polled less than 1 percent of the midwestern vote. The leadership and many of the members of the labor parties then drifted into the new Populist party. The collapse of the Knights, their inability to forge a farmer-labor coalition, the general political incompetence of the labor leaders, and especially the dimming memories of the May Day strikes ended the most realistic dream of a powerful labor party in the Midwest.[54]

53. *Chicago Tribune,* March 31 to April 6, 1887; *Chicago Times,* April 6, 1887; *Milwaukee Sentinel,* April 4 to 7, 10, 1887; *Milwaukee Journal,* April 3, 4, 1888; *Dubuque Herald,* April 3 to 8, 15, 1887, October 26, 1888 (editorial); Commons, *History of Labour,* 2:422–23, 462–68, 482; Gavett, *Milwaukee Labor,* pp. 72–77; Nathan Fine, *Labor and Farmer Parties in the United States* (New York, 1928), pp. 44–54; Zane L. Miller, *Boss Cox's Cincinnati* (New York, 1968), p. 76.
54. The Union Labor party is virtually unknown. See Commons, *History of Labour,* 2:468–70; Herman Nixon, "The Populist Movement in Iowa,"

Throughout the prosperous late eighties and early nineties, bitter strikes frequently shook the old political loyalties of the participants, and redounded to the benefit of the third parties. For example, in the summer of 1892 1,600 sawmill workers near Merrill, Wisconsin, struck for three weeks, demanding a reduction in hours. After losing $50,000 in wages, the men were successful. Robert Schilling, a leading Milwaukee Populist, came to Merrill to lend a hand and spread his gospel; he enjoyed some success, for the Populist vote in Merrill soared from 18 in 1890 to 354 in 1892. In nearby Marinette, however, a three-week strike of 1,300 sawmill workers in 1892 was unsuccessful; 200 new men replaced the strike leaders who formed the nucleus of the third party organization, and that fall the Populist vote fell to 4 percent, compared with 7 percent two years before. In East Liverpool, Ohio, an unsuccessful six-month strike of 3,100 unionized pottery workers in early 1894 stimulated the upsurge of the Populist vote from a mere 23 in 1892 to 384 (or 18 percent of the total) in 1894. This time, however, no strikebreakers came in, and the Populists had organizers nearby.[55]

Long strikes or especially bitter ones, if properly organized, could loosen the party ties of enough men to encourage proselytizing by third-party spokesmen who sympathized with the needs and spirit of the trade unions. The third parties suffered from incompetent leadership and lack of patronage, and were never able to consolidate their gains after the embers of resentment stoked by the original strike had cooled. Since most of the laborers were originally Democrats, the Republicans nearly always benefited either by an influx of new supporters or a weakening of the chief opposition. Unlike the laborites and Populists, the GOP was geared to govern. It could promise more than the temporary re-

Iowa Journal of History (1926) 24:29–32, 55; for the 1888 platforms, see Porter and Johnson, *National Party Platforms,* pp. 83–85.

55. *10th U.S. Labor Report: 1894,* pp. 1242–45, 1014–17; letter of Schilling to M.D. Williams, August 10, 1892, in Ignatius Donnelly MSS, Minnesota Historical Society. While the coal miners near East Liverpool swung to the Populists in 1894 and 1895, the pottery workers, realizing the need for a high tariff, moved into the Republican column in 1895 and 1896, and gave Bryan a cold reception when he came through. *Detroit Free Press,* October 21, 1896; and *19th Report Ohio B.L.S. 1895* (Columbus, 1896), pp.16–24, 30–35.

lief of psychological aches and pains; it promised prosperity and harmony between labor and capital. The Republican theme sounded convincing to scores of thousands of midwestern workers during the hard times of the nineties. They tried the GOP in 1894 and 1896, and were somewhat startled by their own wisdom, for the years from 1897 to 1901 proved to be the most prosperous and the least troubled that midwestern labor had ever known.

10

How the Midwest Was Won:
Money, Morality, and Pluralism in 1896

> The millenium is approaching and
> Bryan is its prophet.
>
> *New York Staats-Zeitung*[1]

Superficially, money was the overriding issue in the contest between William McKinley and William Jennings Bryan for control of the executive branch in 1896. Beneath gold and silver, however, were grave moral questions, and upon this bedrock the real battle occurred. The moralistic tenor of the campaign appeared most strikingly in the nine hundred speeches delivered by the two standard-bearers, who dominated their parties' campaigns more than presidential candidates have ever done before or since. The grassroots oratory followed their lead, as did the press. The most popular editorial topic during the campaign was "The Crime of '73," a silverite slogan attributing America's economic woes to a supposed conspiracy of financiers in 1873 that deprived the people of an adequate money supply. Other moralistic titles such as "Sound Money," "Object Lesson," and "Free Coinage Means Disaster" appeared in thousands of newspapers. Hundreds of nervous editors reflected upon "Revolution," "Free Riot," and "Anarchy," or prepared "Deadly Parallels," and warned of "Repudiation" or the dreaded "Red Flag."[2] Candidates, editors, orators, and voters all agreed that far more was at stake than mere revision of federal monetary policy.

The dynamics of the campaign revolved around Bryan's need to forge a majority coalition of farmers, millenarian reformers,

1. Quoted in *Literary Digest* (August 15, 1896) 13:484.
2. Two aides at Republican headquarters tabulated the titles of tens of thousands of editorials from around the country. The most numerous were: "Crime of '73" (4,598 examples); "Boy Orator" or "Boy Orator of the Platte" (3,866); "Free Coinage" (3,495); "16 to 1" (3,185); "Gold Standard" (1,983 for, 423 against); "Sound Money" (2,308); "Bimetallism" (1,720); "Object Lesson" (972); "Revolution" (480); "Free Coinage Means Disaster" (308); and "Free Riot" (221). *New York Tribune*, November 1, 1896. A perusal of hundreds of editorials indicates that many were commentaries on yesterday's news, others were technical economic analyses, and most were suffused with intense indignation, fear, or moralism. The smaller rural papers often printed editorials sent out by party headquarters.

miners, industrial workers, old-line Democrats and office-hungry politicians. Under the spell of Bryan's rhetoric, the crusading silverites had toppled the conservatives at the Chicago convention in July, yet their fervor had to be sustained four more months to overcome the far more formidable Republican steamroller. In the spring and summer of 1896 the silverite monetary doctrines captured the imagination and excited the utopian longings of pietistic midwestern farmers. Bored with stale high and low tariff arguments, they learned of a new panacea that promised a revolutionary advance in political economy. The economic burdens of the laboring man would be lifted simultaneously with the destruction of his oppressors.

When Bryan's nomination showed the silverites had a leader with charisma the conservatives took fright. By early autumn, however, the belated Republican counteroffensive had undermined confidence in the wisdom and morality of free silver. International markets, not the domestic money supply, regulated prices and profits, and the Republicans endlessly pointed to the happy fact that wheat prices were rising while the money supply remained static. Free silver was denounced as a hollow promise that would certainly lead to economic disaster for banks, insurance companies, mercantile establishments, railroads, and factories—and in the wake of their ruin the workingmen would starve. The only effective policy to overcome the depression, which could be attributed to the irresponsibility of the silverites as much as to the incompetence of Grover Cleveland, was sound money (that is, gold) coupled with a high protective tariff to foster domestic demand and restore full employment and high wages. The silverites, despite their glib talk about the quantity of money and the evils of deflation, were never quite able to explain how newly minted silver would come into the farmers' hands, and could only lamely suggest that urban workers would benefit eventually once the farmers regained prosperity.

The silverites, increasingly on the defensive, changed the thrust of their rhetoric from economics to virtue after Bryan's nomination. Whether free silver was economically sound was not the real question, they said. The root issue was whether the common people should be allowed to decide the matter for themselves, or whether the financial interests of the East and Europe would overpower the people, silence the dissenters, coerce the electorate, and totally corrupt the democratic foundations of American politics. America's sacred heritage of republican virtue—the virtue of Washington, Jefferson, Jackson, and Lincoln—was at stake. The grave charges—the stock argument of radicals in every era—gained sharpness from Bryan's intensely moralistic appeal, and nearly won the election for him. They did establish him as the unquestioned leader of the Democratic party for years to come. Voters who accepted neither the millenial promise nor the validity of free silver wondered if they should not vote for Bryan anyway, to save American democracy. E. C. Wall, a prominent Democratic leader in Wisconsin, overcame his close ties to the pro-Cleveland forces and his own belief in gold to support Bryan, maintaining, "The fight today, is, in my judgment, whether there shall be a republic or not. Whether a few men of wealth shall govern this land or the people."[3]

The Republicans discovered that allegations of massive coercion and fantastic slush funds, whatever their validity, were threatening to pull apart the great coalition they had built during the depression. The pietistic old-stock population could not be abandoned to the enemy. The GOP, aided by articulate gold Democrats and leading ministers, charged that the Chicago platform was, in the words of one religious magazine, "so revolutionary and anarchistic, so subversive of national honor and threatening to the very life of the Republic, that patriotism and loyalty to righteousness constrain a vigorous and unqualified protest."[4] One could vote either for the unimportant Gold Democrat candidate or for William McKinley. The GOP refuted the coercion charges directly by staging massive demonstrations in the streets, proving that urban America freely rejected dishonor, dishonesty, free silver, and Bryan. By election eve the silverites knew they had lost, but ascribed their impending defeat to coercion and resolved to continue their battle for national salvation.[5]

3. E. C. Wall to William F. Vilas, August 13, 1896, William F. Vilas Papers, Wisconsin State Historical Society. Vilas was intensely opposed to Bryan; see Horace Merrill, *William Freeman Vilas* (Madison, 1954), pp. 234–35.

4. *Christian Intelligencer* (New York, Reformed Church magazine), quoted in *Literary Digest* (August 1, 1896) 13:421.

5. The best guide to the election is Stanley Jones, *The Presidential Election*

The organization and conduct of the Democratic campaign exploited fully all the emotionalism and moralism of the silverite crusaders. When William Jennings Bryan, the thirty-six year old meteor of American politics, stunned the nation by capturing the Democratic nomination for president, he realized that bold innovation was necessary for victory in November. By its platform and candidate the Democratic party had repudiated its first president since the Civil War, and everything he stood for. In demanding that the government coin, from all proffered silver, legal dollars at the ratio of 16 to 1 against gold, the silverites rejected the elaborate alliances with high finance, upper-class conservatism, and economic orthodoxy that Cleveland and his New York allies had so carefully nurtured. The advantages to the new policy were great, yet the immediate disadvantages were a heavy burden for the campaign managers. Bryan deliberately repelled the traditional contributors to his party, with the exception of silver-mine owners, who proved less generous than expected, thus crippling his financial resources while the opposition was doubling its war chest. Many traditional Democrats contributed their usual sums, or greater amounts, to the Republicans or to the "Gold Democrats," a rump movement set up by midwestern conservatives as a saving remnant that would some day recover control of the main party. Furthermore, many of the leading metropolitan party organs deserted Bryan, sabotaging his normal channels of communication with the rank and file. As a last blow, the party professionals feared or at least distrusted Bryan, and could not be counted upon to assist his operations.

Bryan rose to the challenge. Seeing himself as the spokesman of the people—indeed, as the savior of the common man—he planned a crusade with daring new tactics that would enlist greater moral support, and more votes, than any American had ever before mobilized. The crusade would be a grass-roots uprising of the producing classes—farmers, laborers, and "honest" businessmen alike—and would have no need for ornate trappings, reactionary newspapers, bulging campaign chests, or the advice of old

of 1896 (Madison, 1964); the fullest bibliography is in Paolo Coletta, *William Jennings Bryan: Political Evangelist, 1860–1908* (Lincoln, 1964), vol. 1.

hacks. A new force, a moral force, would, in alliance with Populists and silverite Republicans, rebuild the Democratic forces from the bottom up. Like all crusaders, Bryan and his cohorts avoided established party leaders and organizations. Outside observers found that "the political machinery that served the party in previous campaigns was almost entirely disregarded, and new and enthusiastic men placed in charge of Mr. Bryan's campaign."[6] Networks of silver clubs, recently established in thousands of midwestern precincts and townships, carried the burden of proselytizing the people with the new gospel. The clubs operated outside the party hierarchy and received little professional supervision. Newcomers to politics, some of them men of high talent, quickly gained the attention of their neighbors. Financed primarily by membership contributions, the three or four thousand midwestern silver clubs distributed millions of documents, conducted schoolhouse lectures on financial topics, rebutted and heckled opposition speakers, sponsored tens of thousands of rallies and parades, and provided forums for unpaid evangelists, aspiring statesman, and office-hungry hangers-on. William Harvey's pamphlet, *Coin's Financial School* was their Bible; Bryan was their messiah. Thanks to Bryan's triple candidacy on the Democratic, Populist, and Silver Republican tickets, the clubs appealed to citizens regardless of party loyalties. Some 60,000 Republicans reportedly joined free silver clubs in Chicago, and another 45,000 downstate; the numbers may have been exaggerated, but not the enthusiasm. Not since the Civil War had party loyalty been so widely disregarded, and traditional party structures been so systematically bypassed.[7]

Educational campaigns sailed on a sea of print. Unable to afford commercial printers, the silver clubs sent lists of addresses to friendly congressmen, who in turn flooded the mails with franked speeches and reports. The clubs bought pamphlets and other literature from regional headquarters in Chicago, reselling them

6. *Washington Post,* November 1, 1896.
7. *Review of Reviews* (1896) 14:264, 304–5, 524–26, 558; William J. Bryan, *The First Battle* (Chicago, 1897), p. 292; *New York Journal,* October 9, 1896, notes the wide circulation of Harvey's tract. On the silver clubs in Illinois, *St. Louis Republic,* October 9, 1896; in Indiana, *Chicago Tribune,* September 28, 1896; in Iowa, *Omaha World-Herald,* October 11, 13, 1896, claiming 20,000 to 40,000 members there.

to their members, who gleaned more insight from a twenty-five cent treatise than from all the free Republican propaganda they were offered. Sorely pressed by the hostile metropolitan press, the Democrats boycotted their betrayers and fell back on the loyal hinterland newspapers. The rural press printed millions of copies of boilerplate "news" and argumentation prepared in Chicago and Washington, but the little papers lacked the prestige, wire service facilities, and circulation needed to communicate Bryan's ideas effectively. Without the established newspapers, or the money and skill to found his own, Bryan's educational plans seemed hopeless. But the candidate brilliantly resolved the crisis by forcing the opposition press to carry his message.[8]

Bryan went to people directly, the first presidential candidate ever to undertake a systematic tour of the critical states. He concentrated on the Midwest, but visited the enemy's eastern strongholds and the border states too, delivering 570 speeches in all, and 317 in October alone. The spellbinder's appearances before enormous audiences, totalling two or three million people, forced the most bitterly antagonistic newspapers to accord him the attention due a newsworthy phenomenon. Furthermore the opposition strategy of attacking Bryan kept him on the front pages. Thus Bryan rallied his followers, forced his name into the headlines, and confounded the enemy. "It used to be the newspapers educated the people," he told a Des Moines rally, "but now the people educate the newspapers."[9]

The crusader did not hesitate to employ the most systematic tactics of the advertising style. In Michigan, Bryan's tour was scheduled so as to give each congressional district a share of his time proportional to its voting population. The state chairman, Daniel Campau, had each voter polled twice, and channeled his meagre funds (mostly from his own pocket) not into expensive displays but into specific get-out-the-vote operations that had been rehearsed since 1892. Campau doubled as national chairman of Bryan's campaign committee, and probably provided more competence than any other advisor.[10]

8. *Review of Reviews* (1896) 14:557–58; *Ann. Cycl. 1896:* 668–70; *New York Tribune,* August 7, 1896.
9. *St. Louis Post Dispatch,* August 8, 1896.
10. *Detroit Free Press,* October 6, 1896. Campau had only $6,800 to

Bryan transcended the role of evangelist for financial unorthodoxy; he led a mass movement for America's redemption. The silverites felt they only needed to win the presidency to achieve their utopia. One man with the people's mandate could sign free silver into law, appoint new judges, defy Wall Street and London, and signal a revolutionary shift in national values. Bryan understood the crusaders' need for a messiah, and he played the role perfectly.

His tours were continuous revivals, often likened to Methodist camp meetings of the old times. A typical appearance, say in a small Indiana city, would be preceded by massive parades of thousands of silverites, many in the uniforms the old army-style campaigns had provided, marching to the blare of dozens of bands, waving banners, flags, placards, and "16 to 1" symbols of every description. Hundreds of wagons brought families in from the farms early in the morning, and perhaps a few special trains carried well-wishers from towns that were not blessed by Bryan's tour managers. The crowds would listen all day to prospective congressmen, legislators, sheriffs, and dog catchers, would hurrah with the haranguers, sway with the spellbinders, and sing familiar tunes and hymns till the moment came. Finally, a few hours late, Bryan's train, the "Idler" would chug in from the last rally twenty miles away. Rambunctious boys, tired farm wives, and hardened men all hushed when their leader appeared. Weary, his rich, well-trained, powerful voice hoarse from abuse, Bryan would apologize that "a large portion of my voice has been left along the line of travel, where it is still calling sinners to repentance." They always laughed then, breaking the tension, readying themselves for a masterful analysis of the complexities of American society. But the candidate spoke only briefly; he could not stay more than five minutes, for there were ten or twenty or even thirty more stops on the day's itinerary, and an equally cruel schedule for weeks to come. No matter. Everyone knew his arguments anyway; the peo-

---

spend, and the Populists and silverites added about $2,000, while the Gold Democrats had $14,600, much more than they could effectively use. The Michigan GOP state committee spent $60,000, while the national and local organizations spent large sums, too. Arthur Millspaugh, *Party Organization and Machinery in Michigan Since 1890* (Baltimore, 1917), pp. 144–45, 151–58. See Jones, *1896 Election*, 401–2.

ple had come to marvel at his appearance, to stand near the man who promised to redeem the land they loved from the grasp of the forces of Evil. A star New York reporter captured the essence of Bryan's style in a dispatch from Indiana:

> Mark the political crusader as he moves along in the wild procession—a tall man in a well-worn coat . . . his eyes burning like coals of fire and his head and his powerful priest-like face radiant with hope and courage. Around him swells the defiant shriek of his followers that "Wall Street shall not prevail against the people!"[11]

Often Bryan likened himself to the sacred figures of the Old and New Testament. "You shall not press down upon the brow of labor this crown of thorns," he cried out to the Chicago convention, his fingers spread over his temples in agony. Then, his audience hypnotized, he spread his arms far apart and called out, "You shall not crucify mankind on a cross of gold!" On other occasions he identified himself with David battling Goliath, or his audiences with the common people who heard Christ gladly while the rich scorned him. In Canton, Ohio, after visiting Major McKinley, he explained to his supporters that their true neighbor was the good samaritan who had compassion for their troubles. He compared his wisdom to Solomon's; the enemy to the lovers of darkness; spiteful Democrats to Judas Iscariot. Senator Daniels of Virginia hit upon an image widely publicized in the silverite press when he hailed Bryan "because he has rolled away the stone from the golden sepulchre in which Democracy was buried." Enthusiasts announced "this country has witnessed a new Pentecost and received a new baptism of fire."[12]

Superficially Bryan's speeches covered a multitude of topics—silver and gold, money and prices, banking, coercion, education, and the unrivalled beauty of the local countryside. At a deeper level, the level at which his audiences listened, his speeches were

11. Bryan, *First Battle*, p. 360; James Creelman of the *New York World* quoted in *Saint Louis Republic*, October 25, 1896; compare Coletta, *Bryan*, 1:168, 173–77.

12. Bryan, *First Battle*, p. 456, for Daniel quote, and 305, 343, 355, 376, 377, 553, 581; Coletta, *Bryan*, 1:141; *Literary Digest* (October 24, 1896) 13:809; for related cartoons. The "Pentecost" quote was mentioned in a minister's letter to the *New York Tribune*, August 28, 1896.

all the same, his words were all about good and evil, the righteous and the wicked, the common people and their oppressors, salvation and damnation. Bryan came to convert the people to the truth that the people can rule and that bimetallism would be the means of redemption. Converts by the thousands found themselves newborn, the scales fallen from their eyes, the truths of society at last visible. The zealous recruits came, Bryan said, "with the enthusiasm of missionaries who go forth to preach the gospel to others." An Illinois leader reported that scores of Republicans "have come forward like sinners in a religious revival and joined us with public denunciations of their old party affiliations." Each of the three hundred members of the Springfield, Illinois, Businessmen's Bimetallic League was "an evangelist in the cause," and competed to see "who can make the greatest number of converts." It was the epic of Saul of Tarsus over again, Bryan explained.[13]

Bryan's revivalism regained thousands of fallen-away Democrats, strengthened the faith of the silverites, and converted legions of others to the cause. The pietistic farmers and townsmen of the Midwest, particularly those who were not wrapped up in the market economy, flocked to see the evangelist who spoke of redemption through free silver. Former Populists in railroad centers, coal towns, lumber camps, and backwoods farming areas responded to his appeal.[14] Bryan made striking gains among third-party Prohibitionists, capturing more of their votes than their own party nominees that year, according to reliable polls.[15]

13. Bryan, *First Battle*, p. 543; *St. Louis Republic*, September 24, October 10, 1896.

14. The *Chicago Tribune*, September 21, 1896, found that, in Wisconsin, "What little silver sentiment there is among the Republicans is generally confined to Americans. Now and then a thriftless Yankee, whose farm is almost always the weediest in the county, and who is to be found in the grocery oftener than in the barn is shouting for silver." Silver sentiment was stronger among Ohio's farmers; N. B. Scott to William McKinley, September 7, 1896, in William McKinley Papers, Library of Congress.

15. In 1896, the Prohibition party split into a "narrow gauge," or single-issue faction, and a "broad gauge" faction that endorsed free silver and numerous other panaceas, and which included most of the party leaders in the Midwest. Although both groups nominated candidates, it seems that most of the narrow gaugers voted for McKinley, and the broad gaugers for Bryan; the two prohibition candidates together received 63,000 fewer votes than the 1892 regional total of 105,000 for Bidwell. See *Indianapolis Sentinel*, September 11, 1896; *Chicago Tribune*, September 21, 26, 1896;

Bryan was the most attractive Democrat that midwestern pietists had ever encountered. He spoke their language, he knew their hopes and fears, he had assumed their burdens. Although Bryan actually polled only slightly more votes that the combined Democratic-Populist totals of 1892, he did best in old-stock pietistic areas. In Ohio he won 48.3 percent of the vote in the forty-three counties with fewest immigrants, a gain of 2.2 points over the combined Democratic and Populist showing in 1895, and a gain of 1.2 points over Cleveland's performance in 1888. The gains were not enough to offset McKinley's growing strength in the cities, but they did forestall a Republican landslide. Bryan (a Presbyterian) even prevented McKinley from making significant gains among Methodists, despite the Republican's well-publicized affiliation with that denomination. In the eight Ohio counties where Methodists predominated, McKinley captured 53.8 percent of the vote in 1896, a slight drop of 0.8 points from Harrison's showing in 1888.[16] In southern Michigan, where Yankee pietism was highly susceptible to Seventh Day Adventism, spiritualism, Christian Science, vegetarianism and food fads, perfectionism, holiness movements, millenarianism, and, of course, prohibition, the Populist and Prohibition parties had been unusually strong, taking up to one-third of the vote. The Prohibition national chairman, Samuel Dickie, ran for Congress from the region in 1890 on the proto-Populist Industrial party slate, and local fusion movements between the two minor parties remained alive. Bryan won wide support there in 1896, and briefly transformed the area into the banner Democratic district of the rural Midwest. Within a few years, however, Bryan's glamor wore thin (he did not endorse prohibition until 1910), and southern Michigan returned to the Republican fold.

The pietists who switched to Bryan in 1896 were responding to an appeal they had long awaited: the call for a purging of the

---

St. Louis Post Dispatch, August 22, 1896; *Omaha World-Herald,* September, 27, 1896; *Washington Post,* October 27, 1896, for poll results, and compare Paul Kleppner, *The Cross of Culture* (New York, 1970), pp. 353–59. On the split see *Daily News Almanac for 1897:* (Chicago, 1897), pp. 116–17.

16. Fayette, Guernsey, Hardin, Harrison, Madison, Morgan, Noble, and Union were the Methodist counties. Without poll results it is quite impossible to accurately estimate how midwestern Methodists voted.

corruption from American politics and society, and the herald-
ing of the millenium. The Nebraskan, although a teetotaler, did
not at this time preach prohibition; he had been aligned through his
party with the wet elements, and he carefully avoided the liquor
issue throughout the campaign. But he did speak to corruption;
indeed that was his basic issue, for he believed "every great economic question is in reality a great moral question."[17] American
society was deranged, he told all his crowds, because wicked pluto-
crats, chiefly Eastern and English financiers, controlled the economy for their own benefit and robbed the farmers, the workers, the
ordinary businessmen of their just rewards for hard work. The
prostration of the economy was ample testimony to perfidy at the
highest level. The "money trust" had seized control of the national
government, reducing the president to a hireling of New York and
London bond syndicates. The federal courts, as evidenced by their
breaking of the Pullman strike and their rejection of the income
tax as unconstitutional, were part of the same nefarious web.
Bryan did not appeal to men on the basis of their aspirations for
upward economic mobility—despite the handful of bankers and
merchants who endorsed his program there was never any illusion
about rustic farmers becoming corporation presidents. His appeal
in the Midwest was fundamentally moralistic, not economic.

In their Chicago platform the silverites pledged remedies for
all the abuses they saw in America. Refusing to compromise in
any way with administration supporters, they condemned "the traf-
ficking with banking syndicates," and "the issuance of notes intending to circulate as money by National banks." The latter
clause, they knew, would outlaw checks and cripple the financial
infrastructure. Evil money-manipulators deserved no less, and the
economy could not long suffer because the true producers of wealth
would be unhurt. The platform declared unconstitutional and "a
crime against free institutions" the "arbitrary interference by Federal authorities in local affairs," which covered both antistrike
injunctions and civil rights bills; both labor unions and Southerners were especially pleased by this plank. Standard Democratic
rhetoric, very much in the Cleveland tradition, appeared in denunciations of "lavish appropriations," "oppressive taxation," "pro-
fligate waste of money," and the McKinley tariff. The federal

17. Bryan, *First Battle*, p. 548.

courts came under attack, and the platform called for an end to life tenure in the federal service (although Bryan said this did not apply to judicial appointments, nevertheless he promised to reconstitute the Supreme Court).[18]

The foremost plank was bimetallism, "the free and unlimited coinage of both silver and gold at the . . . ratio of 16 to 1. . . ." Only with free silver could the nation overthrow the most heinous of all trusts, the money trust. Free silver would remedy the terrible results of the "Crime of '73": deflation, "a heavy increase in the burdens of taxation and of all debts," the "enrichment of the money-lending class at home and abroad," and the "prostration of industry and the impoverishment of the people."[19]

18. Kirk Porter and Donald Johnson, eds., *National Party Platforms: 1840–1964* (Urbana, 1966), pp. 97–100, for text; Bryan, *First Battle*, p. 413. Governor Altgeld identified the five major issues of the campaign, as questions which go "to the foundation of government": "whether the people have surrendered the right of self-government into the hands of the Supreme Court"; federal intervention versus states' rights; the undemocratic power of judges; "whether we shall dissolve in boodle, bribery and corruption"; and "whether British monetary policy shall be made permanent." John Peter Altgeld, *Live Questions* (Chicago, 1899), pp. 687–88 (New York speech of October 17, 1896).

19. The educational effectiveness of the silverite crusade in the Midwest can be gauged from the contents of letters elicited by the *Chicago Record's* poll of every tenth voter. The newspaper tabulated the points contained in the letters without regard to emotional tone or moralistic fervor; the result was a profile of topics that closely resembled the contents and emphasis of the Chicago platform. Some 6,000 Bryanites justified their hero with about 19,000 reasons, of which 41 percent (7,800) specified the need for free coinage of silver at 16 to 1; 15 percent (2,800) demanded an income tax for the rich; 9 percent (1,700) knew Bryan would restore prosperity to the producing classes; 6 percent (1,190) opposed government by court injunction, doubtless with the Pullman strike still rankling; 4 percent (760) echoed Governor Altgeld's opposition to federal interference in state affairs; 4 percent (740) fulminated against Cleveland's deals with the bond syndicates; 4 percent (700) liked the Chicago platform generally; and 2.5 percent wanted either to endorse regulation of monopolies (470), or protest that money was too dear (450), promote free trade (440), or object to the fostering of trusts and money kings (430). In addition, 1 or 2 percent felt that the federal government had recently gained exaggerated power (280), or wanted to halt the spread of the credit system (350), or favored Bryan "because of the identity of the people on the other side" (320), or just personally admired the man (235). Only 1 percent specified that they supported Bryan because they had always been Democrats, although of course, this was an unstated factor for many of the others, while some said that a great purgative panic had to come eventually, so it was better

The silverites explained that free silver, by simply increasing the quantity of hard money in circulation, would raise prices, thus benefiting the farmer and permitting him to increase the demand for industrial production. Prosperity would automatically follow. Simultaneously the reform would punish, if not destroy, all the wicked bankers, bond coupon-clippers, speculators, shylocks, mortgage holders, railroad manipulators, financial juggernauts, and other evildoers who had robbed the American people of republican virtue. Only the dishonest would suffer, so the program would not be in any way unfair. To underline the urgency of the crisis, the silverites insisted that the enemy was at the very moment coercing workers, farmers, and small businessmen through its control of wages, employment, and loans. If the coercion efforts succeeded, there might never again be a chance for Americans to claim their birthright. Armageddon was now. The gold forces, said Bryan, were "a conspiracy against the human race"; the consummation of its diabolical schemes meant "more of misery to the human race than all the wars, pestilences, and famines that have ever occurred in the history of the world." The candidate of the silver forces had no plans to capitulate:

> When you can prove to me that the Creator intended civilization to lapse again into the dark ages; when you can prove to me that the few should ride upon the backs of those who toil. . . . When you can prove to me that the syndicates should be permitted to run the country; that trusts should be permitted to ruin businessmen and then prey upon society, then, and not until then, will I admit that the gold standard will prevail.[20]

The millenial dream, the fervent belief that once free silver came to pass "the door will be open for a progress which will carry civilization up to a higher ground," found its best expression in

---

to have it over right away (210). Although the *Record* poll reached voters irrespective of their opinions, it seems likely that the men who wrote back were the most enthusiastic of the silverites and represented the leadership element in the crusade. *Chicago Record,* October 31, 1896, contains the breakdown. Ideologically, letter writers are typically more extreme and active than the average voter; see Philip Converse, Aage Clausen, and Warren Miller, "Electoral Myth and Reality: The 1964 Election," *American Political Science Review* (1965) 59:332–35.

20. Bryan, *First Battle,* pp. 427, 429, 508.

the utopian fiction of the reformers. Of the futuristic novels and stories that appeared in profusion in the 1890s, none proved more durable or more delightful than the little fantasy written by Frank Baum, a Chicago silverite, in the garb of a modern fairy tale, *The Wonderful Wizard of Oz.*[21]

The tale opens in the present, in gray, deadening, drought-stricken Kansas. A sudden cyclone (silverite triumph at the polls) carries Dorothy (every-woman) into a flawed utopia—a land over-flowing with milk and honey yet controlled by cruel witches. The cyclone lands Dorothy's house atop the wicked Witch of the East, killing her and releasing the Munchkins from serfdom. (The money trust is deposed by Bryan's election, freeing the common people from bondage.) However the wicked Witch of the West remains loose. The good Witch of the North (the northern electorate) tells Dorothy that the Wizard of Oz may help her return to Kansas (to normality). To reach the Emerald City she must follow the yellow brick road, which can be safely traversed only with the magical silver slippers (gold and silver must be in proper parity). Dorothy is protected on her trip by an indelible kiss from the good Witch of the North (an electoral mandate). On the yellow brick road, surely one of the most dangerous routes in American literature, Dorothy encounters the silverite constituents. First the ridiculous stuffed Scarecrow (the farmer), who cannot scare anyone and who fears he has no brains. Actually his behavior shows him to be highly imaginative and responsible (so much for the ridicule of the hayseed in big-city newspapers). The travelers then encounter a vivid symbol of the oppressed industrial worker, the Tin Woodman. The wicked Witch of the East had cast a spell on him so that every time he swung his axe he chopped off part of his body. He is entirely tin now, a purely mechanical being who fears he has lost the power to love. Alone he is helpless—he cannot oil his joints—but in teamwork he proves effective and

21. Ibid., p. 464, for quote. Jay Martin, *Harvests of Change: American Literature 1865–1914* (Englewood Cliffs, 1967), pp. 207–34, who notes (p. 225): "In some senses, the utopian novel became for a brief time the true National Novel." Note that Baum published his book in 1900, during Bryan's "second battle." See Henry Littlefield, "The Wizard of Oz: Parable on Populism," *American Quarterly* (1964) 16:47–58. Care should be taken not to identify Bryan and the silverites with the Populists, who, as noted before, were not very numerous in the Midwest.

compassionate. (The selfish industrial workers, dehumanized by industrialization, need to become aware of their latent compassion, and must cooperate in a farmer-labor coalition.) Finally they encounter the Cowardly Lion, who does frighten people but who says he lacks the courage to do his duty. (He resembles no one more than Bryan himself.) Working together the coalition fights its way to the citadel of power, the Emerald City (the national capital). The Wizard, of course, is a charlatan who tricks people into believing he wields immense power; even his Emerald City is only an optical illusion. (The president is a wire-pulling fake too, and emerald-green paper money is likewise a delusion.) To achieve true freedom for herself and her allies Dorothy must destroy the wicked Witch of the West—who enslaves the girl before being dissolved by a bucket of water. (The western power elite, especially land barons and mortgage holders, are the remaining obstacle; rain relieves the drought and permits the farmer to assert his superior power.) The story ends as the good Witch of the South tells Dorothy that her silver slippers are so powerful that they can fulfill her every wish, and they carry her directly back to her home, quite without help from the fumbling Wizard. Alas, the magic silver slippers are lost in flight when Dorothy returns to Kansas.[22] Utopia thus is possible, with the proper coalition, with the mandate of the North and South, with the silverite panacea; in the process the forces of evil will be vanquished. Some devotees of Bryan claimed:

> He is undoubtedly the Moses to lead [us] out of this sin-cursed land of gold-bugs through the Red Sea of trouble, across the wilderness of trials, over the Jordan of depression and into the land of free silver, unlimited, unrestricted, 16 to 1.[23]

The Republican counterattack equaled the silverite crusade in sincerity and determination, and surpassed it in effectiveness. The Republicans intended to join together all conservative forces

22. And, yes, Dorothy's frisky dog Toto represents the teetotaling Prohibitionists in the silverite coalition. With so much election literature featuring the ratio of 16 ounces of silver to 1 ounce of gold, the colorful utopia just had to be called "Oz."

23. *New York Tribune,* July 18, 1896, quoting from an Arkansas correspondent.

and brand the crusaders as anarchists, dishonest shallow-brained fools, and thoroughly dangerous fanatics. It was a classic counter-crusade. While Bryan preached the overthrow of evil men, the opposition showed that silverite panaceas would wreck the economy for decades, deprive factory workers of their livelihood, cheat honest businessmen, and install a wholly un-American regime. In a positive vein, the Republicans promised that a high tariff would undo the ravages of a Democratic depression. Bryan, finding himself on the defensive, increasingly emphasized the coercion charge and pointed to his huge audiences as proof that the common people, not the anarchists, truly supported him. Governor Altgeld, a candidate for reelection in Illinois and widely considered the brains behind the silver movement, suffered the vilest abuse. Altgeld carefully avoided sensationalism in his speeches in 1896, yet was unable to shake the image of being friendly to anarchism. Never once in the course of the campaign did Bryan venture to defend Altgeld.

Pietistic religious leaders were, on the whole, powerful allies of the countercrusade. They had only recently rejected the millenium promised by the prohibition crusade and had no intention of supporting another unsound movement, especially one that completely ignored temperance. Pastors learned the damage that free silver would wreak on their salaries and endowments, and selected as their most effective sermon topic, the Sunday before election, "Thou Shalt Not Steal." They recoiled at Bryan's sacrilegious prostitution of the holy methods of revivalism. Frank Gunsaulus, a leading Chicago divine, took to the stump to endorse McKinley and expose Bryan's blasphemies:

> The patriotic ministers of this land have some other purpose in the use of the Crown of Thorns and the Cross of the Nazarene than conjuring up with such sacred emblems the unholy spectres of dishonor and revolution.[24]

An eminent Baptist minister expressed the consensus of pietistic leaders on the silverite program:

24. Ibid., August 21, 1896. Gunsaulus was president of the Armour Institute of Technology, and took leave from his college chores to counter-crusade against Bryan.

That platform was made in hell. Dishonesty never came from heaven; anarchy never came from heaven; class making and disunion never came from the upper world.[25]

The liturgical religious leaders were equally hostile to Bryan. The leading Episcopalian magazine, warning of the "corruption of the national currency," the "ruin of national fiscal morality and reputation for honesty," called upon citizens to "uphold and defend the integrity and good faith of this Christian nation" by defeating the Boy Orator.[26] Archbishop Ireland, in a widely circulated open letter, told Catholics that "the monetary question is, indeed, a secondary issue in this campaign." Paramount was "the spirit of socialism that permeates the whole movement"; it was nothing less than "the 'International' of Europe, now taking body in America." Calling upon the traditionalism of Catholics, he warned:

> The war of class against class is upon us, the war of the proletariat against the property-holder. No other meaning than this can be given to the appeals to the "common people," to the "laborer," to the "poor and downtrodden," and to the denunciations against "plutocrats" and "corporations" and "money grabbers" and "bankers." Many adherents . . . do not perceive its meaning; but let them beware; they are lighting torches which, borne in hands of reckless men, may light up in our country the lurid fires of a commune.[27]

The intensely pietistic and millenarian editors of Chicago's leading Methodist magazine, long a spearhead for prohibition, also considered the money issue to be secondary, but drew quite a different moral from the rhetoric Ireland denounced. They liked the spunk it showed. "Apart from the point whether or not the people are right and wise in their demands for free silver," they wrote,

> it is wonderful to witness their grim and determined will to take the reins out of the hands of the syndicated powers which have had their way for so many decades. It is simply magnificent to see prestige and convention majorities turning away from the

25. Bryan, *First Battle,* p. 473.
26. *The Churchman,* of New York, quoted in *Literary Digest* (August 1, 1896) 13:420.
27. Ibid. (October 24, 1896) 13:806.

selfish domination of banks and mints and boards of financial exchange. . . . Even if all the delegates in that Chicago convention were designing and untrustworthy, it is evident that the latter did as they actually did, in the full persuasion that the people—the "common people" if we would say it—demand a change in the financial doctrines and methods of the nation.[28]

A few pietistic ministers, especially ex-Prohibitionists like the pastor of the First Methodist church in Moline, announced for free silver; some lost their pulpits for it. A Kansan wrote Bryan he was the only Presbyterian minister who would vote for him "in these parts," adding "I may loose [sic] my 'Job' for the feeling is intense against men that have no more sense than to vote 'The Anarchistic, Socialistic, repudiation, Demo-popocratic ticket'. . . ."[29] Three days after the Democratic national headquarters discovered it could find only four prominent clergymen who endorsed Bryan, the candidate blasted the preachers of the gospel who, while "enjoyng every luxury themselves," were "indifferent to the cries of distress which come up from the masses of the people." Promptly another barrage of abuse hit Bryan from the pulpits, the Reverend Thomas Dixon portraying the peerless leader as a mouthing, slobbering demagogue, whose patriotism was all in his jawbone, and his congregation stamped its agreement.[30]

McKinley did not let the ministers carry the burden of the countercrusade alone; far from it. McKinley was already the best known politician in the Midwest. In 1894 he had travelled 16,000 miles to 300 cities, and delivered 371 speeches before some two million people. He resolved to match Bryan's great speaking tour, not again by travelling himself, but by bringing the voters to Canton. McKinley adopted the front-porch technique Harrison had used in 1888 and developed it to perfection. From mid-June to election eve hundreds of delegations travelled to Canton to be en-

28. *Northwestern Christian Advocate,* in *Literary Digest* (August 1, 1896) 13:420.

29. Orlando Hart, of Parsons, Kansas, to Bryan, October 31, 1896, in William Jennings Bryan Papers, Library of Congress. Bryan carried that county anyway. Another Methodist minister reportedly lost his Illinois appointment because of his silverite speeches. *St. Louis Republic,* August 22, September 20, 1896.

30. Bryan, *First Battle,* pp. 469, 474; *Omaha World-Herald,* September 18, 1896; Jones, *1896 Election,* pp. 337–40.

tertained by continuous band performances, suitable refreshments, and brilliant rhetoric. McKinley inspired his visitors with original, sophisticated, and carefully researched speeches. Following Harrison's plan, McKinley and his staff examined and edited, or perhaps even drafted, the opening remarks of the spokesmen for the visiting delegations. The candidate thereby controlled the whole tenor of his campaign, had more time for careful planning, and provided fresh news copy every day to balance the coverage given to Bryan.

By remaining at home McKinley escaped the exhausting ordeal of railroad travel, and yet with his 300 speeches achieved as much publicity, and much more favorable comment, than his rival did in twice as many talks scattered over half the country. Every day thousands of cheering visitors left McKinley's lawn a shambles. The railroads reported carrying 9,000 cars filled with 756,000 special passengers to Canton, a remarkable logistics feat even if most came from Ohio and neighboring parts of Pennsylvania. Most of the roads also slashed their excursion fares; the group rate for the 700 mile round trip from Chicago falling to as low as $3.50 each. Saturdays drew the largest crowds, sometimes edging above the 50,000 mark. On September 19, some 6,000 Chicago railway employees visited McKinley, with their employers footing the bill. A few Democrats doubtless took advantage of the free trip. If they did, it was politically dangerous, for William McKinley was the man to show them Bryan's folly; their coworkers returned with souvenir splinters, exciting stories, and unbounded enthusiasm for the "Advance Agent of Prosperity."[31]

The main Republican drive in the Midwest was geared closely to McKinley's work and concentrated on educating the electorate to the dangers of Bryanism and the advantages of protection, while never letting the voters forget the economic miseries a Democratic administration had caused. Abandoning completely the old army-

31. *Cincinnati Commercial Tribune,* November 1, 1896; Joseph P. Smith, ed., *McKinley's Speeches in September* (Canton, 1896), pp. 222–28; *Ann. Cycl. 1896;* 441, 67!; Herbert Croly, *Marcus Alonzo Hanna* (New York, 1912), pp. 214–16; G. W. Steevens, *The Land of the Dollar* (New York, 1897), pp. 128–32. On August 10, McKinley spoke pleasantly with the sixty-man reception committee for Bryan, and shook everyone's hand; he even had a warm handshake for his opponent. *St. Louis Post Dispatch,* August 10, 1896.

style tactics, McKinley decided upon a proselytizing style like that of 1892, only far more intense. "This is a year for press and pen," he announced. "The sword has been sheathed. The only force now needed is the force of reason and the only power to be invoked is that of intelligence and patriotism."[32]

Mark Hanna, one of the first businessmen to throw himself into the political arena (and by far the most successful) directed the overall campaign of education with genius and plenty of money. For the first time Chicago was the operating headquarters of a major party. Charles Dawes, a fresh young politician and an experienced banker, put the Chicago office on a systematic, businesslike basis. Dawes dispensed two million dollars in four months, while the New York branch handled another million and a half. Dawes sent half the money to state campaign committees and spent the rest for literature and speakers.

Under the able direction of Perry Heath, a former editor, the literary bureau in Chicago met a herculean challenge: the systematic education of every American voter in the intricacies and morality of the relatively new question of gold versus silver. Heath surrounded himself with an unusually capable team of writers, including Robert Porter, the superintendent of the 1890 census, Frederick Wines, a Presbyterian minister, statistician and social worker, Eugene Smalley, an editor and historian, and Oscar Austin, a freelance statistician. Together they prepared nearly two hundred pamphlets, chiefly focusing on the money question but covering the tariff as well, and supervised the translation of the pamphlets into a dozen languages.

The Republicans had literature for everybody. Farmers and coal miners, wool growers and steel workers, mechanics and lumberjacks, each could read carefully prepared analyses of the relative effects of gold and silver on his own well-being. Each pamphlet had a press run of a million or more, and aggregated over 200,000,000 copies at a cost of a half-million dollars. Reprints of speeches by sound-money Democrats were in great demand, as was McKinley's letter of acceptance. Evidently most of the pamphlets reached their target audiences and were read and reread. Dawes also distributed millions of posters with colorful designs and clever slogans to all parts of the country. Boiler-plate

32. Smith, *McKinley's Speeches in September,* p. 172.

supplements for smaller newspapers, and a brief daily press release reached a circulation of tens of millions. One hundred full-time employees staffed the headquarters mailing room alone, handling the distribution of material flowing from the printer at the rate of ten or twenty million copies a day; they consigned the material to state committees, which distributed it to the counties and to tens of thousands of precinct workers who made certain that no one was without suitable literature. The operation has never been rivalled in American politics.[33]

Suddenly, about two weeks before election day, Hanna shifted tactics. The debate over money was over, with the gold position victorious; now was the time to crush the crusaders by rebutting their moralistic stance and their charges of coercion and corruption. The inundation of propaganda slackened, and in its stead came a flood of speakers, unnumbered thousands of them. The Chicago headquarters spent $150,000 to pay the travelling expenses of a staff of 1,400 orators, ranging from ex-President Harrison to ambitious young men engaging in their first campaign. In Michigan one hundred speakers furnished by Hanna denounced free silver, free trade and anarchy in unison with 120 orators paid by the state committee. All the candidates, for offices high and low, joined in the attack, as did every glib and eager volunteer. By the climax of the campaign not one county and probably not one township or precinct of the Midwest had missed the educational experience of a political lifetime.[34]

33. *Ann. Cycl. 1896:* 668–70; Charles Dawes, *A Journal of the McKinley Years* (Chicago, 1950), pp. 88–106; *Review of Reviews* (1896) 14:553–55; Croly, *Hanna,* pp. 217–31; *Washington Post,* October 20, 1896; *Chicago Tribune,* October 6, 1896; Millspaugh, *Party Organization,* pp. 142–50; and, generally, Jones, *1896 Election,* pp. 276–83. The farmers were a special target; see Gilbert Fite, "Republican Strategy and the Farm Vote in the Presidential Campaign of 1896," *American Historical Review* (1960) 55: 790–803. Dawes had bound eleven incomplete sets of the pamphlets issued from Chicago; one set is in the Yale Library.

34. The educational impact of the Republican countercrusade was apparent in the 23,500 reasons some 9,000 men gave for supporting McKinley in the *Chicago Record* poll. Fully 40 percent (9,300) demanded sound money and 17 percent (4,100) wanted a protective tariff. Less salient issues included the needs of the farmers and producing classes, mentioned by 6 percent (1,350); the necessity for the federal government to suppress disorders in the states, 5 percent (1,250); and confidence in the Supreme Court, 5 percent (1,100). Only 3 percent (800) mentioned

Hanna had downgraded the usefulness of the flamboyant parades and displays characteristic of the army-style contests. He had promised contributors that the campaign fund would be used in an orderly, businesslike manner, in the way best calculated to win votes. By October, however, the coercion charges were hurting, and threatened to cost several states. The time was due for a demonstration that the silent masses of the people did not support Bryan but stood behind sound money, law and order, and McKinley. The Republicans called upon the Grand Army of the Republic to validate the theme that the cause of national honor and patriotism demanded rejection of Bryan. McKinley sounded the call, telling a delegation of veterans, "The old soldiers this year . . . will stand by the financial honor of the Government, and will no more permit our nation's integrity to be questioned than they would permit that flag [pointing to the stars and stripes] to be assailed."[35] A trainload of ex-generals criss-crossed the region preaching patriotism, home, country, and flag. The *Chicago Tribune* called upon old soldiers to "Stand to your Guns," for "Never, since the rough edge of battle joined in 1861 were loyalty and honor more justly appealed to than now."[36] To climax the patriotic rally, Hanna called for a national "flag day," and on October 31, in every metropolis in the North, columns of marchers, well-dressed but hoarse from cheering, snaked through the flag-draped streets, chanting, shouting, and waving their ban-

---

prosperity solely in terms of restoration of confidence; 4 percent (900) favored tariff reciprocity; 3 percent objected to Bryan's arraying of class against class (650), personally admired McKinley (750), generally approved the GOP platform (640), or cited the traditional competence of the GOP (705). About 2.5 percent explicitly condemned the Democratic platform (565), and only 2 percent specified that they would vote for McKinley because they had always voted Republican before (450). One percent (310) observed that McKinley enjoyed the support of the best men of the community, or that the interests of employer and employee were harmonious (300). Surprisingly few complained that Bryan was too young and inexperienced (120), while a few men feared that the process of transition to free silver would in itself be disastrous (110), and some warned that the Democrats had always been incompetent to handle national affairs (90). *Chicago Record,* October 31, 1896.

35. *St. Louis Post Dispatch,* August 1, 1896.

36. Quoted in Mary Dearing, *Veterans in Politics* (Baton Rouge, 1952), p. 455.

ners. In Chicago an astonished foreigner watched the parade—a hundred thousand marchers!—for five hours:

> They have discovered in this country the effects of the spectacular and auricular, and they have applied it on a characteristically vast scale. You can disregard argument; you can ignore self-interest; you can forget country; you can ever refuse a bribe. But you cannot fail to see and hear and to be struck wellnigh resistless by so imperious and masterful appeal to the senses of your body.[37]

The symbolic displays proved to Altgeld "that the Republicans will stop at nothing." His dreams shattered, the governor was bitter: "they have prostituted the courts, the press and the church, and they have prostituted the American flag to the level of an advertising medium."[38] Bryan himself, attending church services in downstate Illinois, was shocked to see prominent members of the congregation wearing the yellow ribbon of McKinleyism.[39]

McKinley's strategy finally became clear. He was offering pluralism to the American people. The pamphlets promised every ethnic minority that, if they demonstrated their patriotism and good faith by voting for McKinley, the new Republican administration would guarantee their security. Every occupation, every religion, every industry, every section would receive fair treatment, with the protective tariff serving as umbrella for all. Cooperation and compromise, within the framework of sound economics, would be McKinley's principles. He even promised to seek—and later did—international agreements to remonetize silver and establish the bimetallism that the silverites wanted, but on a sound foundation. "The city for the country, and the country for the city, and all for the flag," proclaimed ex-President Harrison. If farmers had grievances, he added, they should "hunt them out and specify them, and hold them up to public judgment, and have faith in your fellow-man," and the Republicans would rectify them. "We have always practiced the Golden Rule," said McKinley, "The best policy is to 'live and let live.' "[40]

37. Steevens, *Land of the Dollar,* p. 192.
38. *New York Tribune,* October 18, 1896; Altgeld, *Live Questions,* p. 688.
39. Bryan, *First Battle,* p. 573.
40. *St. Louis Post Dispatch,* August 29, 1896; *Ann. Cycl. 1896:* 874–75, for Harrison speech.

The crusaders rejected pluralism—there was only one truth, only one common will, and the silverites were the only true custodians of this truth. Bryan felt the opposition had arrayed the moneylenders, the merchants, the wage earners, the financiers, the churches, and the soldiers against the people. Attacking Republican pluralism, he charged, "To them belongs the discredit of making more appeals to class and sectional prejudices than any other party has ever made."[41]

The GOP pushed forward regardless of criticism. In Michigan the gubernatorial nomination went to Detroit's mayor, Hazen Pingree, whose broad appeal to groups traditionally outside the Republican coalition overcame the hostility of party leaders. Mayor Pingree expressed the conciliatory pluralist theme in unmistakable terms:

> There never has been a time in the history of the republic when each one should be more willing to say to his neighbor, "Come and let us reason together."[42]

McKinley's inclusive appeal proved especially important in winning German voters who revolted against Bryan's moralism. The German swing to the Democrats in 1889 and 1890 had exceeded that of any other group and had largely accounted for the magnitude of the Democratic landslide of 1890. While the Germans did not appear more sensitive to the depression than their neighbors, and may have lagged in shifting to the GOP in 1893 and 1894, they did lead the march into McKinley's consensus in 1896.

Except for certain of the socialists, the Germans were intensely hostile to currency debasement, inflation and free silver. They had little use for Yankee utopias, and frequently ridiculed Bryan's "bombastic phrases in Western Methodist camp-meeting style."[43] When Robert Schilling, the Populist-Democratic candidate for Congress, told a Milwaukee audience that it really did not matter whether money was made out of "gold, silver, copper,

---

41. Bryan, *First Battle*, p. 594.
42. *Ann Arbor Democrat,* October 2, 1896, from his acceptance speech.
43. *New York Staats-Zeitung,* quoted in *Literary Digest* (July 25, 1896) 13:390; see also pp. 264–65, 391, 484–85, and 770–71, for other examples of German editorials.

paper, sauerkraut or sausage," he was laughed off the stage. The GOP promptly made "Schilling and Sauerkraut" their campaign slogan in Milwaukee, and swept all but the most faithful German Democrats into the McKinley column. An acute reporter noted that among the German Democrats in Wisconsin the sons were going Republican in 1896; "the fathers, however, talked about personal liberty, the Bennett law, etc.," and proposed to stick it out with the Democrats.[44] One prominent Chicago German newspaper found that, although some Turner clubs were supporting Altgeld and most Germans opposed high tariffs, free silver was alienating them from the Democratic party:

> There are a good many reasons why the Germans do not support the silver movement. They have had to fight against the Prohibitionists, and this may have made them suspicious of all "genuine American" reform movements. The German farmers of the prairie states have seen their American neighbors suddenly go crazy over a movement which the "slow" German did not appreciate because he believes that Methodist revival tactics are out of place in politics.[45]

A leading German Democrat, Henry Raab, tried to explain the conservatism of his constituents in terms of their liturgical religious practices. Speaking a year after his notable triumph in the 1890 election for superintendent of education in Illinois, Raab noted that "the Germans are conservative in their religion. They are strangers to the sensational, the revivals." Rather they sought "to maintain only those ideas and ideals which are not contrary to the institutions of this country," and proposed to defend valiantly their "manners, customs, tastes, traits and language." Their American patriotism, he affirmed, lay in "the courageous struggle against 'bi-metallism' and 'Greenback inflation'; the determination to pay with honest money, that is patriotism."[46] And

44. Hans Sperber and Travis Trittschuh, *American Political Terms* (Detroit, 1962), p. 390, which tells and documents many delightful stories about the origins of catchy political phrases. *New York Tribune*, August 22, 1896; the German shopkeepers in small Wisconsin towns gave heavy support to the Gold Democrats; *Chicago Tribune*, September 21, 1896.

45. *Chicago Abendpost*, April 25, September 2, 1896; *Literary Digest* (August 15, 1896) 13:484.

46. *Illinois Staats-Zeitung*, July 27, 1891.

so in 1896 Raab deserted Bryan, voted for the Gold Democrat ticket, and encouraged his supporters to vote for McKinley.

Apparently the German taste for sound money and distaste for millenarianism cut across all religious, occupational, and political lines. The socialists and trade union activists who did support Bryan were hesitant on the question of free silver—and Johann Most, the most notorious spokesman for dynamite among the anarchists in the United States, finally declared his support for the gold standard! Actually, only a little more than half of the Germans finally cast their votes for McKinley, as table 19 shows. Too many found the idea of supporting their old enemies, the party of prohibition and Bennett laws, too distasteful. Many refused to vote on election day, and heavily German Wisconsin had by far the lowest turnout in the Midwest. Many remained with the Democratic ticket out of confusion about who supported silver (some German Democratic leaders denied that Bryan wanted free silver) or in the expectation that sanity would even-

Table 19

Voting Patterns in Predominantly German Areas, 1888–1896

| | Republican percentage of total vote | | | | |
	1888	1890	1892	1894	1896
Iowa: 14 counties	44%	38%	41%	46%	52%
Iowa: 9 city wards	28	23	34	38	51
Wisconsin: 21 Catholic rural settlements	33	25	30	40	49
Wisconsin: 12 Lutheran rural settlements	35	21	29	37	49
Wisconsin: 11 Milwaukee wards	52	46	52	48	59
Illinois: 5 Chicago wards		55*	38	52	58
General midwestern pattern—all voters	50	47	48	53	55

*Vote for state treasurer; for state superintendent the Republican candidate (Edwards) won only 40 percent of the vote, showing the most ticket splitting in any Midwestern election.

tually return to their old party.[47] Nevertheless the shift of many thousands of Germans into the Republican column in 1896 was the largest and most decisive movement of voters that year. The proud claim of the *Illinois Staats-Zeitung* was not an idle boast:

> The German voters decided the [1896] election in Ohio, Indiana, Michigan, Illinois, Wisconsin, Iowa, Nebraska and Minnesota. . . . They have had many complaints against the Republican party, which . . . sought to combat the influence of the Germans in every way, and annoyed them continually with Prohibition laws, Sunday-closing laws, and school laws. The Germans consequently turned their backs upon the Republicans, with the result that Cleveland was twice elected, and if the Democrats had not inscribed repudiation, bankruptcy, and dishonor upon their colors as a result of their union with the Populists, the Germans would have supported them this time also. . . . It is to be hoped that the Republicans have now learned that the Germans are independent people, and that they will act accordingly.[48]

Not only the Germans, but the conservative Dutch and Swedish farmers as well, were strong for the gold standard; most, however, had long been Republicans, and some of the pietistic Prohibitionists may have shifted toward Bryan. A considerable number of Danes and Norwegians, on the other hand, endorsed free silver. Many had joined the Populist movement, especially the Danes and freethinkers or workers who had been exposed to socialists in the old country.[49]

47. Several of the German newspapers that did support Bryan downplayed or even denied his devotion to free silver and warned that if the Republicans won they would soon outlaw beer. Frederick Luebke, *Immigrants and Politics* (Lincoln, 1969), pp. 161–63; Kleppner, *Cross of Culture,* pp. 323, 329, 333, 364–65. For perceptive accounts of rural Iowa's Germans by a Democratic reporter, see *Omaha World-Herald,* September 7, 19, 27, 1896; See also *Dubuque Herald,* July 25, 1896.

48. Quoted in *Literary Digest* (November 21, 1896) 14:70–71. See also Washington Hesing to William McKinley, July 25, 1896, in William McKinley Papers. Hesing was the gold Democrat who edited the *Illinois Staats-Zeitung* and served as postmaster of Chicago.

49. R. B. Anderson to John Spooner, August 28, 1896, in John Spooner Papers, Library of Congress; *Chicago Skandinaven,* October 10, 1890, and February 2, 1892; Kleppner, *Cross of Culture,* pp. 329, 334–35; James Dowie, *Prairie Grass Dividing* (Rock Island, 1959), p. 170; Kenneth Scott Latourette, *Christianity in a Revolutionary Age* (New York, 1959), 2:133–51.

McKinley's pluralism assured the Republican presidential ticket of increased support from nearly all ethnic groups, though the liturgical-pietistic division remained visible in 1896. Table 20 suggests McKinley's share of the total vote and his gains over Benjamin Harrison among ethnic groups represented by scattered, relatively homogeneous voting units. Although the political behavior of an ethnic group cannot be charted exactly on the basis of such data, nevertheless the picture of sharp Republican gains in immigrant communities is accurate. Greater reliability can come only from interviews, and fortunately the GOP leaked the results of their October poll of Chicago voters' intentions. Table 21 analyzes these poll results by ethnic group. Since McKinley's share of the actual vote fell only four points below the poll's estimates, it can be considered as fairly reliable.[50]

The one major ethnic group in the Midwest that resisted McKinley's blandishments were the Catholic Irish. Although Bryan's apocalyptic style was hardly to their taste, they supported the Democratic ticket in 1896 with their usual enthusiasm, as only a few of the wealthier Jansenistic types bolted to the enemy. The Irish stayed with the Democrats in their hour of crisis, not in the hope of seeing Bryan in the White House, but with the intention of capturing full control of the party they had worked so long to build.

Despite their long experience in America the Irish had achieved little economic security. Factory whistles summoned few Irishmen in the morning, nor were many working as skilled craftsmen or small businessmen. They congregated in the city slums, where the men sought poorly paid unskilled jobs and the womenfolk took in washing or worked as maids to supplement meagre family incomes. Many relied upon charity, and especially on the relief offered by the vote-conscious Democratic machines. Government to the Irishman meant not soft money or high tariffs, but food baskets, bushels of coal, and above all, the hope of the security of a city's public payroll. By the early 1890s the Irish completely

---

50. The Democrats claimed that 90 percent of Chicago's union members (concentrated in construction, printing, and transportation, but not manufacturing) would vote for Bryan, while the GOP said its detailed polls showed 90 percent of nonunion workers were for McKinley. *St. Louis Republic*, October 17, 1896.

controlled the Democratic party in Chicago, and were advancing rapidly in other large cities, and many smaller cities as well. They dominated police and fire departments, were quite numerous in public utilities and street railroads, and their young women were

Table 20

Voting Patterns in Sample Areas, by Religion and Ethnic Group, 1896

	Republican percentage in 1896 (of total vote)	Gain over 1888	over 1892
Predominantly liturgical groups			
Irish			
7 rural Iowa twps.	23%	+3.3%	
Dubuque, Ward 1	28	+7.3	
Chicago, Ward 6	38		+13.1
Chicago, Ward 29	37		+ 9.4
Bohemian			
7 Iowa wards and twps.	28	+7.6	
12 Chicago precincts	42		+21
Polish			
Milwaukee, Ward 14	17	+7.2	
13 Chicago precincts	33		+21
French Catholic			
Bourbonnais, Ill.	77		+19
Predominantly pietistic groups			
Norwegian			
11 rural Iowa twps.	83%	+6.4	
5 recent Wisconsin rural settlements	81	+8.0	
9 older Wisconsin rural settlements	69	+5.1	
6 Chicago precincts	69		?
Swedish			
6 rural Iowa twps.	74	+1.6	
Chicago, Ward 23	59		+16
Rockford, Ill.	89		+25
Negro			
6 Chicago precincts	90		?

rapidly assuming teaching roles in the public school system. They also largely controlled the Catholic church, from the parish house to the convents to the bishoprics. Their flair for hard work and efficient organization in politics amazed and often dismayed onlookers. Of the 393 Irishmen in Chicago's two most heavily German wards, 377 were active in the Democratic machine, while in the 33rd ward "the Germans attend to the voting and the Irish take care of politics."[51]

Table 21

Republican Estimate of October, 1896, Support for McKinley in Chicago, by Ethnic Group

Group	Eligible voters	Percent favoring McKinley
Old Stock	113,500	65%
Germans	93,800	75[d]
Irish	49,700	10
Scandinavian[a]	37,900	70
British[b]	25,200	75
Other[c]	63,000	62
Total	383,000	61
Actual vote, November	350,000	57

a: Swedes (22,900, 80%); Norwegians (10,300, 60%); Danes (4800, 45%).
b: English (13,600, 80%); Scotch (6900, 80%); Canadians (9500, 50%?).
c: Bohemians (16,000, 60%); Dutch (4400, 80%); French (3200, 50%); Poles (16,600, 60%); Jews (6500, 75%); smaller groups (7400, 50%).
d: This estimate seems too high.

Source: GOP National Committee poll, in *New York Herald,* October 29, 1896.

51. *Illinois Staats-Zeitung,* March 20, 1893; E. M. Winston, "The Threatening Conflict with Romanism," *Forum* (1894) 17:430–31; John P. Bocock, "The Irish Conquest of Our Cities," ibid. 17:192–95; Frederick Coudert, "The American Protective Association," ibid. 17:521; Henry C. Merwin, "The Irish in American Life," *Atlantic Monthly* (1896) 77:289–301; Edward Levine, *The Irish and Irish Politicians* (Notre Dame, 1966); Robert Woods, ed., *The City Wilderness* (Boston, 1898).

Loyalty was the cardinal virtue for the Irishman—loyalty to the race, the clan, the church, and the Democratic party. If Bryan repelled the hard-money Germans and the silk-stocking Yankees, so much the better for Irish ambitions to control the party. If the city governments were overly generous in negotiating contracts and padding payrolls, so much the better for the voters in shantytown. Doubtless the non-Irish were annoyed by the ragtag and bobtail appearance of the party. At the 1896 Cook County Democratic convention, inquisitive Republican reporters counted among the 723 delegates some 265 saloon-keepers, 148 patronage holders, 84 ex-jailbirds, 71 unemployed, 36 convicted burglars, 17 accused murderers, 15 ex-policemen, 11 ex-pugilists, 10 men convicted of murder, manslaughter, or mayhem, 7 keepers of gambling houses, 6 farmers, 4 contractors, 4 plumbers, 3 undertakers, 2 doctors, 2 grain dealers, 1 grocer, and 2 proprietors of houses of ill repute.[52] For what it was worth, the Democratic party belonged to the Irish. They realized that a McKinley victory, even a landslide, would not hurt their chances of controlling city halls; all they had to do was hold tight.

The Irish strategy proved brilliantly successful. One month after McKinley's inauguration in Washington, the Democrats ousted the Republican mayors of Chicago, Cincinnati, Columbus, Detroit, and, cruelest blow of all, carried the new president's home town of Canton. Akron, Dayton, Springfield, and Zanesville, Ohio, simultaneously fell to the Democrats, as did half the cities in Michigan and many in Iowa and Wisconsin. Within the next year the Democrats tightened their hold on Indianapolis, regained New York, captured Cleveland and Milwaukee, and swept many of the smaller cities of Illinois and Wisconsin. Often the Irish had to share the fruits of victory, but everywhere their precinct work was yielding rewards. When Kankakee, Illinois, usually Republican by 600 votes, fell to the Democrats by 188 votes, Irish hearts were happy, and nowhere more so than in booming Dixon, Illinois, where the "local Tammany" carried off a miniature landslide in 1898.[53] Bewildered Republicans could only

52. *Civil Service Chronicle* (September, 1896) 2:351, quoting E. F. Donovan in the *Brooklyn Eagle.* The tabulation was prepared and used by Republicans, but the Democrats neither refuted nor denied it.
53. *New York Times,* April 6, 7, 8, 1897; *New York Tribune,* April 8,

admire the political genius of Irishmen who understood the inner workings of municipal government far better than did the upper-class professional reformers. By stomaching Bryan's millenarianism, yet reaping the benefits of McKinley's pluralism, the Irish obtained positions of power in midwestern cities that would last for at least many decades to come.

The Poles and Bohemians, though fewer in number and far less influential than the Irish, also maintained their traditional Democratic allegiance in 1896, though by somewhat smaller margins than in the past. The Democrats organized vigorously in the newer immigrant settlements in 1896, and managed to cooperate successfully with the socialists, who were operating through the Populist party. Bryan's fusion candidacy, of course, increased his support from these otherwise anti-Democratic elements. The predominantly Catholic Polish voters were receptive to appeals that depicted the Republicans as anti-Catholic, anti-labor, and antisaloon. "The Republican ranks consist practically entirely of rich monopolists, who are robbing the poor people," explained the leading Polish newspaper in 1896:

> Shall we then, plain workingmen, entrust offices to them and in this manner help them to continue to oppress us? . . . Go hand in hand with our old friends, the Democrats; that is our only salvation.[54]

The larger cities provided the greatest Republican gains in 1896, thanks to their ethno-religious composition, their industrialized and commercialized economic base, and their relative freedom from the constraints of traditional party loyalties. The fifteen most populous counties in the Midwest, 40 percent of whose voters were liturgical Germans, gave McKinley 56.6 percent of their vote, while the rest of the region gave him only 53.6 percent. This metropolitan lead of 3.0 points of Republican strength over the hinterland contrasted sharply with 1888, when

---

1897; *St. Louis Globe Democrat,* April 6, 1898; *Outlook* (April, 1897) 55:1009–11; *Nation* (April 8, 1897) 64:524; Zane Miller, *Boss Cox's Cincinnati* (New York, 1968), pp. 164–68; *Ann Cycl. 1898:* 454.

54. *Dziennik Chicagoski* (Chicago) April 3, 1896, and March 19, 1897; *Hull House Maps and Papers* (Chicago, 1895), discusses the party affiliations of Chicago's slum-dwellers.

the hinterland was 1.4 points more Republican than the fifteen cities. McKinley would have entered the White House even without the huge pluralities he rolled up in the largest cities, but he would not have won by quite so dramatic a landslide.

McKinley also did well in smaller cities. The *Chicago Tribune* survey of downstate Illinois factory employees revealed crushing Republican leads in nearly every establishment polled. The exceptions were two factories in Moline where McKinley had just recently pulled abreast of Bryan, a brick works in Ottawa (120 to 55 for the silver champion), and the Woodruff bicycle factory in Elgin, where the mechanics preferred Bryan 35 to 15. More typical was the Elgin watch plant, where McKinley held a convincing 755 to 8 lead, with 37 men still undecided in late September on how they would vote.[55] Table 22 shows McKinley's actual share of the total vote in thirty Illinois cities of 4,000 to 12,000 population, contrasted with Harrison's share in 1892. The Ohioan scored his greatest gains in the less prosperous immigrant centers, previously solid Democratic territory, and in the more prosperous old-stock cities, which traditionally had supported Republican candidates.[56] The wealthier immigrant cities, and the poorer old-stock centers were less willing to abandon Bryan, although their inhabitants did mostly vote Republican.

Immigrants and urbanites in the Midwest, being more flexible in their voting habits, more often found themselves on the winning side on election nights than did the farmers and the old-stock

55. *Chicago Tribune*, September 21, 1896. Of 9,750 downstate factory hands, 81.6 percent preferred McKinley, 15.4 percent Bryan, and the rest were undecided. Of 3,482 railroad employees, 86.4 percent preferred McKinley, 11.0 percent Bryan, and 2.6 percent undecided.

56. The sons of the middle-class old-stock pietists favored gold over silver by a 5 to 1 margin, according to straw polls at various colleges. At Hillsdale (Baptist), Franklin (Baptist), Knox (Congregationalist), and Morningside (Methodist) colleges, the students favored gold by 480 to 106, and the faculty favored it by 55 to 3. At Northwestern, Oberlin, Wisconsin, Michigan, and Michigan State, similar ratios were reported. Back East the gold premium soared to about 16 to 1, and at Yale the Gold Democrat ticket outpolled Bryan. Even at the Universities of Nebraska and Virginia, the faculty and students were in McKinley's camp. *New York Tribune*, July 26, October 24, November 2, 1896; *Detroit Free Press*, October 14, 18, 1896; *Saint Louis Republic*, October 28, 1896. The thirty-nine most heavily old-stock small towns in Iowa voted 58.7 percent Republican and 40.5 percent Democratic, virtually the same as in 1888.

voters. The "success score" measures the tendency of a community to line up behind the eventual winners. A community that voted Republican when the GOP won (in 1888, 1894, and 1896), and Democratic when that party won (in 1890 and 1892), is credited with a perfect score of +100. A score of −100 conversely indicates an uncanny ability to fall always on the losing side, a fate that all the counties in the region avoided, although some were on the losing side in four out of five elections (and received a score of −60). A success score of zero simply means that frustration exactly equalled satisfaction over a series of election nights.[57] Table 23 shows the average success scores for sixteen groups of counties, classified according to ethnicity and urbanization.

Table 22

Republican Gains in Medium-Sized Illinois Cities, by Ethnicity and Assessed Valuation, 1892–1896

	Republican share of total vote			
	Predominantly immigrant cities, 4,000 to 12,000 population		Predominantly old-stock cities, 4,000 to 12,000 population	
	Rich[a] (N=4)	Poor[b] (N=10)	Rich[c] (N=7)	Poor[d] (N=9)
1892	46.3%	44.3%	52.6%	48.1%
1896	53.2%	59.0%	61.6%	53.7%
gain	+6.9	+14.7	+9.0	+5.6

a: Alton, Cairo, Freeport, and Braceville-Coal City-Central City. Wealth according to per capita assessed valuation in 1890; "rich" means more than $125.00.
b: Braidwood, Bruce, Galena, Kankakee, Kewanee, LaSalle, Moline, Ottawa, Peru, Waukegan.
c: Canton, Champaign, Dixon, Macomb, Paris, Pekin, Sterling.
d: Beardstown, Centralia, Charlestown, Duquon, Lincoln, Litchfield, Mattoon, Monmouth, Pana.

57. Technically the success score is 100x (# of wins - # of losses)/ (# of elections). See Charles Dollar and Richard Jensen, *Historian's Guide to Statistics* (New York, 1971), chapter 4.

Regionally the average success score for all 533 counties in the five elections from 1888 through 1896 was +23, while 37 counties posted a perfect score of +100.[58] The most striking pattern in table 23 is the poor showing of counties grouped in the upper left quadrant, those with few city people and few immigrants. These four groups of counties had an average success score of only +8, which meant they voted for losers about as often as for winners. The lower left quadrant did much better. These counties, predominantly urban but with relatively few immigrants, had an average score of +21. Slightly better was the performance of the upper right quadrant, the counties with rural populations but

Table 23

Average Success Scores for All Midwestern Counties, 1888–1890–1892–1894–1896, by Urbanization and Nativity

| Proportion urban (1900)[b] | Proportion old-stock white voters, (1910)[a] | | | | Total |
	75–100%	50–75%	25–50%	0–25%	0–100%
Farm, 0%	+10[c]	+11	+29	+34	+20
Rural, 1–20%	3	8	17	40	11
Urban, 20–50%	18	21	33	49	26
City, 50–100%	28	26	39	65	42
Total, 0–100%	12	16	29	47	23

a: Proportion of males over 21 in 1910 whose parents were both native-born whites; the results using the 1900 or 1890 census were only slightly different.

b: Proportion of total population in the county living in towns or cities having more than 2,500 population in 1900; of course, many of the rural inhabitants lived in towns and hamlets and were not farmers.

c: The number of counties in each cell, from left to right, is: top row: 59,35,50,29, sum 173; second row: 40,39,30,8, sum 117; third row: 60,58,31,21, sum 170; fourth row: 5,25,21,22, sum 73; bottom row: 164,157,132,80, grand sum 533. Each cell entry is the mean success score for all counties in the group, *not* weighted for population.

58. In 1888, 65 percent voted for the winner (GOP); in 1890, 44 percent (Democrats); in 1892, 42 percent (Democrats); in 1894, 78 percent (GOP); and in 1896, 71 percent (GOP). Thus the average scores were +30 in 1888, −12 in 1890, −16 in 1892, +56 in 1894, and +42 in 1896.

large concentrations of immigrants; they had an average score of +28. The most impressive scores came in the lower right quadrant, the cities in which most voters were of immigrant stock, chiefly German, Irish, Scandinavian, and British. They accumulated an average score of +46. Indeed, the extreme lower right corner, representing the overwhelmingly immigrant cities, including Chicago, Cleveland, Detroit, and Milwaukee, recorded the highest score of all, +65, which indicates they supported the winners 82.5 percent of the time and the losers 17.5 percent. (Note that 82.5% − 17.5% = 65%). Taking the table as a whole, and moving down each column from farm areas to cities, the success scores increase, indicating that urbanization contributed to political success, even when the proportion of immigrants is held constant. Moving from left to right in any row, from old-stock to immigrant centers, the success scores also increase, indicating that ethnicity also contributed to success, regardless of the level of urbanization. The two factors of urbanization and ethnicity, therefore, independently affected voting flexibility; combined, these factors provided the formula for electoral success. The immigrants and the city-dwellers, singly and together, with their sensitivity to economic conditions, their hostility to pietistic moralism, and their amenability to political pluralism, were the keys to the winning of the Midwest.

The immigrants and the urbanites defined success in politics differently from the old-stock, rural voters. The former groups, except for the Irish among them, shunned political office; the old stock, furthermore, remained securely in control of economic power and social prestige. The critical voting groups did, however, demand high employment rates, high wages, rapid economic growth, tolerance for their customs and cultures, and avoidance of pietistic moralism. They tolerated saloons because they liked beer and distrusted prohibitionists; they supported machine rule because it was effective and responsive to their political demands. They displayed lower levels of partisan loyalty, and greater flexibility in voting, proving themselves willing to swing their support to cooperative candidates. By contrast, the rural and small town pietistic old-stock (and Scandinavian) voters cared more for the style than the substance of public policy. They clung to party loyalties established decades earlier, they abhorred corruption, harbored millenial dreams, and preferred moralistic crusades to pluralistic cooperation. They would rather battle at Armageddon than compromise with the forces of evil.

When McKinley in 1896 called upon "farmers, laborers, mechanics, miners, railroad employees, merchants, professional men and representatives of every rank of people" to heed his candidacy, he explained that "we are all dependent on each other, no matter what our occupations may be. All of us want good times, good wages, good prices, good markets; and then we want good money always."[59] Sound money thus became the symbol of the economic and cultural pluralism and advancement that he knew would sweep the cities and the immigrants into an invincible coalition.

At the same time, Bryan gambled on the support of the pietistic moralists. Ignoring the needs of the immigrants and the cities, he focused his attack on "an arrogance that has seldom been paralleled . . . a tyranny not often before attempted," a conspiracy to force "all mankind [to] bow down and worship the golden calf."[60] He promised moral redemption through free silver, yet was never able to convince the people that his millenium would be as prosperous as McKinley's good society.

The conservatives said that America had become an interdependent, industrial nation, and that farms, factories, shops, mines, and railroads, and yes, banks, offices, schools, stores, and wholesale houses all cooperated to produce genuine wealth; no sector of the society could be punished without harm to everyone. America's values and institutions were sound, and must not be disturbed. Perhaps Bryan's supporters could not understand how a clerk who shuffled papers and tallied numbers in a counting house nine hours a day could benefit mankind half as much as a farmer sweating twelve hours in the fields or a miner digging away underground. "Lawyers do not produce wealth," Bryan said, admitting that he did not produce any either.[61] More likely it seems the silverites were haunted by dread of a great conspiracy, emanating

59. *New York Tribune,* July 4, 1896; Joseph Smith, ed., *McKinley, The People's Choice* (Canton, 1896), p. 38.

60. *St. Louis Republic,* October 4, 1896.

61. Bryan, *First Battle,* p. 538. Although farmers in the cotton and wheat belts suffered greatly during the depression, the midwestern farmers managed much better. Theirs was a diversified agriculture—for example, hog raisers *bought* corn and benefited from lower prices—and the value of

from Europe and the East Coast, that sabotaged virtue with temptations of wealth—wealth ill-gotten by the exploitation of honest workingmen. The relief of these fears could be secured only by a return to general prosperity—an event that did happen shortly after the election.

The upheavals of the 1890s resulted in a long-run realignment of the voting patterns of enough midwesterners to ensure Republican hegemony in the region for decades to come. Historians have speculated whether the Democrats might not have attained the same supremacy if Benjamin Harrison had been reelected in 1892 and had received the blame for the depression. Such speculation assumes, of course, that an equally severe and bitter depression would have occurred had the GOP been in power. In any case, the presence of Grover Cleveland in the White House was not a happenstance of historical fortune. The Democratic triumph of 1892 was a continuation of their landslide of 1890, which in turn was based upon political and cultural issues, not economic conditions. A more fascinating line of speculation is that the Democrats had entered an era of hegemony in 1890, which, save for the depression, would have also lasted for decades.

At a deeper level, the political developments of the 1890s strengthened the spirit of independence that was to characterize twentieth-century politics. Acute observers noticed the change quickly. After the 1894 elections, G. W. Northrup, president of the University of Minnesota, congratulated the American electorate for "doing a good deal more for themselves" than ever before. Sensing the abandonment of the army style of campaigning, he found that voters "do not go to political meetings as much as they used to, because they know that . . . they get simply the foam which rises when the elephants are lashed into angry fury." The

---

their acreage steadily increased. Very few were delinquent on mortgage payments, although many had borrowed as much as Nebraskans or Kansans; the sale of a foreclosed mortgage in the Midwest was a rare event in 1896. *New York Tribune,* August 17, 1896. Tenant farmers, however, did not enjoy the rise in land prices and may have inclined toward Bryan. One wealthy farmer near Decatur, Illinois, reported that "most of the large land owners in the county, Democrats as well as Republicans, are gold bugs. But the renters are largely coming over to Bryan." *St. Louis Republic,* October 12, 1896. Unless new polls are discovered, there will be no way to settle the point.

successive landslides in 1890, 1892, and 1894 had broken the long decades of political stalemate in the nation. Northrup realized that "it makes no difference in one respect which way the landslide goes"; such events "serve this mighty purpose of unfastening men from the party to which they have become riveted with steel rivets so that nothing could move them, and they make it easy for these men ever afterward . . . to vote with perfect independence." Ticket splitting, he thought, would also become common, and nonpartisan reform movements would have their chance to guide municipal government.[62]

Northrup was brilliantly correct. The quick series of landslides, or more precisely the underlying conditions which produced them, loosened the party loyalties of millions of voters and stimulated a revival of antipartyism. Coupled with the moralistic concern with republican virtue that Bryan reawakened in 1896, the spirit of antipartyism—of hostility to bosses, machines, corruption, corporate influence in politics, and professional politicians generally —soon blossomed into the "Progressive Movement."[63] An unexpected consequence of the decline of party loyalty, however, was a sharp decline in turnout and other modes of popular participation between 1900 and 1920, together with a decay in the level and sophistication of information about public affairs among the people, as evidenced by the increasing superficiality and sensationalism of the press.[64]

An antidote to antipartyism also appeared in the 1890s, and for the next three-quarters of a century proved a more potent

62. *Proceedings of the Second National Conference for Good City Government* (Philadelphia, 1895), p. 88.

63. The conservative countercrusade stigmatized the silverite program as anarchistic, including such reputable reforms as the direct election of senators, which long had enjoyed strong support among conservative Democrats. It took years for the stigma to wear off. Many, if not most, of the Progressive crusaders had battled in the trenches against Bryan, including Robert LaFollette, George Norris, Theodore Roosevelt, Jonathan Dolliver, William Allen White, Albert J. Beveridge, Louis Brandeis, and Woodrow Wilson. Only when the spectres of Altgeldism and free silver vanished did they feel free to propose reforms again, or to indulge in crusades.

64. Richard Jensen, "Armies, Admen and Crusaders," *History Teacher* (January 1969), 2:33–50; W. Dean Burnham, "The Changing Shape of the American Political Universe," *American Political Science Review* (1965) 69:7–28; idem, *Critical Elections* (New York, 1970), chapter 4.

force. This was not a backward-looking emphasis on party loyalty, but McKinley's new spirit of pluralism. Born of professional
reaction to the defeats wrought by pietistic moralism inside the
GOP, pluralism carried its champion to the White House and
quickly set the tone of national and midwestern politics. While
antipartyism was essentially pietistic and middle class, pluralism
welcomed liturgical voters to an equal, if not favored, position,
and found roles for men of every occupation and status. While
antipartyism rejected bargaining and compromise in favor of the
unsoiled triumph of a single common will, pluralism sought pragmatic solutions, based on the wisdom of many groups, that everyone could live with. Pluralism facilitated the entry of new groups
into American politics, particularly the Slavs, Italians, Jews, and
Greeks who arrived by the millions in the twenty years after
McKinley's election, and including also the blacks who finally
were brought into the pluralistic mainstream in the 1960s.

The moralists, it is true, won a number of victories, especially
during the First World War, when a single national purpose
tolerated little diversity. The postwar reaction in favor of nor-
malcy, however, ruined the wartime crusaders and brought to
power a nonmoralistic, more pluralistic government run not by
politicians so much as by experts and engineers like Andrew Mel-
lon and Herbert Hoover. Their failure to cope with the strains
created by prohibition and depression led to the final triumph of
pluralism in the New Deal. Franklin Roosevelt perfected Mc-
Kinley's strategy of inclusive pluralism by giving practically every
major economic, ethnic, cultural, and regional interest group in
the country the recognition and legislation it wanted; in the process, the Democrats recaptured the support of the liturgical and
metropolitan electorate that had formed the key to McKinley's
coalition.

In the 1890s, the parties responded to antipartyism and pluralism by abandoning army-style campaign techniques and by ex-
perimenting with crusades and advertising methods. The shift
further undermined partisan loyalties, and the party rapidly lost
its central place in American government. In the span of a decade,
the people abandoned old methods and old loyalties and placed
their future in the hands of new men with fresh ideas and pragmatic principles more suited to the dawning century.

Appendix

The political differences between urban and rural constituencies stemmed from the division of labor. Farmers varied greatly in wealth and income, yet all faced the same general economic conditions—prices, freight rates, weather, new scientific methods, regional market conditions, poor roads—and so far no evidence has appeared to indicate that poor farmers voted against their richer neighbors, once the religious factor is taken into account. In urban areas, however, a heterogeneity of occupations produced a diversity of economic interests, group memberships, and social outlooks. The common laborer, the factory operative, the blacksmith, the retired farmer, the retail merchant, the railroad traffic agent, the physician, and the banker secured their livelihood from quite different sources, and were affected in quite different ways by changing economic conditions and government programs. For some, the tariff was more than a grand political conversation piece—it was a major determinant of income, job security, and economic expectation. Likewise, the money question was highly relevant to the planning of bank clerks and bank depositors, of merchants with a line of credit and farmers with mortgages, of railroad employees and families with insurance policies.

A man's occupation did make a difference on how he voted, even after allowance was made for his religious affiliation. The strongest evidence comes from the interviews taken in the 1870s in northern and central Illinois discussed in chapter 3. Table 24 below shows the Republican share of the major-party preferences of old-stock voters in Geneseo, Illinois, in 1877. Among the church affiliated (nearly all pietistic), the business and professional men were 95 percent Republican, the urban laborers 73 percent, and the nearby farmers 85 percent. Among the men not affiliated with the churches, the business and professional people were 75 percent Republican, the laborers 55 percent, and the farmers 68 percent. For each occupational grouping, church membership produced about a twenty point differential; an equally great differential existed among occupations inside each religious group. A pooling of directory interviews for eight Illinois townships in 1877 and 1878 provides a sufficiently large number of cases to analyze the political complexion of major occupational categories within the pietistic-liturgical-nonaffiliated religious framework. Table 25 shows the proportion of Republicans (of the major party total) for each occupation for each religious group. Note that the differences between pietists and liturgicals outweighed the differences inside the pietist or liturgical category. While the data does not constitute a true sample of the midwestern population, it provides the best information available. There is no evidence to indicate the patterns in any way distort the typical midwestern situation.

Farmers were less Republican than nonfarmers, and provided, in each religious group, a more homogeneous pattern than the nonfarmers. Among the nonfarmers, the proportion of Republicans ranged from a remarkably low 8.0 percent among unskilled liturgical workers, to a high of 81.4 percent among pietistic businessmen. The homogeneity that appears in aggregate election returns vanishes once the population is classified into groups according to the primary factors of religion and occupation. Inside each religious group, the level of Republicanism was fairly high —ranging from pietistic white-collar workers who were 60 percent Republican to businessmen who were 81 percent. Interestingly, the nonmembers of churches showed much less variation,

Table 24

Party Affiliation by Occupational and Religious Status, Geneseo Old-Stock, 1877

	Church affiliated		Not church affiliated		All	
	% Rep.	N	% Rep.	N	% Rep.	N
Business and professional	95.4	151	75.4	221	86.4	472
Urban labor	72.7	11	55.3	74	57.6	85
Farmer	84.6	78	67.6	105	74.9	183
All	90.8	240	69.0	400	77.2	640

Source: Same as table 3, chapter 3.

all tending to cluster around the 50-50 point, with the exception of businessmen and clerical workers. The implication is that without a church affiliation to provide a guide to their "proper" partisanship, the unaffilated divided more or less at random, except when specific, strong occupational ties pulled them toward the GOP.

Table 25

Relative Party Strength by Religion and Occupation, Eight Illinois Townships, 1877–1878

Percent Republican of two-party total; number of cases in parentheses

Occupation	Pietist	Nonaffiliated	Liturgical	All
Nonfarmers				
Business	81.4(N=97)	62.8(105)	51.5(31)	69.1(233)
Professional	75.9(58)	50.0(34)	33.3(9)	63.4(101)
White-collar	60.0(25)	61.9(42)	38.4(13)	57.5(80)
Skilled blue-collar	73.1(145)	55.6(218)	30.4(46)	58.9(409)
Unskilled	65.0(60)	48.0(123)	8.0(113)	36.1(296)
Unknown, retired	65.9(38)	52.6(38)	31.2(16)	54.4(92)
All non-farmers	72.9(423)	55.3(560)	22.8(228)	55.3(1,211)
Farmers				
Farm owners	59.1(279)	49.1(348)	13.1(145)	46.1(772)
Sons of owner	70.6(34)	41.0(61)	0.0(6)	48.5(101)
Renters and laborers	42.5(40)	52.4(84)	7.4(27)	41.7(151)
All farmers	58.4(353)	48.7(493)	11.8(178)	45.6(1,024)
Total population	66.2(776)	52.2(1,053)	18.0(406)	50.9(2,236)

Source: Same as table 4, chapter 3.

Since the Illinois townships analyzed in table 25 were predominantly rural, and contained only one small city, the patterns are even more striking; the division of labor in the Midwest produced sharp political differences, although not as sharp as religion produced. Not surprisingly, businessmen were the staunchest Republicans, with skilled workers closely following professionals as the next most Republican category. One possible economic interpretation of the patterns is that the tariff and monetary policies of the GOP proved highly satisfactory to businessmen, a point strengthened by the surprising willingness of liturgical businessmen to desert the Democratic party, haven of the vast majority of their fellow church members. The professional men—the lawyers, physicians, educators, editors, and clergy—who provided intellectual leadership to the community, though not as directly affected by national economic policies, gravitated toward the viewpoint of the more numerous body of businessmen who dominated the upper middle-class society of the towns and cities. The skilled workers, a special target of Republican programs, were less inclined to the Democrats than their unskilled neighbors, who saw little relationship between national economic policy and their own precarious status. This interpretation is speculative, of course, and when carried into the 1880s or 1890s rests on little direct empirical evidence. However, the polls of factory workers mentioned in chapters 2 and 10 indicate a striking continuity between the high levels of Republican support among Moline factory hands in 1877 and employees in the same plants in 1896.

The factor of class tensions in Midwest politics was complex. Trade unions often were influential in large-city Democratic affairs, and occasionally even formed their own parties. The unions were especially important after major strikes, as was shown in chapter 9. Less explicitly than the unions, the Democratic leadership frequently adopted the rhetoric of class conflict. John Peter Altgeld, a Chicago lawyer with close union ties, was the most notable spokesman, but all the Democrats, even Grover Cleveland, from time to time engaged in crusading oratory against the bloated rich, the grasping trusts, or the over-privileged industries fattening themselves on the helpless consumer through the operation of the overprotective tariff. The Bryan campaign of 1896 offers an opportunity to study this aspect of Democratic rhetoric.

Here the relevant problems are the party variation in relation to class composition and the question of discrimination against Democratic or liturgical workers at the hiring gate. Table 26 shows the distribution of the nonfarmers in the eight Illinois townships, according to occupation for each religious and political grouping. The composition of the parties was noticeably different. Fully three-fourths (76.5 percent) of the Republicans

Table 26

Structure of Political and Religious Groups by Occupation, Eight Illinois Townships, 1877–1878

	Grouping (read down)					
Occupation	All	Rep.	Ind.	Dem.	Pietis-tic	None	Litur-gical
Business	21.1%	24.0%	25.5%	13.3%	23.3%	21.6%	15.3%
Professional	8.5	9.6	8.9	6.8	13.4	7.3	4.6
White-collar	6.8	6.9	7.3	6.3	5.8	7.6	5.3
Skilled blue-collar	32.7	36.0	30.4	30.9	33.8	35.2	21.4
All high and middle status	69.1	76.5	72.1	57.3	76.3	71.7	46.6
Unskilled (specific industry)	8.2	5.8	7.1	12.0	3.1	8.2	16.5
Unskilled (common labor)	15.2	10.2	13.6	22.9	11.0	13.2	30.4
Retired, unknown	7.5	7.5	7.3	7.8	9.6	6.9	6.5
Total	100%	100%	100%	100%	100%	100%	100%
Number of nonfarmers	1717	669	506	542	447	1009	261
Number of farmers	1129	467	105	557	374	553	201
Proportion of farmers among all men in category	39.7%	41.1%	17.2%	50.6%	44.5%	35.5%	43.5%

Source: Same as table 4, chapter 3.

held above-average jobs (professional, business, white collar, skilled labor), in contrast to four-sevenths (57.3 percent) of the Democrats. Along religious lines the differences were even more striking, with three pietists in four (76.3 percent) in the better jobs, contrasted to fewer than half of the liturgicals (46.6 percent). Another way of looking at the pattern is shown in table 27, which indicates the proportion of unskilled and common laborers in each politico-religious category of nonfarmers. In each political group (column) the pietists were least likely to hold unskilled jobs, while the liturgicals were most likely. In each religious grouping (row) the Republicans were least likely and the Democrats most likely to be in unskilled positions. The two factors were cumulative, so that liturgical Democrats had all the disabilities of religion added to those of party, with a consequent unskilled rate of 37.5 percent, and the pietistic Republicans had the advantages of both party and religion, with a consequent rate of only 12.7 percent.

Two interpretations of the patterns in table 27 are possible: either actual discrimination retarded the upward mobility of Democrats and liturgicals, or else unskilled workers tended to prefer the Catholic church and Democratic party. The statistical patterns, which are cross sections at one instant of time, do not permit direct evaluation of the two possibilities. Job discrimination very probably existed on political grounds (see chapter 2), but

Table 27

Unskilled as Proportion of Nonfarmers, by Politico-Religious Groups, Illinois 1877–1878

	Rep.	Indep.	Dem.	Total
Pietists	12.7%	12.5%	18.3%	14.2%
Nonaffiliated	19.1%	20.7%	25.4%	21.4%
Liturgical	17.4%	27.3%	37.5%	33.7%
Total	16.1%	20.7%	29.4%	22.2%

(Number of cases, by row: 307, 24, 116; 309, 449, 251; 52, 33, 176)

Source: Same as table 4, chapter 3.

there is no evidence of it on religious grounds. On the other hand the Democrats made a definite appeal to alienated and unsuccessful workers to cast the blame for their condition on the policies of the Republican administrations; the fact that the data was collected in 1877–78, at the end of a severe depression, suggests that rhetorical appeals may have produced some of the pattern. The question why unskilled workers preferred the Catholic church ought to be rephrased, perhaps, as why Catholics displayed little upward mobility. The evidence from Eastern cities at the time shows that Irish Catholics, especially, were less successful than other immigrant groups in climbing the ladder of economic mobility. Other studies show that Calvinistic Presbyterians were distinctly less affluent than pietistic Presbyterians.[1] The possibility that liturgicals did not strive as hard as pietists is intriguing—and, indeed, one of the subthemes of Max Weber's *The Protestant Ethic and the Spirit of Capitalism.* Until the manuscripts of the 1900 federal census are opened, it will not be possible to interpret differential mobility rates satisfactorily.

Interestingly, there is no evidence from interviews or election returns to show that southerners were significantly more Democratic than other midwesterners, at least in Indiana. In the ten counties in that state in which a majority of the voters were of southern origins, the GOP averaged from 47 to 50 percent of the two-party vote in the 1870s and 1880s, only a point or two below their performance elsewhere in Indiana.[2]

1. Stephan Thernstrom and Richard Sennett, eds., *Nineteenth-Century Cities* (New Haven, 1969). Andrew Greeley and Peter Rossi, *The Education of Catholic Americans* (Chicago, 1966), and William Liu and Nathaniel Pallone, eds., *Catholics/USA* (New York, 1970), demonstrate that the Catholics had caught up by the middle of the twentieth century. Robert Doherty, "Social Bases for the Presbyterian Schism of 1837–1838," *Journal of Social History* (1968) 2:69–79.

2. The counties were Clark, Harrison, Hendricks, Johnson, Lawrence, Monroe, Orange, Pike, Putnam, and Washington. Melvyn Hammarberg, "The Indiana Voter" (Ph.D. diss., U. of Pennsylvania, 1970), provides further demographic and religious analysis for voters in nine counties in 1874. He reports patterns very similar to those given here and notes that loosely affiliated Protestants stood midway politically between church members and the unchurched. Elmer Elbert, "Southern Indiana Politics on the Eve of the Civil War, 1858–1861," (Ph.D. diss., Indiana University, 1967), pp. 207–8, found Republican leaders were more likely to have been southerners than were Democratic leaders in the late 1850s.

> Yet how find, and how, when
> found, learn the facts? . . . They
> must be sought in innumerable
> statesmen's manuals, and political
> text-books, and fragments of
> political biography, debates in
> Congress, abortive attempts at the
> history of the United States,
> newspaper files, volumes of election
> statistics, and all manner of other
> scattered material.
>
> Whitelaw Reid, in *American and English
> Studies* (New York, 1913), 2:206

Whitelaw Reid's century-old advice to students of American politics has proved unquestionably sound. This bibliographical guide attempts to be more specific than Reid, but hardly aspires to total inclusiveness, not even for all the items cited in the footnotes.

1. *Manuscript sources* proved quite disappointing. The politicians of the day discussed elections as readily as they shook hands, yet they seldom entrusted their opinions, plans, or fears to paper. The study focused on voters, and confidential correspondence rarely shed light on their behavior, although some important poll results were uncovered in the Harrison and Usher papers.

The Library of Congress houses the most important collections of relevant manuscripts. However, its holdings of the papers of Grover Cleveland, Benjamin Harrison, and William McKinley were read on microfilm. Each collection contains some significant incoming letters from midwesterners, and the Harrison papers include a large and useful file of newspaper clippings. The William Jennings Bryan papers contain many revealing letters from supporters during and immediately after the 1896 campaign. The Louis Michener papers include several memoranda on the Harrison campaign of 1888. The large John Sherman and John Spooner collections suggested what national issues were especially interesting to minor midwestern politicians.

The State Historical Society of Wisconsin has gathered the next most useful collections of manuscripts. The papers of Jeremiah Rusk, Robert LaFollette, Elisha Keyes, and Ellis B. Usher unveiled the inner workings of Wisconsin party organizations. The Nils P. Haugen papers were the most helpful source on the Norwegian Republicans. Unusually valuable were the William F. Vilas papers, which include many long, remarkably candid and perceptive letters from Edward C. Wall. The Ignatius Donnelly papers, microfilmed by the Minnesota Historical Society, were suggestive on Populist activities.

2. *Newspapers and periodicals* were of primary importance for the study. The hard-working political reporters of the major dailies not only recorded the comings, goings, and utterances of the politicians, but ably described the operation of party organizations, gave incisive summaries of public opinion, reported polls, and tabulated election returns. Well kept, indeed, were the political secrets that did not soon find their way into the newspapers. Editorials, usually written by men of high standing in the party organizations, reflected official strategy and shaped the opinions of the rank and file. It would be a mistake to underrate their significance. N.W. Ayer & Son's *Directory of Newspapers and Periodicals* (Philadelphia, 1885–1897) and Pettingill & Co.'s *Newspaper Directory* (Boston, 1882–1896) list nearly all the midwestern newspapers, their party affiliation, and their average circulation. The usual political affiliation, or bias (1888–1896), of each paper must be noted; those which endorsed Bryan in 1896 are especially indicated.

Chicago: *Herald* (Ind. Dem.); *Illinois Staats-Zeitung* (German, Dem.), the leading German newspaper in the Midwest; *Record* (Ind.), especially fair in 1896; *Skandinaven* (Norwegian, Rep.); *Times* (Dem.), the most liberal major paper in the region; *Tribune* (Rep.), low tariff, high license, and incurably Republican, the *Tribune* gave the best coverage of midwestern politics.

Cincinnati: *Enquirer* (Dem., pro-Bryan), yellow journalism and free silver were its distinctions; *Commercial-Gazette* (Rep.), very powerful editorials, but only fair reporting; *Commercial-Tribune* (Rep.).

Cleveland: *Plain-Dealer* (Dem., pro-Bryan), mediocre reporting.

Des Moines: *Iowa State Register* (Rep.), itself a power in the GOP; excellent coverage of Iowa news.

Detroit: *Free Press* (Dem.); *News* (Dem., pro-Bryan), best reporting in the state; *Patriotic American* (APA weekly).
Dubuque: *Herald* (Dem., pro-Bryan).
Indianapolis: *Freeman* (Negro weekly, Dem.); *Journal* (Rep.), very detailed coverage of Indiana politics; *Sentinel* (Dem., pro-Bryan), equally detailed coverage.
Madison: *Wisconsin State Journal* (Rep.).
Milwaukee: *Herold* (German, Rep.); *Journal* (Dem.); *Sentinel* (Rep.), a very powerful newspaper.
New York: *Herald* (Ind.), excellent reporting, very fair; *Journal* (Dem., pro-Bryan), Hearst's sheet; *Times* (Dem.), very well indexed, fair reporting, good editorials; *Tribune* (Rep.), leading GOP newspaper in the country, and indexed, but poor coverage of the Midwest; *Voice* (Prohibitionist weekly).
Omaha: *World-Herald* (Dem., pro-Bryan), Bryan was editor before his nomination.
Saint Louis: *Globe-Democrat* (Rep.); *Post-Dispatch* (Dem., pro-Bryan); *Republic* (Dem., pro-Bryan).
Springfield: *Illinois State Journal* (Rep.); *Illinois State Register* (Dem.).
In addition, the Chicago Foreign Language Press Survey (80 reels of microfilm, at Chicago Public Library and University of Chicago Library), contains the WPA translations of many editorials from the major foreign language newspapers of that city, 1867 to 1936.

The most informative periodicals of the 1880s and 1890s were: *The Nation; Literary Digest; National Temperance Advocate; Review of Reviews; Public Opinion; Civil Service Chronicle; Arena; North American Review; Forum; Bradstreet's; Political Science Quarterly; Journal of Political Economy;* and *Quarterly Journal of Economics.*

Of special value were religious periodicals, which were scanned for the 1880s and 1890s:

Christian Herald (nondenominational, pietistic)
Independent (nondenominational, pietistic, Republican)
Outlook (before 1893, *Christian Union*) (nondenominational, pietistic)
Homiletic Review (nondenominational, pietistic)
Baptist Quarterly Review (pietistic)

Catholic World (Jansenistic Catholic)
Ecclesiastical Review (liturgical Catholic)
American Catholic Review (liturgical Catholic)
Advance (pietistic Congregational)
Bibliotheca Sacra (Congregational)
Church News (St. Louis, liturgical Episcopalian)
Friends' Review (pietistic Quaker)
Columbus Theological Magazine (liturgical Lutheran)
Lutheran Church Review (pietistic)
Lutheran Quarterly (pietistic)
Lutheran Witness (liturgical)
Methodist Review (pietistic)
Northwestern Christian Advocate (pietistic Methodist)
Observer (pietistic Presbyterian)
Princeton Review (liturgical Presbyterian)
Reformed Quarterly Review (mixed, German Reformed)
Christian Examiner (pietistic Unitarian)

3. *Government publications* were invaluable companions through the maze of midwestern social and economic history. The federal censuses of 1870, 1880, 1890, 1900, and 1910, comprising well over one hundred thick quarto volumes, yielded reams of worksheets crammed with statistics, answered thousands of questions, and raised as many new ones. Compendium volumes for each census were helpful, as were the statistical atlases of 1890, 1900, and 1910. After the twelfth census (1900), a number of special reports appeared, the most used being *Occupations at the Twelth Census* (Washington, 1907) and *Religious Bodies: 1906* (Washington, 1910). S.N.D. North, *History and Present Condition of the Newspaper and Periodical Press of the United States* (Washington, 1884), was a valuable special report from the tenth census.

For demographic data at the township level, state censuses were essential, particularly the *Census of Iowa* (Des Moines, 1875, 1880, 1885, 1895, 1905, 1915), with important election data in the first three volumes; *Tabular Statement of the Census Enumeration [of Wisconsin]* (Madison, 1885, 1895, 1905); and the *Census of Michigan: 1884* and *1894* (Lansing, 1886, 1896).

Each state and the federal government published annual or biennial reports from their bureaus of labor statistics. All of the volumes from 1884 to 1900 were scanned, and provided unexpected riches—for example, tens of thousands of complete interview schedules on wages, working conditions, farming, and economic affairs generally. Convenient summaries of all the state reports appear in the *Third Special Report of the [U.S.] Commissioner of Labor* (Washington, 1893), and in the Department of Labor's *Index of All Reports Issued by Bureaus of Labor Statistics* . . . (Washington, 1902). The *Third [1887], Tenth, [1894],* and *Sixteenth [1901] Annual Reports of the [U.S.] Commissioner of Labor* give details on midwestern strikes, the *Tenth Report* being unusually complete and detailed.

Although they focus on a later period, the *Report* of the Industrial Commission (Washington, 1900–1902), 19 vols., and the *Report* of the Immigration Commission (Washington, 1910–11), 42 vols., contain great quantities of data relevant to the 1890s. On the Pullman strike of 1894, the basic source is the United States Strike Commission, *Report on the Chicago Strike* (Washington, 1895); the Commission was hostile toward Pullman and friendly toward the strikers. The most convenient repository of statistical data, although unfortunately not broken down by states, is Bureau of the Census, *Historical Statistics of the United States: Colonial Times to 1957* (Washington, 1960).

Election returns from ward and township levels, as well as brief biographies of legislators and state officers, make indispensable the official state annual or biennial handbooks: *Iowa Official Register* (Des Moines, 1889–97, annual); *Official Directory . . . of Michigan* (Lansing, 1887–97, biennial); *Annual Report of the Secretary of State . . . of Ohio* (Columbus, 1888–97, annual); and *The Blue Book of . . . Wisconsin* (Madison, 1887–97, biennial). Unfortunately, Illinois began its manual later, and Indiana published detailed election returns only for 1890 in its *Third Biennial Report of the Department of Statistics for 1889–90* (Indianapolis, 1891). Newspapers usually provided the best sources for mayoralty returns.

The *Congressional Record* proved a great disappointment; many petitions from constituencies came in, but mostly concerned with oleomargarine, railroad couplings, and Sunday closing of the Chicago World's Fair. Various state legislative journals

and collections of executive documents were examined, but yielded little of importance.
4. *Collected speeches and letters, autobiographies, and biographies* were used constantly. John Altgeld, *Live Questions* (Chicago, 1899), includes most of his speeches; William Jennings Bryan, *The First Battle* (Chicago, 1897), remains vital for the 1896 campaign; George Parker, ed., *The Writings and Speeches of Grover Cleveland* (New York, 1892), has mediocre coverage; Charles Hedges, ed., *The Speeches of Benjamin Harrison* (New York, 1892), contains all the 1888 campaign speeches; *Speeches and Addresses of William McKinley* (New York, 1893), contains only a few of McKinley's many talks, but four very rare pamphlets (at Yale and the Library of Congress) include nearly all his 1896 campaign speeches: Joseph P. Smith, ed., *McKinley, The People's Choice* (Canton, 1896); *McKinley's Speeches in August* (Canton, 1896); *McKinley's Speeches in September* (Canton, 1896); and *McKinley's Speeches in October* (Canton, 1896); Elting Morison, ed., *The Letters of Theodore Roosevelt* (Cambridge, 1951–54), especially vols. 1 and 2, are fascinating; and Frederic Bancroft, ed., *Speeches, Correspondence and Political Papers of Carl Schurz* (New York, 1913), especially vols. 4 and 5, reveal the Mugwump mind. As a rule, the newspapers were a richer source of texts of speeches than these compilations.

The most used autobiographies and reminiscences were: David Brandt, "Iowa Political Sketches," *Iowa Journal of History* (1955, 1957) 53: 175–83, 341–66, 55:351–66; Cyrenus Cole, *I Remember, I Remember* (Iowa City, 1936), on Iowa politics; Joseph Foraker, *Notes of a Busy Life* (Cincinnati, 1917), on Ohio; Carter Harrison, *Stormy Years* (Indianapolis, 1935), on Chicago; Nils Haugen, *Pioneer and Political Reminiscences* (Madison, 1929), on Wisconsin; Laurence Larson, *The Log Book of a Young Immigrant* (Northfield, Minnesota, 1939), on Norwegian life in Iowa; Robert LaFollette, *Autobiography* (Madison, 1913, [1960 ed.]), which must be used with caution; George Parker, *Recollections of Grover Cleveland* (New York, 1909), on the Democratic campaign organization; and John Sherman, *Recollections of Forty Years . . .* (Chicago, 1895), the detailed stories of the grand old man of the Grand Old Party.

Biographies of greatest value were: Leland Sage, *William Boyd Allison* (Iowa City, 1956); for Altgeld, Harry Barnard, *Eagle Forgotten* (New York, 1938), and Harvey Wish, "The Administration of Governor John Peter Altgeld of Illinois, 1893–1897," (Ph.D. dissertation, Northwestern University, 1936); Paolo Coletta, *William Jennings Bryan* (Lincoln, 1964), vol. 1; William Orcutt, *Burrows of Michigan and the Republican Party* (New York, 1917); James Barnes, *John G. Carlisle* (New York, 1931); Allan Nevins, *Grover Cleveland* (New York, 1932), excellent and highly sympathetic; Horace Merrill, *Bourbon Leader* (Boston, 1957), an excessively critical view of Cleveland; Robert Kelley, *The Transatlantic Persuasion* (New York, 1969), a fresh approach to Cleveland; Ray Ginger, *The Bending Cross* (New Brunswick, 1949), on Eugene Debs; Robert Bolt, *Donald Dickinson* (Grand Rapids, 1970); Thomas Ross, *Jonathan Prentiss Dolliver* (Iowa City, 1958), superb; Matilda Gresham, *Life of Walter Quintin Gresham* (Chicago, 1919), wifely and often unreliable; Herbert Croly, *Marcus Alonzo Hanna* (New York, 1912), excellent; Thomas Beer, *Hanna* (New York, 1929); Harry Sievers, *Benjamin Harrison: Hoosier Statesman* (New York, 1959), excellent; Sievers, *Benjamin Harrison: Hoosier President* (Indianapolis, 1968), weak; Claude Bowers, *The Life of John Worth Kern* (Indianapolis, 1918), a poor biography of a neglected Indiana Democrat; Belle and Fola LaFollette, *Robert LaFollette* (New York, 1953); Chester Destler, *Henry Demarest Lloyd and the Empire of Reform* (Philadelphia, 1963); H. Wayne Morgan, *William McKinley and His America* (Syracuse, 1963), excellent; Elsie Glück, *John Mitchell: Miner* (New York, 1929); Dorothy Fowler, *John Coit Spooner,* (New York, 1961); Richard Current, *Pine Logs and Politics: A Life of Philetus Sawyer, 1816–1900* (Madison, 1950); Horace Merrill, *William Freeman Vilas* (Madison, 1954), excellent; Fred Haynes, *James Baird Weaver* (Iowa City, 1919); and Mary Earhart, *Frances Willard* (Chicago, 1944).

Of course, the *Dictionary of American Biography* (New York, 1928–44), *Dictionary of Wisconsin Biography* (Madison, 1960), *Who Was Who in America* (Chicago, 1942), and the obituaries in the newspapers and in the *Annual Cyclopedia* were consulted frequently, especially for the more obscure personages.

5. *Other sources and collections* often rivalled the newspapers in utility. In particular, [*Appleton's*] *Annual Cyclopedia* (New York, 1862–1903), cited as *Ann. Cycl.*, supplied more facts than any other source; its objectivity, accuracy, scope, convenience, and sometimes even scholarship, make it an unusually impressive source. The [*New York*] *Tribune Almanac* (New York, 1881–99) often was handy, but the *Chicago Daily News Almanac* (Chicago, 1885–98) approached *Ann. Cycl.* and the *Chicago Tribune* in number of footnote citations. It contains precinct returns for all major Chicago elections (and the ethnic breakdown of the city's electorate by precincts in *1889:* 157–62, and by wards in *1894:* 318), as well as convenient biennial ward and township election returns for Wisconsin, Michigan, and Illinois (the only source for Illinois), and for Indiana in 1892. The platforms of the midwestern parties, and lists of organization leaders, together with much other precious information crowd its small-print pages.

In conjunction with the census reports, *Lippincott's Gazeteer of the World* (Philadelphia, 1893) provided information on practically every county, city, village and township in the Midwest. Often it was necessary to turn to the *Rand McNally Commercial Atlas of America* (Chicago, 1922), to find some of the places, but the WPA American Guide series furnished a bit of local color for every county.

Other compilations of value include Kirk Porter and Donald Johnson, *National Party Platforms: 1840–1964* (Urbana, 1966); Joseph P. Smith, ed., *History of the Republican Party in Ohio* (Chicago, 1898); William Henry, ed., *State Platforms of the Two Dominant Political Parties in Indiana, 1850–1900* (Indianapolis, 1902); Benjamin Shambaugh, ed., *Messages and Papers of the Governors of Iowa* (Iowa City, 1903–1905), 7 vols.; George Dawson, ed., *Republican Campaign Text-Book* (New York, 1884, 1888, 1892, 1896), contained probably most of the material used by stump speakers during the presidential canvasses. *The Campaign Text-Book of the Democratic Party* (New York, 1888, 1890, 1892, 1894, 1896) and *The Political Reformation of 1884: A Democratic Campaign Book* (New York, 1884) were the Democratic counterparts. *Campaign Text-Book of the National Democratic Party: 1896* (Chicago, 1896), was the publication of the bolting Gold Democrats. *The Political Prohibitionist* (New York, 1887, 1888, 1889, 1896) is the third party's handbook, of minor value. Yale, the Library of Congress, the Smithsonian Institution, and the Wisconsin State Historical Society possess innumerable campaign leaflets, pamphlets, banners, posters, buttons, torches, and the like; while seldom cited here, they were a lot of fun to look through.

6. *Regional studies* proved indispensable. Paul Kleppner, *The Cross of Culture: A Social Analysis of Midwestern Politics, 1850–1900* (New York, 1970), focuses on Wisconsin, Michigan, and Ohio; it is a major study that nicely complements this book. Horace Merrill, *Bourbon Democracy of the Middle-West, 1865–1896* (Baton Rouge, 1953), covers eight states and thirty years, and suffers from an intense bias against its subject, the conservative Democrats. Lewis Atherton, *Main Street on the Middle Border* (Bloomington, 1954), is a good social history of the midwestern small town in the late nineteenth century. James Bryce, *The American Commonwealth* (New York, 1895), is an outdated classic of middling value. Merle Curti, *The Making of An American Community* (Stanford, 1959), is a sophisticated social history of the Yankees and Norwegians in Trempeleau County, Wisconsin; it does not, unfortunately, cover the 1890s, and generally neglects the role of religion. John Fenton, *Midwest Politics* (New York, 1966), covers the voting history of the region in the twentieth century, but is unreliable on the nineteenth. Henry Hubbard, *The Older Middle West, 1840–1880* (New York, 1936), is rather skimpy on politics in the 1870s. Robert and Helen Lynd, *Middletown* (New York, 1929), contains some historical perspective on the city of Muncie, but neglects basic questions like the roots of party loyalty and prohibition. Richard Power, *Planting Corn Belt Culture* (Indianapolis, 1953), discusses Yankee-Southerner conflict in rural Indiana before 1865. Joseph Schafer, *Wisconsin Domesday Book* (Madison, 1922–37), 5 vols., is a series of excellent township studies for the mid-century. Richard Sennett, *Families Against the City* (Cambridge, 1970), misinterprets Chicago's middle classes; Newell Sims, *A Hoosier Village* (New York, 1912), is a neglected classic, a sociological history of Angola, Indiana. Joseph Rosenstein, "Small-Town Party Politics" (Ph.D. dissertation, University of Chicago, 1950), and W. Lloyd Warner

et al. *Democracy in Jonesville* (New York, 1949), are brilliant sociological studies of Morris City in Grundy County, Illinois. Perhaps the most perceptive analysis of midwestern political culture in the nineteenth century appears in the essays of Frederick Jackson Turner; see his *The Frontier in American History* (New York, 1920). Melvyn Hammarberg, "The Indiana Voter" (Ph.D. diss., U. of Pennsylvania, 1970), correlates partisanship, religion, and demography for individuals in 1874.

Adequate—even good—state histories abound. Emma Thornbrough, *Indiana in the Civil War Era: 1850–1880* (Indianapolis, 1965), is especially thorough. Also valuable were: Logan Esarey, *A History of Indiana* (Indianapolis, 1918); Clifton Phillips, *Indiana in Transition: 1880–1920* (Indianapolis, 1968); Ernest Bogart and Charles Thompson, *The Industrial State: 1870–1893* (Springfield, Ill., 1920), for Illinois; Philip Jordan, *Ohio Comes of Age: 1873–1900* (Columbus, 1943); and Cyrenus Cole, *A History of the People of Iowa* (Cedar Rapids, 1921), by a participant. Unfortunately, Michigan and Wisconsin have been neglected by scholars.

Among the many local histories, the best are: A. T. Andreas, *History of Chicago* (Chicago, 1886), 3 vols.; Bessie Pierce, *A History of Chicago: 1871–1893* (New York, 1957); Bayrd Still, *Milwaukee* (Madison, 1965); Melvin Holli, *Reform in Detroit* (New York, 1969), focusing on Hazen Pingree; Zane Miller, *Boss Cox's Cincinnati* (New York, 1968); and Joseph Dunn, *Greater Indianapolis* (Chicago, 1910), by a participant. Most midwestern counties boast one or more "histories," valuable chiefly for their biographical sketches of prominent citizens and descriptions of townships, churches, newspapers, and industries. Hundreds of these were consulted, and most are listed in Clarence Peterson, *Consolidated Bibliography of County Histories* (Baltimore, 1963). Of special value were the *People's Guides* to Indiana counties, compiled by Cline and McHaffie in the 1870s; *The Past and Present of Rock Island County, Illinois* (Chicago, 1877) is representative of similar guides to Illinois counties. They are of extraordinary value because they record the party, birthplace, occupation, and sometimes age and religion of most inhabitants.

Studies national in scope are numerous. Perhaps the best are Robert Weibe, *The Search for Order, 1877–1920* (New York, 1967), and Samuel Hays, *The Response to Industrialism, 1885–1914* (Chicago, 1957). Useful for the facts are Harold Faulkner, *Politics, Reform and Expansion: 1890–1900* (New York, 1959); John Garraty, *The New Commonwealth, 1877–1890* (New York, 1968); James Rhodes, *History of the United States* (New York, 1919, 1920), vols. 8 and 9, by the perceptive brother-in-law of Mark Hanna; Stanley Hirshson, *Farewell to the Bloody Shirt* (Bloomington, 1962); Ellis Oberholtzer, *A History of the United States Since the Civil War: 1888–1901* (New York, 1937), vol. 5; the unreliable *The Politicos: 1865–1896* (New York, 1938), by Matthew Josephson—now replaced by H. Wayne Morgan, *From Hayes to McKinley* (Syracuse, 1969), which totally ignores the critical developments on the state and local level; and the acute interpretive essays in H. Wayne Morgan, ed., *The Gilded Age* (Syracuse, 1970). G. W. Steevens, *The Land of the Dollar* (New York, 1897), is a good report on the excitement of 1896.

7. *Scholarly studies of elections and politics* include: Walter Burnham, *Presidential Ballots, 1836–1892* (Baltimore, 1955), and Edgar Robinson, *The Presidential Vote: 1896–1932* (Stanford, 1934), for county election returns and overall statistical patterns; Frank Munger, "Two-Party Politics in the State of Indiana," (Ph.D. dissertation, Harvard 1955), a model study focused chiefly on the twentieth century; and a daring though unsuccessful attempt to apply factor analysis, Duncan MacRae and James Meldrum, "Critical Elections in Illinois: 1888–1958," *American Political Science Review* (1960) 54:669–83.

The best books on the party struggles in the 1890s are: Chester Destler, *American Radicalism, 1865–1901* (New London, 1946); Paul Glad, *McKinley, Bryan and the People* (New York, 1964), shallow; Fred Haynes, *Third Party Movements* (Iowa City, 1916), concentrating on Iowa; John Hicks, *The Populist Revolt* (Minneapolis, 1931), which like all studies of the Populists greatly exaggerates their number, rural strength, and importance; Richard Hofstadter, *The Age of Reform* (New York, 1955), a seminal essay directing attention to psychological factors, but unfortunately not grounded on careful research; J. Rogers Hollingsworth, *The Whirligig of Politics: The Democracy of Cleve-*

land and Bryan (Chicago, 1963); Stanley Jones, *The Presidential Election of 1896* (Madison, 1964), which covers the national story down to election day, but largely ignores the voting patterns; George Knoles, *The Presidential Campaign of 1892* (Stanford, 1942), a narrative account in this form, but with many statistics in the original dissertation; George Mayer, *The Republican Party: 1854–1966* (New York, 1967), based upon an exhaustive reading of the manuscripts, but with no new ideas about the 1890s; Jesse Macy, *Party Organization and Machinery* (New York, 1904), still useful; Arthur Millspaugh, *Party Organization and Machinery in Michigan Since 1890* (Baltimore, 1917), an unimaginative treatment of an important theme; Walter Nugent, *The Tolerant Populists* (Chicago, 1963), which overworks its thesis but is filled with fascinating material about Kansas; Joseph Schafer, Jr., "The Presidential Election of 1896," (Ph.D. dissertation, University of Wisconsin, 1941), long the standard account but now displaced by Jones; Robert Marcus, *Grand Old Party: Political Structure in the Gilded Age, 1888–1896* (New York, 1971), which easily demolishes Josephson's *The Politicos;* and Robert Ulrich, "The Bennett Law of 1889," (Ph.D. dissertation, University of Wisconsin, 1965). The role of newspapers and editors in politics has yet to enlist its historian; generally see Frank Mott, *American Journalism* (New York, 1962). Anyone inquiring into the geographical distribution of party newspapers should examine Svennik Hoyer, "The Political Economy of the Norwegian Press," in *Scandinavian Political Studies* (Oslo, 1969) 3:85–143.

A full listing of all the relevant articles about midwestern politics would be tedious. The best include: O. Fritiof Ander, "The Swedish-American Press and the Election of 1892," *Mississippi Valley Historical Review* (1937) 23:533–54; James Barnes, "Myths of the Bryan Campaign," ibid. (1947) 34:267–404, an influential article by the author of one of the best biographies of Bryan's enemies; Carl Degler, "American Political Parties and the Rise of the City," *Journal of American History* (1964) 51:41–59, tends to confuse the urbanization and immigration factors, and neglects entirely cities of less than 45,000 population; Herman Deutsch, "Yankee-Teuton Rivalries in Wisconsin Politics of the Seventies," *Wisconsin Magazine of History* (1931) 14:262–82,

403–18, and his "Disintegrating Forces in Wisconsin Politics of the Early Seventies," in ibid. (1932) 15:168–81, 282–96, 391–411; William Diamond, "Urban and Rural Voting in 1896," *American Historical Review* (1941) 46:281–305, long the only careful statistical analysis of the election, but marred by a neglect of previous or subsequent voting patterns; Gilbert Fite, "Republican Strategy and the Farm Vote in . . . 1896," ibid. (1960) 65:787–806; Thomas Felt, "Suggestions for a Plan of County Organization: Charles Dick Lays the Groundwork for the Campaign of 1896," *Ohio Historical Quarterly* (1960) 69:367–78; Albert House, "The Democratic State Central Committee of Indiana in 1880," *Indiana Magazine of History* (1962) 58:179–210, valuable; Walter Nydegger, "The Election of 1892 in Iowa," *Iowa Journal of History* (1927) 25:358–449; Herman Nixon, "The Populist Movement in Iowa," ibid. (1926) 24:3–103; Joseph Schafer, "Editorial Comment," *Wisconsin Magazine of History* (1927) 10:455–60, on the voting patterns in Wisconsin in 1890; William Whyte, "The Bennett Law Campaign in Wisconsin," ibid. 10:363–90, by a participant; Harvey Wish, "John Peter Altgeld and the Election of 1896," *Journal of the Illinois State Historical Society* (1937) 30:353–84, and his "John Peter Altgeld and the Background of the Campaign of 1896," *Mississippi Valley Historical Review* (1938) 24:503–18; and Roger Wyman, "Wisconsin Ethnic Groups and the Election of 1890," *Wisconsin Magazine of History* (1968) 51:269–93, a computer analysis of voting patterns.

On veterans, pensions and patronage, the most interesting studies are: Wallace Davies, *Patriotism on Parade* (Cambridge, 1955); Mary Dearing, *Veterans in Politics* (Baton Rouge, 1952), exhaustive; Dorothy Fowler, *The Cabinet Politicians: The Postmaster General, 1829–1909* (New York, 1943); and three articles by Donald McMurry, "The Soldier Vote in Iowa in the Election of 1888," *Iowa Journal of History* (1920) 18:335–56, "The Political Significance of the Pension Question, 1885–1895," *Mississippi Valley Historical Review* (1922) 9:19–36, and "The Bureau of Pensions During the Administration of Benjamin Harrison," ibid. 13:343–64.

8. *Secondary works on prohibition* ought to be more numerous. Joan Bland, *The Hibernian Crusade: The Story of the Catholic*

Total Abstinence Union of America (Washington, 1951), is excellent. Charles Camup, "The Temperance Movement in Indiana," *Indiana Magazine of History* (1920) 16:112–51; Dan Clark, "The History of Liquor Legislation in Iowa, 1846–1898," *Iowa Journal of History* (1908) 6:55–87, 339–74, 503–608, is unusually detailed. Ernest Cherrington, *The Evolution of Prohibition* (Westerville, Ohio, 1920), is a chronology. D. Leigh Colvin, *Prohibition in the United States* (New York, 1926), is a good history of the Prohibition party by one of its leaders. Joseph Gusfield, *Symbolic Crusade: Status Politics and the American Temperance Movement* (Urbana, 1963), is an unsuccessful attempt at sociological history. John Krout, *The Origins of Prohibition* (New York, 1925), takes the story to 1851 when the real action began. Peter Odegard, *Pressure Politics* (New York, 1928), is the classic study of the Anti-Saloon League. George Richman, *History of Hancock County, Indiana* (Greenfield, Indiana, 1916), pp. 393–423, is a good account of temperance agitation at the local level. Andrew Sinclair, *Era of Excess: A Social History of the Prohibition Movement* (New York, 1962), unfairly ridicules both wets and drys. Floyd Streeter, "History of Prohibition Legislation in Michigan," *Michigan History Magazine* (1918) 2:289–308, is inadequate. James Timberlake, *Prohibition and the Progressive Movement, 1900–1920* (Cambridge, 1963), fails to connect the two movements closely. Besides the periodicals, two primary sources remain essential starting points. *The Cylopedia of Temperance and Prohibition* (New York, 1891), by many hands, combines moral indignation and detailed history; *One Hundred Years of Temperance* (New York, 1886), is highly revealing of the mind of the crusading dry. The annual *Report* of the WCTU was discreetly silent on only one topic: politics. A very useful compendium is the *Standard Encyclopedia of the Alcohol Problem* (Westerville, Ohio, 1925–1930), 6 vols.

9. *Religious history* is still a sadly neglected field after 1860, as most scholarship neglects the actual beliefs and behavior of the people to focus on the small beginings of the social gospel movement. Only the minor sects and the immigrant churches have received the attention they deserve. Of greatest value were the periodicals, newspapers and the temperance literature cited above, the almanacs, the *Annual Cyclopedia,* the federal census of churches of 1890 and 1906, and the Iowa state census of 1895,

which inquired about religious preferences. Henry Carroll was the leading expert on religious statistics, and his *The Religious Forces of the United States* (New York, 1912), was a reliable guide to census results. Various encyclopedias guided the way through theological thickets, and illustrated the practical force of Christianity by biographies of thousands of ministers and laymen. These sources include: William Cathcart, *The Baptist Encyclopedia* (Philadelphia, 1883), 2 vols.; *Catholic Encyclopedia* (New York, 1907–1912), 15 vols.; *New Catholic Encyclopedia* (New York, 1967), 15 vols., strong on historical material; A. A. Benton, ed., *The Church Cyclopedia* (New York, 1883), Episcopalian; Julius Bodensieck, ed., *The Encyclopedia of the Lutheran Church* (Minneapolis, 1965), 3 vols.; Henry Jacobs and John Haas, *The Lutheran Encyclopedia* (New York, 1899); Erwin Lueker, ed., *Lutheran Cyclopedia* (Saint Louis, 1954), Missouri Synod; Matthew Simpson, *Cyclopedia of Methodism* (Philadelphia, 1880); and Alfred Nevin, *Encyclopedia of the Presbyterian Church in the United States of America* (Philadelphia, 1884).

General studies of greatest value were: James Findlay, *Dwight L. Moody* (Chicago, 1969); Winthrop Hudson, *Religion in America* (New York, 1965); Kenneth Latourette, *Christianity in a Revolutionary Age* (New York, 1958–1962), 5 vols.; Gerhard Lenski, *The Religious Factor* (Garden City, 1963); William McLaughlin, *Modern Revivalism* (Boston, 1959); Sidney Mead, *The Lively Experiment* (New York, 1963); H. Richard Niebuhr, *The Social Sources of Denominationalism* (New York, 1929); Walter Peterson, "Social Aspects of Protestantism in the Mid-West, 1870–1910," (Ph.D. dissertation, University of Iowa, 1951); Earl Raab, ed., *Religious Conflict in America* (Garden City, 1964); Timothy Smith, *Revivalism and Social Reform* (New York, 1957); Rodney Stark and Charles Glock, *American Piety* (Berkeley, 1968).

For particular denominations, the following studies proved of some use: John Cady, *The Origin and Development of the Missionary Baptist Church in Indiana* (Franklin, Indiana, 1942), a good study; S. H. Mitchell, *Historical Sketches of Iowa Baptists* (Burlington, 1886), very dull; Colman Barry, *The Catholic Church and German-Americans* (Washington, 1953); Robert Cross, *The Emergence of Liberal Catholicism in America* (Cambridge, 1958); Philip Gleason, *The Conservative Reformers; German-American Catholics and the Social Order* (Notre Dame, 1968); William Liu and Nathaniel Pallone, eds., *Catholics/U.S.A.* (New York, 1970); Thomas McAvoy, *The Great Crisis in American Catholic History, 1895–1900* (Chicago, 1957); James Moynihan, *The Life of Archbishop James Ireland* (New York, 1953); (Congregationalist) Truman Douglass, *The Pilgrims of Iowa* (Boston, 1911); David Harrell, "The Sectional Origins of the Churches of Christ," *Journal of Southern History* (1964) 30: 261–77; Nathaniel Haynes, *History of the Disciples of Christ in Illinois, 1819–1914* (Cincinnati, 1915); Henry Shaw, *Hoosier Disciples* (Indianapolis, 1966); E. Clowes Chorley, *Men and Movements in the American Episcopal Church* (New York, 1946); George Smythe, *A History of the [Protestant Episcopal] Diocese of Ohio Until the Year 1918* (Cleveland, 1931); Willard Allbeck, *A Century of Lutherans in Ohio* (Yellow Springs, 1966); Walter Beck, *Lutheran Elementary Schools in the United States* (Saint Louis, 1939); Frederick Luebke, "The Immigrant Church as a Factor Contributing to the Conservatism of the Lutheran Church—Missouri Synod," *Concordia Historical Institute Quarterly* (1965) 38:19–28; George Stephenson, *Religious Aspects of Swedish Immigration* (Minneapolis, 1932); Roy Suelflow, *Walking with Wise Men* (Milwaukee, 1967), on the Missouri Synod in Wisconsin; Abdel Wentz, *A Basic History of Lutheranism in America* (Philadelphia, 1964); Wade Barclay, *Early American Methodism: 1769–1844* (New York, 1950) vol. 2; Emory Burke, ed., *The History of American Methodism* (Nashville, 1964), 3 vols.; Richard Cameron, *Methodism and Society in Historical Perspective* (New York, 1961), vol. 1; (Presbyterian) William Harsha, *The Story of Iowa* (Omaha, 1890); L. C. Rudolph, *Hoosier Zion* (New Haven, 1963); Robert Ellis Thompson, *A History of the Presbyterian Churches in the United States* (New York, 1895); Louis Jones, *The Quakers of Iowa* (Iowa City, 1914).

The published minutes of the annual state conferences of the various Protestant denominations were illuminating. State and local histories usually contain chapters on church progress; the best are in the histories of Chicago by Andreas and Indiana by Thornbrough and Phillips cited above. The operation of large Protestant parishes can be inferred from contemporary handbooks, such as Washington Gladden, *The Christian Pastor and the Working Church* (New York, 1898); Washington Gladden, ed., *Parish Problems* (New York, 1887); Thomas Murphy, *Pastoral Theology* (Philadelphia, 1877), for pietistic Presbyterians; William Plumer, *Hints and Helps in Pastoral Theology* (New York, 1874), and Charles Hodge, *Discussions in Church Polity* (New York, 1878), for liturgical Presbyterians. Donald Kinzer, *Episode in Anti-Catholicism* (Seattle, 1964), is a political history of the APA. Of larger scope, though seldom focused on the Midwest, is A. P. Stauffer, "Anti-Catholicism in American Politics, 1865–1900" (Ph.D. dissertation, Harvard University, 1933).

10. *Immigration history* has progressed strongly in the last few decades, but the Germans need far more research. The following works were all quite good: John Allswang, *A House for All Peoples* (Lexington, 1971), follows the voting patterns of Chicago ethnic groups well into the twentieth century; O. Fritiof Ander, "The Swedish-American Press and the American Protective Association," *Church History* (1937) 6:165–79; Kendric Babcock, *The Scandinavian Element in the United States* (Urbana, 1914); Rowland Berthoff, *British Immigrants in Industrial America, 1789–1950* (Cambridge, 1953), especially good on the late nineteenth century; Theodore Blegen, *Norwegian Migration to America* (Northfield, Minn., 1931, 1940) 2 vols.; Albert Faust, *The German Element in the United States* (Boston, 1909); Wellington Fordyce, "Nationality Groups in Cleveland Politics," *Ohio State Archaeological and Historical Quarterly* (1937) 46:109–27; Edwin Levine, *The Irish and Irish Politicians* (Notre Dame, 1966); Frederick Luebke, *Immigrants and Politics: The Germans of Nebraska, 1880–1900* (Lincoln, 1969); M. Justille McDonald, *History of the Irish in Wisconsin in the Nineteenth Century* (Washington, 1954); Stephan Thernstrom and Richard Sennett, eds., *Nineteenth Century Cities* (New Haven, 1969); Brinley Thomas, *Migration and Economic Growth* (Cambridge, England, 1954); Jacob Van der Zee, *The British in Iowa* (Iowa City, 1922); and various books by Carl Wittke, including *The Irish in America* (Baton Rouge, 1951), and *The German-Language Press in America* (Lexington, 1957); Robert Woods, ed., *The City Wilderness* (Boston, 1898), on the Irish.

11. *Economic histories* were not so important for this study, since the newspapers and business magazines gave excellent coverage. However, the following were of value: Margaret Bogue, *Patterns from the Sod: Land Use and Tenure in the Grand Prairie, 1856–1900* (Springfield, Ill., 1959); Chester Destler, "Agricultural Readjustment and Agrarian Unrest in Illinois, 1880–1896," *Agricultural History* (1947) 21:104–16; Davis Dewey, *Financial History of the United States* (New York, 1936); Rendigs Fels, *American Business Cycles: 1865–1897* (Chapel Hill, 1959); Milton Friedman and Anna Schwartz, *A Monetary History of the United States, 1869–1960* (Princeton, 1963); Charles Hoffman, "The Depression of the Nineties," *Journal of Economic History* (1956) 6:137–64; John Hopkins, *Economic History of the Production of Beef Cattle in Iowa* (Iowa City, 1928); Edward Kirkland, *Industry Comes of Age: Business, Labor, and Public Policy, 1860–1897* (New York, 1961); Roy Scott, *The Agrarian Movement in Illinois, 1880–1896* (Urbana, 1962); Fred Shannon, *The Farmer's Last Frontier* (New York, 1945), and his "The Status of the Midwestern Farmer in 1900," *Mississippi Valley Historical Review* (1950) 37:491–510; Albert Stevens, "Analysis of the Phenomenon of the Panic in the United States in 1893," *Quarterly Journal of Economics* (1894) 8:177–48, 252–56; Frank Taussig, *The Tariff History of the United States* (New York, 1931); and Willard Thorp, *Business Annals* (New York, 1926).

12. *Labor histories* were of considerably more use, since they often discussed the political activities of the union leaders, as well as the strikes that upset party loyalties. Two bibliographies were especially valuable: Maurice Neufeld, *A Representative Bibliography of American Labor History* (Ithaca, 1964); and Lloyd Reynolds and Charles Killingsworth, *Trade Union Publications* (Baltimore, 1944-45) 3 vols., which indexes all the union publications, and gives valuable information on many otherwise obscure labor organizations. The reports of the bureaus of labor statistics afforded important insights into the conditions of labor and the patterns of strikes.

Almont Lindsey, *The Pullman Strike* (Chicago, 1942), ignores the political reverberations. Rowland Berthoff, "The Social Order of the Anthracite Region, 1825–1902," *Pennsylvania Magazine of*

History and Biography (1965) 89:261–91, reveals that conditions were somewhat different in the hard-coal areas of Pennsylvania, but neglects the political implications. John Commons et al., *History of Labour in the United States* (New York, 1918–1935), 4 vols., remains the best general history. George Korson in *Minstrels of the Mine Patch* (Philadelphia, 1938) and *Coal Dust on the Fiddle* (Philadelphia, 1943), reveals a great deal about miners' lives through their songs and stories. Carlos Closson, "The Unemployed in American Cities," *Quarterly Journal of Economics* (1894) 8:168–217, 257–60, 453–77, 499–502, contains detailed reports on most large cities. Paul Douglas, *Real Wages in the United States, 1890–1926* (Boston, 1930), is accurate on money wage rates, but exaggerates the rise in the cost of living. Chris Evans, *History of the United Mine Workers of America* (Indianapolis, 1900), contains many documents. Thomas Gavett, *Development of the Labor Movement in Milwaukee* (Madison, 1965), is a model history of the labor stronghold. Herbert Gutman, "The Workers' Search for Power," in H. Wayne Morgan, ed., *The Gilded Age* (Syracuse, 1970), summarizes his extensive work on midwestern mill towns, chiefly in the 1870s. Gerd Korman, *Industrialization, Immigrants and Americanizers* (Madison, 1967), deals with labor in Milwaukee. Henry Demarest Lloyd, *A Strike of Millionaires Against Miners* (Chicago, 1890) is a sensationalist exposé of the Spring Valley lockout of 1889 by the *Chicago Tribune's* famous reporter.

Clarence Long, *Wages and Earnings in the United States, 1860–1890* (Princeton, 1961), is a National Bureau of Economic Research study. Donald McMurry, *Coxey's Army* (Boston, 1929) is a scholarly study of a march as famous, and about as important, as the trek of Johnny Appleseed. John Mitchell, *Organized Labor* (Philadelphia, 1903), is by the outspoken UMW leader. Edward Wittleman, "Chicago Labor in Politics, 1877–1896," *Journal of Political Economy* (1920) 28:407–27, is in need of revision. Andrew Roy, *A History of the Coal Miners of the United States* (Columbus, 1906), is sympathetic to the miners and laudatory of McKinley and Hanna. Albert Rees, *Real Wages in Manufacturing: 1890–1914* (Princeton, 1961), is the N.B.E.R. study that displaces Douglas on the cost-of-living index. Robert Ward and William Rogers, *Labor Revolt in Alabama* (University of Alabama,

1965), covers the coal and railroad strikes of 1894 in Birmingham, with full attention to the political implications, but is weak on economics. Norman Ware, *The Labor Movement in the United States, 1860–1895* (New York, 1929), covers only the Knights of Labor; Frank Warne, *The Coal-Mine Workers* (New York, 1905) and *The Slav Invasion and the Mine Workers* (Philadelphia, 1904), are good, scholarly studies that unfortunately neglect the Midwest; Clifton Yearley, *Britons in American Labor* (Baltimore, 1957), supplements Berthoff's *British Immigrants in Industrial America*.

13. *Political scientists* share with historians a concern with elections, and their insights provided the original stimulus for this study. The historian, however, cannot afford to mechanically retrace the research designs of social scientists. The data will not allow it anyway, for questionnaires cannot be designed for the voters of 1888, nor is participant observation for that time any longer possible. Furthermore, the historical craft has developed unique skills that permit deeper penetrations into the secrets of the past than can be attained by social scientists. By his familiarity with primary documents and his understanding of their context (together with a theory about what is happening) the historian can reconstruct major events, uncover trends, identify key actors, understand their purposes, and discover the values and beliefs of the participants. Knowing their past, and also their future, he can gauge the forces and conflicts animating his characters. Using quotations that capture the mood of the era, together with narratives of carefully selected episodes which, minor in themselves, illustrate the basic processes at work, he can reconstruct a sense of the past that no other method can approach in versimilitude. The richness of the historical method is not lightly to be exchanged for the glittering promises of the social sciences that they will "some day" explain everything.

Some political scientists have made major contributions to the analysis of historical voting patterns. V. O. Key was the foremost exemplar, in *Southern Politics* (New York, 1949), "A Theory of Critical Elections," *Journal of Politics* (1955) 17:3–18, and, with Frank Munger, "Social Determinism and Electoral Decision: The Case of Indiana," in Eugene Burdick and Arthur Brodbeck, eds., *American Voting Behavior* (Glencoe, 1959), pp.

281–99. Harold Gosnell, in *Machine Politics* (Chicago, 1937) and *Grass Roots Politics* (Washington, 1942), introduced numerous statistical techniques. W. Dean Burnham, in several papers and essays, most notably "The Changing Shape of the American Political Universe," *American Political Science Review* (1965) 59: 7–28, and *Critical Elections and the Mainsprings of American Politics* (New York, 1970), expanded the Key tradition. John Fenton, *Midwest Politics,* cited earlier, is a pedestrian application of Key's methods, while Angus Campbell et al., *Elections and the Political Order* (New York, 1966), and Gerald Pomper, *Elections in America* (New York, 1969), advanced the art significantly. Kevin Phillips, *The Emerging Republican Majority* (New Rochelle, 1969), revived an older tradition of analyzing votes by counties, while demonstrating the continuing importance of religion and culture as critical forces in political alignments. A more theoretical statement of the same theme is Raymond Wolfinger, "The Development and Persistence of Ethnic Voting," *American Political Science Review* (1965) 59:896–908. V. O. Key, *Primer of Statistics for Political Scientists* (New York, 1954), introduced the author to the basic techniques, but for an idea of the actual basis of the statistical analysis of the midwestern voting patterns, see Charles Dollar and Richard Jensen, *Historian's Guide to Statistics* (New York, 1971).

The seminal contribution of modern social science is the questionnaire, administered in controlled interviews and analyzed with sophisticated statistical methods. The outstanding studies, particularly for their theoretical statements of the relevant social psychology, are Angus Campbell et al., *The American Voter* (New York, 1960); Bernard Berelson et al., *Voting* (Chicago, 1954); Paul Lazarsfeld et al., *The People's Choice* (New York, 1948). Important syntheses based on this line of research are Robert Lane, *Political Life* (Glencoe, 1959); Lester Millbrath, *Political Participation* (Chicago, 1965), and William Flanigan, *Political Behavior of the American Electorate* (Boston, 1968).

Close observation of campaigns is a research technique best popularized by Theodore White. John Kessel, *The Goldwater Coalition* (Indianapolis, 1968), blending observations with theory, is a model study. Valuable are the essays in Donald Herzberg and Gerald Pomper, eds., *American Party Politics* (New York, 1966);

and William Chambers and Walter Dean Burnham, eds., *The American Party Systems* (New York, 1967). Samuel Eldersveld, *Political Parties* (Chicago, 1964), based on Detroit in the 1950s, brilliantly examined the operations of party machinery. Dan Nimmo, *The Political Persuaders: The Techniques of Modern Election Campaigns* (Englewood Cliffs, 1970), reflects a new interest in campaign techniques. I have generalized my own theory in "Armies, Admen, and Crusaders: Types of Presidential Election Campaigns," *The History Teacher* (January, 1969) 2:33–50. The British experience, contrasted with the American, reveals both the uniqueness and the universality of the latter. M. Ostrogorski, *Democracy and the Organization of Political Parties* (London, 1902), was highly informative on the British system. Also of interest are: H. J. Hanham, *Elections and Party Management: Politics in the Time of Gladstone and Disraeli* (London, 1959); J. R. Vincent, *Pollbooks: How Victorians Voted* (Cambridge, England, 1967); and especially Janet Howarth, "The Liberal Revival in Northhamptonshire, 1880–1895," *The Historical Journal* (1969) 12:78–118. Highly suggestive was David Butler and Donald Stokes, *Political Change in Britain* (New York, 1969), even though it focused on the twentieth century only.

Political philosophy, long a languishing area, revived in the 1950s and 1960s with debates on the merits of pluralism—debates that degenerated into massive campus rioting by the end of the decade. Robert Dahl, *Pluralist Democracy in the United States* (Chicago, 1967), as a summary of Dahl's ideas, was very influential. Leon Epstein, *Political Parties in Western Democracies* (New York, 1967); S.L. Lipset, *Revolution and Counterrevolution* (Garden City, 1970); Gabriel Almond and Sidney Verba, *The Civic Culture* (Princeton, 1963); and Norman Nie, G. Bingham Powell, and Kenneth Prewitt, "Social Structure and Political Participation," *American Political Science Review* (1969) 63:361–78, 808–32, added comparative perspective to the American experience. Norman Pollack, *The Populist Response to Industrial America* (Cambridge, 1962), represents an antipluralist manifesto projected back into the 1890s.

Index

Krauth, Charles Porterfield, 63

Labor politics: in Illinois, 262–63; in Iowa, 265–66; in Wisconsin, 127–28, 142, 265–67. *See also* Knights of Labor; Trade unions
LaCrosse, Wisconsin, 265
LaFollette, Robert, 137, 141, 176, 307 n.63
Language of politics, 11, 168, 170–71. *See also* Oratory; Rhetoric
Larrabee, William, 96, 98–99, 184; and railroad regulation, 100–101, 205
Law and order, 8, 106, 114–16, 118, 119, 194, 290
Lawyers, 180, 305
Liberal Republicans, 91
Licenses, liquor: and Baptists, 80 n.36; in Chicago, 118–19; Episcopalians favor, 77; in Indianapolis, 119; in Iowa, 91, 93, 106–8, 114, 202–3; Jansenists favor, 74; and newspaper editors, 195–97; in Ohio, 115–18, 120; pietists oppose, 72, 191; in Wisconsin, 122. *See also* Local option; Prohibition
Lincoln, Abraham: as symbol, 15, 25, 90, 202, 271
Linton, William, 225, 226
Liturgicals, 58–88; oppose Bryan, 285, 292–93; in cities, 87, 88, 178–79, 182, 300; and depression, 218–19, 304; in 1896, 296–97, 300; in Iowa, 92, 94, 95, 107–8, 112; numbers of, 87, 88; occupations of, 179, 309–15; oppose prohibition, 68, 73, 121, 187; partisanship of, 69, 310–15; and pluralism, 197, 308; theology of, 63–67, 76, 78, 83–84, 206; in towns, 181; vote of, 112, 142–43, 294, 297, 300; in Wisconsin, 123, 125, 146. *See also* Catholics; Episcopalians; Germans, Lutheran; Presbyterians, liturgical
Local option: and Anti-Saloon League, 207; in Iowa, 91, 93, 106, 108, 114, 202; and Jansenists, 74; and professional politicians, 197; and prohibition, 70, 181; in Wisconsin, 122–23, 128

Local politics, xii, 2, 8, 36–39, 48, 70, 169, 172–73, 181, 204–5
Lockouts, 241–43, 250
Logan county, Illinois, 62, 85, 311–14
Lomira, Wisconsin, 142
Lumberjacks, xvi, 228, 288
Lutherans, 64, 67; among elite, 77 n.28; General Synod (pietistic), 62, 63, 67, 73, 82, 184; German, 58, 63, 65, 82–84, 86, 124–26, 130–34, 142–43, 145, 146, 160; Norwegian, 81, 135–36; number of, 86, 87; Swedish, 67, 80, 136; voting patterns of, 61, 62, 81, 142–44; in Wisconsin, 124–36, 142–46

McBride, John, 244 n.9, 258
McGobrick, Bishop, 138
Machines: in Chicago, 36, 38, 223, 298; in Cincinnati, 38, 116, 176; in Cleveland, 38; Democrats control, 180; in Detroit, 36–38; Irish control, 297–300; and McKinley, 177; metropolitan, 36–38; opposition to, 36, 179, 180, 183, 186, 190, 307
McKinley, William: acts in coal strike, 244, 246, 258 n.35; admiration for, 177, 290 n.34; appeals to patriotism, 278; avoids prohibition, 197 n.57; controls GOP, 175, 269; denies coercion charges, 55, 288; discusses prosperity, 151, 156, 158, 214, 216, 305; in 1889, 117; in 1890, 141, 150–52; in 1891, 154–57; in 1892, 158, 171; in 1893, 210–11, 214–15; in 1894, 286; in 1895, 231; in 1896, 269, 286–87, 290; election of, xiii, 52, 57, 268; front porch campaign of, 286–87; as Methodist, 278; in Ohio GOP, 120, 162, 176; promises pluralism, 156, 291, 305, 308; speeches of, 13, 269, 287; uses military rhetoric, 171. *See also* Election of 1896; Tariff, McKinley
McMillan, James, 176
Madison, Wisconsin, 116 n.47, 128
Mahin, John, 102

348

ship of, 81; and prohibition, 80; religion of, 81, 135–36; voting patterns of, 112, 144, 297, 298; in Wisconsin, 122, 135–36, 137, 142, 144
Norwegian Synod, 81, 87, 135–36

Occupation: and mobility, 180–81, 314–16; and partisanship, 179, 309–15. *See also* Class
O'Hara, James, 225, 226
Ohio: Australian ballot in, 42; bribery in, 38–39; coal miners in, 239, 242–44, 249 n.17, 258, 260, 267 n.55; coercion in, 48 n.33; depression in, 211, 217; in 1863, 121; in 1888, 13, 21, 31; in 1889, 116–18; in 1890, 150–52, 141; in 1891, 154–57; in 1892, 158, 169; in 1893, 214–15; in 1894, 267; in 1895, 230–31; in 1896, 278; fraud in, 40; moralists purged in, 176; pottery workers in, 156, 267; professional politicians in, 162, 176, 207; prohibition in, 68–70, 115–18, 120; railroad strike in, 264; religion in, 86, 87; veterans in, 25; WCTU in, 69
Ohio Synod (liturgical), 82, 83 n.41, 125
Old stock: and APA, 232, 236; in 1892, 302; in 1896, 271, 277, 278, 301 n.56, 302; in Iowa, 108, 110, 112, 229 n.52, 301 n.56; lack of success of, 303–4; as Lutherans, 82, 125; occupations of, 180–82; power of, 180–81; vote of, 31–32, 112, 229 n.52, 278, 298, 301 n.56, 302; in Wisconsin, 122, 139. *See also* Pietists; Yankees
Omaha World-Herald, 52, 318
Onahan, William, 119 n.53, 236 n.71
Orange lodges, 232–35
Oratory: army-style, 3, 14–17, 20, 150–51, 165–66; crusading, 106, 155; in 1896, 269, 273–76, 286–87, 289–90; merchandising-style, 167, 172–75. *See also* Language of politics; Rhetoric
Oshkosh, Wisconsin, 5, 128, 139

Palmer, John, 150, 271, 301 n.56
Pamphlets: in army style campaigns, 3–4, 13; in 1888, 4, 11, 13; in 1890, 131; in 1892, 169, 173; in 1896, 53, 55, 273–74, 288–89, 291; in merchandising-style campaigns, 168–69, 173, 175; of prohibitionists, 195
Pana, Illinois, 251 n.20, 255
Panic, fear of, 19, 52–54, 210, 214–15, 280 n.19
Parades: in army-style campaigns, 2–3, 13–14, 165–66, 172; in 1896, 53, 275, 290–91; in 1900, 57; lack of in merchandising-style campaigns, 168–69, 173–74
Park, Edward, 63
Parochial schools: in Illinois, 219–20; in Iowa, 158; and liturgicals, xii, 65, 74, 76, 85; Norwegian, 135–36; in Wisconsin, 123–26, 131–35. *See also* Bennett law; Edwards law
Participation in politics, xi, 2–11, 169, 174, 175, 273, 307. *See also* Turnout
Particularism, theological, 64
Parties, opposition to, 74–75, 84, 163, 190–91, 198, 307
Party loyalty: and army style, xii–xiii, 6–11, 14–16, 45–46; in 1896, 273, 307; and immigrants, 137, 304; and merchandising style, 175, 208; and moralists, 198
Paternalism, 133, 177
Patriotic societies, 220–21, 232, 290
Patriotism in 1896, 271, 290, 293
Patronage: and army style, 11–12, 162, 164; and Bryan, 270, 273, 280; for editors, 6, 162, 166, 205; in 1890, 141; for Germans, 90, 160, 165; and Harrison, 162–63; in Iowa, 90, 113, 205; for Irish, 90, 296–300; and liquor power, 186; and merchandising style, 166, 175; in Michigan, 223–24; for Norwegians, 135, 160; in Ohio, 118; and post office, 162; and veterans, 25, 164
Patrons of industry, 149, 278
Paulist order, 74 n.20, 76 n.25
Payne, Henry, 127, 130, 131